Ecotheology and Nonhuman Ethics in Society

Ecocritical Theory and Practice

Series Editor: Douglas A. Vakoch, California Institute of Integral Studies, USA

Advisory Board: Joni Adamson, Arizona State University, USA; Mageb Al-adwani, King Saud University, Saudi Arabia; Bruce Allen, Seisen University, Japan; Hannes Bergthaller, National Chung-Hsing University, Taiwan; Zélia Bora, Federal University of Paraíba, Brazil; Izabel Brandão, Federal University of Alagoas, Brazil; Byron Caminero-Santangelo, University of Kansas, USA; Jeffrey J. Cohen, George Washington University, USA; Simão Farias Almeida, Federal University of Roraima, Brazil; Julia Fiedorczuk, University of Warsaw, Poland; Camilo Gomides, University of Puerto Rico—Rio Piedras, Puerto Rico; Yves-Charles Grandjeat, Michel de Montaigne-Bordeaux 3 University, France; George Handley, Brigham Young University, USA; Isabel Hoving, Leiden University, The Netherlands; Idom Thomas Inyabri, University of Calabar, Nigeria; Serenella Iovino, University of Turin, Italy; Adrian Ivakhiv, University of Vermont, USA; Daniela Kato, Zhongnan University of Economics and Law, China; Petr Kopecký, University of Ostrava, Czech Republic; Mohammad Nasser Modoodi, Payame Noor University, Iran; Patrick Murphy, University of Central Florida, USA; Serpil Oppermann, Hacettepe University, Turkey; Rebecca Raglon, University of British Columbia, Canada; Anuradha Ramanujan, National University of Singapore, Singapore; Christian Schmitt-Kilb, University of Rostock, Germany; Marian Scholtmeijer, University of Northern British Columbia, Canada; Heike Schwarz, University of Augsburg, Germany; Murali Sivaramakrishnan, Pondicherry University, India; Scott Slovic, University of Idaho, USA; J. Etienne Terblanche, North-West University, South Africa; Julia Tofantšuk, Tallinn University, Estonia; Jennifer Wawrzinek, Free University of Berlin, Germany; Cheng Xiangzhan, Shandong University, China; Yuki Masami, Kanazawa University, Japan; Hubert Zapf, University of Augsburg, Germany

Ecocritical Theory and Practice highlights innovative scholarship at the interface of literary/cultural studies and the environment, seeking to foster an ongoing dialogue between academics and environmental activists.

Titles in the Series

Ecotheology and Nonhuman Ethics in Society: A Community of Compassion, edited by Melissa J. Brotton

The Ethics and Rhetoric of Invasion Ecology, edited by James Stanescu and Kevin Cummings

Disability and the Environment in American Literature: Toward an Ecosomatic Paradigm, edited by Matthew J. C. Cella

Dark Nature: Anti-Pastoral Essays in American Literature and Culture, edited by Richard J. Schneider

Ecotheology and Nonhuman Ethics in Society

A Community of Compassion

Edited by Melissa J. Brotton

LEXINGTON BOOKS
Lanham • Boulder • New York • London

Published by Lexington Books
An imprint of The Rowman & Littlefield Publishing Group, Inc.
4501 Forbes Boulevard, Suite 200, Lanham, Maryland 20706
www.rowman.com

Unit A, Whitacre Mews, 26-34 Stannary Street, London SE11 4AB

Copyright © 2017 by Lexington Books

All rights reserved. No part of this book may be reproduced in any form or by any electronic or mechanical means, including information storage and retrieval systems, without written permission from the publisher, except by a reviewer who may quote passages in a review.

British Library Cataloguing in Publication Information Available

Library of Congress Cataloging-in-Publication Data is Available

ISBN 978-1-4985-2790-3 (cloth : alkaline paper)
ISBN 978-1-4985-2791-0 (electronic)

∞™ The paper used in this publication meets the minimum requirements of American National Standard for Information Sciences Permanence of Paper for Printed Library Materials, ANSI/NISO Z39.48-1992.

Printed in the United States of America

To my sister, Heidi Echo Hudson Brotton, with whom I share a great love for all God's creatures. Remember the salamanders.

Contents

Acknowledgments   vii

Foreword   ix
   David L. Clough

Introduction   1
   Melissa J. Brotton

Part I: Christian Virtues and Nonhuman Ethics   **23**

1. Animal Rights Revisited   25
   Celia Deane-Drummond

2. Whatsoever You Do to the Least of My Brothers: Why it is Wrong to Harm a Fly   43
   Jeffrey A. Lockwood

3. Anthropogenic Climate Change and Animal Welfare   63
   Bryan Ness

4. The Self-Emptying Godhead: Perichoresis, Kenosis, and an Ethic for the Anthropocene   81
   Mick Pope

Part II: Ecotheology in the South   **99**

5. Loving the Mountains: Cultivating Compassion for Places   101
   Andrew R. H. Thompson

6. An Ecotheology of Hunting   117
   Perry Hodgkins Jones

Part III: Liturgical Practices and Hymnody   **129**

7 Singing to Subdue or to Sustain?: Looking for an Ethic of Conservation in Christian Liturgical Song and Hymnody   131
David Kendall

8 Environmental Advocacy and the Absence of the Church   145
Jerry Cappel

Part IV: Catholic Perspectives   **159**

9 Efficacious Ethics: The Trinity, Environment, and Green Design   161
Robert Robin Gottfried

10 Care and Compassion: The Need for an Integral Ecology   179
Cristina Vanin

Part V: Jesus and the Animals in the Gospel of Mark   **197**

11 Liberating Legion: An Ecocritical, Postcolonial reading of Mark 5:1–20   199
Kendra Haloviak Valentine

12 The End of the Road: Jesus, Donkeys, and Galilean Subsistence Farmers   217
Matthew Valdez with Kendra Haloviak Valentine

Index   231

About the Contributors   241

Acknowledgments

I am deeply grateful to each chapter contributor and to John Jones at La Sierra University and to Robert (Robin) Gottfried at The University of the South for their advice during the initial stages of this endeavor. Likewise, Lisa Kohlmeier, Kendra Haloviak Valentine, Maury Jackson, and April Summitt provided needful encouragement early on. The help I received from reference librarians Hilda Smith, Jeff de Vries, and Christina Viramontes at La Sierra University Library was inestimable. As well I am grateful to Margaret Song, Lisa Kohlmeier, Mick Pope, and Bobbi Witham Brotton for being willing to read drafts of the introduction. Thank you also to the series editor, Douglas Vakoch, and to the exceptional team at Lexington Books—Lindsey Porambo, Nick Johns, and Tracy Galloway—for their expertise and timely help. To Bobbi Witham Brotton and Steven J. Brotton, Heidi Echo Brotton Hudson, Mackie Hudson, Jeremy Hudson, Sheri Speare, Voni Witham Slind, and Lana Brandt for their enduring love and support. And abundant gratitude to my Heavenly Father, Who sees every sparrow that falls and every chick too.

Foreword

David L. Clough

We have lived in our current house for eight years now, but it was only two months ago that I first saw a jay visit our garden. The Eurasian jays that live here in England are different from American blue jays: they are mostly a pinky brown but with vivid black and white markings around their eyes, blue and black ripples on the front of their wings, and a black and white tail. As I watched the jay, I saw another first-time visitor: a greater spotted woodpecker, hungry enough to brave our bird feeder and still more strikingly arrayed in black, white, and red. I am always glad to see these birds, but the surprise of finding them in this very familiar context was a particular delight.

I had something of the same feeling when I came across an early fifteenth-century Franciscan commentary on the Ten Commandments for the first time recently. I am not claiming any kind of expertise in relation to fifteenth-century Christian texts, but having spent most of the last decade immersed in reading and writing about nonhuman animals and Christian theology, I was surprised to bump into something new. The text was *Dives and Pauper*, probably written in England between 1405 and 1410.[1] It is constructed as a dialogue between the eponymous figures, and it is unsurprising in a Franciscan text to find that Dives (Latin for "wealthy") comes off consistently worse in the interchange. One of the points Dives puts to Pauper in relation to the fifth commandment is that "It seems to many people that God forbade by this precept all kinds of slaughter, both of man and beast, for he said generally 'Non occides,' 'Thou shalt not kill.'"[2] Pauper suggests a number of plausible reasons why the command should not be understood that way, including the permission given to Noah in Genesis 9 to kill other animals for food. So far, so unsurprising: Augustine had dismissed application of the commandment to nonhuman animals in *The City of God* a thousand years previously.[3] But Pauper goes on to explain to Dives that God forbade the slaughter of beasts cruelly, or for vain pleasures, or wickedness: "God that made all has care of all, and he shall take vengeance on all who misuse his creatures." The passage concludes, "And therefore men should have compassion on beast and bird and not harm them without cause and have regard for the fact that they are God's creatures. And therefore he who for cruelty and vanity beheads beasts and torments beasts or birds more than it is expedient to man's living, they sin very grievously."

Reading those words, I warmed to the anonymous English monk who was their author, apparently deeply formed in the Franciscan attitudes of sisterly and brotherly relationships to fellow animal creatures and speaking to me as a brother in Christ across the six centuries that separated us. As with the jay and the woodpecker, it was a surprise and a delight to happen upon this striking statement of Christian compassion for other animals within theological territory I thought of as well-trodden. Or perhaps my surprise is better understood the other way around entirely: the surprise of discovering a very familiar Christian concern for fellow creatures in a text from so long ago. For the historian Keith Thomas notes that, far from being an anomaly, the attitude toward animal cruelty evident in *Dives and Pauper* is part of "one single, coherent and remarkably constant attitude," which "underlay the great bulk of the preaching and pamphleteering against animal cruelty between the fifteenth and nineteenth centuries," that humans were entitled to domesticate other animals and kill them for food and clothing but should not "tyrannize or cause them unnecessary suffering."[4]

As I reflected further on this early fifteenth-century Christian text and the unity of Christian witness to the compassionate attitudes that Keith Thomas makes clear, my emotions changed from surprised delight to mournful regret and anger. How was it that despite this clear six-hundred-year-old statement of Christian attitudes toward other animals, which represented a consensus position for Christians for the four hundred years that followed, Christian theology and ethics so lost its way that both Christians and their enemies largely accepted without question Peter Singer's accusation in 1975 that Christianity was responsible for extinguishing sympathy for other animals?[5] Singer is wrong in his historical analysis, but given that Christian theologians and the wider church in the twentieth century neglected the strands in the tradition that demonstrate his error, both Singer's mistake and the mistake of the Christians that believed him that their faith had nothing to say about concern for animals is understandable. The theological responses to concern for animals in the decades that followed were valuable and instructive in taking up the cause of other animals as a Christian concern but largely accepted the terms of Singer's analysis that mainstream Christianity had been problematically neglectful of nonhuman animals.[6]

Christian theologians in the twenty-first century therefore need, first, to engage in a reparative project of recalling the roots of concern for nonhuman creatures that run deep through Christian traditions and texts but from which we have become distant through twentieth-century inattention, and, second, to take up the ethics of Christian compassion for other animals in our own particular contexts. Such a reparative project is important to set the record straight, to make clear to Christians the reasons internal to their faith for being concerned about other creatures, to improve the lot of the nonhuman creatures we live alongside, and to persuade those who distance themselves from Christianity on the basis of its supposed neglect of other creatures that they have cause to think again.

For these reasons, we urgently need books like this one, which take up the task of engaging seriously with Christian traditions of compassion for the nonhuman world and with the ethical implications of this concern. Melissa Brotton has assembled an impressive range of contributors who address in diverse ways the challenge of what Christian thought and practice should look like in relation to nonhuman creatures. The chapters in this volume should be a powerful stimulus to a much wider field of Christian theologians and ethicists to take the nonhuman world as a serious object of theological and ethical concern in their teaching and research. The book arrives at an opportune time, which seems to be a tipping point in relation to concern about nonhuman animals and wider environmental concerns, both within the churches and in wider society, with the papal encyclical *Laudato Si'* representative of the wider reception of this compassionate concern. I warmly commend the volume and look forward to the further conversation that it will provoke.

NOTES

1. Priscilla Heath Barnum, ed., *Dives and Pauper* (Oxford: Early English Text Society/Oxford University Press, 1976).
2. This and the quotations that follow are my modern English rendition of Barnum's text, pp. 33–36.
3. Augustine, *The City of God Against the Pagans*, trans. R. W. Dyson (Cambridge: Cambridge University Press, 1998), bk I, ch. 19.
4. Keith Thomas, *Man and the Natural World: Changing Attitudes in England 1500–1800* (London: Penguin, 1984), 153.
5. Peter Singer, *Animal Liberation* (New York: Avon Books, 1975), 200.
6. See, for example, Andrew Linzey, *Christianity and the Rights of Animals* (London: SPCK, 1987), 22.

REFERENCES

Augustine. *The City of God Against the Pagans*. Trans. R. W. Dyson. Cambridge: Cambridge University Press, 1998.
Barnum, Priscilla Heath, ed. *Dives and Pauper*. Oxford: Early English Text Society/Oxford University Press, 1976.
Linzey, Andrew. *Christianity and the Rights of Animals*. London: SPCK, 1987.

Singer, Peter. *Animal Liberation: A New Ethics for Our Treatment of Animals.* New York: Avon Books, 1975.
Thomas, Keith. *Man and the Natural World: Changing Attitudes in England 1500–1800.* London: Penguin, 1984.

Introduction

Melissa J. Brotton

"The Lord is good to all; he has compassion on all he has made."
—Psalm 145: 9 (New International Version)

"The righteous care for the needs of their animals, but the kindest acts of the wicked are cruel."
—Proverbs 12:10 (New International Version)

"Your master never taught you a truer thing," said John; "there is no religion without love, and people may talk as much as they like about their religion, but if it does not teach them to be good to man and beast, it is all a sham—all a sham, James, and it won't stand when things come to be turned inside out and put down for what they are."
—Anna Sewell, *Black Beauty*

When the British Quaker Anna Sewell began to write *Black Beauty* (1877) near the end of her life in 1871, she could hardly have imagined it would become either a children's classic or an animal-rights manifesto though she did hope it would help adults to rethink their mishandling of horses. Written at a period when humans depended on horses for all manner of transportation, agriculture, and industry, from coal mining to canal haulage, this book has been widely credited for raising our social conscience about the treatment of horses and other animals through the author's use of a horse's first-person perspective.[1] Sewell was inspired to write this story about the mistreatment of horses after a friend told her about the American theologian Horace Bushnell's *Essay on Animals*, which had expressed the same concern. Sewell acknowledged Bushnell's influence on her work in a letter to Mrs. Bayly:

> The thoughts you gave me from Horace Bushnell years ago have followed me entirely through the writing of my book, and have, more than anything else, helped me to feel it was worth a great effort to try, at least, to bring the thoughts of men in harmony with the purposes of God on this subject.[2]

Sewell's choice to allow Black Beauty to tell his own story was effective. The story's depiction of various forms of cruelty toward horses, culminating in Beauty's collapse and near death, has had a powerful, lasting effect on Sewell's readers to this day.[3]

Sewell's story reminds us that the nineteenth century's ending in England was an important era for animal welfare and anticruelty legislation just as its beginning was.[4] In 1876 members of Parliament passed an amendment to the Animal Cruelty Act of 1849 that set limits on animal experimentation so that scientists could no longer cut animals open, manipulate, or remove their organs without both good reason and anesthesia. Another popular children's author, the Anglican deacon and mathematician, Charles Lutwidge Dodgson, better known as Lewis Carroll, had written his antivivisection essay one year prior to the passage of this amendment.[5] In his essay Carroll argued that vivisection is a moral issue: "That while we do not deny the absolute right of man to end the lives of lower animals by a painless death, we require good and sufficient cause to be shown for all infliction of pain."[6] Carroll also condemned "the chief evil" of the practice, that of its "effect on the moral character of the operator," which he saw as "distinctly demoralising and brutalising."[7]

Sewell and Carroll were only two of many authors and public figures who raised questions about the treatment of animals in their time and place,[8] questions we are still raising today on a global level. For example, on September 25, 2015, the White House released a statement that China joined with the United States to ban the import and export of ivory.[9] Yet, despite the agreement, news reports show evidence that turning culture around will not be easy, as Chinese businesses launder illegal ivory, and their government wonders what to do with its legal stockpiles.[10] In the meantime the poaching of elephants continues at alarming rates—as many as thirty thousand per year—leading some to believe that African elephants could be extinct very soon.[11]

At the same time, activist groups are combatting the horrific Asian dog-meat trade in which ten to twenty million dogs are slaughtered each year in inhumane ways, not to mention unsanitary. According to a CBS News press release,

> Some are trucked [for] hundreds of miles stuffed six or seven to a crate or small metal cage without food or water. Slaughtering takes place in front of the animals, usually with a club to induce the pain or fear that restaurant owners claim makes their adrenaline-rich meat tastier.[12]

According to SOI Foundation, an animal-rescue group in Thailand, the lucky dogs are clubbed to death while others are skinned or seared alive.[13] A Google search on "dog meat market" results in grisly images of dogs crammed into wire cages on their way to slaughter and tables of already-slaughtered dogs cut into pieces, severed heads and chests with front legs frozen into begging positions as they are prepared to be cooked. According to ABC News, up to 70 percent of the dogs crammed into trucks are stolen from homes, and Western tourists are contributing to the trade, tasting dog meat without knowledge or thought about what the dogs went through.[14] In late 2014, as a result of animal activism, especially by SOI Foundation, Thailand banned the trade and made it a crime.[15] But in the city of Yulin (Guangxi Zhuang) the dog meat festival continues each year with the slaughter of between ten and fifteen thousand dogs within ten days apparently in celebration of the summer solstice.[16]

Another area receiving international attention due to animal activism is male chick maceration.[17] Graphic online videos show day-old chicks carelessly tossed by human hands onto conveyor belts to be crushed or ground up alive. Due to animal activism and public response, some companies and organizations are finally stepping up to end this cruel practice. In the Netherlands, the mass food producer Unilever, for example, is taking steps with animal activists to stop the practice and to be cage-free in the next four years. As well, the president of United Egg Producers (UEP), a major United States cooperation of egg farmers that represent up to 95 percent of America's laying hens, has issued a statement on their commitment to end the practice either by 2020 or "as soon as it is commercially available and economically feasible," according to a Fox News article published on June 13 of this year.[18] This decision by UEP to start ending the practice of chick culling in the United States may have far-reaching effects, as there are initiatives around the world to develop the technologies to support these efforts. Even so, it is clear that economics weighs more than sentient life does on the scales. And will sexing the chicks earlier bring an end to suffering if the chicks inside the eggs are crushed anyways? Will there be a technology developed to produce only female chick eggs to begin with?[19]

AN URGENT CALL TO MERCY

In 2002, Christian journalist Matthew Scully published his book *Dominion*, containing investigative accounts of sports shooting fields, slaughterhouses, and factories with a call to a conscientious redress of evils committed against animals by humans. In his book Scully not only expresses concern about the massive levels at which animal life is taken but also about the thoughtless, overly casual, and calloused mindsets of those who participate in these activities. In one incident at a shooting field, an elephant hunter chats with Scully as he takes aim at an elephant.

> We see the elephant drinking from a water hole some fifty yards from client and camera. "I studied in Limoges for a year," he tells me, "but then decided to come back. To tell you the truth I don't really enjoy hunting that much." The elephant is lifting his trunk toward the hunters. He's caught the scent. He knows. "Swordfishing is my real passion. Hunting, that's just business." He starts to run, falling with a great splash into a kneeling position, his trunk and head under the water, stilled just like that as if in freeze-frame. No need for a second shot. The skinners, charged with moving him, will earn their pay. "I don't like hunting at all, really, especially this"—pointing to the PowerBook. "It's just business."

Scully deplores the lack of deep consideration that even Christians pay to God's creation. "We think too little," he writes, "about the 'reasonable want' and 'reasonable need' that distinguish necessary animal pain from needless, reckless and willful conduct at *their* expense."[20] His book is a call for kind acts reflective of Christ's love that counteract the evils animals suffer by human hands.

> So in every act of kindness we hold in our own hands the mercy of our Maker, whose purposes are in life and not death, whose love does not stop at us but surrounds us, bestowing dignity and beauty and hope on every creature that lives and suffers and perishes.[21]

In the scenes that Scully brings to light we witness living creatures robbed of their dignity of life; sentient creatures born into the world without hope of positive relationship, or, in many cases, of ever smelling fresh air or rolling carefree in the grass like they tend to do when they are not contained. In his book Scully asks whether there is not more of a purpose in God's creation of animals beyond our current uses of them, such as "to awaken humility" and to call us back to a sense of wonder about life and spiritual hope.[22]

The horrors for animals mentioned here cause us to ask how we are to treat these fellow members of our planet. Are they here merely to provide for human wants and needs? Many of us doubt this very much. On social media sites video clips of animals interacting with each other abound. Witnessing lambs, calves, or baby goats as they romp, leap, and play leads us naturally to conclude that they are creatures with their own interests and worthy of our moral regard.[23] And yet most of the domestic animals of the world are considered "livestock," mercilessly warehoused and slaughtered without regard to their emotional or physical well-being.[24] Cultural critic and theologian Ellen Davis has called attention to the misery of animals in concentrated animal feeding operations (CAFOs), describing the state of a typical sow as she stands or lies all day in a filthy, metal cage, her body broken out in lesions,[25] an intelligent animal unable to have any control over where she might wander or walk away from it all. New Testament theologian Sigve Tonstad, responding to scenes of factory animal killings from a Romans 8 perspective, asks, where is compassion in an age where we see "the groaning of creation" more than ever before. Taking a Pauline imperative of "the mercies of God" into account, Tonstad insists, "a believer's ethic of mercy must in the twenty-first century extend to seed, to land, and to the suffering of non-human creatures as a matter of utmost urgency."[26]

Aside from the questions of the treatment of animals are larger questions about the impact of anthropic evil on the earth and its ecosystems. As the field of ecology has developed over the past few decades, we have started to look at how our own systems and patterns of development, industry, consumerism, and agriculture affect earth and its populations. The past two decades have seen ecological studies unfolding in diverse fields of study. Biology, philosophy, ethics, theology, and even English studies are attempting to answer fundamental questions about cultural indifference, environmental justice, factory farming, topsoil erosion, storm systems, ocean acidification, drought, and loss of biodiversity, among many other issues related to what many see as an ecological crisis.

The overwhelming number of issues arising from these studies causes us to wonder whether humans are capable in themselves of saving the earth. From a theological standpoint an even more central question arises in the possibility of accountability to God for our wrongs toward the earth and its creatures. Are humans accountable for acts against nonhumanity? Within Judeo-Christian ethics, this question converges with the concept of a longsuffering Creator, "slow to anger and abounding in love." Are there biblical models for earth care that have relevance for our practices today? Is there hope for building a community of compassion that includes nonhuman beings?

ECOTHEOLOGY AND ANIMAL THEOLOGY

Ecotheology, though informed by earlier conservation[27] and cultural movements, has been developing since the late 1960s largely in response to Lynn White, Jr.'s essay, "The Historical Roots of Our Ecological Crisis," in which he argued that a rampant Western anthropocentrism had developed out of technological advances and a certain interpretation of Genesis 1:28, to subdue the earth and have dominion over it.[28] In his conclusion, White posited an alternative Christian ecology in appealing to the figure of St. Francis as a model for resistance to the deleterious effects of science and technology on nature and for the acceptance of a more humble and equitable posture toward nonhumans.[29] Other pioneer thinkers in ecotheology include Alfred North

Whitehead, John B. Cobb, Jr., Rosemary Radford Ruether, Jürgen Moltmann, Michael Dowd, John F. Haught, and Sally McFague, among others.[30]

Some scholars from the 1970s onward tended to respond to White's essay with defensive or apologetic approaches while others developed "recovery" approaches.[31] David Horrell summarizes these approaches and their strengths and weaknesses; then, based on the work of Ernst Conradie, provides an alternative hermeneutical approach to the Bible's ecological meanings through "doctrinal constructs" and three dimensions of interpretation that include attention to historical context, theological discourse, and scientific inquiry.[32] Richard Bauckhams's comprehensive study, *The Bible and Ecology*, considers perspectives on the earth and the human treatment of animals across Old and New Testaments.[33] Bauckham covers topics such as Edenic context in Genesis 1:28, the creation community in books like the Psalms in which creatures and inanimate entities offer praise to the Creator, God's provision for wild animals, biblical forests, Jesus and the animals, and the fulfillment of past and future ecotopia.

As Bauckham and others have shown, the Bible's ecology can be readily gleaned. The Book of Psalms alone could provide sufficient evidence for a deep creation care ethic. One cannot read more than a few verses without coming across lines describing praise and thanksgiving to God for the created world. Some of these passages address God's provision for wild animals.[34] Others reveal a sense of human wonder about awe-inspiring aspects of nature like stars, mountains, and the sea.[35] Still others draw connections between humans and other sentient beings, noting where certain animals live or how they play.[36] Pastoral psalms metaphorically draw on the protective and peaceful relationship between shepherds and their flocks.[37] In other psalms, the entire created community participates. Sun, moon, stars, trees, rivers, fields, and mountains either join in worship or are called by the poet to sing and clap their hands before God.[38] The whole of the Psalms reveals God's loving relationship to all of his works and creation's enthusiastic response in worship and praise.[39]

Priestly laws in Leviticus and Deuteronomy reveal that humans were not to be careless in taking the life of any animal, whether for food or for religious sacrifice. Animal sacrifice was not to be taken lightly; the annual atonement was a sacred event that involved the whole community.[40] Sacrifices had meaning in that they reminded the people of their standing before God and of his mercy toward them. The animal offerings fulfilled a purpose and did not tend toward needless mass slaughter. The emotional lives of animals were considered in the laws concerning sacrifice. For example, mothers and their young were not to be killed on the same day, the idea being to prevent the distress of one witnessing the death of the other.[41] Agrarian laws expressed care and concern for earth and land, as Ellen Bernstein has effectively demonstrated.[42] Instructions for harvest, especially in the Sabbatical year law, allowed for human poor and wild animals to gather food.[43] The summation of agrarian and priestly laws in the Bible is concerned with what Ellen Davis calls "a wholesome materiality," with codes to preserve and to protect humans, land, and animals.[44]

In the New Testament we also see evidence of God's compassionate purpose for creation community. In his teachings Jesus revealed his regard for animals, such as "foxes," "doves," and "serpents," when he made analogous references to them or mentioned them as exemplars for humans.[45] In Matthew 10:29, Jesus claims that "not a single sparrow can fall to the ground without your Father knowing it."[46] According to Mark 1:13, when Jesus was in the wilderness after his baptism, he was with the wild animals. Richard Bauckham interprets this scene as one of peaceful coexistence.[47] While it is clear from his earthly ministry that Jesus prioritizes people in his saving mission, it is equally clear that his original and ultimate cosmic purpose is toward a kingdom that encompasses and values every living thing through his restorative promise, "Behold, I make all things new."[48]

A field of study related to ecotheology is animal theology, pioneered by animal ethicist Andrew Linzey, who has been defending animal rights from a Christian perspective for four decades beginning with his groundbreaking book, *Animal Rights: A Christian Assessment* (1976).[49] Linzey's work goes beyond that of Albert Schweitzer, credited as the first person to extend a religious theory of ethics to animals in his concept of *Ehrfurcht vor dem Leben*, or "reverence for life,"[50] to creating a systematic theology of animals.[51] In the past decade scholars like Celia Deane-Drummond, David Clough, and Christopher Southgate have likewise produced animal theologies that have opened this field in new directions.[52] Animal theology attends specifically to the treatment and needs of individual animals and species while ecotheology addresses wider problems of habitat, ecosystems, agricultural practices, atmospheric problems, pollution, and deforestation. But there is a great deal of overlap between the two, as the concerns of animals are related to those of the environment. Maintaining the distinction between ecotheology and animal theology is important because the immediate interests and needs of animals often conflict with those of ecosystems and environments.[53]

NONHUMAN ETHICS

In *Animal Liberation* (1975), Australian philosopher Peter Singer, in the spirit of forerunners Jeremy Bentham and John Stuart Mill, extended the classical utilitarian approach of equal consideration of interests to animals based on their sentience, or their capacity to experience pleasure or pain, by exposing the inhumane treatment of animals in factory farms and research facilities.[54] *Animal Liberation* has been reissued four times with its most recent, fortieth-anniversary edition in 2015. Reading it today, I feel as if it could have been published for the first time yesterday, so relevant it is to our current animal crisis in the world and in the United States.

While Peter Singer considers animal moral interests from a utilitarian, or consequentialist view, American philosopher Tom Regan extends deontological ethics (those based on Kant's theory of duty)[55] to animals and argues that certain animals, as subjects of life experience, hold inherent value and therefore have rights.[56] Regan's conditions for inherent rights indicate that a subject of a life must be more than responsive and must also possess certain cognitive functions such as the ability to remember, to perceive, to emote, and to experience pleasure and pain.[57]

Other post-Kantian theorists like Christine Korsgaard and, more recently, Julian Franklin, have expanded on the idea of the inherent value of animals. Korsgaard reasons that sentient creatures have moral standing by natural extension of human moral identity.[58] She critiques Kant's view that only humans are ends-in-themselves because moral obligation and value arise from "the legislative will," which only humans, as rational creatures, possess. Although animals cannot participate in lawmaking, they can be the recipients of universal legislative acts extended to them through Kant's own concept of "passive citizens"[59] and through Korsgaard's expansion of self-awareness as an ability to situate oneself in a social order or a community and to matter to oneself.

Like Regan and Korsgaard, Julian H. Franklin makes a case for animal consideration through the appeal to human duty based on the notion that Kant confused the subjects of the categorical imperative with its recipients. Furthermore, Franklin believes that while an argument from compassion is admirable and important, it does not go far enough without a solid grounding in reason, as it "will always lack a proper base of discrimination."[60]

Aside from nonhuman ethics based on consequences and those based on a sense of duty is a third perspective based on character virtues.[61] In other words, to do what is right depends upon being a particular kind of person, one who is honest, responsible, and unselfish, for example.[62] Daniel C. Russell notes, "What sets virtue ethics apart is that it treats ethics as concerned with one's whole life—and not just those occasions when something with a distinctive 'moral' quality is at stake."[63] The Irish philosopher and novelist Iris Murdoch found the closest thing to *good* person in *humble* person. "Humility," Murdoch wrote, "is a rare virtue and an unfashionable one and one which is often hard to discern. Only rarely does one meet somebody in whom it positively shines, in whom one apprehends with amazement the absence of the avaricious tentacles of the self."[64] Likewise, farmer and poet Wendell Berry considers that the health of the world's future will depend in large part on a type of person—the "responsible consumer."[65]

An approach related to virtue ethics is care ethics, formalized by Carol Gilligan and Nel Noddings in the early 1980s and later influenced by writers such as Virginia Held, Annette Baier, and Sarah Ruddick.[66] Care ethics is relational and reparative in essence according to Joan Tronto and also to Bernice Fischer, while some theorists stress the interconnectedness between the provider and the recipient. Daniel Engster describes the benefits of the care perspective as applied to animal ethics.

> By grounding human beings' moral duties to animals in our relationships with them, care theorists sidestep debates about whether or not animals possess the necessary cognitive capacities to qualify for rights possession. They likewise evade disputes about whether or not social utility actually supports abolishing factory farming, eliminating animal testing, and the like. In care ethics, our duties to animals arise out of the concrete, empirically verifiable relationships we have with them.[67]

In Engster's view, we have a duty to help animals that we have made dependent on us. This way of seeing care ethics obligates us to care for our own companion or agrarian animals but not necessarily for wild animals, such as skunks or raccoons, unless they become unable to help themselves in some way, for example, by being caught in a soccer net.

Some ecofeminists see care theory as going beyond the rationalist foundation of rights theory to a valuing of emotion and relational qualities such as compassion and empathy.[68] Marti Kheel, for example, rejects the need for a rationalist claim for the "ecology of care" and instead begins with an inverse premise of care as an underlying ethos with failure to care as anomaly. Based on a medical model, Kheel's "feminist holist" care ethic values individuals and embraces emotion as a natural response to the suffering of individual animals in the meat industry, on fur farms, or in research facilities.[69]

Finally, we will turn to wisdom as a separate approach from virtue ethics, as it appears to be gaining ground that way. Like virtue, wisdom can be traced back in the Western tradition to Aristotle's *Nicomachean Ethics* and his notions of *phronĕsis*, practical wisdom, and *sophia*, reasoning about universal truths. The wisdom literature of the Old Testament, such as Job, Psalms, Proverbs, and Ecclesiastes, as well as prophetical books, such as Amos and Joel, also offer deep principles related to living a good life and taking beneficial actions for the long term. In discussing nonhuman ethics, the concept of wisdom is valuable in its own right, especially in the context of theology and biblical studies.[70]

CONTRIBUTIONS

The authors in this book draw connections between theology, philosophy, and ethics in the context of environmental concerns and the future of earth and its nonhumans. Though coming from diverse disciplines and faith communities, they collectively engage with ethical approaches to the treatment of nonhuman others in the world with the concept of compassion emerging from scripture, doctrine, tradition, and worship. Many of them move from theory to practice as they call attention to reparative actions that humans can take to love and to help our world, its places, and its creatures.

The chapters in the first section examine current ethical theories and their relationships to Christian principles as they relate to nonhumans in a variety of situations. Is it necessary to invoke rights language in order for humans to act responsibly toward animals? Celia Deane-Drummond considers the literature on animals in culture and moves beyond the animal-rights language of theorists like Andrew Linzey and Tom Regan to that of a Christian virtue ethic based on the priority of love that is other-focused. An understanding of our theological connections with animals may provide the ground needed to shape a moral community that includes human and nonhuman others.

Entomologist Jeffrey A. Lockwood discusses the three most common approaches to ethics and how they apply to insects. Does sentience theory hold up for bugs? Does an appreciation for aesthetics offer adequate justification for choosing not to hurt or destroy them? As Jesus called for humans to treat others with kindness and consideration of their needs, do ants, butterflies, grasshoppers, and ladybugs fall within the realm of our consideration? Lockwood weighs the strengths and weaknesses of the various approaches and calls us to consider justice as a master virtue that through principal can extend to animal others, including "the least of these."

Bryan Ness looks at the welfare of animals in the context of anthropogenic climate change and Old and New Testament scripture, and he challenges evangelical Christian complacency toward the loss of biodiversity. Promoting Clare Palmer's Laissez Faire Intuition as an ethical system for wild animals, Ness provides a hybrid approach to determining animal intervention under conditions of stress such as climate change. He then turns to practical considerations and offers reasonable predictions and recommendations for assisting and managing domestic and wild animals with the increasing problems brought on by global warming. For Ness, all is not lost and much can still be done to salvage species.

Mick Pope develops a Trinitarian global ethic grounded in scientific theory, the perichoretic (co-indwelling) nature of the Trinity and the kenotic (self-emptying) character of God. Using the work of Hans Küng, Stuart Kauffman, John Walton, and Jürgen Moltmann, Pope advances a global, Christian ethic to stand up against the rapid decline of earth and its resources.

Seeing the creation afresh, as the resting place of God and His temple in the Shabbat, for example, helps us redefine who we are in God. Jesus's incarnation, denial of self, and example of life through the indwelling of the Holy Spirit offers the model needed for helping earth with its many problems today. God's relation to his created beings, similar to that of his Trinitarian nature, empowers humans to perform the self-emptying acts needed if nonhumans are to survive in this age.

In the following section, Nonhuman Ethics in the South, Andrew R. H. Thompson explores the culture of Appalachia from the standpoint of loving a place and *The Foxfire Book*, comprised of narrative material from locals about their everyday lives and histories, including folklore, recipes, home remedies, and interviews. What does it mean to love Appalachia, a place of rich natural resources historically exploited by the mining industry? Thompson begins by looking at the pastoral letters of the local Catholic bishops that detail the suffering of people and land. He then moves to a discussion of compassion for place and proposes a theocentric understanding through the works of H. Richard Niebuhr and James M. Gustafson and a cultivated practice of compassion toward a place through Iris Murdoch and Wendell Berry's moral disciplines. Reading the *Foxfire* series invites us into the practice of loving place, as these texts reveal the deep connections between the people of Appalachia, their land, and the divine value placed on them. Perry Hodgkins Jones discusses the seeming irony of a Christian ethics of hunting in the Southeastern United States, where game hunting is a popular pastime. Can the church condone its members acting as predators to nonhumans in God's created order? By looking at ethical approaches taken by Elizabeth Johnson and David Clough, along with a close study of hunting culture in the United States, Hodgkins Jones explores two sides of this complex issue: On the one hand, hunters are some of the most ardent protectors of habitats, and, on the other, hunting for only sport is questionable in a nation where food is abundantly available. By considering Johnson's concept of "deep incarnation" and Clough's vision of nonhuman redemption and human accountability to God, it is possible to see that hunters can act ethically toward the creatures they kill. According to this view, an ethic of hunting may even allow for humans to understand where their food comes from and to act responsibly, moving them away from the sense of power and pride and toward a sanctified participation that leads to awe and reverence toward creation. Even so, Hodgkins Jones argues, the hunting community must understand their duty and follow the rules in order to ensure that they are contributing to the preservation of wildlife and ecosystems in place of destroying them.

The following section, Liturgical Approaches and Hymnody, contains studies of past and current ecological themes in worship and song. David Kendall opens this section with a focus on three approaches to creation care in hymn and chant repertoires from medieval times through the present. Looking across the approaches, Kendall sees a movement toward a more responsive ethic of care for creation. Reading hymns from the perspective of creation care shows the value of hymnody as a subject worthy of ecotheological treatment, as it reflects changes in environmental consciousness, especially from the past two centuries.

Does ecology need a place at the pulpit? Reverend Jerry Cappel asks how the church can effectively respond to growing environmental challenges and injustices. While a lot of good work goes on in "green teams," the fact remains that a solid focus on ecological concerns remains a marginal issue for most church attendees, and even the clergy seem to dismiss such concerns or to consign them to the secular or political spheres. In order for the church to become more engaged with earth's challenges, we need a paradigm shift from obligation to celebration. Restoration of the priority of creation care to liturgical practice is "work for clergy, teachers, musicians and worship leaders," as we recognize our calling to "faith and faithfulness" and our place as creation caretakers in right standing with our Creator.

Economist Robert Robin Gottfried opens Catholic Perspectives with a discussion of the Trinity and its relationship to contemporary virtuous design in city structures like buildings and parks. The wise and practical care of our earthly home depends on our relationship to the Creator, who cares for and sustains us.

Cristina Vanin discusses four creation-care doctrines in Pope Francis's *Laudato Si'* as foundational to an integral Christian ecology. The future of earth's home depends on our responsiveness to the ecological crisis at hand due to our embracing of a technocratic culture and its alienating influence to the detriment of the earth, its poor, and its creatures. By recognizing our cultural sin of being outside of God's will when we devalue the earth and its resources, we can learn to repent and to attend to lifestyles that resist consumerist, anthropocentric ways while we take up our social obligations to others in love and service. This response resonates with St. Francis's vision of healing and transformation.

The final section of this book considers Jesus's own relation to the animal kingdom in two stories from the Gospel of Mark. First, Kendra Haloviak Valentine reads Mark 5:1–20, the story of Jesus and Legion through ecocritical and postcolonial lenses, asking why it is that Jesus would choose to negotiate with demons and allow them to destroy two thousand pigs. Does the liberation of Legion serve ecological and political purposes as well as spiritual ones? Using Mary Douglas's anthropological work on purity and pollution and Roland Boer's economic context of ancient Israel, Haloviak Valentine reveals the story of Legion's spiritual deliverance as economic and ecological liberation for an entire biotic community. In delivering Legion,

Jesus provides the possibility for a more sustainable future for people and their land.

In the final chapter, Matthew Valdez (with Kendra Haloviak Valentine) provides a sociopolitical reading of the triumphal entry scene depicted in Mark 11:1–11 by taking into account Mark's ecological perspective through his narrative symbols that reveal Jesus's solidarity with the peasant subsistence farmers of his day. Jesus's choice to ride on a donkey symbolize the overturning of the existing oppressive order, represented by a corrupted temple order, even before Jesus enters the temple. Valdez moves beyond Mark's text to consider present-day evils of factory farming and CAFOs to ask questions that may reveal inconsistencies in our social fabric. The chapter ends with a hopeful vision and a call to expand our vision of Christian care to the nonhuman world.

FROM FAITH TO ACTION: OVERCOMING EVIL WITH GOOD

What can we do? Understanding that Christian ecology expands from theory to service, Anne Marie Dalton and Henry C. Simmons write, "[p]ractices of hope come to life in real people, in real places, in real communities, in real time. These are the sources of global change."[71] Worship, biblical texts, doctrine, and music that focus on creation care remind us of our role as stewards and shape our ecological imaginaries.[72] Various denominations and faith communities have made commitments to creation care, and it is important to recognize and to value the distinct contributions each provides to the conversation. For example, Cristina Vanin, in her chapter here, covers four Catholic doctrines on creation care, including conversion, virtues, culture, and nurturance of spirituality in the context of ecology. The uniqueness of Mormon ecology, according to George B. Handley, consists in its nondualist interpretation of body and spirit and in a conception of the Fall as opportunity for joy within redemptive hope.[73] In Adventist faith the emphasis on the seventh-day Sabbath with its natural connection to the literal creation week, vegetarianism, medical missions, and preparation for our roles as caretakers of the new earth provide a solid foundation for creation-care vision and practice.[74]

Universities can do much toward fostering a culture of creation care through service learning and community action. British theological ethicist and Methodist preacher David Clough directs CreatureKind, an online project for the promotion of farm-animal welfare in connection with church communities. CreatureKind's vision is to help church members value farm animals as living beings and to contribute to their health and safety.[75] At the small, private university where I work we offer several courses on human and animal ethics as a natural outgrowth of our school's faith and mission.

Health psychologist Leslie R. Martin teaches an ethics course in which students either contract with local animal welfare groups or work on projects related to animal issues.[76] Biologist John Perumal helps students grow vertical gardens, cook vegetarian meals, and clean city streets. In my Pets and People freshman seminar, students create their own pet-care manuals that include pages on safety, routine vaccinations, and spaying and neutering.[77]

Many people in my community who provide services to animals also see their actions as integral to their faith. A mother-daughter team have a nonprofit organization called Taking it to the Streets with Lori and Shira, devoted to the care of street people and their animals. Aside from providing dogs and cats with their vaccines and alterations, they also distribute blankets, backpacks, food, water, collars, and leashes to the homeless on a daily basis and at their free "street stores." Lori says, "I believe that the work we do represents Judaism at its best. We may not be out there as a religious organization, but I feel that we represent our faith well."[78] As well, Marie Sanner manages a chapter of Cats in Need of Human Care, a nonprofit organization that rescues cats and dogs. Of her work, Marie says, "The reason I do rescue is because I want to help God's creatures that have been abused and not taken care of."[79] David Loop of Sierra Pacific Furbabies freely shares with others how his conversion while in prison led him to start his animal rescue: "Living in a cage in one of the harshest prisons in California, my life dependent on the actions of others, I developed a profound belief in the power of prayer." David's rescue work has received local and international media attention, as he goes into dark and tight places to rescue tiny kittens.[80] "Rescue work became my passion," he says, "as I could relate to the helpless animals that relied on us as their protectors."[81]

CONCLUSION: LOVING OUR ENEMIES

I write in the wake of the killing of Cecil the lion just outside his habitat at Hwange National Park and that of Harambe, the seventeen-year-old gorilla at the Cincinnati Zoo, shot by zoo officials for possibly endangering a child who had climbed and fallen into his habitat.[82] In both cases the strong protests and public outcry, which included media bashing, led to the protection of the humans involved in the acts. In the case of Walter Palmer, whose arrow and gun killed Cecil, angry demonstrators caused the shutdown of his dental office for several months, and police monitored his return to practice.[83] In the case of Harambe's death, the media withheld the names of the mother and son.[84] Both incidents brought attention to the plight of wild animals. Within five months of Cecil's death, the U.S. Fish and Wildlife Service moved to protect two species of lion by adding them to the endangered species list,[85] and in the case of Harambe petitions and animal groups raised awareness of problems related to animal captivity.

On the one hand the human response to nonhuman tragedy reveals the rightful, deep emotional connection and moral obligation we feel toward creatures in the wild and in captivity. But on the other hand, the methods used in these cases to bring about the desired end are not tenable for thinking Christians. True Christian ecology is called to a much higher response toward humans as well as toward nonhumans. In taking our stand against violence toward nonhumans, we are also called to extend love even to those who move against our beliefs and causes. In taking up the cross of love for our enemies, we may find hope that acts of compassion toward human others may ultimately have the desired effect we seek toward the animal world. Christianity is a relational religion that begins in the here and now.[86] Thus, the beginning of this process for any individual Christian is in humility, repentance, and prayer to receive this love.

The readings in this book remind us of the importance of biodiversity, local church efforts, scriptural inheritance, and community involvement in the context of our environmental challenges. While we strive to promote the welfare of earth and its creatures, I feel it is important to acknowledge freedom of choice as an ultimate, underlying biblical principle. The main value of making a book like this consists in its diversity of views and backgrounds, many of which accord in mutual concern about how we relate to our common home and its nonhuman inhabitants. The climate of incivility and hate we have recently witnessed calls us to recognize and to respect the freedoms of those who may disagree with us even while we retain our own convictions. It is my hope that the viewpoints and the principles addressed here will do much to inspire change of heart in the spirit of that freedom and love recognized by Bible champions through the ages as we seek together to help our world.

NOTES

1. Claudia Durst Johnson and Vernon E. Johnson write that *Black Beauty* did more than any other novel to influence the animal movement in terms of increased work in animal societies and anticruelty legislation. *The Social Impact of the Novel* (Westport, CT: Greenwood Press, 2002). "Many of the cruel practices horses endured in *Black Beauty* helped lead to legislation banning the behavior." (Stephanie Libo, "Black Beauty: The Tale of a Horse that Changed the Perspective of a Nation," *Living Green Magazine*, November 30, 2012, accessed July 1, 2016, http://livinggreenmag.com/2012/11/30/people-solutions/black-beauty-the-tale-of-a-horse-that-changed-the-perspective-of-a-nation/.

2. Quoted in Fred Glueckstein's *Of Men, Women and Horses* (Bloomington, IN: Xlibris, 2006), 25.

3. *Black Beauty* was selected as NPR's Backseat Book Club book in 2012. See Michele Norris's account covering the book's influence and her interview with children's author Jane Smiley on *All Things Considered*: "How 'Black Beauty' Changed the Way We See Horses," *NPR Books, Backseat Book Club: Youthful Reads for Junior Brainiacs*, November 2, 2012,

accessed June 27, 2016, http://www.npr.org/2012/11/02/163971063/how-black-beauty-changed-the-way-we-see-horses.

    4. The work of Richard Martin, William Wilberforce, Fowell Buxton, and others in Parliament led to the passing of the Anti-Cruelty to Cattle Act on July 22, 1821. Not quite two years later, these men, under the leadership of Reverend Arthur Broome, formed the Society for the Prevention of Cruelty to Animals, ironically, at Old Slaughter's Pub. Bernard Unti, "Amazing Grace: The Work of William Wilberforce," in *Every Living Thing: How Pope Francis, Evangelicals, and Other Christian Leaders are Inspiring All of Us to Care for Animals* (Canton, MI: Front Edge Publishing, 2015), 253–57. See also Andrew Linzey and Tom Regan, *Animals and Christianity: A Book of Readings* (Eugene, OR: Wipf and Stock Publishers, 1990), x-xi.

    5. Lewis Carroll, "Some Popular Fallacies about Vivisection," in *The Fortnightly Review*, New Series, ed. John Morley, 17 (June 23, 1875): 847–52.

    6. Ibid., 853.

    7. Ibid.

    8. Linzey and Regan discuss the goal of the 1875 newly established Victoria Street Society (later, the National Anti-Vivisecton Society) to regulate and put an end to vivisection. Among the members were Victor Hugo, Cardinal Manning, Robert Browning, Lord Alfred Tennyson, Thomas Carlyle, and John Ruskin with others (*Animals and Christianity*, x-xi).

    9. Office of the Press Secretary, The White House, "Fact Sheet: President Xi Jinping's State Visit to the United States," *The White House*, September 25, 2015, accessed June 29, 2016, https://www.whitehouse.gov/the-press-office/2015/09/25/fact-sheet-president-xi-jinpings-state-visit-united-states.

    10. Laurel Neme, "Why Shutting Down China's Ivory Trade Won't Be Easy," January 8, 2016, accessed July 4, 2016, http://news.nationalgeographic.com/2016/01/160108-illegal-ivory-trade-china-hong-kong-elephant-action-league-rhino-horn/.

    11. According to Dune Ives, former senior director of Vulcan Philanthropy (currently the executive director of the Lonely Whale Foundation), "more than 30,000 of these awe-inspiring animals are poached each year by AK 47's, coordinated helicopter attacks, and mass cyanide poisoning." "World Elephant Day," Vulcan.inc, August 12, 2015, accessed July 5, 2016, https://medium.com/@vulcaninc/what-if-there-were-no-elephants-left-d7fa11c3190d#.s3gfoaao8.

    12. "Annual dog meat festival in China under new scrutiny," *CBS News*, April 4, 2016, accessed June 28, 2016, http://www.cbsnews.com/news/annual-dog-meat-festival-in-china-under-new-scrutiny/.

    13. Iskhander Razak, "Dog cruelty: Rise in slaughter of stolen pets as Western tourists fuel South-East Asia dog meat market," *ABC News*, January 21, 2016, accessed June 29, 2016, http://www.abc.net.au/news/2016-01-22/dog-cruelty-stolen-pets-tourists-fuelling-growth-in-meat/7088380.

    14. Razak, "Dog cruelty."

    15. Razak, "Dog cruelty."

    16. Among the many news items related to the issue of the Yulin dog meat festival, see, Samuel Osborne, "Yulin Dog Meat Festival 2016: New pictures emerge of 'nightmare' conditions for animals involved in Chinese event," *Independent*, April 7, 2016, accessed July 5, 2016, http://www.bbc.com/news/world-asia-china-33220235.

    17. The practice of large-scale egg producers whereby male chicks are identified and ground up alive through a machine because they have no economic value to egg companies. This practice, along with other ways of killing male chicks, has been approved by the American Veterinary Medical Association. See *AVMA Guidelines for the Euthanasia of Animals*, (Schaumberg, IL: The American Veterinary Medical Association, 2013), 63, https://www.avma.org/KB/Policies/Documents/euthanasia.pdf.

    18. "U.S. egg producers to eliminate routine killing of male chicks by 2020," FoxNews.com, June 13, 2016, accessed June 26, 2016, http://www.foxnews.com/leisure/2016/06/13/us-egg-producers-to-eliminate-routine-killing-male-chicks-by-2020/.

    19. Germany has recently decided to continue the practice in spite of animal advocacy. Researcher and veterinarian Maria-Elisabeth Krautwald-Junghanns at Leipzig University is hoping her efforts will ultimately result in female-only incubation. Brigitte Osterath, "Practice of killing male chicks to continue, German parliament decides," *Made for Minds*, Deutsche

Welle, March 18, 2016, accessed July 1, 2016, http://www.dw.com/en/about-dw/profile/s-30688.

20. Matthew Scully, *The Power of Man, the Suffering of Animals, and the Call to Mercy.* New York: St. Martin's Griffin, 2002, 85.

21. Scully, *Dominion*, 398.

22. Scully, *Dominion*, 398.

23. Marc Bekoff has been on the forefront of showing that animals have emotional lives worthy of our compassionate consideration. See, for example, Marc Bekoff, *The Animal Manifesto: Six Reasons for Expanding our Compassion Footprint* (Novato, CA: New World Library, 2010); Marc Bekoff, *The Emotional Lives of Animals: A Leading Scientist Explores Animal Joy, Sorrow, and Empathy—and Why They Matter* (Novato, CA: New World Library, 2007), and Marc Bekoff and Jessica Pierce, *Wild Justice: The Moral Lives of Animals* (Chicago: University of Chicago Press, 1992).

24. See Peter Singer, *The Most Good You Can Do* (New Haven, CT: Yale University Press, 2015), 137. Singer reports that 9.1 billion animals are raised and slaughtered yearly in the United States alone. He especially laments the animals that die before they get to the slaughterhouses due to various stresses placed upon them by factory farming practices and transportation (138).

25. Ellen F. Davis, *Scripture, Culture, and Agriculture: An Agrarian Reading of the Bible* (Cambridge: Cambridge University Press, 2010), 98.

26. Sigve K. Tonstad, *The Letter to the Romans: Paul Among the Ecologists* (Sheffield, UK: Sheffield Phoenix Press, 2016), 308. For a fascinating study on the theology of seeds, see 295–304 as well as Ellen Davis, *Scripture, Culture and Agriculture*, 48–53.

27. Anne Marie Dalton and Henry C. Simmons provide a comprehensive history of the development of ecotheology in the United States. *Ecotheology and the Practice of Hope*, (Albany: State University of New York Press, 2011), 19-37.

28. Celia Deane-Drummond defines *ecotheology* as "that reflection on different facets of theology in as much as they take their bearings from cultural concerns about the environment and humanity's relationship with the natural world." *Eco-Theology* (London: Anselm Academic, 2008), x.

29. Lynn White, Jr., "The Historical Roots of our Ecological Crisis," *Science*, New Series, 155, no. 3767 (March 10, 1967), 1204.

30. While ecotheology includes studies in various world religions and their traditions, as shown in Paul Waldau and Kimberley Patton's remarkable edition, *A Communion of Subjects: Animals in Religion, Science, and Ethics* (New York: Columbia University Press, 2006) and as represented in the membership of the International Society for the Study of Religion, Nature, and Culture, I have chosen to limit the scope of this book to the Judeo-Christian tradition while appreciating the crosscurrents of thought between traditions.

31. David G. Horrell, *The Bible and the Environment* (London: Equinox, 2010), 11.

32. Ibid., 125. See also Ernst Conradie, "What on Earth is an Ecological Hermeneutics? Some Broad Parameters," *Ecological Hermeneutics: Biblical, Historical, and Theological Perspectives* . Eds. David G. Horrell, Cherryl Hunt, Christopher Southgate, and Francesca Stavrakopoulou. (London: T and T Clark, 2010), 295-314.

33. Richard Bauckham, *The Bible and Ecology: Rediscovering the Community of Creation* (Waco, TX: Baylor University Press, 2010).

34. Ps. 104:11, 21; Ps. 147:9.

35. Ps. 19:1–6

36. Ps. 104: 17–18, 26.

37. Ps. 23:1–6; Ps. 100:3; Ps. 119:76.

38. Ps. 96:12; Ps. 98:8; Ps. 148.

39. This is not to say that the Psalms do not also reflect real-world violence in nature or predator-prey relationships, which they do, but, taken as a whole, the Psalms reveal God as caretaker over his created works, including humans, fields, rivers, mountains, and animals, domestic and wild. See Richard Bauckham, *The Bible and Ecology*, 87–92.

40. Ex. 12: 3–7; Ex. 29:10–14.

41. Lv. 22: 22–28.

42. Ellen Bernstein, "A Biblical Land Ethic? A Response to Aldo Leopold," *Ecotheology in the Humanities: An Interdisciplinary Approach to Understanding the Divine and Nature* (Lanham, MD: Lexington Books, 2016), 25–52. See also Ellen Davis, *Scripture, Culture, and Agriculture: An Agrarian Reading of the Bible* (Cambridge: Cambridge University Press, 2009).

43. Lv. 23:22; Lv. 25:3–8.

44. Ellen Davis, *Scripture, Culture, and Agriculture*, 82.

45. Mt. 8:20; Lk. 9:58;

46. Mt. 10:29 (English Standard Version).

47. Richard Bauckham, 126–29.

48. Revelation 21:5 (New King James Version).

49. Andrew Linzey's distinguished career has been devoted to making connections between Christianity and animal rights since his 1976 work, *Animal Rights: A Christian Assessment*. He has authored more than twenty books since then on animal ethics in the context of Christianity, the Bible and ecology. He is a member of the faculty of theology at Oxford and the director for the Oxford Centre of Animal Ethics. He is also Professor of Animal Theology at the University of Winchester.

50. The Albert Schweitzer Fellowship page suggests that the term *ehrfurcht* contains overtones of power that are not captured by *reverence*. "It holds reverberations of the feelings we experience on the tops of high mountains, in a storm at sea, or in a tropical tornado." "Philosophy," The Albert Schweitzer Fellowship, 2016, accessed June 29, 2016, http://www.schweitzerfellowship.org/about/albert-schweitzer/philosophy/.

51. For a brief history of Linzey's career see the introduction to *Creatures of the Same God: Explorations in Animal Theology* (Brooklyn, NY: Lantern Books, 2009).

52. See Celia Deane-Drummond and David Clough, *Creaturely Theology: On God, Humans and Other Animals* (London; SCM Press, 2009); David Clough, *On Animals: Volume 1: Systematic Theology*, (London: Bloomsbury, 2012); Christopher Southgate, *The Groaning of Creation: God, Evolution, and the Problem of Evil* (Louisville, KY: Westminster John Knox Press, 2008). These scholars and others span the gap between ecotheology and animal theology.

53. And yet the two areas of study are related. David Clough discusses the relevance of animal theology to larger systems with the idea of concentric circles outward from animals to vegetation to the universe. We are simply choosing to stop and pay attention to one of the rings like we do in looking at human theology. Introduction, *On Animals: Volume 1: Systematic Theology*, (London: Bloomsbury, 2012), xxiii.

54. While acknowledging the soundness of other ethical perspectives, Singer argues that "the limit of sentience . . . is the only defensible boundary of concern for the interests of others" and that other characteristics, such as the capacity for reason, can be only arbitrary considerations. Peter Singer, *Practical Ethics*, 2nd edition, Cambridge: Cambridge University Press, 1993), 58. See also *Animal Liberation: A New Ethics for Our Treatment of Animals* (New York: HarperCollins, 1975).

55. Deontology stems from the work of Immanuel Kant, who theorized that humans should only ever act in ways they would wish to become universal laws. Humans should treat all other humans as ends in themselves rather than as means to ends.

56. See Tom Regan, *The Case for Animal Rights* (Berkeley: The University of California Press, 1983).

57. Tom Regan, 283.

58. Christine Korsgaard, "The Origin of Value and the Scope of Obligation," in *The Sources of Normativity* by Christine Korsgarrd, ed. Onora O'Neill (Cambridge: Cambridge University Press, 1996), 131–32.

59. "Laws are by their very nature universal, according to Kant, and a universal law can extend its protection to someone who did not participate, and could not have participated, in its legislation" (Ibid., 96).

60. Julian H. Franklin, *Animal Rights and Moral Philosophy* (New York: Columbia University Press, 2004), xiii, 77–88.

61. Daniel C. Russell, *The Cambridge Companion to Virtue Ethics* (Cambridge: Cambridge University Press, 2013), 1.

62. The study of virtue ethics stems from Aristotle's *Nicomachean Ethics* in which the achievement of virtue is paramount to the acquisitions of goods. Aristotle's virtues include courage, temperance, generosity, friendliness, and magnanimity, to name a few. Because Aristotle's virtues are dispositional, it is truer to Aristotle's meaning to read them as practical and not as theoretical. Garth Kemerling, "Aristotle: Ethics and Virtues," *The Philosophy Pages*, accessed June 18, 2016, http://www.philosophypages.com/hy/2s.htm.

63. Ibid., 2.

64. Iris Murdoch, *The Sovereignty of Good* (London: Routledge, 2001), 101.

65. Wendell Berry, *The Unsettling of America: Culture and Agriculture* (Berkeley, CA: Counterpoint Press, 1977), 19–29.

66. Maureen Sander-Staudt, "Care Ethics," in *Internet Encyclopedia of Philsophy: A Peer-Reviewed Academic Resource*, by James Fieser and Bradley Dowden, accessed July 1, 2016, http://www.iep.utm.edu/care-eth/.

67. Daniel Engster, "Care Ethics and Animal Welfare," *Journal of Social Philosophy*, 37, no. 4 (Winter 2006):521.

68. Maureen Sander-Staudt, "Care Ethics."

69. Marti Kheel, *Nature Ethics: An Ecofeminist Perspective* (Lanham, MD: Rowman & Littlefield, 2008).

70. For example, Celia Deane-Drummond makes use of wisdom in the opposing concepts of "Divine Sophia" and "Shadow Sophia" to integrate theories of theodicy in her book *Eco-Theology* (London: Anselm Academic, 2008) as she does in *Christ and Evolution: Wonder and Wisdom* (Minneapolis, MN: Fortress Press, 2009).

71. Dalton and Simmons, 126.

72. Charles Taylor's concept of the *social imaginary* finds currency in the literature of ecotheology. See Dalton and Simmons, *Ecotheology and the Practice of Hope*, 1–18; Doug Sikkema, "Ecotheology and Enchantment: How Wendell Berry Helps Re-vision the World," in *Ecotheology and the Humanities: An Interdisciplinary Approach to Understanding the Divine and Nature*, ed. Melissa J. Brotton (Lanham, MD: Lexington, 2016), 73–86. For an illuminating study of how liturgical practices may shape "religious imaginaries," see Karen Dieleman, *Religious Imaginaries: The Liturgical and Poetic Practices of Elizabeth Barrett Browning, Christina Rossetti, and Adelaide Proctor* (Athens: Ohio University Press, 2012).

73. George B. Handley, "The Environmental Ethics of Mormon Belief," *BYU Studies* 40, no. 2 (2001):191.

74. See Young-Chun Kim, "Sanctification as Impetus for Creation Care in Adventism," in *Ecotheology in the Humanities: An Interdisciplinary Approach to Understanding the Divine and Nature*, ed. Melissa J. Brotton (Lanham, MD: Lexington, 2016), 53–70.

75. See the CreatureKind website at http://becreaturekind.org.

76. Leslie R. Martin's course's name is Science, Ethics, and Ethical Extensionism.

77. Because we live in a community with a huge homeless animal population, we feel it is vital to provide education to our students about American standards of veterinary care, including population control.

78. Lori Rich, email message to the author, June 29, 2016.

79. Marie Sanner, text message to the author, July 4, 2016.

80. One story made the NBC nightly news on Tuesday, December 15, 2015. See Heather Navarro and Tony Shin, "Crews Capture Kitten Stuck in Storm Drain for More Than 28 Hours in Fontana," *Watch Live: NBC4 News*, December 15, 2015, accessed July 5, 2016, http://www.nbclosangeles.com/news/local/trapped-kitten-rescue-social-media-fontana-storm-drain-362065651.html.

81. David Loop, email message sent to the author, July 5, 2016.

82. Emanuella Grinberg, "In gorilla's death, critics blame mother, Cincinnati Zoo," *CNN*, May 30, 2016, accessed June 29, 2016, http://www.cnn.com/2016/05/29/us/cincinnati-zoo-gorilla-shot/. The child was released from the hospital unharmed.

83. Ed Payne, "Walter Palmer, the man who killed Cecil the lion, returns to his dental practice," *CNN News*, September 8, 2015, accessed June 30, 2016, http://www.cnn.com/2015/09/08/us/walter-palmer-dentist-cecil-lion-return/.

84. Emanuella Grinberg, "In gorilla's death, critics blame mother, Cincinnati Zoo."

85. In effect in the *Federal Register* since January 22, 2016. "Lions Are Now Protected Under the Endangered Species Act," Endangered Species, U.S. Fish and Wildlife Service, accessed June 30, 2016, https://www.fws.gov/endangered/what-we-do/lion.html.

86. Lk. 17:21. David Clough expresses this thought in *On Animals: Volume 1: Systematic Theology* (London: Bloomsbury, 2012), 170: Concerning Christ's statements on the kingdom of Heaven in Matthew's gospel, "because the kingdom of heaven has come near (4.17), the righteousness of his followers must exceed that of the scribes and Pharisees (5.20), those who wish to enter must do the will of the Father (7.21), those who seek it must give up everything for it (13.44–5) and those who wait must be wise in their preparations like the bridesmaids who took oil for their lamps (25.1–4)."

REFERENCES

American Veterinary Medical Association. *AVMA Guidelines for the Euthanasia of Animals*. Schaumberg, IL: The American Veterinary Medical Association, 2013. https://www.avma.org/KB/Policies/Documents/euthanasia.pdf.

"Annual dog meat festival in China under new scrutiny." *CBS News*. April 4, 2016. Accessed June 28, 2016. http://www.cbsnews.com/news/annual-dog-meat- festival-in-china-under-new-scrutiny/.

Bauckham, Richard. *The Bible and Ecology: Rediscovering the Community of Creation*. Waco, TX: Baylor University Press, 2010.

Bekoff, Marc. *The Animal Manifesto: Six Reasons for Expanding our Compassion Footprint*. Novato, CA: New World Library, 2010.

———. *The Emotional Lives of Animals: A Leading Scientist Explores Animal Joy, Sorrow, and Empathy—and Why They Matter*. Novato, CA: New World Library, 2007.

Bekoff, Marc and Jessica Pierce. *Wild Justice: The Moral Lives of Animals*. Chicago: University of Chicago Press, 1992.

Bernstein, Ellen. "A Biblical Land Ethic? A Response to Aldo Leopold." In *Ecotheology in the Humanities: An Interdisciplinary Approach to Understanding the Divine and Nature*. Edited by Melissa J. Brotton. Lanham, MD: Lexington Books, 2016, 25–52.

———. *Ecology and the Jewish Spirit: Where Nature and the Sacred Meet*. Woodstock, VT: Jewish Lights Publishing, 2008.

Berry, Wendell. *The Unsettling of America: Culture and Agriculture*. Berkeley, CA: Counterpoint Press, 1977, 19–29.

Carroll, Lewis. "Some Popular Fallacies about Vivisection." In *The Fortnightly Review*, New Series. Edited by John Morley, 17 (June 23, 1875): 847–52.

Clough, David L. *On Animals: Volume 1: Systematic Theology*. London: Bloomsbury, 2012.

Conradie, Ernst. "What on Earth is an Ecological Hermeneutics? Some Broad Parameters." *Ecological Hermeneutics: Biblical, Historical, and Theological Perspectives*. Edited by David G. Horrell, Cherryl Hunt, Christopher Southgate, and Francesca Stavrakopoulou. London: T & T Clark, 2010, 295–314.

Dalton, Anne Marie and Henry C. Simmons. *Ecotheology and the Practice of Hope*. Albany: State University of New York Press, 2010.

Davis, Ellen F. *Scripture, Culture, and Agriculture: An Agrarian Reading of the Bible*. Cambridge: Cambridge University Press, 2010.

Deane-Drummond, Celia. *Introduction to Eco-Theology*. London: Anselm Academic, 2008.

———. *Christ and Evolution: Wonder and Wisdom*. Minneapolis, MN: Fortress Press, 2009.

Deane-Drummond, Celia and David Clough. *Creaturely Theology: On God, Humans and Other Animals*. London: SCM Press, 2009.

Dieleman, Karen. *Religious Imaginaries: The Liturgical and Poetic Practices of Elizabeth Barrett Browning, Christina Rossetti, and Adelaide Proctor.* Athens: Ohio University Press, 2012.
Engster, Daniel. "Care Ethics and Animal Welfare." *Journal of Social Philosophy*, 37, no. 4 (Winter 2006).
Franklin, Julian H. *Animal Rights and Moral Philosophy.* New York: Columbia University Press, 2004.
Glueckstein, Fred. *Of Men, Women and Horses.* Bloomington, IN: Xlibris, 2006.
Grinberg, Emanuella. "In gorilla's death, critics blame mother, Cincinnati Zoo." *CNN News.* May 30, 2016. Accessed June 29, 2016. http://www.cnn.com/2016/05/29/us/cincinnati-zoo-gorilla-shot/.
Handley, George B. "The Environmental Ethics of Mormon Belief." *BYU Studies* 40, no. 2 (2001): 187–211.
Horrell, David G. *The Bible and the Environment: Towards a Critical Ecological Biblical Theology.* London: Equinox, 2010.
Ives, Dune. "World Elephant Day." Vulcan.inc. August 12, 2015. Accessed July 5, 2016. https://medium.com/@vulcaninc/what-if-there-were-no-elephants-left-d7fa11c3190d#.s3gfoaao8.
Johnson, Claudia D. and Vernon E. Johnson. *The Social Impact of the Novel.* Westport, CT: Greenwood Press, 2002.
Kheel, Marti. *Nature Ethics: An Ecofeminist Perspective.* Lanham, MD: Rowman & Littlefield, 2008.
Kemerling, Garth. "Aristotle: Ethics and Virtues." *The Philosophy Pages.* Accessed June 18, 2016. http://www.philosophypages.com/hy/2s.htm.
Kim, Young-Chun. "Sanctification as Impetus for Creation Care in Adventism." In *Ecotheology in the Humanities: An Interdisciplinary Approach to Understanding the Divine and Nature.* Edited by Melissa J. Brotton. Lanham, MD: Lexington Books, 2016, 53–70.
Korsgaard, Christine. "The Origin of Value and the Scope of Obligation." In *The Sources of Normativity* by Christine Korsgarrd. Edited by Onora O'Neill. Cambridge: Cambridge University Press, 1996.
Libo, Stephanie. "Black Beauty: The Tale of a Horse that Changed the Perspective of a Nation." *Living Green Magazine.* November 30, 2012. Accessed July 1, 2016. http://livinggreenmag.com/2012/11/30/people-solutions/black-beauty-the-tale-of- a-horse-that-changed-the-perspective-of-a-nation/.
Linzey, Andrew. *Animal Rights: A Christian Assessment.* London, UK: SCM Press, 1976.
———. *Creatures of the Same God: Explorations in Animal Theology.* Brooklyn, NY: Lantern Books, 2009.
Linzey, Andrew, and Tom Regan. *Animals and Christianity: A Book of Readings.* Eugene, OR: Wipf and Stock Publishers, 1990.
"Lions Are Now Protected Under the Endangered Species Act." *Endangered Species. U.S. Fish and Wildlife Service.* Accessed June 30, 2016. https://www.fws.gov/endangered/what-we-do/lion.html.
Murdoch, Iris. *The Sovereignty of Good.* 2nd ed. London: Routledge, 2001.
Neme, Laurel. "Why Shutting Down China's Ivory Trade Won't Be Easy." January 8, 2016. Accessed July 4, 2016. http://news.nationalgeographic.com/2016/01/160108-illegal-ivory-trade- china-hong-kong-elephant-action-league-rhino-horn/.
Norris, Michele. "How 'Black Beauty' Changed the Way We See Horses." *NPR Books, Backseat Book Club: Youthful Reads for Junior Brainiacs.* November 2, 2012. Accessed June 27, 2016. http://www.npr.org/2012/11/02/163971063/how-black- beauty-changed-the-way-we-see-horses.
Office of the Press Secretary. The White House "Fact Sheet: President Xi Jinping's State Visit to the United States." *The White House.* September 25, 2015. Accessed June 29, 2016. https://www.whitehouse.gov/the-press-office/2015/09/25/fact-sheet-president-xi-jinpings-state-visit-united-states.

Osborne, Samuel. "Yulin Dog Meat Festival 2016: New pictures emerge of 'nightmare' conditions for animals involved in Chinese event." *Independent*. April 7, 2016. Accessed July 5, 2016. http://www.bbc.com/news/world-asia- china- 33220235.

Osterath, Brigitte. "Practice of killing male chicks to continue, German parliament decides." *Made for Minds*. Deutsche Welle. March 18, 2016. Accessed July 1, 2016. http://www.dw.com/en/about-dw/profile/s-30688.

Payne, Ed. "Walter Palmer, the man who killed Cecil the lion, returns to his dental practice." *CNN News*. September 8, 2015. Accessed June 30, 2016. http://www.cnn.com/2015/09/08/us/walter-palmer-dentist-cecil-lion- return/.

"Philosophy." *The Albert Schweitzer Fellowship 2016*. Accessed June 29, 2016. http://www.schweitzerfellowship.org/about/albert- schweitzer/philosophy/.

Razak, Iskhander. "Dog cruelty: Rise in slaughter of stolen pets as Western tourists fuel South-East Asia dog meat market." *ABC News*. January 21, 2016. Accessed June 29, 2016. http://www.abc.net.au/news/2016–01–22/dog-cruelty-stolen-pets-tourists-fuelling-growth-in-meat/7088380.

Regan, Tom. *The Case for Animal Rights*. Berkeley: University of California Press, 1983.

Russell, Daniel C. *The Cambridge Companion to Virtue Ethics*. Cambridge: Cambridge University Press, 2013.

Sander-Staudt, Maureen. "Care Ethics." In *Internet Encyclopedia of Philosophy: A Peer-Reviewed Academic Resource*. By James Fieser and Bradley Dowden. Accessed July 1, 2016. http://www.iep.utm.edu/care-eth/.

Sikkema, Doug. "Ecotheology and Enchantment: How Wendell Berry Helps Re-vision the World." In *Ecotheology and the Humanities: An Interdisciplinary Approach to Understanding the Divine and Nature*. Edited by Melissa J. Brotton. Lanham, MD: Lexington Books, 2016, 73–86.

Scully, Matthew. *Dominion: The Power of Man, the Suffering of Animals, and the Call to Mercy*. New York: St. Martin's Griffin, 2002.

Singer, Peter. *Animal Liberation: A New Ethics for Our Treatment of Animals*. New York: HarperCollins, 1975.

———. *The Most Good You Can Do*. New Haven, CT: Yale University Press, 2015.

———. *Practical Ethics*. 2nd edition. Cambridge: Cambridge University Press, 1993.

Southgate, Christopher. *The Groaning of Creation: God, Evolution, and the Problem of Evil*. Louisville, KY: Westminster John Knox Press, 2008.

Tonstad, Sigve K. *The Letter to the Romans: Paul Among the Ecologists*. Sheffield, UK: Sheffield Phoenix Press, 2016.

Unti, Bernard. "Amazing Grace: The Work of William Wilberforce." In *Every Living Thing: How Pope Francis, Evangelicals, and Other Christian Leaders are Inspiring All of Us to Care for Animals*. Edited by Christine Gutleben. Canton, MI: Front Edge Publishing, 2015.

"U.S. egg producers to eliminate routine killing of male chicks by 2020." *FoxNews.com*. June 13, 2016. Accessed June 26, 2016. http://www.foxnews.com/leisure/2016/06/13/us-egg-producers-to- eliminate-routine-killing-male-chicks-by-2020/.

Waldau, Paul, and Kimberley Patton. *A Communion of Subjects: Animals in Religion, Science, and Ethics*. New York: Columbia University Press, 2006.

White, Lynn, Jr. "The Historical Roots of our Ecological Crisis," *Science*. 155, no. 3767 (March 10, 1967): 1203–7.

Part I

Christian Virtues and Nonhuman Ethics

Chapter One

Animal Rights Revisited

Celia Deane-Drummond

The place of animals in humanities literature, including religious literature, is beginning to be recognized and acknowledged. While this literature calls to mind the importance of the animal in human culture, it seeks to persuade toward a more sensitive treatment of animals indirectly, as opposed to the more aggressive use of the language of rights in the work of Tom Regan, Andrew Linzey, and others that has dominated much of the literature on animal ethics. This chapter will consider the place of animal liberation and rights language in as much as it presumes the validity of human rights premised on a particular and questionable ontology of the human. In place of animal rights, I argue for a Christian virtue ethic that flows from a particular self-conscious theological orientation, namely, the priority of love in our relations with others, including other animals.

A few years ago I met a senior scientist actively engaged in medical research on mice. One of the first questions he somewhat nervously asked me when he found out that I was interested in questions about the theological place of other animals was whether I supported animal rights. My instinctive answer was that I did not but that I did support human responsibilities toward other animals. But what might these responsibilities entail? And what does this tell us about what it means to be human? The association of animal rights with violent actions by humans toward human others engaged in research on animal kinds that may entail their killing is one unfortunate outcome of the animal rights movement and one of the reasons why some of those who take a theological position on this topic are sometimes skeptical about the value of animal-rights.[1] The purpose of this chapter is not to explore the practical or even political issues associated with animal rights but to probe more deeply and critically the various philosophical and theological arguments that have been used by its supporters in order to uncover their implicit anthropology. In other words, to put this more plainly, how has what might seem to be a compassionate stance in favor of other animals ended up promoting violence toward other humans?

This opens up the constructive possibility for a virtue ethic that is more deeply grounded in theological anthropology in as much as it is concerned about who we are and how we perceive ourselves as much as what we do. In practical terms, this includes a strong focus on other regard; in Christian terms, *the priority of love* that then shapes what justice toward animals might require.

The exclusion of animals from the moral community in the history of Western thought is well documented. Historically and even today other animals have been thought of as devoid of certain categories, such as reason and autonomy, which have then been used as criteria for exclusion from moral concern. The increasing awareness of the actual capacities of other animal kinds, coincident with the rise in the civil rights movements in the nineteenth century opposing sexual and racial discrimination, opened the way for the emergence of explicitly named *animal* rights in the twentieth and twenty-first centuries, mirroring wider discussions of human rights. Champions of animal rights point to specific legal gains in animal welfare that they credit to the success of their campaigns. Examples include the 1988 Swedish Animal Welfare Act, the 1990 Veal Crate Ban in the UK, the 1992 International Dolphin Conservation Act and so on. Yet we might ask ourselves if such gains might have been wrought through a different approach to moral philosophy that had rather less tendency toward violent outbursts toward human opponents.

THE CASE FOR ANIMAL RIGHTS

David De Grazia distinguishes three uses of the term *rights* in relation to other animals, each of which shows an increasing demand in practical terms. The first, weakest kind he terms *moral status*, that is, other animals are to be included in the human sphere of moral concern.[2] This presupposes that other animals have inherent value, so that our duties to them are direct rather than simply indirect. For example, it might be possible to argue, as medieval authors such as Thomas Aquinas certainly did, that we need to be kind to animals because if we are violent toward animals, then we are more likely to be violent toward humans.[3] This is an *indirect* approach to moral worth that was subsequently endorsed by Immanuel Kant, since according to this view, other animals are not morally bound in the same community as human beings. Kant believed that our indirect duties to other animals reflect human ownership. Hence, the belief that animals are property is reinforced and subsequently embedded in many legal frameworks in the liberal, Western world. Theologically, of course, Aquinas is rather more complex than such an ethical directive implies since he still valued other creatures as created by God and displaying that goodness. But once theological reasons for restraint disappeared following secularising Enlightenment tendencies toward a rejection of religious authority, the temptation to use animals in a purely instrumental way became strong. Opposing such a stance by arguing that humans have *direct* duties to other animals, as they have moral status *in their own right*, independent of whether humans value them for instrumental or other reasons, is therefore a prerequisite for animal welfare. Is De Grazia correct, however, in calling this recognition of moral status the lowest tier of animal *rights*? It is certainly a prerequisite for it, but the term *right* seems odd unless we think of it as a right to be morally considerable. However, those who hold this position would not necessarily associate themselves with animal rights as such.

The second term that De Grazia associates with animal rights has to do with what he terms the *equal consideration sense*.[4] According to this view, suffering or interests of other creatures count, and all creatures are morally equivalent according to the degree to which they are capable of sentience or having interests. The priority given to *interests* and *sentience* is associated with Peter Singer, who was one of the first to draw on Jeremy Bentham in order to highlight the moral significance of animal suffering.[5] Singer judges the validity of an action according to the sum total of suffering or happiness; so that for him to treat a human animal any differently from other animals in judging a particular claim makes no sense. In fact those who do so suffer from a discriminatory attitude in favor of human beings that he castigates as *speciesism*. Above all, Singer is convinced that his attack on speciesism is the only philosophically reasonable position to hold, citing those such as R. G. Frey or Michael Allen Fox, who seemed to have changed their mind in favor of a version of his own view. For Singer, reliance on other bases for ethical action that draw on emotion or respect for animals are bound to falter, as he believes that they are less universal compared with reason.[6] Yet, he is assuming that his view is the only reasonable one, which clearly it is not.

Many others have built on Singer's work but have used other criteria for equal regard, such as De Grazia's own developed position and that of Sapontzis on other animals having particular interests.[7] But are any of these positions really *arguments* for animal "rights" as such? R. G. Frey has argued against imputing rights to other animals on the basis that they cannot have interests in that such interests are, according to him, related to particular desires and emotions associated with thought and language.[8] Rejecting the mapping of human interests onto that of other animals and then using this as a basis for a rejection of animal rights seems somewhat forced, especially as Frey's subsequent development of *quality of life* criteria for other animals seems to fall under the same general bracket as interests or sentience.[9] He argues, in other words, that an experiential subject has a quality of life that is related to "richness in its scope and its capacity for enrichment," regardless of the creatures under consideration. In this view, healthy adult humans have more of this quality than do other animals due to their more complex psychological capacities.[10] But what precisely will this do for animals if equal consideration is taken seriously? The filter in each case is still focused through the lens of a utilitarian ethic; in other words, what might over time lead to the least suffering in the case of sentience, or the most promotion of interests, or the promotion of the highest quality of life and so on. Significantly, Frey argues that quality-of-life criteria, in effect, exclude ways of thinking about moral consideration that rely on traditional demarcation lines between humans and other animals; hence, he claims:

> moral standing, I think, has nothing to do with agency on the part of the subject, nothing to do with the capacity to display virtues in the course of one's behaviour or with the capacity to make contracts, nothing to do with the possession of moral rights. . . . In my view moral standing or moral considerability turns upon whether a creature is an experiential subject, with an unfolding series of experiences that, depending on their quality; can make that creature's life go well or badly. Such a creature has a welfare that can be positively or negatively affected, depending on what is done to it.[11]

Frey's rejection of contractual or virtue approaches to moral standing and his promotion of equal consideration is remarkably similar to the consequentialist approach taken by Singer or De Grazia except that now quality of life replaces sentience or having interests. Singer's promotion of his case for animal liberation by naming his opponents "speciesist," in parallel with other discriminatory practices, such as "racist" and "sexist," has parallels in the way De Grazia reinforces this approach by suggesting that the onus is on those who support differential treatment of human beings to employ specific *reasons* why their position is to be preferred.[12] He also believes that if we take the option of inequality, then this opens the door to abuse. But the problem of all calculations of utilitarian value is that the sum total of happiness will depend, ultimately, on the prior suppositions of what counts as happiness for those who hold particular views, so this provides no guarantee that animal welfare will be protected. It is another reason why Singer and Frey arrived at apparently very different views about whether the social and political realities that they confronted need to be changed or not, for their calculation of outcomes was different. Further, as Stephen Clark points out, an individual action is unlikely to make any difference whatsoever to the final state of play in utilitarian calculation, thus undercutting the basis on which to make changes in lifestyle.[13]

But before engaging in more detailed analysis of the outcomes of the different alternatives, the third sense in which animal rights is used that De

Grazia terms the *utility trumping sense* needs to be considered. According to this view, the vital interest of a particular animal needs to be protected regardless of the consequences to the wider social community. Tom Regan is arguably the pioneer of this position, and it is worth noting that he defends his view as the *only* animal rights position in contrast to two other positions, namely, indirect duty or direct utilitarian arguments of Singer.[14] He supports his argument by distinguishing *moral patients* from *moral agents*, where the former "lack the prerequisites that would enable them to control their own behaviour in ways that would make them morally accountable for what they do."[15]

What unites both patients and agents in the moral community is what he terms being *subjects of a life* that is shaped by beliefs and desires, perception, memory, a sense of the future, including one's own future.[16] Accordingly, his view claims that the inherent value of moral patients is independent of their usefulness to others or the extent to which they possess favored virtues. In this way "All who have inherent value have it equally, whether they be moral agents or moral patients."[17] He reinforces this position by arguing for what he calls "the respect principle," so that the value of a life is respected as inherently good rather than for specific qualities that it may or may not have.[18] While his insistence on an extension of moral concern to include other animals is one that aligns with softer versions, and his casting of subjects of a life focuses on the inherent value of individual creatures rather than on the particular characteristics that they bear, such as sentience or interests, its consequences are much more drastic than that of Singer's position since *any* instrumental use of animals is abhorrent regardless of the benefits that are claimed. So if subjects pass these criteria, then Regan argues that their interests need to be protected *regardless* of social consequences. But the difficulty we immediately come up against is that the rights of one form of life will clash with another in predator-prey relationships, so how are humans as moral agents to be arbitrary judges of which creatures have the "right" to survive?[19] The practical outcome of this view is drastic, namely, the dissolution of all forms of animal husbandry, scientific or experimental use of animals, and all killing of animals unless it is strictly a matter of human life or death.

BEYOND ANIMAL RIGHTS

If we use for the time being De Grazia's classification scheme and consider the first circle of animal rights, namely, that animals are worthy of inclusion in the moral sphere, then other animals are recognized as those beings that are worthy of direct consideration rather than simply because of their usefulness to humans. But what purpose is *rights* language serving here? Why not simply talk about moral standing or why animals matter, terms favored by authors such as Stephen Clark or Mary Midgley? Midgley argues that the term *rights* is so flexible in its meaning that it is difficult to defend using the term as a basis for an argument.[20] In the legal sphere human rights are associated with particular duties so that a defense of animal rights in this sense becomes problematic. She goes on to suggest that "the ambiguity of terms like 'right,' then, does not just express a mistake, but a deep and imperfectly understood connection between law and morality."[21] However, she admits that even if terms are obscure, if they are connected with particular practical outcomes, they may be effective, so "they are like strong tools caught up and used as levers to remove a particular obstacle, without the thought of their other properties." But tensions will remain as long as the terms are unclear so that: "Such concepts can then prove misleading or useless. Other ideas must be forged to supplement or replace them." She believes that the word "right" cannot be salvaged in a useful or clear way but only in a wide sense to draw attention to problems rather than to solve them. Hence, "In its moral sense, it oscillates uncontrollably between applications which are too wide to resolve conflicts ('the right to life, liberty and the pursuit of happiness') and ones which are too narrow to be plausible ('the basic human right to stay at home on Bank Holiday')."[22]

If the next focus is on the second sense in which "rights" might be used, that is, in terms of equal consideration, then this raises both theoretical and practical issues that need to be dealt with. In theoretical terms *equality* as a term has a nebulous pedigree that arguably is almost as conflictual as that associated with rights. While De Grazia argues that equal regard in favor of humans needs to be defended by those who object to its extension to other animals, Midgley's case rests on the way equality has been understood as applying to rectify injustices *within* a group, rather than outside it. Equality as a term is also associated with contractual approaches to the moral community that De Grazia rejects. Midgely believes that once we attempt to extend the case for equality outside the sphere in which it was originally formed and framed, then it becomes difficult to operate in practice since it leads to unrealistic political objectives that can then be dismissed.[23] The notion of equality also relies on a pooled sense of self-interest, so that it might become worse for those who are excluded. In other words, gains may be felt in one domain, but there is loss for those outside the immediate circle. This is precisely what seems to have happened in the case of equal regard for sentience, for example. In this case, all those humans who lack sentience through illness, accident or old age are in a lower moral category compared with other sentient animals. While often known as the "case from marginal humans" in order to argue for the inclusion of other animals in moral considerability, the use of the term *marginal* in itself displays a particular *unethical* attitude toward those who have lost such capacities. Consideration of other animals has therefore thrown the spotlight back on how we deal with others in the human community who are particularly vulnerable. This applies regardless of the particular criteria used, be it sentience, quality of life, or interests, for where they involve consequentialist arguments, the apparent diminishment of the most vulnerable humans by ranking their significance lower than that of other animals shows some of the reasons why there has been so much hostility by advocates of those with disabilities toward animal rights. Peter Singer, of course, is careful to avoid using terms such as *rights*, but his liberationist position can easily be interpreted according to such a view, and in the public domain, at least, there seems little discrimination. Further, his view is no less damaging toward those who are excluded in the human community by his particular version of what counts in terms of equal regard, namely, the maximization of sentience, regardless of membership of species.

It is hardly surprising, therefore, that the most thoughtful positions taken by those concerned about the moral significance of other animals are those that cast doubt on the use of the term *animal rights* as a strategy for mobilizing action in favor of animal welfare.[24] It is also clear to many that there are particular "rights" of humans that do not apply to other animals, such as the right to worship and rights commensurate with abilities to form highly complex religious, political, and social communities. But are such differences more about interests rather than rights, thus casting further doubt on the fruitfulness of such terminology? Moreover, once doubt is cast on the use of the language of rights in the softest sense of the word of moral inclusion, what about the harder versions of Tom Regan or others like him? His is an ethical position that is based on a deontological value of creaturely kinds, but the line in or out of moral concern is drawn according to their capacity to be subjects of a life. It is possible to argue against this view on the basis that animals are not subjects of a life, but this view is becoming much harder to sustain in the light of animal ethology. The question circles back once more on whether subjectivity can really be used in order to separate those in or out of the moral domain in a way that renders all those with such subjectivity apparently equivalent status. In all this discussion there is a failure to appreciate adequately the embeddedness of human rights discourse in social networks that are not shared by other animals. Hence, even to attempt to extend such a view to individual animals, while disregarding such networks, commits what might be termed a category mistake. The closest that we might comfortably get to a version of "natural rights" is through a modified version of natural law theory and wild justice, but even natural law theory did not emerge from simple observation of the basic needs of other animals; rather, it elevated participation in the divine law by reasonable creatures.[25]

Andrew Linzey has written extensively on animal rights from a theological point of view, arguing for what he terms *theos-rights*. Hence, rather than casting doubt on the potential usefulness of this term, he has reinforced it and reified it still further by coming up with theological reasons to support animal rights. His position aligns with that of Tom Regan, which is the "hardest" version of animal rights. There are some reasons why theologians might possibly warm to Regan's approach, not least because he has stressed the need to value lives according to the principle of respect rather than because of their utility for others. This is a variant on Kant's affirmation of human beings as ends rather than as means to an end except this time it is extended to include other animal kinds. A Christian affirmation of the goodness of all creation might be reason enough to respect life. But Linzey uses Regan's position to argue not just for all creaturely life, or even animal life, but only for those closest to humans—namely, mammals. Linzey's basic argument, which has been rehearsed many times before, is that God as Creator has rights in creation, therefore creatures that are filled with the Spirit are of inherent value to God.[26] These creatures, which he defines as Spirit-filled, breathing, and made of flesh and blood, therefore make a moral claim on us, not just because they are creaturely but because they are given inherent value by God. In his view it is *God* who has chosen to give value to such creatures. His theological position is one associated with a particular theological anthropology in which humans simply receive the status to be in the image of God by divine *fiat*. He contrasts this with perceiving humans as having certain capacities in order to relate to God in a particular way and through such capacities becoming included in the divine image. Linzey seems to object to the latter on the basis that it invests too much in humanity rather than in God.

Wenberg, correctly in my view, objects to Linzey's position not only because there is no reason why God could not affirm particular capacities in humans but also because "it renders divine valuation essentially arbitrary."[27] Another objection relates to the criteria with which apparently divine affirmation is concluded. There is, for example, no theological basis for Linzey's elevation of the "flesh" as either being of inherent divine significance or of being restricted to warm-blooded animals that suckle their young. I will return to more recent attempts to associate Christology with other animals below, but for the time being it is worth noting that associating rights language with divine beneficence is itself problematic. In other words, what is the basis for using rights, a highly ambivalent term, with God's activity?[28] This is particularly the case since the language of rights arises where there is a breakdown of trust in human societies; hence, it seems to me that to apply this either to the animal or to the divine domain seems at best strange, at worst foolhardy. In addition, rights language has legalistic connotations that are difficult to associate with the reciprocity found in human relationships with companion animals, a topic that Linzey seems to avoid. Stephen Webb believes that Linzey is inconsistent in practice in that although he claims to base his argument on theos-rights, this is in tension with other aspects of his work that stress generosity that also seems to shape his approach. While Webb is correct that there is a tension running throughout Linzey's work, Linzey has remained a firm advocate of animal rights even in his most recent publications.[29] An alternative view is that Linzey's language of generosity echoes the particular way he envisages rights as that which are given unconditionally by God with little thought to particular capacities other than being flesh-bearing creatures. In much the same way, for Linzey, humans are called to imitate such unconditional generosity toward mammals. The selection of God's special action and human vocation seem to circle back to a preconceived and somewhat arbitrary definition of what counts in moral terms, namely, being a member of warm-blooded mammalian species.

But there is, perhaps, an even deeper problematic in the language of animal rights that its proponents seem to ignore, namely, that it relies on animal protection almost entirely through extensions of what are deemed valid in the human sphere. Terms such as *rights*, *justice*, *equality*, *respect*, *interests*, and so on all originated in specific moral discourse among sophisticated human societies. It is therefore still highly anthropocentric in orientation and has not escaped the particular way in which such terms have evolved even while presuming to cast doubt on affirmations of human nature in the name of unwarranted "speciesism." The onus, therefore, contra de Grazia, is not so much on those who argue for some distinction between humans and other animals in order to argue *why* equal consideration does not apply to all creatures,[30] but rather on those who claim that equal regard applies *outside* the human moral sphere in which it historically originated; in other words, to show why equal regard needs to be extended. The animal rights view is also peculiarly influenced by what might be called a liberal philosophy, aiming at autonomy, equality, and rights in a way that is a faded mirror image of liberal Western culture. I am not necessarily claiming that we should avoid the use of such terms at any cost but rather that we become far more self-reflective in the way language is used across different species categories. To claim, as some do, that evolutionary science has simply proved that species barriers no longer exist is to mistake genetic similarity with equivalence in biological and evolutionary terms. The biological and ecological separation of species either through geographic isolation or other means is well known in population genetics.[31] Hence, even where there are strong genetic similarities, very small genetic differences, such as that involved in gene regulation, for example, can lead to wide divergences between different species. In other words it is a falsification of evolutionary science to isolate genetic similarity and to call on this as a way to argue against any specifically species interests. A comparison between capacities in other social animals and the lineage *Homo* needs to be qualified by recognizing the time scale of moral evolution as well as the time of divergence from a common ancestor: sophisticated moral frameworks took place relatively late in the evolution of our species, many thousands of years even after *H. sapiens* first appeared and after many millions of years' divergence from our closest living primate cousin, the chimpanzee.[32]

THE PRIORITY OF LOVE

The Christian tradition of compassion for animals sits somewhat uneasily alongside other aspects of the tradition that are more instrumental in tone. Yet a survey of the Christian tradition shows that compassion cannot be avoided.[33] Yet perhaps this idea needs to be pushed further and insistence given not just on *compassion for* other animals but rather on the *priority of love*.[34] Compassion forces humanity to be sensitive to the suffering of other animals, and from this stance it would resist all those practices that attempt to abuse or torment them. This is, of course, vitally important, but does it go far enough in rethinking the relationship between humans and other animals? Love implies something stronger and emerges from a sense of shared creaturely belonging. With Alasdair MacIntyre, we should not think of vulnerability or dependence as *diminishing* what it means to be human but as woven into what it *means* to be human by admitting that humans are also dependent animals. In this way the priority of love will open up a sense of responsibility toward those who have various functions impaired, but their worth will not be judged by the measure of that impairment.[35] This is where Singer's utilitarian view of sentience is so fatally flawed since just because someone is no longer capable of a conscious acknowledgment of suffering, at least according to an objective assessment of such capabilities, does not mean that they are dispensable or outside the circle of love. This is where a theological account is more convincing for a religious believer compared with a humanist account since humanism is only able to go as far as what might seem reasonably to be the case. The priority of love of the type I am indicating here is one that is *in excess* of the reasonable, in excess of the simply compassionate, and is more akin to a grace-filled, theological love ethic that then undergirds the way other virtues, such as justice and prudence, take shape.

Alasdair MacIntyre acknowledges that the classical virtues point in this direction, so that "to participate in this network of relationships of giving and receiving as the virtues require, I have to understand that what I am called upon to give may be quite disproportionate to what I have received and that those to whom I am called upon to give may well be those from whom I shall receive nothing."[36] Here the measure of giving reflects the particular *need* of the recipient rather than being subject to reciprocal goods. What is remarkable in MacIntyre's account is that while he acknowledges to a limited extent the astonishing degree to which some other animals share in what used to be thought of as human characteristics, this then reshapes his virtue ethic so that it deals with unfortunate humans rather than having any direct implications on how humans treat other animals. His network of relationships is, on the one hand, open in acknowledging the lives of other animals but, on the other hand, closed in seeming to omit other animals from his discussion of those beings to whom humans are called to be responsible. But if we widen that network of relational others in a way that is inclusive, rather than exclusive, then the self-conscious acknowledgement of the priority of love can begin to take shape beyond narrowly conceived versions of human societies as restricted to other members of the same species. Here rules and principles are relevant only in as much as they serve to point in the general direction of what needs to be done rather than filling out in detail what is required.[37]

The central place of Christian love has shaped a significant discourse in Christian ethics ever since St. Paul named it in New Testament literature as the first of the three theological virtues.[38] The term *agape* is what is meant here though in contemporary society the language of autonomy or justice is more likely to find secular resonance. While I do not wish to deny their significance, I suggest that the specific Christian emphasis on the theological priority of love should not be forgotten, not least because an ethic unharnessed from acknowledgement of our deepest emotional bonds will falter in its detachment from human animality. By this I mean not so much that Christian love emerges from naturalistic feelings of love but that the grace of God needs to be viewed as *embodied* rather than disembodied. Agape love takes its pattern and form from the love expressed in the particular life of Jesus Christ and his approach to death as one who freely gives away his life.[39] Loving concern for others as that which lends shape to the way humans act applies across a range of different moral discourses, including various accounts of ethics of care put forward as feminist alternatives to too strong an emphasis on detached reasoning and justice.[40] Agape love also looks for specific, *concrete* ways of loving in particular scenarios and therefore avoids the utilitarian tendency to lump together the sum total of suffering and happiness, as if my own contribution could make little difference. It is also prepared to listen to others and endure all things, as I Corinthians 13 insists, recalling the first of the Ten Commandments, to love God, and the second, to love neighbor. Agape love in this view does not presuppose or require mutuality in the manner that friendship more commonly does.[41]

I am not suggesting here that agape love, in opening up the possibility of other regard, is *all sufficient* in shaping the particular way human beings respond to the demands of vulnerable others, be they humans or other animals. Rather, agape love sets the stage for the expression of other virtues that are then needed in discerning what might be done, namely, a prudential exercise of justice, where other animals are thought to be morally considerable as recipients of justice making, and in some cases may be agents of a kind of wild justice.[42] Aquinas taught that charity is the mother of all virtues and named love of God as the foundation of all charity.[43] A religious sense of the capacity for *agape* goes much further than the kind of empathy that is observed in other social animals and communities, even if we might admire the extent to which other regard is possible in species other than humans.

Naming agape as the first moment prior to considerations of justice also highlights that justice in the Christian tradition is more than an objective set of rules. However, Timothy Jackson makes the tension between a Christian perspective on justice, as expressed experientially and witnessed in the incarnation, compared with secular philosophical traditions, too stark, for in my view the latter need not necessarily "destroy a Christian account of justice and the love on which it trades."[44] Although he is correct to point to the priority of love, justice as virtue is compatible and complementary to other, more objective versions of what justice making requires rather than in competition with them. Of course, there may be some philosophical schools that can be accommodated more readily than others, but the theological task is to interpret these in a new way without reducing the task to these traditions, rather than to set up barriers between theology and philosophical reflection. Accordingly, capability approaches to justice are, in my view, more compatible with what might be termed *naming the intrinsic value* of created beings compared with contractual approaches. In this sense the former are also rather more compatible with an understanding of Christ as incarnate in the created world.[45]

For the moment the point I am making is that justice as virtue flows from attention to the theological virtue of *agape* and goes beyond what might be anticipated from purely reciprocal patterns of justice making. Justice as virtue points to a term preferred in the biblical text, namely, *the righteousness (dikaiosune) of God*. In this way Jackson gives a good description of virtue when he claims that "Justice as righteousness has the narrative unity and pathos of a loving personality (or perhaps of a society of such persons) rather than the solidity of a physical object, or even the immutability of a Platonic form. One can have abstract theories about inanimate things or general predicates, but not about virtuous persons."[46] In texts such as the Epistle to Galatians, the overflowing love of God expressed in God's self-communication is the source of making righteous; it seems, therefore, to have a transformative influence on human beings.[47] Jackson believes that this points to a merging of justice as righteousness and agape, but he resists making this move in as much as he believes that justice needs to be kept distinct from love, so that love governs justice, where justice becomes what is due.[48] Thomas Aquinas argued no less, namely, that love needs to govern justice as virtue, but that the measure of our justice making can also be ordered rationally according to particular principles.[49]

CONCLUSIONS

This chapter attempts to lay out the basic arguments of those supportive of animal rights along with associated arguments for animal liberation in order to show how such reflections impinge on our own self-understanding and perception of what it means to be human. For although the rhetoric is about animal liberation, those who support this position argue that it is entirely reasonable and even necessary for humans *as humans* to act as if the perceived barriers between species no longer exists. But this creates new ethical problems, where particularly vulnerable human beings are in danger of being treated as dispensable. A rationale for widening the zone of protection for other animals showing similar characteristics in an inclusive way is therefore not as obvious as proponents of animal rights suggest. Animal rights goes further in that animals as inherently valuable subjects of a life comes to the fore, so that all animals showing such subjectivity are to be protected as a matter of course, regardless of the social or economic consequences. A theological gloss on this position is to render rights as given by God, rather than humanity. Human dependency and vulnerability are part of what it means to be human and express virtues. But from a Christian point of view a deliberate and self-conscious alternative to animal rights is one that takes into account the priority of love in the theological tradition. By "love" I mean, here, agape love or other regard that goes deeper than an attitude of compassion. It is this love that serves to shape what justice as virtue might be like, and, ultimately, it acts like a filter of deliberation in seeking out what might be the most reasonable alternative positions on justice making for animals. Such a love is metaphorical and poetic when applied to thinking about God but becomes more practical when thinking about how humans are to act. The full meaning of agape love is one that only makes proper sense when interpreted according to a communitarian understanding of human relationships to all others, including God. A key problem with animal rights is its focus on individual animal subjects to such an extent that the communal basis for human being and acting is largely missing.[50] Kinship reminds us of what we might call the liminal space between humans, other animals and other creaturely kinds in a way that carves out a particular place for specifically human wisdom to find expression. Such wisdom is not divorced from natural wisdom in other creatures and human beings but from the perspective of Christian theology, at least, seeks to echo a Christological wisdom born of a pneumatology that is grounded in a theological pattern of relating that we find in the life, death and resurrection of Jesus Christ.

NOTES

1. Michael Northcott, "'They Shall Not Hurt or Destroy in All My Holy Mountain' (Isaiah 65.25): Killing for Philosophy and a Creaturely Theology of Non-Violence," in *Creaturely Theology: On God, Humans and Other Animals*, eds. Celia Deane-Drummond and David Clough (London: SCM Press, 2009), 231–48.
2. David De Grazia, *Animal Rights: A Very Short Introduction* (Oxford: Oxford University Press, 2002), 15–17.
3. Thomas Aquinas, *Summa Theologiae*, trans. Thomas Gilby (London: Blackfriars, 1966), 28: I–II.102.6. Here Aquinas puts the initial emphasis on pity for animal suffering, which he recognizes as also encouraging pity toward other humans who are also suffering.
4. De Grazia, *Animal Rights*, 15.
5. Peter Singer, *Animal Liberation*, 2nd ed. (London: Pimlico, 1995). This book was first published in 1975. In the intervening years Singer has witnessed the rise of animal liberation movements of all sorts, inspired to a great extent by his book. His preface to the second edition is unrepentant of any negative impacts that may have ensued, but at the same time he is "uncomfortable" with the idea that his book was some sort of "blueprint" for animal liberation, but this is not because he has witnessed any negative aspects but because he wants to give credit to the activists that have made animal liberation as strong a movement as it has become (xvi). While he denounces the violence associated with some portions of animal liberation (xxiv), he does not acknowledge how his own theory might lead logically to that conclusion.
6. Singer, *Animal Liberation*, 243.
7. See David De Grazia, *Taking Animals Seriously: Mental Life and Moral Status* (Cambridge: Cambridge University Press, 1996). See also S. F. Sapontzis, *Morals, Reasons and Animals* (Philadelphia: Temple University Press, 1987).
8. R. G. Frey, *Interests and Rights: The Case Against Animals* (Oxford: Clarendon Press, 1980). See comment in Mary Midgley, *Animals and Why They Matter* (Athens: University of Georgia Press, 1983), 54–55.
9. R. G. Frey, "Animals," in *The Oxford Handbook of Practical Ethics*, ed. Hugh La Follette (New York: Oxford University Press, 2003), 161–87.
10. Frey, "Animals," 175.
11. Frey, "Animals," 174.
12. De Grazia, *Animal Rights*, 21.
13. Stephen Clark, *Animals and their Moral Standing* (London: Routledge, 1997), 97–100.
14. Tom Regan, *The Case for Animal Rights* (Berkeley: University of California Press, 1983), 151.
15. Regan, *The Case for Animal Rights*, 152.
16. Regan, *The Case for Animal Rights* 243. Frey's "quality of life" or De Grazia's "interests" also assume a measure of subjectivity though Regan's list is rather more comprehensive.
17. Regan, *The Case for Animal Rights*, 240.
18. Regan, *The Case for Animal Rights*, 258–62.
19. A point raised by Clark, 102–3, in his discussion of Regan.
20. Midgley, *Animals and Why They Matter*, 47.
21. Midgley, *Animals and Why They Matter*, 62.
22. Midgley, *Animals and Why They Matter*, 63.
23. Midgley, *Animals and Why They Matter*, 67–68.
24. Robert Wenberg, *God, Humans, and Animals: An Invitation to Enlarge our Moral Universe* (Grand Rapids, MI: Eerdmans, 2003), 155.
25. Aquinas, I–II.96.2, states, "natural law is a kind of sharing by us in the Eternal Law, from which human law falls short." The first principle of natural law cannot be changed, that good is sought and evil avoided (Aquinas, I–II.94.5). The sheer variety of interpretations of natural law theory and its evolution through history might give another pause for thought in assuming that a single version of natural rights might be effective in promoting justice among other animals.
26. See Andrew Linzey, *Animal Rights: A Christian Assessment* (London: SCM Press, 1976); *Christianity and the Rights of Animals* (London: SPCK, 1987); *Animal Theology* (Lon-

don: SCM Press, 1994); *Why Animal Suffering Matters* (Oxford: Oxford University Press, 2009).

27. Wenberg, *God, Humans, and Animals*, 166.

28. A similar objection is to be found in Stephen Webb, *On God and Dogs: A Christian Theology of Compassion for Animals* (Oxford: Oxford University Press, 1998), 40.

29. In Linzey's most recent book, *Why Animal Suffering Matters*, he still insists on both the importance of rights as well as other ways of framing the discourse. In this book he argues against humans as causal agents in all forms of animal suffering but refrains from using the utilitarian calculus to support this position.

30. De Grazia, *Animal Rights*, 21, makes this claim but also seeks to defend against counter-arguments on 23–34. He names Midgley's position as an appeal to "social bonds," where positive identification provides a stronger basis for action. He argues against this on the grounds that humans still have a duty not to harm those outside our immediate socially bonded sphere. However, what De Grazia seems to miss in this argument is that the grounds for ethical distinction is not simply about social bonding, though this is partly what is at stake, but that the basis for any rights talk has its origin in complex human societies in a way that is difficult to translate into the social world of other animals. What needs to be made clear, therefore, is the basis for social concern between humans and other animal kinds and the responsibilities between different social communities (Deane-Drummond, *The Wisdom of the Liminal: Evolution and Other Animals in Human Becoming* (Grand Rapids, MI: Eerdmans, 2014).

31. Speciation in animals is most commonly allopatric, that is through geographical isolation. However, rarely it may be sympatric, that is, occur in the same habitat by chromosomal or genetic changes that lead to reproductive isolation. An even rarer form known as parapatric speciation occurs at a boundary of climatic regions (Coyne and Orr 2004).

32. J. Wentzel van Huyssteen, *Alone in the World? Human Uniqueness in Science and Theology* (Grand Rapids, MI: Eerdmans, 2006). While the possibility of human symbolic capacities and simpler moral systems are likely to be earlier than van Huyssteen supposed in this book, the development of sophisticated moral frameworks came later.

33. This applies across different Christian perspectives, as illustrated by Stephen Webb's *On God and Dogs: A Christian Theology of Compassion for Animals* (Oxford: Oxford University Press, 1998) and Deborah Jones's *The School of Compassion: A Roman Catholic Theology of Animals* (Leominster: Gracewing, 2009).

34. I am taking this term from the title of Timothy Jackson's (2003) book, *The Priority of Love: Christian Charity and Social Justice*. This book provides a solid theological argument for the importance of agape love as that which shapes the way social justice is conceived. In the preface he recounts the particular significance of how the roadside death of a dog opened up his understanding of the immense love of God for all creaturely kinds (xii–xiii). One might have expected, therefore, that his book would deal with how human beings might be called to express love and justice toward other animals, but disappointingly this aspect is virtually absent from his account.

35. Alasdair MacIntyre, *Dependent Rational Animals: Why Human Beings Need the Virtues* (London: Duckworth, 2009).

36. MacIntyre, *Dependent Rational Animals*, 108.

37. MacIntyre's comment that natural law also includes being faithful to the virtues need not distract us here (111). However, those who reject natural law sometimes do so on the assumption that it is either naturalistic or that it amounts to a wooden application of a rule-based ethic, both of which are false, or at least only applicable to selected interpretations of natural law.

38. Opinions differ as to what extent Christian love has dominated discussion of theological ethics. Some argue it has held a limited place, such as Edward Collins Vacek, *Love: Human and Divine: The Heart of Christian Ethics* (Washington, DC: University of Georgetown Press, 1994); others, such as Richard Hays, that it has held an overly dominant role ("Christology and Ethics in Galatians: The Law of Christ," *Catholic Biblical Quarterly*, 49 no. 2 (1996): 269–90). Timothy Jackson argues, convincingly in my view, that Stanley Hauerwas's demotion of the role of love in ethics is exaggerated; what needs to be checked is a way of articulating love in the way that it becomes idolized. Timothy Jackson, *The Priority of Love: Christian Charity and Social Justice* (Princeton, NJ: Princeton University Press, 2003), 16–17. Nonetheless, Hauer-

was's *Cross Currents* article cited by Jackson was published in 1972, a period when a secular emphasis on "free love" was probably at its height, and in that context its meaning could easily be misunderstood. See Stanley Hauerwas, "Love's Not All You Need," *Cross Currents*, 22 (Summer/Fall 1972): 225–37.

39. While self-sacrificing behavior has been criticized by feminist scholars as encouraging the oppression of women, if the pendulum swings too far in the direction of self-assertion, the bonds of social relationship will begin to break down rather than be reinforced. Christ's offering is one that seeks to build up relationships in a way that is freely chosen, done in solidarity with victims of abuse rather than to reinforce that abuse. In this one might say that Christ identifies with the senseless suffering of other creatures.

40. See, for example, Nel Noddings, *Caring: A Feminine Approach to Ethics and Education* (Berkeley: University of California Press, 1984); Lisa Cahill, *Sex, Gender, and Christian Ethics* (Cambridge: Cambridge University Press, 1996); Carol Gilligan, *In a Different Voice: Psychological Theory and Women's Development* Cambridge, MA: Harvard University Press, 1982) to name a few. For a critical engagement with dualist implications of Noddings and Gilligan see Mary Jeanne Larrabee, *An Ethic of Care* (New York: Routledge, 1993) and for further commentary C. Deane-Drummond, *Genetics and Christian Ethics* (Cambridge: Cambridge University Press, 2006).

41. I have argued elsewhere that friendship love understood from a theological perspective does not necessarily have to be seen as preference based, and, once we view it in this manner, then this opens up the possibility of closer relationships with other animals (Deane-Drummond 2006).

42. Celia Deane-Drummond, "Natural Law Revisited: Wild Justice and Human Obligations for Other Animals," *Journal of the Society for Christian Ethics* 35, no. 2 (2015): 159–73, doi:10.1353/sce.2015.0045.

43. "Charity is called the end of all the other virtues because it directs them all to its own end. And since a mother is one who conceives in herself from another, charity is called the mother of the other virtues, because from desire of the ultimate end it conceives their acts by charging them with life" (Aquinas, II–II.23.8). Citing Ephesians 3.19, Aquinas (II–II.24.1) also names charity as being rooted in the will orientated toward the end, meaning that which God intends, hence charity is "ruled not by reason, as are the human virtues, but by the wisdom of God, it goes beyond reason."

44. Timothy Jackson, *The Priority of Love: Christian Charity and Social Justice* (Princeton, NJ: Princeton University Press, 2003), 31.

45. I am not suggesting that a contractual or procedural approach to justice, such as that of John Rawls, is incompatible with Christian theology but that alternatives may be more fruitful in the light of Christian reflection on the significance of the incarnation ("Deep Incarnation and Eco-Justice as Theodrama: A Dialogue between Hans urs von Balthasar and Martha Nussbaum." Deane-Drummond, 2010).

46. Jackson, *The Priority of Love*, 32.

47. Hays, 269–90.

48. Jackson, *The Priority of Love*, 38.

49. An outline of what a Thomistic theory of justice entails is outside the scope of this chapter. I have discussed this in other contexts, such as in *The Ethics of Nature* (Oxford: Blackwell, 2004).

50. Elisabeth Anderson picks up this discussion in a helpful way in her analysis of the tension between animal welfare, animal rights and environmentalism. Her notion that a *qualified* sense of rights emerges in different social contexts seems far more reasonable than the somewhat spurious argument for animal rights based on marginal cases. Elisabeth Anderson, "Animal Rights and the Values of Non-Human Life," in *Animal Rights: Current Debates and New Directions*, eds. Cass R. Sunstein and Martha R. Nussbaum (Oxford: Oxford University Press, 2004), 277–98.

REFERENCES

Anderson, Elisabeth. "Animal Rights and the Values of Non-Human Life." In *Animal Rights: Current Debates and New Directions*. Edited by Cass R. Sunstein and Martha C. Nussbaum, 277–98. Oxford: Oxford University Press, 2004.
Aquinas, Thomas. *Summa Theologiae*, Vol. 28, *Law and Political Theory*, I-II.90–97. Translated by Thomas Gilby. London: Blackfriars, 1966.
———. *Summa Theologiae*, Vol. 29, *The Old Law*, I–II.98–105. Translated by David Bourke. London: Blackfriars, 1969.
———. *Summa Theologiae*, Vol. 34, *Charity*, II–II.23–33. Translated by R. J. Batton. London: Blackfriars. 1975.
Cahill, Lisa. *Sex, Gender and Christian Ethics*. Cambridge: Cambridge University Press, 1996.
Clark, Stephen. *Animals and their Moral Standing*. London: Routledge, 1997.
Coyne, Jerry A. and H. Allen Orr. *Speciation*. Sunderland, MA: Sinauer Associates, 2004.
De Grazia, David. *Taking Animals Seriously: Mental Life and Moral Status*. Cambridge: Cambridge University Press, 1996.
———. *Animal Rights: A Very Short Introduction.* Oxford: Oxford University Press, 2002.
Deane-Drummond, Celia. *The Ethics of Nature*. Oxford: Blackwell, 2004.
———. *Genetics and Christian Ethics*. Cambridge: Cambridge University Press, 2006.
———. "Deep Incarnation and Eco-Justice as Theodrama: A Dialogue between Hans urs von Balthasar and Martha Nussbaum." In *Ecological Awareness*. Edited by Sigurd Bergmann and Heather Eaton, 193–206. London: LIT Verlag, 2010.
———. *The Wisdom of the Liminal: Evolution and Other Animals in Human Becoming*. Grand Rapids, MI: Eerdmans, 2014.
———. "Natural Law Revisited: Wild Justice and Human Obligations for Other Animals." *Journal of the Society for Christian Ethics* 35, no. 2 (2015):159–73. doi: 10.1353/sce.2015.0045.
Frey, R. G. *Interests and Rights: The Case Against Animals*. Oxford: Clarendon Press, 1980.
———. "Animals." In *The Oxford Handbook of Practical Ethics*. Edited by Hugh La Follette. 161–87. New York: Oxford University Press, 2003.
Gilligan, Carol. *In a Different Voice: Psychological Theory and Women's Development*. Cambridge, MA: Harvard University Press, 1982.
Hauerwas, Stanley. "Love's Not All You Need." *Cross Currents* 22 (Summer/Fall): 225–37, 1972.
Hays, Richard. "Christology and Ethics in Galatians: The Law of Christ." *Catholic Biblical Quarterly* 49 (2): 269–90, 1987.
———. *The Moral Vision of the New Testament*. San Francisco: Harper Collins, 1996.
Jackson, Timothy. *The Priority of Love: Christian Charity and Social Justice*. Princeton, NJ: Princeton University Press, 2003.
Jones, Deborah. *The School of Compassion: A Roman Catholic Theology of Animals.* Leominster, UK: Gracewing, 2009.
Larrabee, Mary Jeanne. *An Ethic of Care*. New York: Routledge, 1993.
Linzey, Andrew. *Animals Rights: A Christian Assessment.* London: SCM Press, 1976.
———. *Christianity and the Rights of Animals*. London: SPCK, 1987.
———. *Animal Theology*. London: SCM Press, 1994.
———. *Why Animal Suffering Matters*. Oxford: Oxford University Press, 2009.
MacIntyre, Alasdair. *Dependent Rational Animals: Why Human Beings Need the Virtues*. London: Duckworth, 2009.
Midgley, Mary. *Animals and Why They Matter*. Athens: University of Georgia Press, 1983.
Noddings, Nel. *Caring: A Feminine Approach to Ethics and Moral Education*. Berkeley: University of California Press, 1984.
Northcott, Michael. "'They Shall Not Hurt or Destroy in All My Holy Mountain' (Isaiah 65.25): Killing for Philosophy and a Creaturely Theology of Non-Violence." In *Creaturely Theology: On God, Humans and Other Animals*. Edited by Celia Deane-Drummond and David Clough, 231–48. London: SCM Press, 2009.
Regan, Tom. *The Case for Animal Rights*. Berkeley: University of California Press, 1983.

Sapontzis, S. F. *Morals, Reasons and Animals*. Philadelphia: Temple University Press, 1987.
Singer, Peter. *Animal Liberation*. 2nd ed. London: Pimlico, 1995.
Vacek, Edward Collins. *Love: Human and Divine: The Heart of Christian Ethics*. Washington, DC: Georgetown University Press, 1994.
van Huyssteen, J. Wentzel. *Alone in the World? Human Uniqueness in Science and Theology*. Grand Rapids, MI: Eerdmans, 2006.
Webb, Stephen. *On God and Dogs: A Christian Theology of Compassion for Animals*. Oxford: Oxford University Press, 1998.
Wenberg, Robert N. *God, Humans and Animals: An Invitation to Enlarge Our Moral Universe*. Grand Rapids, MI: Eerdmans, 2003.

Chapter Two

Whatsoever You Do to the Least of My Brothers

Why it is Wrong to Harm a Fly

Jeffrey A. Lockwood

A familiar form of praise regarding an individual's compassion or gentleness is that he or she "wouldn't harm a fly"—an idiom that extends back at least three hundred years.[1] The expression needs little explication, as we all know that flies are merely insects, they can be annoying, and they can transmit pathogens. So if one is unwilling to hurt such an inconsequential, even deleterious, creature, then the individual is surely kind toward fellow humans. Conversely, a worrisome child (or a morally depraved adult) might be said to "pull wings off flies."[2] The wanton maiming of a creature—even an insect—reflects poorly on a person's character. However, in everyday life, swatting or spraying a fly does not seem to undermine one's character.

The task of the moral philosopher is to engage commonplace or folk judgments—and then determine if there is a sound line of argument from first principles to justify our intuitions. And so the challenge that I undertake is one of seeking compelling reasons why it would be praiseworthy to avoid harming a pesky (or any other) insect and why it would be blameworthy to willfully mutilate (but not intentionally kill) an insect. In addition to these intriguing entomological cases regarding ethical behavior, there is potentially much to gain with regard to clarifying our relationship to the natural world.

Analysis of ethical theories is often sharpened by the careful consideration of marginal cases. For example, nobody would expect different, philosophically viable theories to provide divergent judgments regarding the morality of torturing innocent children to death solely to satisfy one's own desire to inflict suffering. However, we are not surprised to find that various theories come to contrasting conclusions about abortion and capital punishment.[3] Along similar lines, it's not a simple matter as to whether there are circumstances in which we ought to torture an individual who has knowledge of a pending act of terrorism (how sure are we of the individual's knowledge, how much pain can be justified, how imminent is the attack, how many lives are at risk, and so forth?).[4] Such borderline cases force the ethicist to clarify the terms and limits of a theory, oftentimes resulting in caveats or modifications and sometimes yielding a "bite the bullet" response when a conclusion conflicts with our initial intuitions.

And so it is that insects provide a kind of limit case with which we can probe the boundaries of ethical theories concerning our treatment of other beings and elements of the natural world. In fact, insects might represent an ideal test insofar as they are a kind of minimalist animal. Some other invertebrates (e.g., worms and bivalves) might be perceived as being incrementally more marginal, as insects are capable of reasonably complex behaviors, including learning.[5] Clams, for example, have such extraordinarily simple nervous systems and external anatomies that we don't perceive them to be like us in any relevant way. So, in a sense, insects are the fetuses and comatose patients of environmental and animal ethics.

Our treatment of other animals is a seemingly incoherent amalgamation of social norms, some of which might have compelling moral reasons but many of which apparently reflect conventions without much, if any, clear justification. Imagine that there's a fly on the kitchen counter. You are concerned that it might deposit pathogens (germs). So, you grab the fly swatter and slowly stalk the insect, raise the swatter stealthily, and then slap the creature. Next, imagine that there's a duck floating on a pond. You enjoy roasted duck. So, you grab your shotgun from the floor of the blind, slowly shift into shooting position, raise the weapon to your shoulder, and then pull the trigger. Few people would object strongly to the first killing, but many would find it a character flaw to shoot a sitting duck.[6] Why does the standard of "fair chase" or sportsmanship apply to ducks but not to flies?

Imagine that you're sitting on your deck reading the paper and a gnat has been flitting around your head. It is an annoying distraction, but it isn't a hazard to your health. The creature finally lands on the arm of your chair, so you grab a section of newspaper and swat the pest. Now imagine that you're on the deck and a vagrant dog has been barking incessantly. You can't concentrate on the paper or enjoy your reading. The animal isn't endangering you or your property. Finally, it comes into the yard, so you get your pistol from the house and shoot the cur, killing it instantly. Few people would strongly condemn the first killing but would find shooting the annoying stray to be repugnant. Why does the legitimacy of pest control apply to gnats but not to mutts?

To make sense of the fly/duck and gnat/dog cases, we need to find a relevant moral difference between the animals.[7] The problem is akin to the practice of enslaving blacks or underpaying women. Without a substantive difference, these practices cannot be morally justified—and neither race nor gender constitutes a compelling difference (one could just as easily contend that whites and men should be disenfranchised). Likewise, having six (versus two or four) legs, having four (versus two or zero) wings, and being small (versus large) don't seem to be relevant moral differences. We'll need to determine if any of the available moral theories can identify such a difference. And if successful, then can the theory also take into account the following case?

Imagine that you're on a hike with some friends. Everyone stops for a rest and on a nearby log there is a cricket. One of the hikers sees the insect, reaches into her backpack, extracts a can of insecticide and sprays the creature. "I find insects just so creepy," she explains. It's not as if she stomped on a squirrel or pulled a slingshot from her pack and plunked a robin. But surely a moral theory that finds nothing wrong with her action would require some very unexpected and highly dubious principles.

Next, we'll see if utilitarianism, deontology, or virtue ethics might provide a reasonable account for our decision to not harm—or to dismember, swat, or spray—a fly.

STANDARD ETHICAL THEORIES

This section will cover the three ethical theories that prevail in Western philosophy: utilitarianism (acting to achieve the greatest good for the greatest number), deontology (intending to act in accord with moral duty), and virtue ethics (acting from laudable character traits), and apply them to entomological ethics.

Utilitarianism

Utilitarianism takes various forms (e.g., act and rule utilitarianism), but the central concept is that an ethical action provides the greatest good for the greatest number.[8] The "good" can be understood as whatever assures happiness (physical, psychological, or cultural well-being), and the "number" might be understood as all of those beings that can experience whatever is good. What we seek is to either minimize harm or maximize pleasure in one or more of its possible manifestations. The theory is consequentialist insofar as the morality of an action is solely a function of its actual results.

Insects and the Greatest Good

Insects are presumably incapable of emotional experiences and unable to appreciate higher goods (e.g., beauty, tradition, or faith). However, insects may feel some kinds of pain.[9] Their experience is surely unlike our own, but nonetheless these creatures appear to be discomforted by some treatments, and they can learn to associate stimuli with presumably discomforting events (e.g., electrical shock), a phenomenon which provides prima facie evidence of pain. So, although their pain is unlike ours (the same might be said of newborns), it should factor into a utilitarian analysis. Consider the sheer number of insects that we kill with a backyard fogger, for example. If each individual experiences some modicum of pain during its neurotoxically induced demise, this would entail that we can't do just anything to large numbers of insects—at least without some overriding consideration.

A utilitarian might offer two provisions to this ethical constraint. First, if we take too seriously the potential suffering of insects, this would prevent mowing lawns, harvesting fields, and taking walks. Thousands of insects might be dismembered by a spinning blade and dozens could be crushed by human feet. But human happiness counts as well, and we must be permitted to feed ourselves and lead our lives in ways that bring us happiness (e.g., taking walks).[10] The utilitarian calculus has to include the degree or quality of the good, and here's where things get morally messy.

One can reasonably contend that many instantiations of individual human happiness trump large numbers of harmed insects. There is, however, presumably some extremely large numbers of slowly dying insects (e.g., ten thousand variously dismembered grasshoppers) that would offset a miniscule increase in a human individual's pleasure (e.g., the smell of freshly cut grass). The problem is that it's just not clear how many sliced up insects offset the pleasure that comes from having a manicured yard.

Nor does the utilitarian calculus explain why it is wrong to pull wings off flies if doing so provides great happiness to the human. Utilitarianism has an apples-and-oranges problem. Given the epistemic constraints, there is no compelling reason to presume that insect suffering from being dewinged (apples) is greater than the pleasure, however perverse, that accrues to the dewinger (oranges).

Another reply to the utilitarian's justification of wholesale killing of insects by reference to human needs is to refer to the Jains. The monks sweep the path in front of themselves to avoid stepping on insects and refrain from candlelight to avoid incinerating insects.[11] This religious practice demonstrates that it is possible to live without harming insects. However, the remarkable devotion of the Jain monks is arguably made possible only by having a larger social context in which such extreme practices are viable (e.g., other people provide their food). And utilitarianism entails the greatest good for the greatest number, not merely what is good for some sorts of humans and creatures (e.g., Jains, ants, and moths).

Second, the utilitarian might contend that swatting a fly provides an instantaneous death. So if these creatures have no sense of their own lives—no perception of a self or future to be frustrated—then killing them isn't an ethical problem as long as some other being has pleasure as a consequence (e.g., not being pestered). But pulling off their wings or poisoning their nervous systems is quite another matter, and we often kill insects through protracted processes.

And so utilitarianism provides no clear explanation of why quickly crushing (versus spraying) the cricket during the hike would be wrong. After all, the individual's discomfort with the creepiness of insects is mitigated, and the insect is killed instantly. Moreover, the utilitarian seems unable to explain why it would be praiseworthy to be the sort of person who literally wouldn't harm a cricket (or a fly).[12]

There is another, rather strange, challenge to the utilitarian view of how we ought to treat insects. In the practice of "crush fetishism," men derive sexual gratification from squashing creatures (usually invertebrates) or, more typically, watching women do so. A spokesperson for this fetish argued that "normal" people cause extensive suffering to livestock to satisfy their desire for sensory pleasure to eat meat.[13] The crush fetishist also derives pleasure from killing animals, but their creatures of instrumental pleasure are typically insects. So, who has the stronger utilitarian case? If we take the pleasure of a tasty steak to be on a par with the pleasure of sexual gratification, then crush fetishism is defensible. This seems a most disturbing result of consequentialist ethics.

It would appear that utilitarianism provides some ethical insight in terms of how we ought to consider actions that involve killing many insects to satisfy vastly fewer people. Some practices (e.g., pesticide applications to vital food crops) are likely countenanced by the fact that we must compete (and kill) in order to live and to experience the good. But this raises the further question of how we go about killing. Choosing the chemical that kills most quickly or the biological agent that kills only the pest species seems morally compulsory but somehow misses the mark (a bit like feeling good about using drones to destroy presumptive enemies while doing less harm to innocent bystanders than conventional bombing).

Most importantly, utilitarianism does not provide a compelling rationale for why we'd praise the person who gently removes a fly from the house (some individuals might find pleasure in doing so, but if others don't, then there's no ethical obligation) or condemn a person who pulls wings from flies (if they find this practice more pleasing than the insect's resultant suffering). At the scale of the individual insect, the epistemic constraints regarding the "greatest good" are such that utility provides little moral guidance.

Deontology

Deontology is an alternative ethical theory. Unlike utilitarianism, which is consequentialist (the outcome of an action is all that matters), deontology is concerned with our intentions; an action is right if done for the right reasons, being in accord with moral duty.[14] This theory is often framed in terms of rights. An individual can have both positive rights which require others to act (e.g., if another being has the right to be fed, we're obligated to provide food) and negative rights which require others to refrain from acting (e.g., if another being has a right to life, we're obligated to refrain from poisoning their food). In western societies, where human liberty is vital, we tend to think in terms of rights, rather than duties. But the right to food means nothing unless it entails a duty for others to provide sustenance to the extent reasonably possible (after all, "ought" implies "can"—we are not morally obligated to do things beyond our capacities). However, rights and duties are not perfectly paired.

There are imperfect duties, such as the obligation to be charitable.[15] We might have a duty to be charitable, but no individual has the right to claim another's charity. That is, if a panhandler asks for money, a passerby is not obligated to make a contribution. However, the individual is morally wrong to never act charitably (again, given the person's capacity to do so). Another disconnection between rights and duties involves supererogatory (beyond the call of duty) actions such as heroic rescues.[16] The drowning person does not have a right to be saved (setting aside there being a lifeguard whose special duties involve rescuing). If a person jumps into the water and saves the victim, the savior is morally praiseworthy, but if a bystander does not risk her life, she's not blameworthy.

Rights, Duties—and Insects

To understand our duties to insects, one approach is to express deontology in the simple, but not wholly inaccurate, form of the Golden Rule. Perhaps we are obligated to do unto insects as we would have others do unto us. In fact, this is how a parent might admonish a child who's pulling wings off a fly: "Would you like it if someone pulled you apart?" The problem is whether the projection of "liking" onto the fly is justified. If the child is pulling apart a doll, the wrongness is not a matter of what the doll is experiencing (which is nothing) but merely a concern for destroying something of economic value—and a fly doesn't have much, if any, such value.

And so, deontologists face an epistemic gap much like the utilitarians—we don't know what an insect likes or experiences. Cutting off an insect's leg apparently doesn't produce pain (there is no evidence of limping or sensitivity in the amputated limb), but crushing pressure does yield behaviors that are reasonably interpreted as distress.[17] Perhaps pulling the wings off flies is like our getting a haircut, and while a forced haircut might violate an individual's right to self-determination, a fly seemingly lacks such autonomy. Removing its wings results in it becoming less flylike and unable to perform its normal functions. But here the deontologist has to make the case that the fly has a right to do fly things—and why should this be?

One answer is that natural rights are conferred by virtue of some intrinsic quality. Rationality and sentience—or perhaps just being a human—can ground the right to life, for example. Our capacity to make plans means that others can harm us by denying our autonomous goals. Flies, on the other hand, aren't project pursuers with the capacity to have their intentions frustrated. But perhaps we're asking more than is reasonable to ground the notion of rights—and our corresponding duties.

It has been argued that the only requirement for being morally considerable (i.e., possessing some minimal rights) is the capacity to be made better or worse off insofar as a particular being is concerned.[18] Depriving an engine of oil makes a car worse off but only with regard to our interests in using it for transportation. However, most (perhaps all) living things have a condition that can be better or worse with regard to themselves. A wingless fly will struggle to escape predators, locate food, or find mates—and it has an autonomous interest in survival and reproduction.

If we turn to a religious perspective, Albert Schweitzer's "reverence for life" yields a similar ethic.[19] Schweitzer's contention was that we could be certain that we want to go on living and that we share this desire with all living beings (including plants, so having a desire, like being concerned, does not entail consciousness). This has been formulated as a biocentric Golden Rule in which we have a duty to care for and respect all living things the same as we would wish for ourselves. But of course, we wish to eat, which means killing. And so we again run into the problem that we encountered with utilitarianism: How do we resolve competing consequentialist goods or, in the present case, deontological rights?

We surely have a right to protect our psychological and physical well-being. So there is no duty to allow flies to buzz around our heads or to occupy our kitchens (negative duties), let alone having a positive duty to introduce them into our homes. If we have a right to avoid psychological trauma, then the creeped-out hiker was justified in killing the cricket (shooing it away might elicit greater anxiety as its location would become unknown). There must be reasonable constraints on our desires and limits to our needs—as well as those of other creatures. But finding these boundaries is an enormous challenge.

What deontology offers in terms of why it is unethical to remove a fly's wings or ethical to avoid harming a fly is not entirely satisfying. Perhaps we have a negative duty to refrain from gratuitously killing or mutilating other life forms and maybe acts of removing—rather than swatting—flies are supererogatory (i.e., heroic). But these formulations of duty seem too weak to fully account for our intuitions about harming insects.

Virtue Ethics

Virtue ethicists take a very different approach to right action than do utilitarians or deontologists. Rather than specifying rules or principles that make an action right, the key is developing into an individual with certain character traits.[20] And then, a moral act is simply that which a virtuous person does. In the Western intellectual tradition, virtue ethics played an important role for the ancient Greeks. Later, the four cardinal virtues of the Greeks (prudence, justice, temperance, and courage) were conjoined with the theological virtues of faith, hope, and love to yield the seven Christian or heavenly virtues of the Catholic catechism.[21]

Virtue ethics has seen something of a renaissance in contemporary environmental discourse, where neither utility nor rights/duties have provided a compelling framework.[22] Insects can be perceived as being vital elements in the context of the environment, given their diversity and ecological importance. And so it stands to reason that our treatment of insects might be understood through the lens of the virtues.

The Virtuous Treatment of Insects

Virtue ethics requires that we cultivate particular character traits (virtues) while avoiding others (vices) in order to fully realize our human potential thereby knowing and doing what is right. In short, to "not harm a fly" is important because this reflects virtue (e.g. regard for others), while to "pull wings off flies" promulgates vice (e.g., disregard of others). However, one might object that we don't really know whether insects warrant such regard. Perhaps they deserve no greater consideration than rag dolls. And it is here that virtue ethics would appear to have a significant advantage over utilitarianism or deontology as an ethical framework in its capacity to sidestep the problem of being mistaken about facts that bog down the other theories.

One of the most important features of virtue ethics in terms of providing an account of our moral intuitions about the treatment of insects is that we can avoid the epistemic problem of not knowing what another creature experiences. The key lies in how one becomes virtuous and hence moral. The path to virtue is practice. Through repetition, we live out the virtues until they become our very nature, at which point our actions are emergently moral. Even if we are mistaken as to whether insects feel pain, as long as our belief about their lives is reasonable (rational deliberation underwrites virtue, and it is plausible that these animals can suffer), then refraining from harming flies or choosing to remove rather than swat them constitutes a virtuous practice.[23]

In a similar sense, the child who believes the doll has experiences (this might be a reasonable belief for a child) is practicing the virtues by not "hurting" the doll. So virtue is always relativized to the capacity or potential of the individual. What is brave for a firefighter to do might be foolhardy for a bystander. What constitutes praiseworthy tolerance for a person with entomophobic tendencies (e.g., refraining from spraying a cricket) might represent nothing particularly virtuous for other people.

There is, of course, a reasonable limit to what is required of us (whatever our context), and Aristotle recognized the importance of practical judgment. In fact, the virtues were framed in terms of instantiating the golden mean between extremes (e.g., courage lying between rashness and cowardice). So for most of us, allowing a fly to crawl across one's food would be excessively tolerant, and spraying a cricket in the forest would be excessively intolerant.

A crucial point for ethics in terms of interacting with insects is that they provide ideal opportunities to cultivate virtue. We are able to develop a range of positive character traits through frequent practice, given our abundant encounters with these creatures. Furthermore, insects stretch our virtuous capacities by often being perceived as alien, off-putting, frightful, or disgusting.[24] It is easy to resist harming kittens and it is not difficult, albeit rather rare, to save a puppy. So there is little challenge and hence limited potential for refining our virtues. However, choosing to step over an ant on the sidewalk, refraining from spraying a grasshopper in the garden, opening a window to let an annoying fly escape, or removing a wayward spider from the basement requires far greater consideration.

The Practices of Entomological Virtue

If practice makes perfect, what are some of the ways in which deliberate and reflective interactions with insects can cultivate the virtues?

By choosing not to harm insects, we manifest a form of the Aristotelian virtue of temperance (*sōphrosunē*).[25] Although the ancients were concerned with moderation of bodily pleasures, today temperance often manifests as capacity to accept differences in appearances and beliefs among our fellow humans. To "live and let live" is taken to be a virtue. Xenophobia (fear of the unfamiliar) is a contemporary vice, and perhaps spiders in basements are a kind of practice field for being tolerant of gay men kissing, women in burkas, and people speaking Spanish. I have previously argued that, "if kids learn that they can coexist with radically different creatures, maybe they'll figure out that they can live among not-like-us humans."[26]

If nothing else, a close encounter with an insect can be an opportunity to practice self-restraint. Aristotle argued that this capacity, although not itself a virtue (one could restrain oneself from doing something good), was vital to developing the virtues.[27] More to the point, one must achieve self-mastery or the ability to act according to rational deliberation. Insects can most certainly elicit irrational responses,[28] so they provide abundant opportunities for us to practice responding to other beings in ways that aren't driven by unreflective emotional outbursts. And this leads us to the next virtue.

Our encounters with insects also cultivate the Aristotelean virtue of gentleness (*praótēs*). Although this quality primarily concerned anger, the fundamental notion is again that we should be ruled by reason rather than emotion.[29] And certainly our responses to insects ought to be informed by consideration of their actual danger to our well-being, rather than an ungrounded fear or disgust. We might also see our interactions with insects in terms of the Roman virtue of *clementia*, or mercy—acting with mildness and setting aside previous transgressions.[30] That we were once stung by a wasp or annoyed by a fly is therefore not an ethical basis for seeking to spray all stinging insects or to pull wings from flies in retribution.

The next virtue is rather more complicated in an entomological context. In dealing with insects and deciding how to treat these little animals, we must admit that there is much that we do not know about them. In a sense, each encounter entails humility regarding these radically "other" life forms. Returning for a moment to the matter of our not knowing whether insects can feel pain, it seems clear that if we care about suffering (and this seems morally obligatory in all theories), we ought to be curious about and attempt to know what sorts of beings can suffer.[31]

And so, although Aristotle did not specifically consider epistemic humility, he advocated *alētheia*, or truthfulness, about one's abilities and accomplishments.[32] Perhaps this virtue might be combined with the intellectual virtue of *episteme* or knowledge.[33] And here we might turn to the *Apology* in which Socrates compared himself to a pretentious accuser: "I am wiser than this man; it is likely that neither of us knows anything worthwhile, but he thinks he knows something when he does not."[34]

Entomologists can attest to the capacity of insects to elicit a sense of wonder and to evoke curiosity. Interestingly, Aristotle's intellectual virtues don't include curiosity. But perhaps there is a secondary place for this capacity insofar as knowledge (*episteme*) must be acquired, and presumably one must be interested in the world in order to learn.

But perhaps this is stretching Aristotle's approach to virtue beyond plausible limits. Other philosophers have proposed virtues that do not echo those of the ancient Greeks. The post-Enlightenment celebration of science provides strong endorsement for the cultivation of wonder and curiosity. Elias Baumgarten has cogently argued that curiosity—a desire to know—is a moral virtue.[35] He considers what would be (in)appropriate objects of curiosity and, by this account, insects are most certainly suitable sources of wonder. This is not to say that everyone must be curious about insects, only that these animals have a compelling potential to provide abundant and appropriate opportunities for us to practice curiosity. Baumgarten sees curiosity as being parallel to the final contemporary virtue that we'll consider—the appreciation of beauty.

Dominic Melver Lopes makes the case that possessing aesthetic taste is a virtue; this capacity is intrinsically good for humans insofar as it contributes to our well-being.[36] And insects provide, once again, both frequent and potentially challenging opportunities for aesthetic appreciation. Many people have argued for the beauty of insects, including, perhaps most famously, Walt Whitman: "I believe a leaf of grass is no less than the journey work of the stars, And the pismire [an ant] is equally perfect."[37] The famed conservationists Paul and Anne Erhlich have maintained that "some tiny wasps and flies, if seen under a microscope, appear to be fashioned out of solid gold."[38] And again, the capacity to appreciate beauty is exercised more vigorously in observing the features of insects than in contemplating a field of wildflowers. Hence, insects have the capacity to refine and extend our aesthetic judgments through frequent practice.

The Virtues of Virtue Ethics

Virtue ethics has the capacity to make sense of diverse arguments regarding how we ought to treat other creatures. The various arguments concerning our moral obligations to animals can be categorized as being either direct or indirect.[39] Direct theories posit that animals are sentient and hence qualify as moral patients. Many in this camp hold that animals are not morally equivalent to humans because they lack some important qualities (e.g., rights, rationality, self-consciousness, and moral sensibility) but nonetheless deserve moral consideration.

Indirect theories deny that animals have moral standing in and of themselves with René Descartes being the most (in)famous philosopher in this camp. He specifically dismissed insects: "it is more probable that worms and flies and caterpillars move mechanically than that they all have immortal souls."[40] However, there might still be ethical considerations in how we treat animals. A weak version pertains to their being (mis)perceived as suffering, such that we harm empathetic people who see us apparently mistreating animals. A strong consideration of our interactions with animals is a basis for our treatment of people. Because animals have relevant analogical features to humans (not including sentience by this account), those who practice cruelty toward animals are more likely to behave similarly to people. And here we can salvage Descartes, who maintained that we can judge the heart of a man by his treatment of animals.[41]

Although virtue ethics are not usually enlisted in discussions of animals, this approach provides a conceptual umbrella that makes sense of both direct and indirect theories. If insects are sentient, then taking care to "not harm a fly" and certainly refraining from pulling off its wings would be meaningful ways of practicing compassion. If insects aren't sentient (and again, we don't know), then acting as if they can suffer is a way of rehearsing the ways in which we treat those beings capable of suffering.

Virtue ethics might also make sense of one of the better known religious injunctions concerning how we ought to treat one another—and perhaps, with some plausible extrapolation, how we ought to treat nonhumans, including insects. In "The Judgment of the Nations" (Matthew 25: 33–40), Jesus explains:

> Then the King will say to those on his right, "Come, you who are blessed by my Father; take your inheritance, the kingdom prepared for you since the creation of the world. For I was hungry and you gave me something to eat, I was thirsty and you gave me something to drink, I was a stranger and you invited me in, I needed clothes and you clothed me, I was sick and you looked after me, I was in prison and you came to visit me."
>
> Then the righteous will answer him, "Lord, when did we see you hungry and feed you, or thirsty and give you something to drink? When did we see you a stranger and invite you in, or needing clothes and clothe you? When did we see you sick or in prison and go to visit you?"
>
> The King will reply, "Truly I tell you, whatever you did for one of the least of these brothers and sisters of mine, you did for me."

By this account, how one treats the poor, hungry, ill, and imprisoned is the standard against one's worthiness or virtue is measured. There were (and are) abundant opportunities to treat "the least" with compassion, mercy, generosity, and kindness. Moreover, it has been pointed out that Jesus called upon people to practice loving actions that require no special training. We are not expected to heal the sick or free the imprisoned—merely to visit them, which is within anyone's ability (as noted by John Chrysostom, the influential fourth-century Archbishop of Constantinople).[42]

So where does this leave insects? Saint Francis of Assisi considered all living beings to be his brethren. In his "Canticle to the Sun," he prays: "Be praised, my Lord, through all Your creatures" and refers to even inanimate elements of nature as his "brothers and sisters."[43] By extension, it does not seem implausible for a Christian to perceive that a fly is among the "least of my brothers" and that interactions with insects would be a means of practicing the virtues of mercy, kindness, compassion, gentleness, and love.

Objections to Virtue Ethics

The application of virtue ethics to our treatment of insects is not without potential pitfalls,[44] and I'll address three that seem particularly pertinent to the entomological context.

The first concern is the anthropocentric core of virtue ethics. In effect, insects are valuable because they are a means to our ends. That is, these creatures merely provide frequent and challenging opportunities for us to practice the virtues. In an important sense the virtues themselves are also means with the ultimate end being *eudaimonia* or happiness.[45]

This objection has been levied against the use of virtue ethics to address environmental issues as well, and perhaps a similar response obtains. In pragmatic terms, neither utilitarianism nor deontology has provided frameworks leading to responsible actions based on the current state of the environment.[46] Although these have been the dominant ethical frameworks throughout modern times, the condition of the environment would appear to be rather strong evidence that neither theory has greatly constrained human behavior.

Furthermore, utility, if not entirely anthropocentric, leans heavily on human capacities insofar as "the good" invariably includes and typically emphasizes our well-being. Any conceptualization of what is good that excludes humans is nonstarter (e.g., the misanthropic ideals of some radical environmentalists). Likewise, every formulation of rights includes humans. I am unaware of any deontological framework that proposes a right for a nonhuman that does not also pertain to humans.

Finally, "anthropocentrism" cannot be considered a de facto defeater of an ethical system. There is no self-evident reason that an anthropocentric moral theory is fatally flawed. Those who wish to defeat virtues ethics on these grounds need to explain why it is mistaken to adopt anthropocentric ethics. Even the much-celebrated ethical perspectives (these are not rigorously explicated theories) of Aldo Leopold, Rachel Carson, and Wendell Berry are, upon careful consideration, rooted in human well-being.[47]

A second objection regarding virtue ethics is the problem of the ever-expanding list of candidate virtues, many of which are overlapping or even redundant, although the greater concern is the possibility of conflicting virtues. Conventionally, the tension between justice and mercy is raised as a problem,[48] and there is a sense in which this conflict pertains to what we do about a pesky fly. Surely it is no virtue in allowing our food to be contaminated or our mental state to be harried, but then neither is it virtuous to act out of anger or annoyance.

The problem of such dilemmas is shared with deontology in which duties conflict. Advocates of both ethical theories can reply, there is a virtue or duty that should prevail if one possesses sufficient philosophical discernment. This line of defense holds that in any given instance, there is actually no deep, genuine, or irresolvable dilemma, only a failure to fully understand what is morally required.[49] For virtue ethics, one might also appeal to a kind of master virtue—practical wisdom (*phronesis*), which one develops in the course of leading a good life. In addition, virtue must be relativized to the capacities of an individual, so there is no universal solution to the apparent dilemma of the annoying fly.

Third, one might object that we have not exhausted the potential of either utilitarianism or deontology. And, to be fair, the critique of these theories in this chapter is a bit quick, and proponents might have compelling replies to the shortcomings that were identified in the context of entomological ethics. In addition, if/when neurophysiologists or other scientists provide convincing evidence for (or against) insect pain and thereby close the epistemic gap, then it might be possible to factor the experiences of these creatures into the utilitarian calculus or the analysis of rights. But even so, this knowledge would not undermine the viability of virtue ethics.

With respect to utilitarianism, virtue ethics does not dismiss the importance of the greatest good (for the greatest number). Many of the virtues would seem to be consistent with positive consequences. Acting with beneficence, compassion, and gentleness would seem to have considerable potential to yield pleasurable outcomes. The crucial difference is that for the virtue ethicist, the consequences neither motivate nor justify the action—they are merely a fortuitous result of one's cultivating a virtuous character.

As for deontology, again virtue ethics will often be in accord with various moral duties. Among the virtues, honesty is often included in one way or another (e.g., Aristotle's *alētheia*, or truthfulness, about oneself and truth-telling is a classic duty in Kantian deontology).[50] But again, the motivation and justification differs between the two ethical theories. The person cultivating the virtues tells the truth not out of a rational, considered duty but because doing so is in accord with leading a good life. Likewise the deontologist might refrain from harming a fly because of a duty to act respectfully toward living things while the virtue ethicist does so in consideration of cultivating his or her character.

There may well be more devastating objections to framing our treatment of insects in terms of virtue ethics. However, it appears that this moral theory has considerable potential to account for our folk intuitions regarding flies and perhaps avoids some of the shortcomings of the dominant, alternative frameworks.

CONCLUSION

This overview of ethical theory is constrained by space limitations. Unpacking the strengths and weaknesses of the major moral frameworks, let alone important alternative approaches such as feminist ethics and non-Western approaches as they pertain to the treatment of insects, would require a book-length treatment. Not being a theologian, I only speculated how religiously informed morals may also contribute to our understanding. However, it appears that virtue ethics might align with some Christian perspectives regarding our relationships to nonhuman beings.

One of the great challenges of using virtue ethics as a guide to leading a good life is sorting out which character traits ought to be included. Perhaps practical wisdom (*phronesis*) provides a means of selecting the most appropriate virtues for various individuals and challenges. But there is also the possibility that a "master virtue" could be used to guide our practice, and Aristotle proposed that justice (*dikaiosunē*) could play this role.[51] The just individual possesses the virtues and the ability to apply them in the community.

One of the essential forms of justice concerns the distribution of resources. Aristotle limited his analysis to fellow humans and material goods, but the underlying principle plausibly extends to other animals and psychological/emotional resources. The fundamental notions are that of the mean (providing neither too much nor too little) and dessert (unequal individuals should not be treated equally).

Insects are not our equals, but this does not imply that their value is zero. At least they deserve to be left unharmed when rational consideration reveals that they represent no risk to ourselves. This may be too low of an ethical bar, but it is a standard of justice that we often fail to meet. And perhaps such attentiveness is consistent with Christian values, as well: "What is the price of two sparrows—one copper coin? But not a single sparrow can fall to the ground without your Father knowing it" (Matthew 10:29).

NOTES

1. "Wouldn't harm a fly," *Know Your Phrase*, accessed August 15, 2015, http://www.knowyourphrase.com/phrase-meanings/Wouldnt-Harm-a-Fly.html.

2. For an interesting discussion of how people perceive this behavior see: "Why do children sometimes pull wings off flies, pull legs off daddy-long-legs, etc.?" *Democratic Underground*, accessed August 15, 2015, http://www.democraticunderground.com/1018473628.

3. Christopher Kaczor, *The Ethics of Abortion: Women's Rights, Human Life, and the Question of Justice* (New York: Routledge, 2010); Matthew Kramer, *The Ethics of Capital Punishment: A Philosophical Investigation of Evil and its Consequences* (New York: Oxford University Press, 2014).

4. J. Jeremy Wisnewski and R. D. Emerick, *The Ethics of Torture* (New York: Bloomsbury, 2009).

5. Daniel R. Papaj and Alcinda C. Lewis, eds., *Insect Learning: Ecology and Evolutionary Perspectives* (New York: Springer, 2012).

6. John F. Organ, R. M. Muth, J. E. Dizard, S. J. Williamson, and T. A. Decker, "Fair Chase and Humane Treatment: Balancing the Ethics of Hunting and Trapping," *Transactions of the North American Wildlife and Natural Resources Conference*, 63 (1998): 528–43.

7. Tom L. Beauchamp and R. G. Frey, eds., *The Oxford Handbook of Animal Ethics* (New York: Oxford University Press, 2014). Lori Gruen, *The Stanford Encyclopedia of Philosophy*, s.v. "The Moral Status of Animals," accessed August 15, 2015, http://plato.stanford.edu/archives/fall2014/entries/moral-animal/.

8. Walter Sinnott-Armstrong, *The Stanford Encyclopedia of Philosophy*, s.v. "Consequentialism," ed. Edward N. Zalta, accessed August 15, 2015, http://plato.stanford.edu/archives/spr2014/entries/consequentialism/.

9. C. H. Eisemann, W. K. Jorgensen, D. J. Merritt, M. J. Rice, B. W. Cribb, P. D. Webb, and M. P. Zalucki, "Do Insects Feel Pain?—A Biological View," *Experientia* 40 (1984): 164–67. J. A. Lockwood, "The Moral Standing of Insects and the Ethics of Extinction," *Florida Entomologist* 70 (1987): 70–89.

10. Tatjana Visak and Robert Garner, eds., *The Ethics of Killing Animals* (New York: Oxford University Press, 2015).

11. Padmanabh S. Jaini, *Jaina Path of Purification* (New Delhi: Motilal Banarsidass, 2014).

12. A rule-based utilitarianism might hold the best potential of providing some rationale: Brad Hooker, *The Stanford Encyclopedia of Philosophy*, s.v. "Rule Consequentialism," ed. Edward N. Zalta, accessed August 15, 2015, http://plato.stanford.edu/archives/spr2011/entries/consequentialism-rule/.

13. Hugh Raffles, *Insectopedia* (New York: Pantheon, 2010), 267–90.

14. Larry Alexander and Michael Moore, *The Stanford Encyclopedia of Philosophy*, s.v. "Deontological Ethics," ed. Edward N. Zalta, accessed August 15, 2015, http://plato.stanford.edu/archives/spr2015/entries/ethics-deontological/.

15. D. Heyd, *Supererogation: Its Status in Ethical Theory* (Cambridge: Cambridge University Press, 1982).

16. E. Pybus, "'Saints and Heroes,'" *Philosophy*, 57 (1982): 193–99.

17. Lockwood, "The Moral Standing of Insects and the Ethics of Extinction."

18. L. E. Johnson, *A Morally Deep World: An Essay on Moral Significance and Environmental Ethics* (New York: Cambridge University Press, 1991).

19. Albert Schweitzer, *Out of My Life and Thought: An Autobiography* (Baltimore: Johns Hopkins University Press, 2009)

20. Rosalind, Hursthouse, *The Stanford Encyclopedia of Philosophy*, s.v. "Virtue Ethics," ed. Edward N. Zalta, accessed August 15, 2015, http://plato.stanford.edu/archives/fall2013/entries/ethics-virtue/.

21. *New Advent: Catholic Encyclopedia*, s.v. "Virtue," accessed July 18, 2016, http://www.newadvent.org/cathen/15472a.htm.

22. Geoffrey B. Frasz, "Environmental Virtue Ethics: A New Direction for Environmental Ethics," *Environmental Ethics* 15 (1993): 259–74. Philip Cafaro and Ronald Sandler, eds., *Environmental Virtue Ethics* (Lanham, MD: Rowman & Littlefield, 2005).

23. I have made a similar argument, in greater detail, concerning the case of an individual encountering a scattering of trash placed along a roadside by an avant-garde artist and mistaking the art installation for strewn garbage and removing the material. The epistemic error does not negate the virtuous quality of the act, as the individual reasonably interpreted the situation and cultivated the virtues of care, humility, and aesthetic appreciation. See J. A. Lockwood and A. V. Latchininsky, "Philosophical Justification for the Extirpation of Non-Indigenous Species: The Case of the Grasshopper *Schistocerca nitens* (Orthoptera) on the Island of Nihoa, Hawaii," *Journal of Insect Conservation* 12 (2008): 429–45; D. S. Maier and J. A. Lockwood, "Conservation as Picking up Trash in Nature," *Environmental Philosophy* 12 (2015): 99–119.

24. Jeffrey A. Lockwood, *The Infested Mind: Why Humans Fear, Loathe, and Love Insects* (New York: Oxford University Press, 2013), 174.

25. Howard J. Curzer, "Aristotle's Account of the Virtue of Temperance in *Nicomachean Ethics* III 10–11," *Journal of the History of Philosophy*, 35 (1997): 5–25.

26. Lockwood, *The Infested Mind.*

27. Christopher Toner, "Akrasia Revisited: An Interpretation and Defense of Aristotle," *The Southern Journal of Philosophy* 41 (2003): 283–306.

28. Lockwood, *The Infested Mind.*

29. Aristotle, *Nichomachean Ethics*, 1125a–b, accessed August 15, 2015, http://www.perseus.tufts.edu/hopper/text?doc=Perseus%3Atext%3A1999.01.0054%3Abekker%20page%3D1125b.

30. Susanna Braund, ed., *Seneca: De Clementia* (New York: Oxford University Press, 2011).

31. Linda Zagzebsky, *On Epistemology* (Belmont, CA: Wadsworth, 2009).
32. Aristotle, *Nicomachean Ethics*, 1125a–b, accessed August 15, 2015, http://www.perseus.tufts.edu/hopper/text?doc=Perseus%3Atext%3A1999.01.0054%3Abekker%20page%3D1125b.
33. Aristotle, *Nicomachean Ethics*, trans. Joe Sachs (Indianapolis, IN: Focus, 2002), 116–20.
34. Plato, *Euthyphro, Apology, Crito, Meno, Phaedo*, ed. G. M. A. Grube, trans. G. M. A. Grube, *Plato: Five Dialogues: Euthyphro, Apology, Crito, Meno, Phaedo* (Indianapolis, IN: Hackett, 2002).
35. Elias Baumgarten, "Curiosity as a Moral Virtue," *International Journal of Applied Philosophy* 15 (2001), 169–84, DOI:10.5840/ijap200115215.
36. Dominic McIver Lopes, "Virtues of Art: Good Taste," *Proceedings of the Aristotelian Society* 82 (2008): 197–211.
37. Walt Whitman, *Leaves of Grass* (Seattle, WA: CreateSpace, 2014) 51.
38. Anne Ehrlich and Paul Ehrlich, "Preserving biodiversity just for the beauty of nature," *Mother Earth News*, July/August 1981, accessed August 15, 2015, http://www.motherearthnews.com/nature-and-environment/the-beauty-of-nature-zmaz81jazraw.aspx.
39. Scott D. Wilson, *Internet Encyclopedia of Philosophy*, s.v. "Animal ethics," accessed August 15, 2015, http://www.iep.utm.edu/anim-eth/#SH1c.
40. Thomas Regan and Peter Singer, eds., *Animal Rights and Human Obligations* (Englewood Cliffs, NJ: Prentice Hall, 1989), 18.
41. Regan and Singer, *Animal Rights and Human Obligations*.
42. "Matthew, Chapter XXV," *People's Bible Notes*, accessed August 15, 2015, http://www.kingjamesbibleonline.org/Matthew-25-35/.
43. Francis of Assisi, "Canticle of Brother Sun," *Francis and Clare: The Complete Works*, The Classics of Western Spirituality: A Library of the Great Spiritual Masters, eds. Richard J. Payne and John Farina (Mahwah, NJ: Paulist Press, 1982), 38–39, accessed July 18, 2016, https://books.google.com/books?id=sznaF957ieQC&pg=PA37&source=gbs_toc_r&cad=4#v=onepage&q&f=false.
44. Hursthouse, "Virtue Ethics."
45. Hursthouse, "Virtue Ethics."
46. There is extensive documentation of environmental problems, but here are three particularly relevant references: Lester R. Brown, *World on the Edge: How to Prevent Environmental and Economic Collapse* (New York: W. W. Norton, 2011). Dave Foreman, *Man Swarm and The Killing of Wildlife* (Durango, CO: Raven's Eye Press, 2011). Naomi Klein, *This Changes Everything: Capitalism vs. The Climate* (New York: Simon & Schuster, 2015).
47. Although there is insufficient space to delve into this, even a cursory reading of *A Sand County Almanac*, *Silent Spring*, or *The Unsettling of America* will make evident that these leading thinkers framed their concerns primarily, if not exclusively, in terms of human interests.
48. Robin Antony Duff, "Justice, Mercy, and Forgiveness," *Criminal Justice Ethics* 9 (1990): 51–63.
49. Hursthouse, "Virtue Ethics."
50. Hursthouse, "Virtue Ethics;" Alexander and Moore, "Deontological Ethics."
51. Michael Slote, *The Stanford Encyclopedia of Philosophy*, s.v. "Justice as a Virtue," accessed August 15, 2015, http://plato.stanford.edu/archives/fall2014/entries/justice-virtue/.

REFERENCES

Aristotle. *Nichomachean Ethics*. 1125a–b. Accessed August 15, 2015. http://www.perseus.tufts.edu/hopper/text?doc=Perseus%3Atext%3A1999.01.0054%3Abekker%20page%3D1125b.
Aristotle. *Nicomachean Ethics*. Translated by Joe Sachs. Indianapolis, IN: Focus, 2002.

Baumgarten, Elias. "Curiosity as a Moral Virtue." *International Journal of Applied Philosophy* 15 (2001): 169–84, DOI:10.5840/ijap200115215.

Beauchamp, Tom L., and R. G. Frey, eds. *The Oxford Handbook of Animal Ethics*. New York: Oxford University Press, 2014.

Braund, Susanna, ed. *Seneca: De Clementia*. New York: Oxford University Press, 2011.

Brown, Lester R. *World on the Edge: How to Prevent Environmental and Economic Collapse*. New York: W. W. Norton, 2011.

Cafaro, Philip, and Ronald Sandler, eds. *Environmental Virtue Ethics*. Lanham, MD: Rowman & Littlefield, 2005.

Curzer, Howard J. "Aristotle's Account of the Virtue of Temperance in *Nicomachean Ethics* III 10–11." *Journal of the History of Philosophy* 35 (1997): 5–25.

Duff, Robin Antony. "Justice, Mercy, and Forgiveness." *Criminal Justice Ethics* 9 (1990): 51–63.

Ehrlich, Anne, and Paul Ehrlich. "Preserving Biodiversity Just for the Beauty of Nature." *Mother Earth News*. July/August 1981. Accessed August 15, 2015. http://www.motherearthnews.com/nature-and-environment/the-beauty-of-nature-zmaz81jazraw.aspx.

Eisemann, C. H., W. K. Jorgensen, D. J. Merritt, M. J. Rice, B. W. Cribb, P. D. Webb, and M. P. Zalucki. "Do Insects Feel Pain?—A Biological View." *Experientia* 40 (1984).

Foreman, Dave. *Man Swarm and the Killing of Wildlife*. Durango, CO: Raven's Eye Press, 2011.

Francis of Assisi. "Canticle of Brother Sun." *Francis and Clare: The Complete Works*. The Classics of Western Spirituality: A Library of the Great Spiritual Masters. Edited by Richard J. Payne and John Farina. Mahwah, NJ: Paulist Press, 1982, 38–39. Accessed July 18, 2016. https://books.google.com/books?id=sznaF957ieQC&pg=PA37&source=gbs_toc_r&cad=4#v=onepage&q&f=false.

Frasz, Geoffrey B. "Environmental Virtue Ethics: A New Direction for Environmental Ethics." *Environmental Ethics* 15 (1993): 259–74.

Heyd, D. *Supererogation: Its Status in Ethical Theory*. Cambridge: Cambridge University Press, 1982.

Jaini, Padmanabh S. *Jaina Path of Purification*. New Delhi: Motilal Banarsidass, 2014.

Johnson, L. E. *A Morally Deep World: An Essay on Moral Significance and Environmental Ethics*. New York: Cambridge University Press, 1991.

Kaczor, Christopher. *The Ethics of Abortion: Women's Rights, Human Life, and the Question of Justice*. New York: Routledge, 2010.

Klein, Naomi. *This Changes Everything: Capitalism vs. The Climate*. New York: Simon & Schuster, 2015.

Kramer, Matthew. *The Ethics of Capital Punishment: A Philosophical Investigation of Evil and its Consequences*. New York: Oxford University Press, 2014.

Lockwood, Jeffrey A. *The Infested Mind: Why Humans Fear, Loathe, and Love Insects*. New York: Oxford University Press, 2013.

———. "The Moral Standing of Insects and the Ethics of Extinction." *Florida Entomologist* 70 (1987): 70–89.

Lopes, Dominic McIver. "Virtues of Art: Good Taste." *Proceedings of the Aristotelian Society* 82 (2008): 197–211.

Organ, John F., R. M. Muth, J. E. Dizard, S. J. Williamson, and T. A. Decker. "Fair Chase and Humane Treatment: Balancing the Ethics of Hunting and Trapping." *Transactions of the North American Wildlife and Natural Resources Conference*, 63 (1998): 528–43.

Papaj, Daniel R. and Alcinda C. Lewis, eds. *Insect Learning: Ecology and Evolutionary Perspectives*. New York: Springer, 2012.

Pybus, E. "Saints and Heroes." *Philosophy*, 57 (1982): 193–99.

Raffles, Hugh. *Insectopedia*. New York: Pantheon, 2010.

Regan, Thomas and Peter Singer, eds. *Animal Rights and Human Obligations*. Englewood Cliffs, NJ: Prentice Hall, 1989.

Schweitzer, Albert. *Out of My Life and Thought: An Autobiography*. Baltimore: Johns Hopkins University Press, 2009.

Toner, Christopher. "Akrasia Revisited: An Interpretation and Defense of Aristotle." *The Southern Journal of Philosophy* 41 (2003): 283–306.
Visak, Tatjana and Robert Garner, eds. *The Ethics of Killing Animals*. New York: Oxford University Press, 2015.
Whitman, Walt. *Leaves of Grass*. Seattle, WA: CreateSpace, 2014.
Wisnewski, J. Jeremy, and R. D. Emerick. *The Ethics of Torture*. New York: Bloomsbury, 2009.
"Wouldn't harm a fly." *Know Your Phrase*. Accessed August 15, 2015. http://www.knowyourphrase.com/phrase-meanings/Wouldnt-Harm-a-Fly.html.
"Why do children sometimes pull wings off flies, pull legs off daddy-long-legs, etc.?" *Democratic Underground*. Accessed August 15, 2015. http://www.democraticunderground.com/1018473628.
Zagzebsky, Linda. *On Epistemology*. Belmont, CA: Wadsworth, 2009.

Chapter Three

Anthropogenic Climate Change and Animal Welfare

Bryan Ness

The effects of anthropogenic climate change are often viewed through a heavily anthropocentric lens, and even when the rest of the biosphere is considered, it is often in reference to biodiversity and ecosystem integrity in a strictly utilitarian fashion. Lost in the discussion are the more specific concerns about the rights of individual organisms that will be affected by climate change, many of which will face an uncertain future of potentially shrinking habitat and the need to relocate geographically to find more hospitable habitats. Whether simply displaced or set firmly on the road to extinction, individual animals will undoubtedly suffer. Sources of trauma potentially include having to tolerate suboptimum climatic conditions leading to chronic heat stress and dehydration, disruption of breeding cycles and gradual starvation due to increasing scarcity of food or prey. Both domesticated and wild animals will likely experience increased suffering from disease, as well, since most parasites and disease vectors will likely experience range expansions as temperatures rise. Since climate change is largely driven by humans, humans bear a responsibility to identify the animal welfare problems that will occur and to develop plans to alleviate as much suffering as possible.

One of the principles upheld in Old Testament Levitical law was the act of giving back to the earth and its creatures as exemplified by the Sabbatical years (every seventh year) in which the land was to be left fallow in part to provide food for wild animals. The biblical story of Noah also exemplifies God's concern for the animal world by commanding Noah to save some animals of every species. Our ethical response clearly needs to include maintaining biodiversity and ecological stability but also needs to focus on the potential for individual animal suffering and how we can alleviate it wherever possible. Because the specific effects of climate change are so uncertain, we must develop contingency plans for a variety of potential actions, including assisted geographic relocation of animal populations, identification of potential new habitats, assisted reproduction, control of invasive species and development of treatments for the increased incidence of diseases and parasites. Animal welfare issues will become increasingly complex under the rapidly changing conditions brought on by global warming, and many times actions deemed necessary to alleviate animal suffering may introduce ancillary suffering or may result in the suffering of other species. Even studies designed to better understand animals of concern have the potential to introduce animal welfare issues of their own. For example, tracking or data-logging devices attached or surgically inserted into an animal may reduce their fitness and quality of life, and capture and biopsy methods may introduce additional trauma. These and related concerns must be addressed if we are to behave ethically in response to the suffering we are indirectly imposing on wild animals through anthropogenic climate change.

Although the general public in the United States still harbors some doubt about the reality of climate change, and even fewer believe that it is caused by humans, scientists are in large agreement that anthropogenic[1] climate change is happening.[2] The specific consequences of climate change are also not completely certain, but climate-modeling research over the past forty years has provided an accurate range of consequences that are largely dependent on our response to the problem. According to the latest report from the IPCC (Intergovernmental Panel on Climate Change), if we simply continue to release CO_2 at roughly the current rate and don't reduce outputs until around 2080, global temperature is predicted to rise by as much as 3° C (5.4° F), and sea levels are predicted to rise by as much as 0.6 m (2.0 feet) by 2100.[3] Recent projections by James Hansen and his colleagues suggest that sea level changes may be much worse than previously projected with a possible 0.59 m (1.9 feet) rise in sea levels by as early as 2065.[4] Climate change is predicted to result in numerous other changes, including ocean acidification, increased global precipitation, increased storm intensities and shifts in seasonal and annual rainfall patterns. All of these will have profound impacts on global ecology and thus on animal welfare.

Among Christians, and especially evangelicals, there is even less acknowledgment of anthropogenic climate change. Although 69 percent of Catholics believe global warming is happening, only 51 percent of evangelicals agree.[5] Oddly, a somewhat greater percentage of evangelicals agree with regulating "carbon dioxide (the primary greenhouse gas) as a pollutant" (72 percent) and that we should "provide tax rebates for people who purchase energy-efficient vehicles or solar panels" (74 percent).[6] In part, this ambivalence toward anthropogenic climate change could stem from a traditional reading of the book of Genesis, where God tells man, "Be fruitful and increase in number; fill the earth and subdue it. Rule over the fish of the sea and the birds of the air and over every living creature that moves on the ground."[7] It can be (and has been) interpreted here that man has been given dominion to exploit the earth for his personal benefit. It was this interpretation that Lynn White, Jr., blames for our all our modern environmental crises, the Judeo-Christian teleology, which has permeated Western philosophy.[8]

Evangelical eschatology may also be partly to blame, as it is often expressed by evangelicals that God will not allow us to destroy the earth and that even if we did destroy the earth, God has promised us a new one on His return.[9] There is also a strong tendency among evangelicals to distrust science; since they do not believe in evolutionary theory, they extend this disbelief to the scientific enterprise in other fields. This is especially the case with climate science since many of the predictions are based on past climate data spanning tens of thousands of years into the past, a timespan not allowed for in the short-term interpretations of Genesis so prevalent among conservative evangelicals.[10]

Christians also use a variety of other rationalizations to prevent becoming involved in caring for the environment. These include that environmentalism is too closely associated with the New Age Movement (based on a fear of spiritualism), it is too closely related to pantheism, it will lead to a world government,[11] it will lead to greater support for abortion[12] and that people are more important than caring for nature.[13] [14] Although some of the items on this list may seem trivial or not clearly connected with environmentalism, they do have considerable weight in many faith communities, leading to a sometimes antagonistic relationship with the environmental community.[15]

In spite of this, there are theologians who see the biblical creation account and other references as more of an admonition of stewardship. Yes, man was given the earth to "exploit" for his benefit but only within certain bounds. Mankind is not free to simply plunder the natural world but to use it wisely, all the while preserving it for future generations. There are even indications that mankind is to care for nature for its own sake. The Genesis account of the Noachian flood hints at God's concern for not just humans and the animals that humans find useful, but all animals.

> The Lord then said to Noah, "Go into the ark, you and your whole family, because I have found you righteous in this generation. Take with you seven of every kind of clean animal, a male and its mate, and two of every kind of unclean animal, a male and its mate, and also seven of every kind of bird, male and female, to keep their various kinds alive throughout the earth.[16]

Of what use to Noah would unclean animals be since according to Levitical law, unclean animals were not to be used for food? That God commanded Noah to save both clean and unclean animals suggests that part of mankind's role on earth is to care for all of nature.

An additional Levitical injunction was the observance of Sabbath years:

> The Lord said to Moses on Mount Sinai, "Speak to the Israelites and say to them: 'When you enter the land I am going to give you, the land itself must observe a Sabbath to the Lord. For six years sow your fields, and for six years prune your vineyards and gather their crops. But in the seventh year the land is to have a Sabbath of rest, a Sabbath to the Lord. Do not sow your fields or prune your vineyards. Do not reap what grows of itself or harvest the grapes of your untended vines. The land is to have a year of rest. Whatever the land yields during the Sabbath year will be food for you–for yourself, your manservant and maidservant, and the hired worker and temporary resident who live among you, as well as for your livestock and the wild animals in your land. Whatever the land produces may be eaten.'"[17]

This injunction recognizes not only the now well-known need to allow fields to lie fallow to maintain long-term productivity but also acknowledges that wild animals are valuable in themselves with its specific mention of them as benefiting from what grows in the fields during the Sabbath year. Although the injunction is described in greatest detail here, it is again mentioned in seven other places in the Old Testament, a testimony to its apparent relevance.[18]

Respect for wild animals is also hinted at in how the Old Testament describes the use of wild animals. It is clear that the trapping of animals was permissible for food, but hunting for sport appears to be entirely absent from the Bible. Even those biblical figures portrayed as hunters, e.g. Nimrod and Esau, are typically not looked upon favorably, and none of the major figures in the Bible is mentioned as being a hunter.[19]

Although the New Testament says very little about man's obligations to the natural world, there are hints here as well concerning mankind's responsibilities. When Paul says in the book of Romans, "We know that the whole creation has been groaning as in the pains of childbirth right up to the present time," it seems clear that not only are humans suffering from "the fall" but that nature is too. Nature looks for deliverance just as much as mankind does.[20] A common metaphor used by Jesus in His parables is that of the steward, left by the master to care for his property and possessions, and generalizing this concept to the earth implies mankind's continued responsibility, given at creation, to continue to care for the earth. Jesus emphasizes the importance of this stewardship role in statements like this:

> Who then is the faithful and wise servant, whom the master has put in charge of the servants in his household to give them their food at the proper time? It will be good for that servant whose master finds him doing so when he returns.[21]

Probably the strongest statement supporting mankind's obligation to care for the earth occurs in Revelation, where John describes the final judgment scene when Jesus comes as king and announces his displeasure with those who have been actively destroying the earth, instead of caring for it:

> The nations were angry;
> and your wrath has come.
> The time has come for judging the dead,
> and for rewarding your servants the prophets
> and your saints and those who reverence your name,
> both small and great—
> *and for destroying those who destroy the earth.*[22]

APPLICABILITY OF ANIMAL ETHICS TO WILD SPECIES

The application of animal ethics principles to domesticated animals is well established both theologically and philosophically, but how these principles should be applied to wild species is less certain. As suggested above, the Old Testament does seem to teach respect for wild animals, but to what degree should this respect be applied, and what should it look like in practice? Until the latter half of the twentieth century, ethical obligations to wild animals were very little discussed. Even once wild animals were brought into the discussion, the primary obligation according to most treatments has been to not disturb or harm them—essentially a rule of non-interference.

A good example of an ethical system for wild animals is Clare Palmer's LFI (laissez-faire intuition):

> where (a) we have *prima facie* duties not to harm any animals (though these duties can be outweighed in certain circumstances); (b) there are normally no requirements to assist wild-living wild animals, though we are usually *permitted* to do so; and (c) we are often *required* to assist domesticated animals and (on occasions) other animals that fall into what I will call the human/animal "contact zone," where human actions have affected animals' lives negatively.[23]

By "contact zone" Palmer means any kind of influence a human might have on a wild animal. Most commonly this would involve some sort of literal contact, as in actually encountering the animal in some manner, a most obvious example being hitting a deer while driving. When contact of this sort has caused obvious harm, as in the case of the injured deer, the human has an obligation to assist in some manner, such as contacting wildlife rescue for assistance in healing and rehabilitating the deer, or if the injuries are too extensive, possibly to euthanize the deer as painlessly as possible. A contact zone need not involve physical contact, though, if the animal is harmed due to distant human actions, such as fish dying in a pristine mountain lake acidified from acid rain caused by emissions from a coal-fired power plant miles away. The fish in this pristine mountain lake are now in the human contact zone, obligating us to assist the animals that are harmed.

But what if the contact zone is even larger? Bill Mckibben suggests that anthropogenic climate change could constitute the development of a global contact zone that would include all animals.

> The idea of nature will not survive the new global pollution—the carbon dioxide and the CFCs and the like. This new rupture with nature is different not only in scope but also in kind from salmon tins in an English stream. We have changed the atmosphere, and thus we are changing the weather. By changing the weather, we make every spot on earth man made and artificial. We have deprived nature of its independence, and that is fatal to its meaning. Nature's independence is its meaning; without it there is nothing but us.[24]

Unfortunately, due to the complex effects of climate change on animals and the habitats in which they live, there will often be difficult decisions to make that might involve causing harm to some animals in order to prevent greater harm to other animals. This can be troubling, especially when some of these harms might include culling of animals to control population growth or eradication of alien or invasive species. Many of the more prominent animal ethics philosophies of the end of the twentieth and the beginning of the twenty-first century prohibit causing pain to any animals, especially if they are sentient, and generally also prohibit killing animals although such is sometimes allowed if it is essential to save large numbers of other individuals and if it is done painlessly. These conflicts are a consequence of the differing goals of animal liberation[25] and environmental ethics, which necessarily clash in a far-reaching crisis like climate change.

What is most difficult to integrate into environmental ethics is sentientism, the emphasis common in animal liberation that sentient animals have special rights above those of nonsentient animals. In contrast, is the more holistic approach of environmentalists like Aldo Leopold, who states, "a thing is right when it tends to preserve the integrity, stability, and beauty of the biotic community. It is wrong when it tends otherwise,"[26] thus shifting the emphasis from individual animals to the entire system. J. Baird Callicott further emphasizes this, saying, "in every case the effect upon ecological systems is the decisive factor in the determination of the ethical quality of actions."[27]

Expanding on the ideas of Leopold and especially Callicott, Gary Varner concludes the following, many of which run counter to the concerns of animal liberationists: (1) hunting of some sort is essential to control overpopulation of wild species,[28] (2) large predators that kill sentient animals are essential to properly functioning biotic communities,[29] and (3) special attention must be paid to endangered species.[30] As should be apparent from these conclusions, whether an animal is sentient or not is not specified, and controlling overpopulation by hunting would lead to a certain amount of suffering for individual sentient animals. Both of these problems contain values important to animal liberationists. It should also be noted that in this holistic approach domestic animals are assumed to continue as wards of humans rather than being released or phased out, as some animal liberationists advocate. Domestic animals will no doubt be affected by climate change, so humans must remain committed to reducing their suffering as well.

Given the tension between concern for the suffering of individual sentient animals and the concern for preservation of whole biotic communities, especially those containing endangered species, what will be needed is a hybrid approach to the problem.

> Here, a hybrid "ethical" approach is suggested; this is not a rigorous ethical theory but rather a set of recommendations aimed at improving the general acceptability of conservation activities that have the potential to impact negatively on individual wild animals. It is based on the utilitarian ethic in that actions are not classified as right or wrong *per se*, but rather as better or worse, and incremental improvements in the welfare of wild animals affected by conservation practices are considered better than no improvements at all.[31]

The flowchart below represents one way of approaching animal welfare in a complex setting like global climate change, emphasizing that it is a dynamic process that may require reassessment (figure 3.1).

Given the pervasive nature of climate change, I propose that humans are obligated to assist animals globally, whether they be domestic animals, to whom we already owe obligations, or wild animals, which are now in our contact zone. This is a monumental responsibility and certainly one which might have been avoided with more foresight. We still have time to reduce the effects of climate change by reducing our CO_2 emissions, but given the world political situation, this seems less and less likely. It is time to plan how to fulfill our obligations to the animals of the world. The remainder of this chapter will comprise an overview of the kinds of harms animals are likely to suffer with options about how we might be able to respond. I will first review some of the major harms to domestic animals and what can be done to alleviate those harms. Then I will include some specific examples that involve wild animals and consider potential options for remediation.

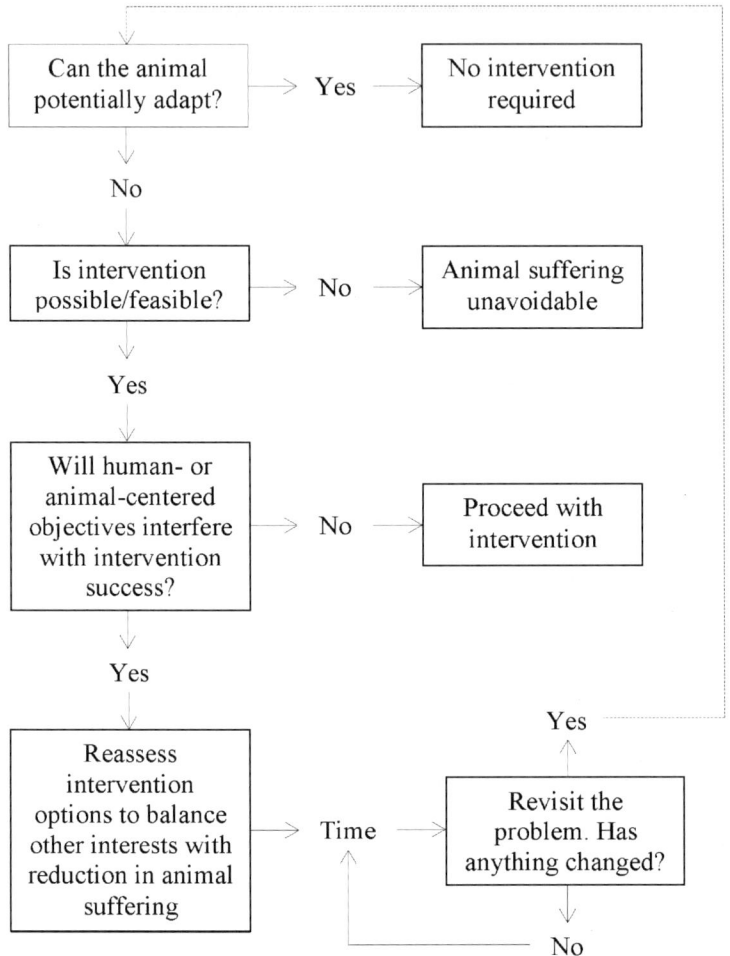

Figure 3.1. This flowchart outlines the process for determining whether intervention on behalf of an animal, or group of animals, is required as a result of climate change. If the animal can adapt to the changes imposed by climate change, then no intervention is required. If the animal cannot adapt, then it must be determined whether intervention is even possible. Is it technically possible? Is it economically feasible? If the answer to either of these questions is no, then animal suffering in this case is unavoidable. If the answer to both questions is yes, then other objectives must be assessed. Will the intervention have an unacceptably negative affect on humans? Will the intervention have unacceptably negative effects on other animals? If not, then intervention should proceed. If the answer to either of these questions is yes, then a partial intervention of some sort must be designed that will not interfere with other objectives and which will reduce animal suffering as much as possible. Over time the intervention should be reassessed, and if anything has changed, the situation should be reevaluated.

CLIMATE CHANGE AND DOMESTIC ANIMAL WELFARE

Companion animals that live in close association with humans, typically in their own dwellings, will face the same challenges from climate change as humans themselves, but other domesticated animals such as horses, cattle, pigs, chickens, and other agricultural animals will face unique risks. The most obvious primary challenge to animals maintained outdoors will be thermoregulation. As average temperatures rise, the effects of heat stress will increase. One of the most direct effects on cattle, in this regard, is growth and reproduction. Higher temperatures reduce rumination efficiency and nutrient absorption, which throws off overall energy balance, causing reduced growth weight and weight loss.[32] Climate change will affect reproduction in cattle in myriad ways, which may vary somewhat between temperate and tropical climes, including endocrine disruptions, poor follicular development, low-quality sperm, reduced libido, poor estrus expression, lowered conception rate, and reduced perinatal survival.[33]

Elevated temperatures may also lead to the emergence of new pathogens and the increased incidence of current pathogens and parasites.[34] Mathematical modeling of parasite/host dynamics under climate change predictions suggest there may be tipping points that could lead to dramatically increased parasite loads, due to "nonlinear responses in infection dynamics."[35] The interplay between agricultural animals and their parasites/pathogens is also affected by geographical shifts in animal husbandry caused by shifting climate patterns. For every 1° C (1.8° F) increase in mean annual temperature, an approximate 100 km (62 miles) latitudinal shift in natural biological communities occurs. Such changes can bring about new associations between naturally occurring parasites/pathogens and domestic animals.[36]

A variety of strategies for mitigating the effects of climate change have potential, including improved shelters, modification of feeding regimen (e.g., increased fiber; vitamin, antioxidant, and mineral supplementation, cooled drinking water, and modified feeding schedule), hormone treatments, and better care during pregnancy.[37] In almost all cases this will mean increased costs for production, but these will lead not only to improved animal welfare, but also to increased production rates. A longer-term solution may be to identify underlying genetic markers for heat-stress tolerance and breed for these traits.[38] There are over one thousand local breeds[39] of cattle worldwide from which to draw genetic resources, so the potential for improving the more widely used breeds is good.[40]

Although the primary focus has been on cattle, many of the same concerns exist for other agricultural animals, but because the value per animal is lower for many of the smaller animals, and they are typically housed in a more controlled environment, less research has focused on how climate change will affect them. Many of the same proposed solutions for cattle would likely be just as applicable to these animals.

CLIMATE CHANGE AND WILD ANIMAL WELFARE

Unfortunately, as will be apparent when looking at specific wild animals, there is much less that can be done to counteract the effects of climate change on wild species. The consensus among scientists is that we are well past the point where we will be able to fully reverse climate change, and since the political will to act decisively even now is lacking, there is every indication that we are committed to a considerable amount of climate change. Much animal suffering due to climate change is already apparent, and the problems will only get worse as we approach the end of the twenty-first century. Rather than make a complete catalog of ways that climate will affect wildlife, I will review two specific examples as case studies: polar bears and amphibians (especially frogs). These examples will not only stand as proxies for all other wild animals but should also serve as a reminder that due to the interconnectedness of organisms within their biotic communities, harm to these animals often results in concomitant harm to other animals. This is one of the major reasons to approach the dilemma of climate change and animal suffering from a holistic ecological ethic.

Polar bears (*Ursus maritimus*) are probably the most iconic animal face of the natural tragedy of climate change. They are found only in the circumpolar arctic and spend the bulk of their time on sea ice, returning to land during the ice-free summer period in some cases, where they subsist on their fat reserves. Polar bears are the top predators of the arctic, and since their prey (seals and sea lions) are only accessible from the sea ice, the longer the ice-free period, the less food is available. The current population of polar bears is estimated at twenty thousand to twenty-five thousand.[41] In addition to the climate threats discussed below, as a top predator they are exposed to various human pollutants,[42] and they face threats from oil and gas development and overhunting.[43]

One of the reasons that so much attention is paid to polar bears is that the polar regions are experiencing the largest temperature changes on the globe, as predicted by climate change models.

> Because Polar Bears depend on sea-ice, habitat that literally "melts" as temperatures warm, there is an unambiguous relationship between GHGs,[44] temperature, habitat availability, and persistence of the species. Projections of their future, therefore, are more straightforward for Polar Bears than may be possible for other species.[45]

The primary threat, therefore, from climate change, is loss of sea ice that will lead directly to starvation of the affected bears. Since sea ice coverage from year to year fluctuates widely, it is difficult to predict when polar bears will be at the greatest risk, which is why a comprehensive monitoring plan is important.[46] In addition to utilizing all the typical aspects of field monitoring, Vongraven, et al. also advocate using traditional ecological knowledge or indigenous knowledge.[47]

The most straightforward way to alleviate climate change harms to polar bears is to provide supplemental food to bears that are starving although the costs can be very high, conservatively estimated to be $32,000 per day for the most accessible population, and supplemental feeding might need to be maintained for several months.[48] Less feasible might be rehabilitation in captivity followed by release back into the wild or relocation. Relocation may be an untenable option considering that in bad years, when bears are in need of human intervention, there may be minimal availability of viable locations.[49] The ultimate option may end up being capture of as many remaining polar bears as possible and maintaining them in zoos. At some point, if climate change continues apace, there may no longer be adequate habitat for polar bears to survive in the wild. Most animals, as climate change occurs, are expected to migrate (or could be relocated by humans) to reach climate conditions that are appropriate for them, but with the polar bear already living at the extreme edge of its acceptable habitat, climate change simply forces the inevitable.

One issue of concern for any species that must be aggressively monitored and managed is the effects these activities might have on the individual animals. Monitoring can involve capture, radio tagging or collaring, biopsy procedures or other invasive or ongoing interference, any of which could be stressful or painful for individual animals. The extent of the trauma and pain must be balanced against the benefits of the information obtained.[50] Nathaniel Kalluk, an Inuit from Resolute Bay, Nunavut, Canada, has seen collared polar bears be unable to hunt seal at breathing holes effectively.[51]

Frogs, as typical amphibians, require regular access to fresh water in order to maintain the moistness of their skin and for reproduction, as almost all species of frogs lay their eggs in water. The greatest diversity of frogs is in the tropics with decreasing species diversity approaching northern and southern temperate zones. They are entirely absent in the colder arctic regions, Antarctica, and many oceanic islands. Of all groups of vertebrates, amphibians have the largest percentage of species (32.5 percent) listed as globally threatened by the International Union for Conservation of Nature in 2004,[52] which increased to 40 percent by 2010,[53] and 43 percent of amphibian species exhibit population declines.[54] The three main factors affecting amphibian numbers are climate change, chytridiomycosis[55] and anthropogenic land-use changes, and of these three climate change seems to have the largest effect.[56] Interactions among these three factors could potentially amplify the effects synergistically. Adequate data are lacking though to be sure that climate change is playing the largest role in species decline although there is enough evidence to suggest that climate change at least has indirect and/or sublethal effects, which might include changes in phenology, range shifts, and reduction in body size.[57] A potential interaction between climate change and other factors has also been proposed.[58]

Given the potential impacts of climate change, with increasing temperature being paramount, alleviating heat and water stress would be the most obvious intervention. One way this could be accomplished is by relocation to either higher latitudes or elevations where temperature and overall climate would presumably be similar to what it was in the species' original range before climate change. Such a process, though, is extremely complex and costly, with many interacting issues from ethics, law, biology, and ecology.[59] Our past record of transplanting species, whether intentionally or unintentionally, has been fraught with problems, so although relocation is appealing in theory, it may be of limited usefulness. A more tenable approach for frogs might be to sample broadly for chytridiomycosis, to identify those frog populations that are free of the disease, and to focus our efforts on preserving those areas intact as refuges where other climate change mitigations might be implemented.[60] Since chytridiomycosis might become more prevalent as the climate warms, intensive monitoring of designated refuges should be implemented, and methods for combatting the infection should be developed as soon as possible.

Proposed ways of mitigating the direct effects of climate warming on frogs include "(i) installation of microclimate and microhabitat refuges; (ii) enhancement and restoration of breeding sites; and, (iii) manipulation of water levels at breeding sites."[61] Some of these methods have been used successfully in a few cases while those that have not been tried have a good theoretical basis for working. The second of the above approaches may be exacerbated by other aspects of climate change, such as changes in rainfall amounts and timing, which are common cues for breeding activity, where breeding sites may be temporary pools of water. Since controlling rainfall is not possible, a workaround might be establishing permanent pools of water so breeding can take place even if inadequate rainfall occurs.[62]

Remediation may face unique challenges in north temperate regions, since although the overall climate is warming, winters nevertheless may be colder and harsher. In a multiyear habitat management program for an Idaho Great Basin population of the ESA candidate species, the Columbia spotted frog (*Rana luteiventris*), it was found that although habitat restoration efforts were moderately successful, recovery was slower than expected.[63] Even after nine years, full recovery of the population had not yet occurred, most likely due to harsher winters, later springs, and higher fall temperatures than normal, among other factors.

CONCLUSION

Climate change is a reality, and humans are in large part responsible. Since the effects of climate change are so far-reaching, humans have an obligation to alleviate the consequent animal suffering. Unfortunately, as should be apparent from this chapter, the effects are so pervasive that for many animals there may be no feasible long-term solutions. For example, although polar bears may be helped in the short term at great effort and monetary expense, predictions are that there will come a time when no more suitable polar bear habitat will be left. Although we might be able to save the species by moving individual bears into zoos, this represents a less-than-desirable outcome, and it is not clear that their quality of life could ever approach what it would be in the wild. What about the thousands of other species of vertebrates, each with their own issues with respect to climate change? Some may adapt, some may be able to migrate to more hospitable climate zones, but many, like the polar bear, may find themselves locked into either extinction or long-term survival in zoos. To be realistic, zoos do not represent an infinite resource, and funds are not unlimited either, meaning that choices as to which species to save and which to let go will be an ongoing ethical challenge. Then there are the millions of invertebrate species that are intimately tied to very specific biological communities. When those communities are gone, will these species also go extinct?

We have known about anthropogenic climate change for well over forty years now, and had we immediately begun the process of reducing carbon emissions, along with reductions in other greenhouse gases, we might have had some chance of preventing or at least reducing climate change. The two standard objections from society in general have been, (1) we aren't certain enough to warrant taking action, and (2) it will cost too much to reduce greenhouse gas emissions. The standard objections from most Judeo-Christians were either that God would not allow climate change to occur, or that if it does occur, it is of no concern because God will remake the earth someday anyway. A proper understanding of ecotheology answers these objections, reminding us that we are stewards of God's creation. We cannot sit by and allow mankind to destroy the earth. Unfortunately, now the costs of preventing climate change are even higher, and our obligation to alleviate animal suffering must now be added to the cost of neglecting to act sooner.

NOTES

1. Anthropogenic means "human-caused."
2. Although 63 percent of Americans consistently agree that climate change is happening, only 42 percent agree that it is primarily human caused, and these percentages vary regionally. See Peter D. Howe, et al., "Geographic Variation in Opinions on Climate Change at State and Local Scales in the USA," *Nature Climate Change* 5 (June 2015): 596. Among scientists, based on testimony before Congress, 86 percent believe climate change is happening, and 78 percent believe that it is anthropocentric, at least in part. See Xinsheng Liu, et al. "Scientists' Views and Positions on Global Warming and Climate Change: A Content Analysis of Congressional Testimonies." *Climatic Change* 131, no. 4 (2015): 496.
3. IPCC. *Climate Change 2014: Synthesis Report*. Contribution of Working Groups I, II and III to the Fifth Assessment Report of the Intergovernmental Panel on Climate Change (Geneva, Switzerland: IPCC, 2014), 11.
4. J. Hansen, et al., "Ice Melt, Sea Level Rise and Superstorms: Evidence from Paleoclimate Data, Climate Modeling, and Modern Observations that 2°C Global Warming is Highly Dangerous," *Atmospheric Chemistry and Physics. Discussions* 15 (2015): 20082, accessed August 6, 2015, http://www.atmos-chem-phys-discuss.net/15/20059/2015/acpd-15-20059-2015.pdf.
5. Anthony Leiserowitz, Edward Maibach, and Connie Roser-Renouf, Geoff Feinberg and Seth Rosenthal. *Climate change in the American Christian Mind* (New Haven, CT: Yale Project on Climate Change Communication, 2015), 4.
6. Leiserowitz, et al., *Climate Change in the American Christian Mind*, 5.
7. Genesis 1:28, New Iinternational Version.
8. Lynn White, Jr., "The Historical Roots of Our Ecologic Crisis," *Science* 155, no. 3767 (1967): 1205.
9. John Copeland Nagle, "The Evangelical Debate Over Climate Change," *University of St. Thomas Law Journal* 5, no. 1 (2008), 69–70.
10. Nagle, "The Evangelical Debate Over Climate Change," 71–75.
11. Any political action that might be construed to require international cooperation prompts conservative evangelicals to posit slippery slope arguments or conspiracy theories that mesh with their particular interpretations of predicted apocalyptic events.
12. Since overpopulation is often cited as a root cause of our environmental crises, family planning and birth control are often central components of comprehensive environmental planning. Since, in the secular world, abortion is an assumed component of family planning, this can be a prominent concern for those Christian groups that strongly oppose abortion.
13. Calvin B. DeWitt, "Christian Environmental Stewardship: Preparing the Way for Action," *Perspectives on Science and Christian Faith* 46, no. 2 (1994): 80–89.
14. The tendency for Christians to see mankind as the pinnacle of creation often leads to difficulty in recognizing the connection between humans and the rest of nature. Christians often see humans as separate from nature, thus leading to less motivation to feel responsible for protecting and conserving nature. This often leads to a kind of "magical thinking" that sees God as caring for humans, rather than nature supporting our existence.
15. For a more thorough treatment of these and other concerns, see chapter 8, "Environmental Advocacy and the Absence of the Church."
16. Genesis 7:1–3, NIV.
17. Leviticus 25:1–7, NIV.
18. See also Ellen Bernstein, "A Biblical Land Ethic?" in *Ecotheology in the Humanities: An Interdisciplinary Approach to Understanding the Divine and Nature*, ed. Melissa J. Brotton (Lanham, MD: Lexington Books, 2016): 25–52.
19. Sidney B. Hoenig, "The Sport of Hunting: A Humane Game?" *Tradition: A Journal of Orthodox Jewish Thought* 11, no. 3 (1970): 14.
20. Romans 8:22, NIV.
21. Matthew 24:45–46, NIV.
22. Revelation 11:18, NIV (emphasis added).

23. Clare Palmer, *Animal Ethics in Context* (New York: Columbia University Press, 2010), 5.
24. Bill McKibben, *The End of Nature* (New York: Random House, 1989), 50.
25. Animal liberation is a common term used to encompass both animal rights and animal welfare philosophies.
26. Aldo Leopold, *A Sand County Almanac* (Oxford: Oxford University Press, 2001), 189.
27. J. Baird Callicott, "Animal Liberation: A Triangular Affair," *Environmental Ethics* 2, no. 4 (1980): 320.
28. The ecotheology of hunting is covered in greater detail in chapter 6.
29. Some animal ethicists have advocated modifying the ecology to prevent the depredations of large predators although only in theory as how to accomplish it is far from clear. Some Christian theologians view texts such as Isaiah 65:25 (NIV):

"...
The wolf and the lamb will feed together,
and the lion will eat straw like the ox,
but dust will be the serpent's food.
They will neither harm nor destroy
on all my holy mountain,"
says the Lord.

as prophesies of a future age where God will transform earth's ecological systems and do away with predation.

30. Gary Varner, "Environmental Ethics, Hunting, and the Place of Animals," in *The Oxford Handbook of Animal Ethics*, eds. Tom L. Beauchamp and R. G. Frey (Oxford: Oxford University Press, 2011), 860.
31. Ngaio J. Beausoleil, "Balancing the Need for Conservation and the Welfare of Individual Animals," in *Dilemmas in Animal Welfare*, eds. Michael C. Appleby, Daniel M. Weary, and Peter Sandøe (Oxforshire, UK: CABI, 2014), 133.
32. V. Sejian, et al., "Strategies for Alleviating Abiotic Stress in Livestock," in *Livestock Production and Climate Change*, eds. Pradeep K. Malik, Raghavendra Bhatta, Junichi Takahashi, Richard A. Kohn, and Cadaba S. Prasad (Oxforshire, UK: CABI, 2015), 28.
33. Jyotirmoy Ghosh, Sujoy K. Dhara and Pradeep K. Malik, "Climate Change: Effects on Animal Reproduction," in *Livestock Production and Climate Change*, eds. Pradeep K. Malik, Raghavendra Bhatta, Junichi Takahashi, Richard A. Kohn, and Cadaba S. Prasad (Oxforshire, United Kingdom: CABI, 2015), 188.
34. Sejian, et al., "Strategies for Alleviating Abiotic Stress in Livestock," 30.
35. Naomi J. Fox, et al., "Climate-Driven Tipping-Points Could Lead to Sudden, High-Intensity Parasite Outbreaks," *Royal Society Open Science*, 2, 140296 (2015), 13, accessed August 13, 2015.http://dx.doi.org/10.1098/rsos.140296
36. Philippe Dorchies, "Global Climatic Changes, Animal Health and Zoonosis," *Scientia Parasitologica* 16, nos. 1–2 (2015): 10, accessed August 13, 2015.http://scientia.zooparaz.net/2015_16_01/01-11-sp-1-2015-Dorchies.pdf.
37. Sejian, et al., "Strategies for Alleviating Abiotic Stress in Livestock," 37.
38. Sejian, et al., "Strategies for Alleviating Abiotic Stress in Livestock," 38–40.
39. A local breed is a breed reported in only one country according to the Domestic Animal Diversity Information System of the Food and Agriculture Organization of the United Nations. See Food and Agricultural Organization of the United Nations, Commission on Genetic Resources for Food and Agriculture, *Report of a Consultation on the Definition of Breed Categories*, 7th session (Rome, October 24–26, 2012), 6, accessed August 13, 2015. http://www.fao.org/docrep/meeting/026/me588e.pdf.
40. Paul J. Boettcher, et al., "Genetic Resources and Genomics for Adaptation of Livestock to Climate Change," *Frontiers in Genetics* 5, no. 461 (2015): 2, accessed August 13, 2015.http://dx.doi.org/10.3389/fgene.2014.00461.

41. S. Schliebe, et al. (IUCN SSC Polar Bear Specialist Group), "Ursus maritimus," *The IUCN Red List of Threatened Species*, Version 2015.2, last modified June 30, 2008. Accessed August 13, 2015, http://www.iucnredlist.org/details/22823/0.

42. They are particularly vulnerable to PCBs (polychlorinated biphenyls), which are concentrated in the fat of their prey and apparently depress their immune systems and may also cause endocrine suppression.

43. Subsistence hunting is allowed and is carefully monitored, but since total population levels have been falling and accurate estimates are difficult, it is uncertain whether current guidelines are sufficient to protect the bears.

44. Greenhouse Gases.

45. Steven C. Amstrup, "Polar Bears and Climate Change: Certainties, Uncertainties, and Hope in a Warming World," in *Gyrfalcons and Ptarmigan in a Changing World, Volume I*, eds. R. T. Watson, T. J. Cade, M. Fuller, G. Hunt, and E. Potapov (Boise, ID: The Peregrine Fund, 2011), 16.

46. Dag Vongraven, et al., "A Circumpolar Monitoring Framework for Polar Bears," *Ursus*. 26 (2012), 1–66.

47. Vongraven, et al., "A Circumpolar Monitoring Framework for Polar Bears," 48.

48. Andrew E. Derocher, et al., "Rapid Ecosystem Change and Polar Bear Conservation," *Conservation Letters* 6, no. 5 (2013), 372.

49. Andrew E. Derocher, et al., "Rapid Ecosystem Change and Polar Bear Conservation," 373.

50. Rory P. Wilson and Clive R. McMahon, "Measuring Devices on Wild Animals: What Constitutes Acceptable Practice?" *Frontiers in Ecology and the Environment* 4, no. 3 (2006): 153.

51. Martin, Keavy, *Stories in a New Skin: Approaches to Inuit Literature* (Winnipeg: University of Manitoba Press, 2012), 1.

52. Simon N. Stuart, et al., "Status and Trends of Amphibian Declines and Extinctions Worldwide," *Science*, 306, no. 5702 (2004), 1783.

53. Michael Hoffmann, et al., "The Impact of Conservation on the Status of the World's Vertebrates," *Science* 330, no. 6010 (2010): 1505.

54. David B. Wake and Vance T. Vredenburg, "Are We in the Midst of the Sixth Mass Extinction? A View from the World of Amphibians," *Proceedings of the National Academy of Sciences of the USA* 105, Suppl. 1 (2008): 11466.

55. Chytridiomycosis is caused by the chytrid fungus *Batrachochytrium dendrobatidis*. It is believed to have originated in Africa as an infection in African frogs in the genus *Xenopus*, which was subsequently spread to other parts of the world through international trade. See Ché Weldon, et al., "Origin of the Amphibian Chytrid Fungus," *Emerging Infectious Diseases* 10, no. 12 (2004): 2100–2105.

56. Christian Hof, et al., "Additive Threats from Pathogens, Climate and Land-Use Change for Global Amphibian Diversity," *Nature* 480 (2011): 516.

57. Yiming Li, Jeremy M. Cohen, and Jason R. Rohr, "Review and Synthesis of the Effects of Climate Change on Amphibians," *Integrative Zoology* 8, no. 2 (2013): 148–50, 155.

58. Li, Cohen, and Rohr, "Review and Synthesis of the Effects of Climate Change on Amphibians," 151–53.

59. Mark W. Schwartz, et al., "Managed Relocation: Integrating the Scientific, Regulatory, and Ethical Challenges," *Bioscience* 62, no. 8 (2012): 732–43.

60. Héctor Zumbado-Ulate, et al., "Extremely Low Prevalence of *Batrachochytrium dendrobatidis* in Frog Populations from Neotropical Dry Forest of Costa Rica Supports the Existence of a Climatic Refuge from Disease," *EcoHealth* 11, no. 4 (2014): 600.

61. Luke P. Shoo, et al., "Engineering a Future for Amphibians Under Climate Change," *Journal of Applied Ecology* 48, no. 2 (2011): 488.

62. Shoo, et al., "Engineering a Future for Amphibians Under Climate Change," 489.

63. David S. Pilliod, and Rick D. Scherer, "Managing Habitat to Slow or Reverse Population Declines of the Columbia Spotted Frog in the Northern Great Basin," *Journal of Wildlife Management* 79, no. 4 (2015): 587–88.

REFERENCES

Amstrup, Steven C. "Polar Bears and Climate Change: Certainties, Uncertainties, and Hope in a Warming World." In *Gyrfalcons and Ptarmigan in a Changing World, Volume I*. Edited by R. T. Watson, T. J. Cade, M. Fuller, G. Hunt, and E. Potapov. Boise, ID: The Peregrine Fund, 2011, 11–20.

Beausoleil, Ngaio J. "Balancing the Need for Conservation and the Welfare of Individual Animals." In *Dilemmas in Animal Welfare*. Edited by Michael C. Appleby, Daniel M. Weary, and Peter Sandøe. Oxfordshire, UK: CABI, 2014, 124–47.

Bernstein, Ellen. "A Biblical Land Ethic?" In *Ecotheology in the Humanities: An Interdisciplinary Approach to Understanding the Divine and Nature*. Edited by Melissa J. Brotton. Lanham, MD: Lexington Books, 2016, 25–52.

Boettcher, Paul J., et al. "Genetic Resources and Genomics for Adaptation of Livestock to Climate Change." *Frontiers in Genetics* 5, no. 461 (2015): 1–3. Accessed August 13, 2015. http://dx.doi.org/10.3389/fgene.2014.00461.

Callicott, J. Baird. "Animal Liberation: A Triangular Affair." *Environmental Ethics* 2, no. 4 (1980): 311–38.

Derocher, Andrew E., et al. "Rapid Ecosystem Change and Polar Bear Conservation." *Conservation Letters* 6, no. 5 (2013): 368–75.

DeWitt, Calvin B. "Christian Environmental Stewardship: Preparing the Way for Action." *Perspectives on Science and Christian Faith* 46, no. 2 (1994): 80–89.

Dorchies, Philippe. "Global Climatic Changes, Animal Health and Zoonosis." *Scientia Parasitologica* 16, nos. 1–2 (2015): 1–11. Accessed August 13, 2015. http://scientia.zooparaz.net/2015_16_01/01-11-sp-1-2015-Dorchies.pdf.

Food and Agriculture Organization of the United Nations. Commission on Genetic Resources for Food and Agriculture. *Report of a Consultation on the Definition of Breed Categories*. 7th session. Rome, October 24–26, 2012, 6. Accessed August 13, 2015. http://www.fao.org/docrep/meeting/026/me588e.pdf.

Fox, Naomi J., et al. "Climate-Driven Tipping-Points Could Lead to Sudden, High-Intensity Parasite Outbreaks." *Royal Society Open Science* 2, 140296 (2015): 1–14. Accessed August 13, 2015. http://dx.doi.org/10.1098/rsos.140296.

Ghosh, Jyotirmoy, Sujoy K. Dhara, and Pradeep K. Malik. "Climate Change: Effects on Animal Reproduction." In *Livestock Production and Climate Change*. Edited by Pradeep K. Malik, Raghavendra Bhatta, Junichi Takahashi, Richard A. Kohn, and Cadaba S. Prasad. Oxforshire, UK: CABI, 2015, 183–201.

Hansen, J., et al. "Ice Melt, Sea Level Rise and Superstorms: Evidence from Paleoclimate Data, Climate Modeling, and Modern Observations that 2°C Global Warming is Highly Dangerous." *Atmospheric Chemistry and Physics. Discussions*, 15 (2015): 20059–20179. Accessed August 6, 2015, http://www.atmos-chem-phys-discuss.net/15/20059/2015/acpd-15-20059-2015.pdf.

Hoenig, Sidney B. "The Sport of Hunting: A Humane Game?" *Tradition: A Journal of Orthodox Jewish Thought* 11, no. 3 (1970): 13–21.

Hof, Christian, Miguel B. Araújo, Walter Jetz, and Carsten Rahbek. "Additive Threats from Pathogens, Climate and Land-Use Change for Global Amphibian Diversity." *Nature* 480 (2011): 516–21.

Hoffmann, Michael, et al. "The Impact of Conservation on the Status of the World's Vertebrates." *Science* 330, no. 6010 (2010): 1503–9.

Howe, Peter D., et al. "Geographic Variation in Opinions on Climate Change at State and Local Scales in the USA." *Nature Climate Change* 5 (June 2015): 596–603.

IPCC. *Climate Change 2014: Synthesis Report*. Contribution of Working Groups I, II and III to the Fifth Assessment Report of the Intergovernmental Panel on Climate Change. Geneva, Switzerland: IPCC, 2014.

Keavy, Martin. *Stories in a New Skin: Approaches to Inuit Literature*. Winnipeg: University of Manitoba Press, 2012.

Leiserowitz, Anthony, et al. *Climate change in the American Christian Mind*. New Haven, CT: Yale Project on Climate Change Communication, 2015.

Leopold, Aldo. *A Sand County Almanac*. Oxford: Oxford University Press, 2001.
Li, Yiming, Jeremy M. Cohen, and Jason R. Rohr. "Review and Synthesis of the Effects of Climate Change on Amphibians." *Integrative Zoology* 8, no. 2 (2013): 145–61.
Liu, Xinsheng, et al. "Scientists' Views and Positions on Global Warming and Climate Change: A Content Analysis of Congressional Testimonies." *Climatic Change* 131, no. 4 (2015): 487–503.
McKibben, Bill. *The End of Nature*. New York: Random House, 1989.
Nagle, John Copeland. "The Evangelical Debate Over Climate Change." *University of St. Thomas Law Journal* 5, no. 1 (2008): 53–86.
Palmer, Clare. *Animal Ethics in Context*. New York: Columbia University Press, 2010.
Pilliod, David S. and Rick D. Scherer. "Managing Habitat to Slow or Reverse Population Declines of the Columbia Spotted Frog in the Northern Great Basin." *Journal of Wildlife Management* 79, no. 4 (2015): 579–90.
Schliebe, S., Ø. Wiig, A. Derocher, and N. Lunn (IUCN SSC Polar Bear Specialist Group), "Ursus maritimus," *The IUCN Red List of Threatened Species*, Version 2015.2. Last modified June 30, 2008, http://www.iucnredlist.org/details/22823/0.
Schwartz, Mark W., et al. "Managed Relocation: Integrating the Scientific, Regulatory, and Ethical Challenges." *Bioscience* 62, no. 8 (2012): 732–43.
Sejian, V., et al. "Strategies for Alleviating Abiotic Stress in Livestock." In *Livestock Production and Climate Change*. Edited by Pradeep K. Malik, Raghavendra Bhatta, Junichi Takahashi Richard A. Kohn, and Cadaba S. Prasad, 25-60. Oxforshire, United Kingdom: CABI, 2015.
Shoo, Luke P., et al. "Engineering a Future for Amphibians Under Climate Change." *Journal of Applied Ecology* 48, no. 2 (2011): 487–92.
Stuart, Simon N., et al. "Status and Trends of Amphibian Declines and Extinctions Worldwide." *Science* 306, no. 5702 (2004): 1783–86.
Varner, Gary. "Environmental Ethics, Hunting, and the Place of Animals." In *The Oxford Handbook of Animal Ethics*. Edited by Tom L. Beauchamp and R. G. Frey, 855–76. Oxford: Oxford University Press, 2011.
Vongraven, Dag, et al. "A Circumpolar Monitoring Framework for Polar Bears." *Ursus* 26 (2012): 1–66.
Wake, David B. and Vance T. Vredenburg. "Are We in the Midst of the Sixth Mass Extinction? A View from the World of Amphibians." *Proceedings of the National Academy of Sciences of the USA* 105, Suppl. 1 (2008): 11466–11473.
Weldon, Ché, et al. "Origin of the Amphibian Chytrid Fungus." *Emerging Infectious Diseases* 10, no. 12 (2004): 2100–2105.
White, Lynn, Jr. "The Historical Roots of Our Ecologic Crisis." *Science* 155, no. 3767 (March 10, 1967): 1203–7.
Wilson, Rory P. and Clive R. McMahon. "Measuring Devices on Wild Animals: What Constitutes Acceptable Practice?" *Frontiers in Ecology and the Environment* 4, no. 3 (2006): 147–54.
Zumbado-Ulate, Héctor, et al. "Extremely Low Prevalence of *Batrachochytrium dendrobatidis* in Frog Populations from Neotropical Dry Forest of Costa Rica Supports the Existence of a Climatic Refuge from Disease." *EcoHealth* 11, no. 4 (2014): 593–602.

Chapter Four

The Self-Emptying Godhead

Perichoresis, Kenosis, and an Ethic for the Anthropocene

Mick Pope

The Earth has now entered the Anthropocene, an era of ecological crisis in which humanity is *a*, if not *the* major geological force. The Anthropocene is characterized by the threatened or actual breaching of the nine planetary boundaries[1] that support a safe habitation for the continuation of human existence. In 1990, Catholic theologian Hans Küng called for a global ethic to deal with this ecological crisis. More recently, in his encyclical on the environment, *Laudato Si'*, Pope Francis unmasked the idols of modernity, namely those attitudes associated with a utilitarian view of nature as primarily a resource to be exploited.[2] These idols, or "myths," as Pope Francis refers to them are associated with nature's reductionism and function collectively as a methodology delivering great advancements (even if failing to deal with the consequences) and also as a hermeneutic eroding meaning and desacralizing nature. In this chapter, I will develop a Christian ethic for the Anthropocene based upon three aspects. The first, derived from scientific theory, is emergence, the idea that higher-order descriptions of reality are epistemologically and ontologically nonreductive. Hence, ethics is a real thing and not reducible to lower-order considerations. Second, the dynamical, relational model of the Trinity, known as perichoresis, demonstrates that the basis for ethics is a God who is relationship within Godself and that this relationship is extended to human and nonhuman creation. This perichoretic Trinity cannot be reduced to creation itself (as in panentheism or emanationism), but neither is it the impassible God of classical theism, as in a God who is incapable of suffering with his creation. Instead, this model is based on the ever-present Trinity who cares for, suffers with, and reenchants, or resacralizes, creation. Third, the shape of Christian ethics is self-emptying or kenotic, as demonstrated in creation (the Father), redemption (the Son), and creativity (the Holy Spirit). Therefore the Father, Son, and Holy Spirit together as one interact selflessly with creation, and Christians, in turn, model selflessness in actions toward other humans and nonhumans.

THEORIES OF THE ANTHROPOCENE

The Anthropocene concept implies that we live in a human-dominated geological epoch.[3] A number of historical explanations for the Anthropocene have been suggested.[4] One of these involves a theory that megafaunal (creatures of the ice age, like mammoths, etc.) extinctions occurred between fifty thousand and ten thousand years before present (BP), when modern humans migrated to new continents and came into contact with large mammals that, not having coevolved with humans, were vulnerable to being outcompeted or killed by them. This understanding places the ethical problem of the Anthropocene into our very natures and challenges the concept of evolved instincts, raising the possibility for a biblical doctrine of sin and "the Fall" that go beyond the scope of this study.

Other theories are tied to agricultural events such as the origins of farming (11,000 years BP), extensive farming (8,000 years BP), rice production (6,500 years BP), and the formation of anthropogenic soils, leading up to present-day farming, which has generated extensive land-clearing and emissions in carbon dioxide and methane.[5] One theory of the Anthropocene is rather euphemistically referred to as "New-Old World collision" and is associated with a global carbon dioxide minimum in 1610, the result of European invasion of the Americas and deaths of up to fifty million people due to European diseases, ways of life, enslavement, and famine. Such an explanation ties the concept of the Anthropocene to empire, colonialism, and genocide. More modern theories include reference to the beginning of the Industrial Revolution in 1760, nuclear weapon detonations since 1945, and the introduction of persistent industrial chemicals since about 1950. The later dates are associated with what is known as the "Great Acceleration,"[6] an increase in socioeconomic trends such as population, energy use, fertilizer consumption, water use, etc., which is associated with a rapid increase in greenhouse gas emissions, surface temperatures, ocean acidification, marine fish capture, nitrogen emissions into coastal zones, and terrestrial biosphere degradation as well as other environmental hazards. Theories of the Anthropocene suggest that humanity is now pushing against seven of the nine planetary boundaries and threatening our safe operating space on the Earth.[7]

THE NEED FOR CHRISTIAN ETHICS IN THE ANTHROPOCENE

In 1990, Catholic theologian Hans Küng called for a world ethic together with peace and dialogue among religions.[8] Such an ethic, he states, is needed to address environmental and social issues such as war and famine.[9] Küng does not seek to develop an idealistic concept of religion or to extract an essence of faith in order to construct a global ethic. Rather, he sees the need to stress what unites religions if they are to remain credible in the present context.[10] Interestingly, the warm welcome that Pope Francis's encyclical *Laudato Si'* has received attests to the fact that there is still a place in secular society for moral leadership from a religious source.[11]

Küng identifies that the West is "faced with a vacuum of meaning, values and norms," which presents a problem for individuals and for our political system.[12] This vacuum is due to the failure of state socialism, neocapitalism, and ideas of unlimited growth or endless progress, which have led to environmental degradation while Enlightenment reason has turned in on itself. Without any sense of the sacred, the idea of rationality espoused by the Enlightenment had the effect of seeing nature as a machine, contra to newer and more holistic understandings of the way the world functions.[13] Because of this inheritance, we face "catastrophic economic, social, political and ecological developments" that "necessitate a world ethic if humanity is to survive on this earth."[14] At the very least, such an ethic might prevent further calamities because of what Küng calls "extremely dangerous technological limit experiences," as "technological progress has increased so terrifically that it constantly threatens to overtake political forms."[15] This global ethic of planetary responsibility replaces an ethic of success and fulfills Kant's categorical imperative of not treating humans as a means to an end. Such an imperative can be extended to nonhumans as well: animals, for example, can be viewed as ends in themselves.[16] This ethic is other-focussed on neighbor, on the world around us, and on future generations. We need to think and act in a global context. Küng believes we need to transcend our own self-tendencies such as self-determination, discovery, realization, and personal fulfilment. In particular, his curious phrase is "human beings must become more than they are; they must become more than human!"[17]

So what room is there for religion in the development of this global ethic? Küng acknowledges that religion has been a hindrance to progress at times but also that the nonreligious can have a basic ethical orientation.[18] And yet the issue remains that there is no ready source to ground such a global ethic without religion. Quoting biologist Hubert Markl, Küng observes, "Science cannot teach us such norms" as we require for a global ethic.[19] There is no quasi-innate "categorical imperative" to appeal to. Küng's global ethic, which must be genuinely and uniquely Christian, turns on two key theological ideas. The first is the concept of the triune nature of God because it is uniquely Christian. The second idea addresses Küng's insistence on the need to transcend our own self-impulses, which sometimes requires us to sacrifice our own self-interests and, on occasion, even our lives.[20] This is the idea of kenosis, or self-emptying, as exemplified by Jesus. An ethic of self-emptying has value because it addresses the concern that Christianity can be authoritarian and narrow-minded instead of agreeable to make room for dialogue in a pluralistic world.

SECULAR GLOBAL ETHIC MODELS

Like Küng, Stuart Kauffman recognises that we lack a global ethic, but Kauffman seeks to develop one along scientific lines in place of religious ones.[21] Kauffman rejects the idea of a God who intervenes in the world.[22] Instead, he adopts religious ideas and language, and he maintains that God is equated with the "natural creativity in the universe."[23] Kauffman rightly states that a system of reductionism, such as that of Stephen Weinberg,[24] cannot provide us with an ethical framework.[25] Such reductionism means, following Hume, that there is no *ought* from *is*.

To deal with this problem, Kauffman suggests that life, purpose, and meaning are all emergent phenomena, where emergence means, in essence, that the whole is greater than the sum of its parts. Such emergence comes in two forms. Epistemological emergence says that while lower-level descriptions of higher-level phenomena are possible, new knowledge is generated at the higher levels. For example, we cannot determine whether the purpose of the heart is to make a thumping noise or to pump blood on the basis of physics alone but need to think like a biologist does.[26] Hence, our fuller understanding of the heart relies on thinking at the higher level of the delivery of oxygen and nutrients to tissues rather than at the lower level of the motion of quarks and leptons.

On the other hand, ontological emergence says that genuinely new things emerge from the lower levels that are not reducible to these lower levels. Take, for example, the evolution of the Earth's biosphere. Kauffman claims that no full set of equations can be written down and solved to deduce the evolution of the Earth's biosphere.[27] We cannot see ahead of time all of the novelties that will arise nor list all of the variables that need to be put into the equations. Hence, the number of simulations required to represent exactly the state of the biosphere is infinite, and there is no way of selecting from among these infinite number of simulations the correct one, as the computer required to calculate these simulations would be as large as the universe itself, natural selection is not only epistemologically emergent (we learn new things) but also ontologically emergent (genuinely new things appear) so it is not possible to precisely determine the future state of the universe based on present conditions. We cannot keep rerunning the universe for a different result. Part of the evolution of the biosphere includes agency, meaning, and purpose. Take, for example, a bacterium swimming in a glucose gradient. By altering its behavior to swim up the gradient, the bacterium is exhibiting purpose (obtaining more food), agency (changing course to swim to more food), and a concept of meaning (the glucose gradient means more food). If life is truly emergent, as Kauffman argues, then agency and purpose must also be emergent. The more complex the organism, the more complex the agency and purpose. Hence, while there is the concept of *is*, a description of the state of things, in physics, in contrast, emergence suggests that because ideas of agency and purpose naturally arise from the state of things, we can say that *ought* emerges from *is*, or that ethics and morality are real things.

Emergence is a potentially useful tool for developing a Christian ethic for the Anthropocene. Murphy and Ellis develop such an ethic at length, suggesting that theology is an emergent discipline at the top of the hierarchy.[28] Although Kauffman maintains a physicalist emergent model, his adoption of Christian and teleological language suggests that without a transcendent being, there is no basis for a global ethic. Kauffman assumes that the universe is a closed system and that the discovery of proximate causes excludes the possibility of final causes. His model of divine action is special and episodic when contrasted with the ongoing providential care of God demonstrated in scripture (e.g., Psalm 104, Acts 17:28). It also appears somewhat arbitrary to suggest that agency can be attributed to a bacterium but denied to God; in other words Kauffman accepts causation as emergent or bottom-up, but a priori denies divine causation as a top-down mechanism, as in God can operate in a lawlike manner or above our ideas of law. One possible example of this, as Conway Morris notes, is convergent evolution, in which similar features in animals are produced by similar evolutionary forces but in different environments. An example would be the canine teeth that evolved in both placental and marsupial mammals. Morris goes on to suggest that similar to the impact of predation on teeth, or the physics of air on flight mechanisms, a "mental air" produced the convergent evolution of intelligence in different animals. Why can't this be conceived as top-down divine causation?[29] The concept of bottom-up emergent causation is therefore not incompatible with a view of God that is immanent in guiding the process either from a bottom-up (emergent) manner or a top-down (convergent) manner. Such a view will be developed further below.

PERICHORESIS AND THE CREATION TEMPLE

Because the Trinity is unique to Christianity, it should lie at the center of Christian theology.[30] Clark H. Pinnock states that the Trinity is "an insight arising from the narrative of salvation, which is God's self-revelation."[31] Likewise, Keith Ward notes that "the idea of the Trinity does not supersede [Old Testament] monotheism; it interprets it in the light of a specific set of revelatory events and experiences."[32] See, for example, 1 Corinthians 8:6, in which Paul fits Jesus into Jewish monotheism by inserting him into the Shema (Deuteronomy 6:4-5).[33] We will deal with two conceptions of the Trinity. The economic Trinity refers to the revealed nature of the Godhead, made known in scripture, particularly in the incarnation. Another idea of Trinity, according to Thomas F. Torrance, is the immanent, or theological Trinity, which focuses on God's ontological nature, the inner being or life of the Trinity.[34] This conception of Trinity is logically prior to the economic Trinity but not directly apprehended by humans. John Webster proposes that the proper order of understanding Trinitarian theology is essence—persons—external processions.[35] He sees a danger in seizing on God's economic activity as an unshakeable foundation. Instead he wants to begin by attending to the special nature of God's unity. Webster emphasizes that God is understood to be self-sufficient and enjoys plenitude of life within Godself. Likewise, he posits God's love may not be a needy love, requiring an external subject to create and love. However, Webster's immanent Trinity appears too static and distant in his suggestion that a creature's dignity is simply found in being itself rather than being the subject of divine love. Webster also appears to suggest that as God did not need to create anything, the creation does not evoke a response in the inner being of God once it has been created. Impassibility does not do God or his relationship to creation in Scripture justice and is more Hellenistic in its metaphysics.[36] Love is necessarily risky and open to suffering.[37] "God is love" is essential to any model of the Trinity.[38] But there is a problem with starting our theologizing with the immanent Trinity in that it is not shaped enough by the biblical account of the economic Trinity. With God's identity of love as foundational, it makes more sense to oppose Webster's view and posit, rather, that we gain insight about the immanent Trinity from the economic Trinity.

A fruitful model of the immanent Trinity is perichoresis, which John of Damascus describes as the "mutual interpenetration of divine and human nature in Jesus, the God-human being, and for the reciprocal indwelling of the Father, the Son, and the Holy Spirit," following John 14:11.[39] Torrance defines perichoresis as the way in which the three persons of the Trinity exist in one another, applying equally to all three persons.[40] Perichoresis links the soteriological (economic) with the ontological (immanent) because it is an "*implication* of the unity-in-variety of the divine economic involvement in the world."[41] Perichoresis preserves the creator/creature distinction because mutual indwelling is not possible for material creatures as it is for God, who is spirit.[42] Perichoresis represents a relationship that is wholly spiritual and intensely personal since God is spirit (John 4:24) and love (1 John 4:8). God is known only in a circle of reciprocal relations that are completely *homoousial* so that the Father is not truly known apart from the Son and Spirit. Note also that perichoresis is not antithetical to hypostatic distinctions within the Godhead but requires them since these distinctions are needed for perichoretic relationships.[43] Hence, while the dimension of personhood emphasises distinction, the interpenetrating unity secures against separation.[44] In this view God is always Father but not always creator, for God as Father to the Son is prior to God's creative act.[45] Creation is contingent, and God does not need the creation to be Father. His eternal purpose of love was to freely create a universe where he has made us as his creation in his image and likeness to share in divine fellowship. God's creative power is not a bare exercise of power by a lonely God but an exercise of love. The historical economic love of Trinity directs us back to ontological love within the Trinity apart from God's relationship to the world.

God the Father is eminently creator, Jesus is creation's exemplar and efficient cause, and the Spirit is creation's perfecting cause.[46] In the beginning God created the heavens and the earth (Genesis 1:1); all things are from him (1 Corinthians 8:6), and all things have their being from him (Acts 17:28). Creation proceeds according to God's word, and all that he commands is so and is good. God's creative acts are doxological (Psalm 19:1) and call for a doxological response (Revelation 4:11). That God exists and has made all that is reflects his invisible powers in creation and acts as a witness against idolatry (Romans 1:20f). The author of Psalm 104 reflects on the initial act of creation and ordering and also upon God's ongoing providential care in both human and nonhuman affairs.

The Spirit, as one with the Father and Son, hovers over the creation like a mother hen over its chicks (Genesis 1:2). The Spirit is breathed into Adam (Genesis 2:7) to make him a *nephesh chayyah* (living being). This is the pattern for all human beings, as Job notes (Job 33:4). The Spirit also has an ongoing role in the maintenance of life: without it all creatures return to the dust (Psalm 104:29–30), including human beings (Job 34:14–15). It would, however, be inappropriate to make the Spirit some kind of élan vital, or life force, which animates living things and is measurable by some experiment. Instead, the Spirit is a divine person of creativity that supervenes over all living things and yet is deeply personal.

The Son, spoken of as the logos, was with God in the beginning, and all things were made through the logos (John 1:1–3). Hence, the incarnation of the logos as the agent of salvation links creation theology to soteriology. While all things are from (*ek*) God and for (*eis*) him; all things are by (*dio*) Christ and through (*dio*) him (1 Corinthians 8:6).

The creation is not only the work of the triune creator but is also the temple of the triune creator. John Walton connects God's ceasing from his work on the seventh day (*shabbat*; Genesis 2:2) with rest (*nuach*), as is found in Exodus 20:11, where God *rested* on the seventh day and blessed it as a *Sabbath*. This temple language is found in the pilgrim Psalm of ascents, Psalm 132. In verses 7 and 8, "dwelling place" is paralleled with "resting place" (*menuha*), and footstool is paralleled with the ark. Likewise, in verse 14 resting place is paralleled with God's throne.[47] Hence, creation itself is a temple, the divine throne room from which God rules. The Jerusalem temple is creation in miniature with the water basin reflecting the sea and the pillars possibly pillars of the earth (1 Kings 7). The Hebrew word for light (*or*) used in connection with the tabernacle lamp (e.g. Exodus 25:6) is the same used for the celestial bodies on the fourth day of creation (Genesis 1:15–17).[48] Some might argue that there is a movement in the bible from the cosmos to the individual. The birth of the church represents the coming of the Spirit on individual believers (Acts 2). The biblical trajectory is of an imminent God above the waters (Genesis 1:2), taking up rest in creation (Genesis 2:1–3), centered on a royal garden (Genesis 3:8).

While various theophanies occurred during the Patriarchal period, God became associated first with leading the Exodus (Exodus 13:21) and then with descending upon the Tabernacle (Exodus 40:34–38). When Solomon dedicated the temple, he acknowledged that it could not contain God (1 Kings 8:27). While individuals have the Spirit, the church collectively is the temple in the New Testament (1 Corinthians 3:16–17, *humin* is you, plural). The telos of creation is that it should once more be a temple. The original center of this temple, the Garden of Eden (Genesis 2), is subsumed into a city, the New Jerusalem (Revelation 21:22). So God rules from his cosmic temple through his representatives. Rikk Watts notes there are very close parallels with the account of the formation of human beings from the dust and the breathing in of the divine breath and contemporary ancient Near Eastern accounts.[49] This is a "monotheistic anthropology," where humans are installed as the divine image to be his presence in the temple-cosmos. So we see that the key to reenchanting nature, and hence an ethic for the Anthropocene, is to recognize that, biblically speaking, creation is the divine temple in which God's image is installed. This thought is further clarified in that the verbs *work* and *take care of* in Genesis 2:15 are best understood as sacred service.[50] Our tending of creation is therefore holy work in God's image, shaped by God's character, and located in God's temple.

So what role does perichoresis play in creation temple theology? The perichoretic nature of the immanent Trinity means that it is open to the other, outside of Godself. Pinnock notes that God is not static, nor standoffish but is rather "loving relationality and sheer liveliness. . . . As loving communion, God calls into being a world that has the potential of realizing loving relationality within itself."[51] Hence, the creation God indwells bears his stamp in the sorts of relationships that are observed. Pinnock further suggests that God creates in a way that is consistent with his relational being. Creation is a work of art that God delights in (see Ps 104:31), and creatures also share in God's delight when they are "struck by the giftedness of their own existence." It makes them want to "dance and play," a possible allusion to Ps. 104:26 and the frolicking of Leviathan.[52] This self-reflection is manifest supremely in God's image reflected in human beings.

Pinnock notes that human beings, as creatures of God's Spirit are the only creatures able to identify as the "I" capable of responding to the divine "Thou."[53] God is everywhere present—nowhere more so than in human beings who, because of their intelligence, deeper and richer experiences, freedom and openness to God, stand at the pinnacle of creation and serve as a fuller dwelling place for God than do other life forms.

Notwithstanding this difference between human and nonhuman creatures, the Trinity helps us understand relative autonomy of the world as a whole and its relatedness to the Father.[54] The world was created in distinction from the Father so as to be able to relate and respond freely to him. The perichoretic Trinity seems to point to this because God is free and constitutes a genuinely responsive relationship within himself. The creation was not necessary, but God's perichoretic nature suggests the possibility of creating a world with which God can freely relate. Further, the world is ontologically distinct from God and not an emanation. In this way, God can freely enter in and take delight in a world capable of echoing his interpersonal relationships. As Pinnock notes, "God is delighted by the way that nature can mirror the divine and exhibit its traces," which includes spontaneity and openness among creatures, reciprocal relationships, and more.[55] We must reject, however, any identification between God and creation, as it is nowhere suggested in the scriptures that the two are homoousial, to say nothing of the issues it raises with the problem of evil.

Jürgen Moltmann wants to take perichoresis a step further and speaks not just of persons but of divine spaces for the other two divine persons in claiming that "they also mutually cede the other's life and movement and make themselves inhabitable for one another."[56] Moltmann is trying to further explore the deep coinherence and reciprocity of the Trinity with an eye on creation. Inspired by the Kabbalah, he suggests that "God gives space, God makes room . . . God withdraws himself in order to go out of himself" and before he creates "he has already made himself the receptive and sustaining *space* for those he has created."[57] Here we see echoes of Acts 17:28, that we move and have our being in God. If this understanding of the perichoretic nature of the immanent Trinity is true, then creation models the Trinity in the following ways: (a) God creates the world to inhabit and relate to and, hence, immanently coinheres in the world, and (b) the Trinity makes space for creation so that it in general, and humanity in particular, move within God and have their being in him. The understanding of coinherence and the perichorectic understanding of divine immanence advanced here are therefore not contradictory and do not identify creature and creator as homoousial because they describe the colocation of creature and creator, not their consubstantiation or, less still the emanation of the former from the latter. Note also that this immanent colocation is not stating the same idea as panentheism. We are in God insofar as he is immanent to all things, upholds all things and relates to all things.

THE KENOTIC TRINITY

We have seen already that in creation God makes room for the other. This idea can be developed further in viewing creation as kenosis. The origin of kenosis is found in the Christological hymn in Philippians 2:5–11, where in verse 7 Christ emptied himself (*eauton ekenôsen*). Scholars are divided as to whether this emptying refers to the incarnation, i.e., becoming human, or to Christ's humiliation ("he humbled himself"), which refers to the cross. Sarah Coakley suggests that it is the former. If she is right, then metaphysical issues arise concerning what divine powers are lost. Otherwise, the passage is largely ethical in content.[58] However, it appears that this is a false dilemma. Firstly, Jesus was in (*huparxôn*) the form (*morphê*) of God but did not regard equality to be grasped, unlike Adam (verse 6). Instead he emptied himself (*eauton ekenôsen*), taking the form (*morphen*) of a slave (*doulos*). There is a lack of a connective and (*kai*) in the Greek, although translations like the NASB provide one, between taking the form of a slave and the second phrase of verse 7, being made into the likeness (*homoiômata*) of a human (*anthrôpos*). Hence, it is likely that Jesus's slave status was the act of becoming human. The presence of the connective *kai* links the two statements about Jesus being human (*anthrôpos*): a direct consequence of him being in human form is that he humbled himself to death in a dishonorable manner on a Roman cross. Hence, kenosis in this case was moving from divine form and equality to slavery, or from humanity to a humble death and, hence, onto exaltation. Kenosis is both a question of a change in ontological status (form of God to form of a slave/human) and an ethical example (Jesus as model for humans). Paul seems less interested in questions of what the former change means ontologically than he does ethically and functionally—for the very reason (*dio*) of Jesus's death, he is given the name of all names.

As Coakley notes, kenosis has also come to be understood, more broadly, as part of all three persons of the perichoretic Trinity although this is done in a variety of ways with a variety of philosophical and theological underpinnings.[59] The first important extension is that of creation as kenosis, which we have already discussed in the context of the perichoretic Trinity as making room for the other to exist. Acts 17:28 lends itself to such an idea without necessarily insisting upon panentheism or process thought. Polkinghorne examines the tension between kenosis and action, love and power within the Godhead.[60] Overemphasis on love leads to process theology, which ultimately subverts eschatology for both humans and the rest of creation. God either becomes too much a part of creation and therefore impotent, or God becomes too focused on love and wooing creation, so there is no assurance his will is achieved. By contrast, overemphasis on power leads to a form of classical Theism that makes it difficult to ascribe love to God in any useful, analogical way.[61] The application of kenotic thinking to the Trinity and creation aids us in thinking more deeply about *creatio continua*, theodicy and divine action. Theology after Darwin requires that we accept that there is a continual unfolding of new forms and that this process involves evolutionary blind alleys and suffering. In direct analogy with free will, Polkinghorne advocates for what he calls *free process* and offers it as a defence to the problem of physical or natural evil.[62] There is then a sense in which God gives way or makes room for the other to be and to evolve, exploring new possibilities. God making room for other is an emergent process, as discussed earlier, where genuinely new things emerge. Polkinghorne sees this process as distancing God from evil and suffering and yet leaving the process open to divine guidance.[63] In Polkinghorne's view, creaturely action is both energetic and informational while the divine (the incarnation notwithstanding) is pure information input.[64] In other words, God does not act in any physical manner that we can directly detect; his action is hidden to us. Such information will give rise to new patterns in the biosphere by directing its development although this understanding implies that life is to be understood primarily as information, i.e., that is stored in DNA. We can then align Genesis 1:2, for example, with God shaping an emergent process while allowing for the result to be genuinely new. As Coakley observes, Polkinghorne wants a noninterventionist God.[65] While such a concept of God might work for *creatio continua*, how does it fit with an eschaton that is both continuous with the old, *creatio ex vetere*, but is also new and different? Such difficulties notwithstanding, Polkinghorne identifies four kenotic principles of creation.[66] *Kenosis of omnipotence* means that God exercises general providence while leaving the other room to be. This means that there are some things that occur which are not God's (prescriptive) will. As Stephen Evans has commented, our views of omnipotence have been too shaped by our theology. What if omnipotence is precisely the idea that God can create creatures that are genuinely independent of him?[67] *Kenosis of simple eternity* suggests that God adds a temporal pole at creation in order to relate to creation.[68] Hence, God must interact with temporal creatures in a temporal manner, within time though he remains outside of it.[69] Third, *kenosis of omniscience* means that the future is emergent and not yet. Polkinghorne importantly stresses that while the future is not exhaustively known even to God, God is not unprepared for the future, as Scripture attests and that this limitation is embraced within the Godhead and not imposed from without. Lest this lapse into process theology, we must insist that God is not passive but is able to bring about the future that God wants, the eschaton, and is also able to genuinely respond to petitionary prayer. This leads to Polkinghorne's last kenotic application, that of the *kenosis of causal status*. In the incarnation, the son became a cause among causes although we might argue, post baptism, the Son with the blessing of the Father in the power of the Spirit was more than just a supersized human in terms of his causal powers. In creation, "God allows creatures their part in bringing about the future," and so there must be "an interweaving of providential and creaturely causalities."[70]

KENOTIC ETHICS

So where does such a view leave us with regards to an ethic for the Anthropocene? Kenosis within the Godhead's action toward creation means that as the *imago Dei* is, so must our ethic be. Following Kauffman, but recovering emergence by way of Polkinghorne and others, kenosis must be emergent and yet also guided. Even so, Holmes Rolston suggests that nature is cruciform but not kenotic.[71] The struggle for existence occurs at all levels, but only higher forms have the capacity for suffering. Nature is cruciform because of suffering, not in spite of it, for there "is a great divine 'yes' behind and within every 'no' of crushing nature."[72] However, there is no self-emptying in nature any more than there is selfishness, for nature just is.[73] Only humans can be kenotic among creatures because action has to be freely chosen. Interestingly, Malcolm Jeeves explores the idea of kenosis as evolved.[74] He notes that neither neuroscience nor scripture insist upon dualism, and hence the study of neuroscience is essential to understanding the evolution of kenosis. At the same time, there are both Christians and non-Christians who have rejected reductionism.[75] Following primatologist Frans de Waal, Jeeves notes that requisites for morality occur in nature, such as a sense of fairness, empathy and social norms, and all of these have a firmly neurobiological basis.[76] Altruism can be spread to future generations, where it passes on reproductive success.[77] However, it is also the case that there is more to neurobiology than bottom-up causation, and studies have shown that top-down causation can also occur, that habits can change the brain. This leads many to suggest that free will and altruism are real things.[78] This understanding is perfectly consonant with the thesis of this chapter, that kenosis is embedded in our natures but that it has to be practiced.

Ellis defines kenotic behavior as a way of being in tune with the nature of God. Kenosis is "a joyous, kind, and loving attitude that is willing to give up selfish desires and to make sacrifices on behalf of others for the common good and the glory of God, doing this in a generous and creative way, avoiding the pitfalls of pride, and guided and inspired by the love of God and the gift of grace."[79] How do we practice this kenotic ethic? Rather than allow for the typical forms of nature management in which nature is treated as a resource, Rolston demands that we limit our inherited (via evolutionary altruism) desire for self-actualisation so that it does not become self-aggrandizement on a colossal scale. This self-limitation applies as much to our hubristic attempts to manage our damage, such as the effects of geoengineering, as to the damage itself and involves humans recognising the claims of nonhumans. This returns us to Genesis 1 temple cosmos theology and the shared blessing to be fruitful and multiply (Genesis 1:22, 28). Such kenosis is our Christian calling for this millennium.[80] How might this look in the Anthropocene? A full investigation is beyond the scope of this chapter, but a few brief comments illustrate the idea of sacrificially making room for the other. The first would be that human beings have to limit their population. Even if society were to be 100 percent carbon neutral, human beings require food, potable water, and space for habitation, sanitation, garbage disposal, roads, and so forth. The human impulse to reproduce is strong, and Christians often have a tendency to have large families. Unless solutions can be found to reduce urban spread and resource usage, human population will have to decline by sensible and noncoercive means. Second, human societies will need to become less consumptive. Gluttony, aside from being among one of the seven deadly sins, can be extended to excessive or wasteful production (for example, about 40 percent of food produced in the United States is wasted) or energy profligacy. These are issues of personal piety and sacrifice as well as policy and societal structure. Third, kenosis can extend to human dietary choices. While we might argue about the eschatological fate of animals, vegetarianism has long been adopted by Christians to minimize violence toward the nonhuman. For example, going vegetarian can reduce the rate of cow slaughter (and thereby the number of cows killed each year) by lessening the demand for beef. The various aspects of the Anthropocene demand not that we follow Jesus's dietary example in the eating of fish at the end of his ministry (e.g. John 21), but rather that we empty our demands for meat protein in a reduced meat or nonmeat diet.[81]

Fourth, human habitation needs to be designed with nature in mind. High-density housing could be adopted to reduce urban sprawl and impact on wild areas although research constantly shows the human need for contact with nature. Planting native flora in parks to encourage native fauna and control of pests and creating various animal corridors to reduce road kill allow humans to live more closely with nonhumans. Even dangerous animals can cohabit with humans, as Richard Turere of the Masai community has recently demonstrated with his way of deterring lions from taking their livestock.[82]

Fifth, our way of dealing with the damage we have done needs to be kenotic. Fossil fuels are an extractive and ultimately dominating way of producing our energy, whereas wind, solar, and other renewable energy sources are more in harmony with the Earth system. As Tim Flannery has noted, geoengineering is hubristic and likely ineffective.[83] Instead, he advocates for so-called third-way technologies such as bio char and reforestation that represent enhancement or revitalization of natural processes rather than the artificial use of iron as an ocean fertilizer or sulphur as a stratospheric aerosol. Kenosis places profound limits even on the use of technology that ecomodernists would have us believe will be our salvation. By way of analogy, as in the incident on Mount Carmel in 1 Kings 18, will our technology be as manipulative as that of the prophets of Baal,[84] turning to the same ideology that caused our woes, or will we be Yahwehistic or, more properly, kenotic, like the perichoretic Triune God?

CONCLUSION

In order to face the present ecological crisis of the Anthropocene, we need also to face the present crisis of anthropology. Are we the result of four billion years of random evolution, where meaning is meaningless? Can meaning appear ex nihilio through this material process, or are meaning, purpose and ethics the imprint of the divine being on the cosmos? Seeing the Godhead not as a remote monad but as a dynamic, loving interrelationship who is open to the other and models to the other sacrifice and self-limitation provides us with a basis for a Christian ethic for the Anthropocene. We must make room for the other, be it through dialogue with other humans or through concern for nonhumans whose existence we threaten. To be a part of dialogue in how to address the Anthropocene, in how to achieve Küng's peace among religions means being more committed to the distinctives of Christian theology, not less. This means that exploring doctrines such as perichoresis and kenosis is essential.

NOTES

1. According to a team led by Johann Rockström, the nine planetary boundaries are climate change, biodiversity loss, changes to biogeochemical cycles, ocean acidification, land use changes, fresh water loss, ozone depletion, atmospheric aerosols, and novel entities (pollutants). Johann Rockström, Will Steffen, Kevin Noone, et al., "Planetary Boundaries: Exploring the Safe Operating Space for Humanity," *Ecology and Society* 14, no. 2, (2009): 32. http://www.ecologyandsociety.org/vol14/iss2/art32/.

2. Pope Francis lists "individualism, unlimited progress, competition, consumerism," and "the unregulated market" as "'myths' of modernity." Pope Francis, *Laudato Si': On Care for Our Common Home*, (Rome: Vatican Press, 2015), 210, accessed May 24, 2015, http://w2.vatican.va/content/francesco/en/encyclicals/documents/papa-francesco_20150524_enciclica-laudato-si.html.

3. Paul Crutzen, "Geology of Mankind," *Nature* 415 (2002): 23.

4. Simon L. Lewis and Mark A Maslin, "Defining the Anthropocene," *Nature* 519 (2015): 171–80.
5. William F. Ruddiman, *Plows, Plagues and Petroleum: How Humans Took Control of the Climate* (Princeton, NJ: Princeton University Press, 2010).
6. Will Steffen, Wendy Broadgate, Lisa Deutsch, et al, "The Trajectory of the Anthropocene: The Great Acceleration," *The Anthropocene Review* 2 (2015): 1–18.
7. Will Steffen, Katherine Richardson, Johann Rockström, et al., "Planetary Boundaries: Guiding Human Development on a Changing Planet," *Science* 347 (2015): 1–17, accessed January 15, 2015, DOI: *10.1126/science.1259855.*
8. Hans Küng, *Global Responsibility: In Search of a New World Ethic* (London: SCM Press, 1991), xv.
9. Küng, *Global Responsibility*, 2.
10. Küng, *Global Responsibility*, xvi.
11. Pope Francis, *Laudato Si': On Care for Our Common Home* Vatican, Website, May 24, 2015, http://w2.vatican.va/content/francesco/en/encyclicals/documents/papa-francesco_20150524_enciclica-laudato-si.html.
12. Küng, *Global Responsibility*, 9–10.
13. Küng, *Global Responsibility*, 6–15.
14. Küng, *Global Responsibility*, 25.
15. Küng, *Global Responsibility*, 15.
16. Küng, *Global Responsibility*, 25f.
17. Küng, *Global Responsibility*, 31.
18. Küng, *Global Responsibility*, 37.
19. Küng, *Global Responsibility*, 41.
20. Küng, *Global Responsibility*, 43.
21. Stuart Kauffman, *Reinventing the Sacred: A New View of Science, Reason and Religion* (New York: Basic Books, 2010), 273.
22. Kauffman, *Reinventing the Sacred*, 71.
23. Kauffman, *Reinventing the Sacred*, iii.
24. Stephen Weinberg's claim is, "All the explanatory arrows point downward, from societies to people, to organs, to cells, to biochemistry, to chemistry, and ultimately to physics." Stephen Weinberg, *Dreams of a Final Theory: The Scientist's Search for the Ultimate Laws of Nature* (New York: Vintage, 1993), 168.
25. Kauffman, *Reinventing the Sacred*, ix.
26. Kauffman, *Reinventing the Sacred*, 34.
27. Kauffman, *Reinventing the Sacred*, 37.
28. Nancey Murphy and George F. R. Ellis, *On The Moral Nature of the Universe: Theology, Cosmology and Ethics* (Minneapolis, MN: Fortress Press, 1996).
29. Simon Conway Morris, *Life's Solutions: Inevitable Humans in a Lonely Universe* (Cambridge: Cambridge University Press, 2005).
30. Stanley J. Grenz, *Theology for the Community of God* (Grand Rapids, MI: Wm. B. Eerdmans Publishing, 1999), 53.
31. Clark H. Pinnock, *Flame of Love: A Theology of the Holy Spirit* (Downers Grove, IL: IVP, 1996), 26.
32. Keith Ward, *Religion and Creation* (Oxford: Clarendon Press, 1996), 327.
33. N. T. Wright, *Paul and the Faithfulness of God: Parts I and* II (Minneapolis, MN: Fortress Press, 2013), 365.
34. Thomas F. Torrance, *Christian Doctrine of God, One Being Three Persons* (Edinburgh, NY: Bloomsbury T & T Clark, 2001), 7.
35. John Webster, "Trinity and Creation," *International Journal of Systematic Theology* 12 (1): 4–19.
36. Thomas R. Thompson and Cornelius Plantinga, Jr., "Trinity and Kenosis," in *Exploring Kenotic Christology: The Self-Emptying of God*, ed. C. Stephen Evans (Oxford: Oxford University Press, 2006), 172–73.
37. Paul S. Fiddes, "Creation out of Love," in *The Work of Love: Creation as Kenosis*, ed. John Polkinghorne (Grand Rapids, MI: Wm. B. Eerdmans Publishing, 2001), 184–91.

38. Thompson and Plantinga, "Trinity and Kenosis," 173.
39. Jürgen Moltmann, *Science and Wisdom* (Minneapolis, MN: Fortress Press, 2009), 117.
40. Torrance, *Christian Doctrine*, 168–69.
41. Colin Gunton, *The One, The Three and the Many: God, Creation and the Culture of Modernity* (Cambridge: Cambridge University Press, 1993), 163.
42. Torrance, *Christian Doctrine*, 171.
43. Torrance, *Christian Doctrine*, 174–75.
44. Thompson and Plantinga, "Trinity and Kenosis," 184.
45. Torrance, *Christian Doctrine*, 207.
46. Webster, "Trinity and Creation."
47. John Walton, *The Lost World of Genesis One: Ancient Cosmology and the Origins Debate* (Downers Grove, IL: IVP, 2009), 71–74.
48. Walton, *The Lost World of Genesis*, 81–82.
49. Rikk Watts, "The New Exodus/New Creation Restoration of the Image of God: A Biblical-Theological Perspective on Salvation," in *What Does it Mean to be Saved?* ed. John G. Stackhouse, Jr. (Grand Rapids, MI: Baker Academic, 2002), 18–22.
50. John Walton, *The Lost World of Adam and Eve: Genesis 2–3 and the Origins Debate* (Downers Grove, IL: IVP, 2015), 104–15.
51. Pinnock, *Flame of Love*, 23.
52. Pinnock, *Flame of Love*, 55.
53. Pinnock, *Flame of Love*, 73.
54. Pinnock, *Flame of Love*, 56.
55. Pinnock, *Flame of Love*, 57.
56. Moltmann, *Science and Wisdom*, 118.
57. Moltmann, *Science and Wisdom*, 119–210.
58. Sarah Coakley, "Kenosis: Theological Meaning and Gender Connotations," in *The Work of Love: Creation as Kenosis*, ed. John Polkinghorne (Grand Rapids, MI: Wm. B. Eerdmans Publishing, 2001), 194.
59. Coakley, "Kenosis," 198–203.
60. John Polkinghorne, "Kenotic Creation and Divine Action," in *The Work of Love: Creation as Kenosis*, ed. John Polkinghorne (Grand Rapids, MI: Wm. B. Eerdmans Publishing, 2001), 91.
61. Polkinghorne, "Kenotic Creation and Divine Action," 92.
62. Polkinghorne, "Kenotic Creation and Divine Action," 95.
63. Polkinghorne, "Kenotic Creation and Divine Action," 97.
64. Polkinghorne, "Kenotic Creation and Divine Action," 101.
65. Coakley, "Kenosis," 201.
66. Polkinghorne, "Kenotic Creation and Divine Action," 102–5.
67. C. Stephen Evans, "Kenotic Christology and the Nature of God," in *Exploring Kenotic Christology: The Self-Emptying of God*, ed. C. Stephen Evans (Oxford: Oxford University Press, 2006), 207–8.
68. As William Lane Craig has argued at length, tensed facts cannot be expressed in a tenseless fashion. See "Omniscience, Tensed Facts, and Divine Eternity," *Reasonable Faith with William Lane Craig*, accessed May 21, 2016, http://www.reasonablefaith.org/omniscience-tensed-facts-and-divine-eternity.
69. William Lane Craig, *Time and Eternity: Exploring God's Relationship to Time* (Wheaton, IL: Crossway, 2001).
70. Polkinghorne, "Kenotic Creation and Divine Action," 105.
71. Holmes Rolston, III, "Kenosis and Nature," in *The Work of Love: Creation as Kenosis*, ed. John Polkinghorne (Grand Rapids, MI: Wm. B. Eerdmans Publishing, 2001), 58–65.
72. Rolston, "Kenosis and Nature," 59.
73. Rolston, "Kenosis and Nature," 61.
74. Malcolm Jeeves, "The Nature of Persons and the Emergence of Kenotic Behavior," in *The Work of Love: Creation as Kenosis,* ed. John Polkinghorne (Grand Rapids, MI: Wm. B. Eerdmans Publishing Co., 2001), 66–89.
75. Jeeves, "The Nature of Persons and the Emergence of Kenotic Behavior," 75.

76. Jeeves, "The Nature of Persons and the Emergence of Kenotic Behavior," 82–83.
77. Jeeves, "The Nature of Persons and the Emergence of Kenotic Behavior," 79.
78. Jeeves, "The Nature of Persons and the Emergence of Kenotic Behavior," 86–87.
79. George F. R. Ellis, "Kenosis as a Unifying Theme for Life and Cosmology," in *The Work of Love: Creation as Kenosis*, ed. John Polkinghorne (Grand Rapids, MI: Wm. B. Eerdmans Publishing, 2001), 108.
80. Rolston, "Kenosis and Nature," 66–89.
81. Andy Alexis-Baker, "Didn't Jesus Eat Fish?" in *A Faith Embracing All Creatures: Addressing Commonly Asked Questions about Christian Care for Animals*, ed. Tripp York and Andy Alexis-Baker (Eugene, Oregon: Cascade Books: 2012), 70–71.
82. Richard Turere, *My Invention that Made Peace with Lions*, Filmed February 2013, TED Video, 7:20, accessed July 23, 2016, http://www.ted.com/talks/richard_turere_a_peace_treaty_with_the_lions.
83. Tim Flannery, *Atmosphere of Hope: Searching for Solutions to the Climate Crisis* (Boston: Atlantic Monthly Press, 2015).
84. The drought of 1 Kings 17 was divine judgment on Israel for breaking the covenant by worshiping the storm god Baal. The contest between the prophets of Baal and Elijah in 1 Kings 18 to light the sacrificial burnt offering through invocations to Baal with prayer and bloodletting. This invocation was a way of manipulating Baal to achieve their ends in contrast to Yahweh's intentions spoken through Elijah.

REFERENCES

Alexis-Baker, Andy. "Didn't Jesus Eat Fish?" In *A Faith Embracing All Creatures: Addressing Commonly Asked Questions about Christian Care for Animals*. Edited by Tripp York and Andy Alexis-Baker. Eugene, OR: Cascade Books: 2012.
Coakley, Sarah. "Kenosis: Theological Meaning and Gender Connotations." In *The Work of Love: Creation as Kenosis*. Edited by John Polkinghorne. Grand Rapids, MI: Wm. B. Eerdmans Publishing, 2001.
Craig, William Lane. *Time and Eternity: Exploring God's Relationship to Time*. Wheaton, IL: Crossway, 2001.
Crutzen, Paul. "Geology of Mankind." *Nature* 415 (2002): 23.
Ellis, George F. R. "Kenosis as a Unifying Theme for Life and Cosmology." In *The Work of Love: Creation as Kenosis*. Edited by John Polkinghorne. Grand Rapids, MI: Wm. B. Eerdmans Publishing, 2001.
Evans, C. Stephen. "Kenotic Christology and the Nature of God." In *Exploring Kenotic Christology: The Self-Emptying of God*. Edited by C. Stephen Evans. Oxford: Oxford University Press, 2006.
Fiddes, Paul S. "Creation out of Love." In *The Work of Love: Creation as Kenosis*. Edited by John Polkinghorne. Grand Rapids, MI: Wm. B. Eerdmans Publishing, 2001.
Flannery, Tim. *Atmosphere of Hope: Searching for Solutions to the Climate Crisis*. Boston: Atlantic Monthly Press, 2015.
Grenz, Stanley J. *Theology for the Community of God*. Grand Rapids, MI: Wm. B. Eerdmans Publishing, 1999.
Gunton, Colin. *The One, The Three and the Many: God, Creation and the Culture of Modernity*. Cambridge: Cambridge University Press, 1993.
Jeeves, Malcolm. "The Nature of Persons and the Emergence of Kenotic Behavior." In *The Work of Love: Creation as Kenosis*. Edited by John Polkinghorne. Grand Rapids, MI: Wm. B. Eerdmans Publishing Co., 2001.
Kauffman, Stuart. *Reinventing the Sacred: A New View of Science, Reason and Religion*. New York: Basic Books, 2010.
Küng, Hans. *Global Responsibility: In Search of a New World Ethic*. London: SCM Press, 1991.
Lewis, Simon L. and Mark A Maslin. "Defining the Anthropocene." *Nature* 519 (2015): 171–80.

Moltmann, Jürgen. *Science and Wisdom*. Minneapolis, MN: Fortress Press, 2009.
Morris, Simon Conway. *Life's Solutions: Inevitable Humans in a Lonely Universe*. Cambridge: Cambridge University Press, 2005.
Murphy, Nancey and George F. R. Ellis. *On The Moral Nature of the Universe: Theology, Cosmology and Ethics*. Minneapolis, MN: Fortress Press, 1996.
Pinnock, Clark H. *Flame of Love: A Theology of the Holy Spirit*. Downers Grove, IL: IVP, 1996.
Polkinghorne, John. "Kenotic Creation and Divine Action." In *The Work of Love: Creation as Kenosis*. Edited by John Polkinghorne. Grand Rapids, MI: Wm. B. Eerdmans Publishing, 2001.
Pope Francis. *Laudato Si': On Care for Our Common Home*. The Holy See. Accessed May 24, 2015. http://w2.vatican.va/content/francesco/en/encyclicals/documents/papa-francesco_20150524_enciclica-laudato-si.html.
Pope, Mick. "With Heads Craning Forward: The Eschaton and the Non-human Creation in Romans 8." In *Ecotheology in the Humanities: An Interdisciplinary Approach to Understanding the Divine in Nature*. Edited by Melissa J. Brotton. Lanham, MD: Lexington Books, 2016.
Rockström, Johann, Will Steffen, Kevin Noone, et al., "Planetary Boundaries: Exploring the Safe Operating Space for Humanity," *Ecology and Society* 14, no. 2, (2009): 32. http://www.ecologyandsociety.org/vol14/iss2/art32/.
Rolston, Holmes, III. "Kenosis and Nature." In *The Work of Love: Creation as Kenosis*. Edited by John Polkinghorne. Grand Rapids, MI: Wm. B. Eerdmans Publishing Co., 2001.
Ruddiman, William F. *Plows, Plagues and Petroleum: How Humans Took Control of the Climate*. Princeton, NJ: Princeton University Press, 2010.
Steffen, Will, Wendy Broadgate, Lisa Deutsch, et al. "The Trajectory of the Anthropocene: The Great Acceleration." *The Anthropocene Review* 2 (2015): 1–18.
Steffen, Will, Katherine Richardson, Johan Rockström, et al. "Planetary Boundaries: Guiding Human Development on a Changing Planet." *Science* 347 (2015): 1–17. DOI: 10.1126/science.1259855.
Stuart, Tristram. *The Global Food Waste Scandal*. May 2012. TED Video. 14:15. https://www.ted.com/talks/tristram_stuart_the_global_food_waste_scandal.
———. *Waste: Uncovering the Global Food Scandal*. New York: W. W. Norton, 2009.
Thompson, Thomas R. and Cornelius Plantinga, Jr. "Trinity and Kenosis." In *Exploring Kenotic Christology: The Self-Emptying of God*. Edited by C. Stephen Evans. Oxford: Oxford University Press, 2006.
Torrance, Thomas F. *Christian Doctrine of God, One Being Three Persons*. Edinburgh, UK: Bloomsbury T & T Clark, 2001.
Turere, Richard. *My Invention that Made Peace with Lions*. February 2013. TED Video, 7:20. http://www.ted.com/talks/richard_turere_a_peace_treaty_with_the_lions.
Walton, John. *The Lost World of Genesis One: Ancient Cosmology and the Origins Debate*. Downers Grove, IL: IVP, 2009.
———. *The Lost World of Adam and Eve: Genesis 2–3 and the Origins Debate*. Downers Grove, IL: IVP, 2015.
Ward, Keith. *Religion and Creation*. Oxford: Clarendon Press, 1996.
Watts, Rikk. "The New Exodus/New Creation Restoration of the Image of God: A Biblical-Theological Perspective on Salvation." In *What Does it Mean to be Saved?* Edited by John G. Stackhouse, Jr. Grand Rapids, MI: Baker Academic, 2002.
Webster, John. "Trinity and Creation." *International Journal of Systematic Theology*. 12, no. 1: 4–19.
Weinberg, Steven. *Dreams of a Final Theory: The Scientist's Search for the Ultimate Laws of Nature*. New York: Vintage, 1994.
Wright, N. T. *Paul and the Faithfulness of God: Parts I and II*. Minneapolis, MN: Fortress Press, 2013.

Part II

Ecotheology in the South

Chapter Five

Loving the Mountains

Cultivating Compassion for Places

Andrew R. H. Thompson

On cars, walls, and guitar cases throughout the Appalachian Mountains and beyond, one can find bumper stickers reading "I [heart] Mountains." Distributed by the West Virginia Highlands Conservancy, the sticker represents a certain place-based consciousness that actively opposes the environmental harms of a number of particularly Appalachian concerns: the abuses of the mining industry (including mountaintop removal coal mining), hydraulic fracturing for natural gas, other energy production, and forest and wilderness conservation.

The sentiment the sticker expresses, that of loving the mountains, or any place, is a commonly invoked one, especially with respect to environmental issues like these. In his influential essay, "The Land Ethic," Aldo Leopold reflects, "It is inconceivable to me that an ethical relation to land can exist without love, respect, and admiration for land."[1] Author Wendell Berry similarly argues that it is impossible "that humans would ever take good care of anything that they don't love."[2] Many who invoke this image of loving places, including Berry and Leopold, ascribe environmental problems to a fundamental disconnect from the land, an exploitative attitude that instrumentalizes places. They see an attitude of love for place, and, more importantly, for specific places in their particularity, as a necessary corrective to this pathology.[3]

The character of this love rarely receives explicit consideration. The significant attention devoted to love for persons from a wide range of philosophical and religious perspectives is too extensive to address here. Yet love for place, as commonplace as it is in environmental literature, has had no such attention.

Often, however, the implicit understanding of this love seems to resemble compassion. For the purposes of this chapter, I submit that compassion can be assumed to involve an emotional and moral (that is, determinative of one's actions) response to the suffering of another (below I will also suggest that this response is commonly seen as a cultivated attitude, rather than an abstract principle for discrete decisions). Given this understanding of compassion, exhortations to love places in response to the harms being enacted upon them can be heard as calls of a compassionate nature. Like compassion, love of places is paradigmatically summoned by those places' suffering.

This compassionate love for places in response to suffering is illustrated most clearly in approaches like those of liberation theologian Leonardo Boff, who urges attention to the cry of the earth that, along with the cry of the poor, demands integral liberation from their mutual oppression.[4] With respect to Appalachian issues, a similar perspective is expressed by the Catholic Bishops of Appalachia. In two pastoral letters, *This Land is Home to Me* (1975) and *At Home in the Web of Life* (1995), the bishops speak of the mountains' struggle and the combined cry of suffering of the land and people.[5] They see people and land united in a single "web of life," both victims of a materialistic society, and praise those "friends of the web of life" who have "loved the hills and hollows."[6]

Still, though, compassionate love for places remains relatively ambiguous. What might it mean to "love the hills and hollows" of Appalachia? Can the idea of compassion be readily translated from human relationships to relationships with places? In this chapter, I will articulate an understanding of compassion for places that is consistent with the sentiments evoked by the Highlands Conservancy and the authors noted above while addressing the conceptual problems raised by this application of compassion. After defending the usefulness of this application of compassion in spite of these problems, I will describe an understanding of place and of compassion for places based on the theocentrism of H. Richard Niebuhr and James M. Gustafson.[7] I will argue that the identity and value of places inhere in their relationship to the creator of all and the source of all value, and that in this context compassion entails relating to places—and especially to their suffering—in a way appropriate to that fundamental relationship. Returning to the specific context of Appalachia, I will suggest that practices like planting by astrological signs, making moonshine, and basket weaving may be capable of cultivating this attitude of compassion for the mountains. As one ethnographer of Appalachia muses, "we can't go back now, but we can listen to what they have to say and learn from it. That's one reason why we asked Beulah Perry to show us how to make a basket."[8]

THE PROBLEM OF PLACE

I begin by indicating the special problems that arise when the notion of love, and specifically compassionate love, is applied to place. Without attempting a comprehensive definition of compassion, if it is understood generally to involve an emotional and moral (that is, determinative of one's actions) response to the suffering of another, it becomes clear that places are an unusual object of compassion. To begin with, can a place be properly said to suffer? Compassion may be plausibly said to extend beyond humans to many nonhuman creatures; yet can it be meaningfully applied to the nonsentient and inanimate constituents of a place? This question leads to another more fundamental one: what is a place beyond these constituents? In other words, is a place something greater than the sum of its parts? With respect to compassion, is it possible to have compassion for a place, rather than simply for its constituent parts? What might this mean?

Before turning to substantive answers to these questions, I consider two responses that attempt to make them irrelevant. First, it may be argued that a place really is nothing beyond its constituents: it is simply the sum of its parts, nothing more. The idea of loving a place *as* place, then, is meaningless or misleading. We do better, this argument would suggest, to have compassion on some of the inhabitants of a place and to concern ourselves with the degree to which such compassion ought to extend—to sentient creatures? Creatures that can be said to have "well-being"? All living creatures? Compassion for the place itself as place, then, would add nothing to the matter.

Not surprisingly, I do not find this argument persuasive. I believe place is meaningful and useful as an object of compassion for two reasons. First, as I will argue in greater length below, place is a unifying concept. Attention to—and compassion toward—a place as place is attention to the integrity of the place's various components in one whole. Integrity is the fundamental insight of the field of ecology, which is built on ever more expansive wholes. Ecological research continually indicates the dependence of organisms and ecosystems on one another in more and more complex and intertwined relationships. Likewise, time and again ecological crises illustrate the errors that result from addressing only one element of an ecosystem in abstraction from or to the neglect of other elements. While compassion for specific constituents of a place may focus our attention and action on particular harms, compassion for the place itself reminds us of those constituents' relations to the larger whole and is therefore an essential complement to the more specific compassion.

Moreover, the holism of compassion for a place is a helpful, and in any case, a necessary context for deliberating on the actions compassion requires. If compassion in ecotheology is to be useful, it must help agents decide between competing ecological goods. An attitude of compassion toward the constituent parts of a place may serve to guide decisions in favor of one or the other of those parts; yet without compassion for the place itself, such deliberation is ignorant of the larger goods at stake and therefore could be dangerously narrow.

With respect to the unity of the idea of place, and, specifically, what constitutes the good (or, alternatively, the suffering) of a place, two caveats are in order. First, it is important to guard against a view that would see this unity as necessarily harmonious. The complex interdependence of organisms and ecosystems, which includes predation and disease, resists such a characterization. What is good for a place is not necessarily good for all its constituents; this is precisely why compassion for a place is an essential corollary to compassion for its inhabitants. The second caveat is related to the first: what is good for a place often depends on scale. Whether the relevant place is a particular acre of forest or a mountain or a region matters significantly in determining what compassion entails. The cultivated approach to compassion I will describe below suggests a certain relatively local scale. Here the point is simply to note that just as the good of a place may not conduce to the good of specific inhabitants, it also may not be the same when viewed on a larger scale.

Place is necessarily unitive; it is also irreducibly particular. This is the second reason that compassion for a place as place is a morally helpful concept. Attention to place calls us to attend to the lived, embodied experience of particular locales in a way other categories cannot. Even the category of ecosystems, which may reflect the same integrity or unity as place, does not carry this same emphasis on particularity. Ecosystems are assemblages of systems, processes, and organisms. As a category, ecosystem is useful because of its generality: this ecosystem can be compared with other ecosystems that are similar in relevant ways. This is why it would seem odd to speak of loving an ecosystem. The category of ecosystem abstracts precisely the particularity that place emphasizes. Thus place inhabits a region between the atomistic particularity of specific individuals and the abstract generality of ecosystems. Compassion for place, as a moral concept, upholds the importance of both integrity and particularity.

As with the unitive function of place, the particularity of place also merits a caveat. The local tendency noted above notwithstanding, it is important that the emphasis on place and particularity not be construed too exclusively. A parochial focus on one particular place to the exclusion or detriment of other places is both ecologically and theologically misguided. Any responsible ecology must recognize the interdependence of places, such that to care for or protect one place at the expense of another is inconsistent. Similarly, the theocentric approach to place that I will suggest, by positing a transcendent source of value and identity for places, clearly opposes any inclination toward isolationism. Because all beings, and by extension, all places are equally valued, any exclusive focus on one particular place seriously misunderstands this approach.

I have argued that compassion for places is a useful concept because of the unity and particularity that place entails. On the other hand, it may be that when authors like Boff and others describe something like compassion for places, they intend it metaphorically. Perhaps we ought to concede that love for places is qualitatively different from compassion for sentient beings—more like attention or a sense of affection or attachment. This is a second way of avoiding the difficulties described above in applying compassionate love to a place as place, and it is certainly a plausible option. Such a metaphorical approach, however, misses the real possibilities for responsive and empathetic action presented by a more literal interpretation of compassion for place. The understanding of compassion I will propose can respond to the difficulties without sacrificing the profound emotional and moral content of a robust notion of compassion.

LOVING PLACES

What, then, might it mean to love a place as place, an object of compassion that exists beyond its individual constituents? I propose a theocentric understanding of compassion for places based on the thought of Christian ethicists H. Richard Niebuhr and James M. Gustafson. In particular, Niebuhr's relational theory of identity and Gustafson's interpretation of it for ethics ground my approach as it seeks to respond to the peculiar difficulties raised above.

Niebuhr suggests that human moral action is fundamentally characterized by response to other actions, and, indeed, that our very identity as agents is sought in these responses.[9] The problem, he argues, is that "the radical action by which I am and by which I am present with this body, this mind . . . is not identifiable with any of the finite actions that constitute the particular elements in physical, mental, personal existence."[10] As beings that are essentially responsive, humans are nonetheless unable to find the foundation of their being, a coherent and enduring self, in any particular actions, their own or those of others. We act and respond in a multiplicity of interconnected roles and relationships, but our identity exists beyond any or all of these roles. It must therefore be sought elsewhere.

The response to the question "How is it possible to be *one* self in the multiplicity of events and one's interpretations of them?" cannot be found in any finite actions or in the self alone.[11] Unified identity can only be found in "the radical action whereby I am I, and things are as they are," which, for theists, is God.[12] Coherence as a self is found not in any of the finite relationships in which one responds but rather in this fundamental relationship.

Niebuhr's understanding of value is similarly relational. Rather than being purely objective (inhering completely in the valued object) or purely subjective (existing completely in the perception of the valuer), Niebuhr insists that value is a characteristic of relationships: "value is present wherever being confronts being, wherever there is becoming in the midst of plural, interdependent, and interacting existences. It is not a function of being as such but of being in relation to being."[13] It makes sense to speak of something as having value only insofar as it has value *for* or *to* something else. As with identity, the question becomes where coherence is to be found in this network of related and often competing valuations; again, the response for theists is God, the center of value: "the starting point is that transcendent absolute for whom, or for which, whatever is, is good. . . . With this beginning the value theory of monotheistic theology is enabled to proceed to the construction of many relative value systems, each of them tentative, experimental, and objective."[14] The center of value is the value that defines all derivative values. Everything is valuable insofar as it is valued by and with respect to this center (and for Niebur the center is universally inclusive, thus "whatever is, is good"—that is, valued).

Thus, although value and identity are not the same thing for Niebuhr, they are functionally similar. In both, unity in the midst of competing claims and relationships is found in a single, transcendent source. For Niebuhr this source is identified with the Christian God; what is essential, though, is that it is found beyond any finite, particular relation or role. No particular characteristic or claim defines one's identity except the fundamental relationship to "that radical action by which I am;" no particular value relationship defines one's ultimate value except that with the center of value. The particular strength of this perspective is that it incorporates and upholds all finite relationships and roles even as it relativizes them with respect to the fundamental relationship. By organizing all values around a single transcendent value, the theocentric perspective "destabilizes or fractures the privileged point of view from the inside."[15] Because the center of value and identity is not wholly understood in terms of one particular value or role—because the center is transcendent—the theocentric perspective is capable of radically relativizing its own interpretations in ways unavailable to other worldviews.

I wish to suggest that Niebuhr's understanding of identity and value can be fruitfully applied to the multiplicity that characterizes place. That is, with respect to the question of how place is to be understood in relation to its constituent parts, I argue that it can be understood in the same way that human identity and value can be understood, which, in Niebuhr's view, is in an equally multifaceted way. Just as a coherent human identity and valuation are sought in relation to a transcendent source, the identity and value of a place as place are found not in any one of its constituent parts, nor in their sum, but rather in a transcendent source of value. This source can be identified with a Christian God, but it need not be so defined; indeed, Niebuhr's understanding of God as the principle of being and source of value is quite broad and emphatically resists identification with any particular imagination. Again, what is essential is that it exists beyond any particular feature or relationship. With all its various features and relationships, the identity and coherence of a place exist in its relation to its transcendent source, its creator; its value originates in the transcendent, unifying center of value that values all things in relation to one another and to itself.

This move toward a transcendent center of value is, in some ways, counterintuitive for environmental concern. After all, God's transcendence is often blamed for attitudes that dismiss and instrumentalize nonhuman values. Many environmental thinkers therefore emphasize the immanence of the divine in nature. Niebuhr consistently maintains, however, that this transcendent center is active and revealed in all facets of creation and values them all equally. Where this conception differs from other, more immanent ones is in the insistence that, while all creation is valued and capable of revealing divine purposes, the source of this value and the primary purposes behind the created order always transcend any part of that order. This guards against identifying any finite goals as ultimate ones, or, in Niebuhr's words, "absolutizing the relative."[16] It also reminds us that while attributes like "harmony," "integrity," and "order" may be meaningful from the divine, transcendent perspective, they may not be perceptible in any limited part of creation.

But what does such a conception mean with respect to compassion for a place? How does this Niebuhrian approach to place affect our emotional and moral response to places? For Niebuhr, himself, this fundamental relationship means that "God is acting in all actions upon you." The appropriate response, then, is to "respond to all actions upon you as to respond to his action."[17] Niebuhrian ethicist James M. Gustafson modifies this dictum to apply it to environmental action: "We are to relate ourselves and all things in a manner appropriate to our and their relations to God."[18] Elsewhere he explains how this is to be discerned: "The divine ordering is perceived, insofar as it is humanly possible, in and through the ordering of nature, culture, history, and personal living."[19]

Gustafson's version seems useful in understanding how humans might relate compassionately to places. If the identity of a place and its value are grounded in its relation to a creator or source of value, beyond any finite relationships, characteristics, or constituent parts, then an appropriate human approach to a place relates to it in a way appropriate to this fundamental relationship, insofar as it can be known. As Gustafson notes, we might perceive some sense of this relationship in the "ordering"—that is, the particular, finite relationships between places and among the constituent parts within places—that we can encounter in nature, culture, history, and "personal living," by which I understand direct personal experience of a place.

Just as suffering is frequently understood to be a paradigmatic occasion for compassion, Gustafson argues that this fundamental relationship can be best perceived negatively in the experience of disvalue. Although a clear understanding of the value or identity of a place is beyond human discernment, we can perceive threats to the well-being of species or of creation in general more readily than we can articulate what well-being requires.[20] While we may not be able fully to articulate what beauty or integrity are in a specific place, we may experience an immediate perception of ugliness or brokenness that help clarify our understanding of that place and its value.

Finally, for both Gustafson and Niebuhr, the first and most important step to perceiving this divine fundamental relationship and conforming our relationships to it is removing ourselves and our own interests from the center of our identities and value systems.[21] Niebuhr argues the guiding image of dramatic action in which the self is the protagonist is unable to give any clarity to our understanding of ourselves or the world; only the transcendent source and value center he describes can provide such clarity.[22] If compassion requires conforming our relationships with places to the fundamental relationship between those places and their creator and source of value, it first requires removing ourselves and our interests from the center of our relationships.

CULTIVATING COMPASSION

Niebuhr and Gustafson thus provide a foundation for a compassionate relation to place that begins to respond to the above problems of place. If the coherent identity of a place exists fundamentally in its relationship to a transcendent creator and source of value, then compassion means perceiving that relationship and conforming our own actions and attitudes to it. What this compassion requires may be most clear in a negative sense: we may best see how to be more compassionate toward a place by experiencing the ways it has been damaged or degraded, that is, by experiencing its suffering. The remainder of this chapter considers how this approach to compassion might actually be fostered and enacted.

Compassion is frequently understood to be the product of disciplined practice rather than a characteristic of discrete actions. That is, it is often more an agent-oriented value than an act-oriented one. This is especially evident in some forms of Buddhism, for example, where compassion is developed as part of the path to enlightenment, but it can be seen in reflections in other traditions as well. Compassion is not an abstract principle that is simply enacted on individual occasions; it is a virtue cultivated over a lifetime of practice. Similarly, my understanding of compassion for places does not carry specific prescriptions for what compassion entails in particular situations. Rather, it is an attitude or virtue that is shaped by—and then shapes—an agent's actions. This attitude is cultivated by particular kinds of practices; it is to these practices that we now turn.

For philosopher Iris Murdoch, the moral life involves the careful cultivation of attention to particular individuals, "a patient and just discernment and exploration of what confronts one, which is the result not simply of opening one's eyes but of a certainly perfectly familiar kind of moral discipline."[23] Goodness is known not in the abstract but only in this practiced discipline of attentiveness that she identifies as love or compassion. Murdoch's understanding of love bears significant resemblance to the kind of compassion I have been describing, and her description of the disciplined cultivation of love is helpful in understanding what is involved in relating compassionately to places. In terms similar to Niebuhr and Gustafson's invocation of a divine transcendent center of value, she describes the Good as a central focus of attention that clarifies our vision of all other finite beings, whether a blade of grass or another person.[24] Like Niebuhr and Gustafson, Murdoch too believes that excessive self-centeredness obstructs this clarity of vision, and thus she describes love as the practice of "really looking," attending to a particular reality without "returning surreptitiously to the self with consolations of self-pity, resentment, fantasy and despair." As a paradigmatic example, she suggests attention to nature, "a self-forgetful pleasure in the sheer alien pointless independent existence of animals, birds, stones and trees."[25]

Murdoch's image of "sheer alien pointless independent existence" risks envisioning nature as pristine or our experience of it as unmediated by our own beliefs and presuppositions. As Gustafson points out, there is no such experience; every encounter with nature already involves the "cultural penetrations of nature."[26] Further, human beings inevitably interact with their environment. The pristine wilderness witnessed by an uninvolved observer is a fantasy. If, however, we understand Murdoch's compassion to include careful interaction with nature, rather than a bystander's appreciation of a scenic landscape, this can be a useful model for the compassionate attention to place I have described. Murdoch's invocation of the Platonic notion of a craft (*techné*) as a way of cultivating loving attention suggests this interpretation.[27] By learning and practicing a craft, one is taken away from self-concern to a clear-eyed appreciation of the reality of the thing that is loved. In Niebuhr and Gustafson's terms, *technai* can shift our attention away from particular constituents of a place and, more importantly, from self-interest and self-involvement, to relate to places in ways appropriate to their relation to God, the transcendent source and center of value.

There may be no better exponent of this kind of active, loving attention to a place than Wendell Berry. Berry poignantly describes the patience and discipline required to stand in a place and ask of it, "What is this place? What is in it? What is its nature? How should men live in it? What must I do?"[28]

The answers come only gradually and partially, if at all; it is the asking itself, the humility required to learn from a place, that is essential. This discipline of humility and patience it leads to is the skill to use and care for this part of creation responsibly.[29] Thus Berry's approach is not a bystander's admiration of a pristine landscape; only by interacting with and working in a place does one really come to know it.[30] His description of the proper relationship to a place is an eloquent expression of the kind of loving attention I have been discussing and is worth quoting at length:

> Only in . . . silence and darkness can [one] recover the sense of the world's longevity, of its ability to thrive without him, of his inferiority to it and his dependence on it. Perhaps then, having heard that silence and seen that darkness, he will grow humble before the place and begin to take it in—to learn from it what it is. As its sounds come into his hearing, and its lights and colors come into his vision, and its odors come into his nostrils, then he may come into its presence as he never has before, and he will arrive in his place and will want to remain.[31]

This is a demanding vision; yet surely this is what it would mean truly to love a place.

Thus the compassion for places I described above, based on Niebuhr and Gustafson's theocentrism, is more fully realized in the disciplined cultivation seen in Murdoch and Berry. By approaching a place with humility and patience and interacting with it through crafts of the sort Murdoch identifies and Berry describes at length, one can come to know the place well enough to develop a relationship with it that begins to conform to the divine relationship.

Returning to the example of Appalachia and loving the mountains, it is important that this approach to compassion for places not be understood as a romantic connection to place of the sort that is so often invoked in discussions of that region. I am not suggesting that only those born or raised in a place are capable of intimately knowing it or that the people of Appalachia have, as has often been claimed, some innate connection to their homeplace. Rather, the focus is on practices of attention and care. I am arguing that actively interacting with a place is essential to discerning God's relationship with that place and conforming our relationship to that fundamental one. This is not an innate connection to place; rather, it is practiced a way of being in place. I will consider examples of crafts that inform and strengthen a love of Appalachia below, but they might include farming, harvesting ginseng in the mountains, or studying firsthand the biology of the region. Even deep mining might represent the kind of attentive connection to the mountains that carries one away from selfish interests to allow a place truly to speak. It is hard to imagine a more intimate experience of the mountains than that of underground mining, and to deny that this could be the sort of craft through which one cultivates loving attention to a place seems prejudiced. On the other hand, it does not seem to me that the mechanized practices and enormous scale of mountaintop removal allow for the kind of attention that Murdoch describes. The question of whether smaller-scale surface mining might be a way of actively loving the mountains I will leave unanswered; perhaps only a miner could answer this question definitively.

Loving the mountains, or loving any place, means seeing that place's identity and value theocentrically; beyond any particular features or constituent parts, places have coherent identity and value in their relationship to the creator and source of value. This way of understanding a place, then, entails relating to it in a way appropriate to its relation to God. This relationship has significant characteristics typically associated with compassion: attention to the other that shifts focus away from the self; a special sensitivity to the suffering of the other; and the patient, humble discipline to cultivate these attitudes through concrete practices. Wendell Berry and Iris Murdoch describe this process of cultivation. For the agrarian Berry, the paradigmatic *techné* through which one comes to know a place is, of course, through farming—literally cultivating a place. Murdoch offers the examples of art, such as literature and painting, and learning a language such as *technai*, capable of cultivating true vision.[32] In this section I have indicated briefly some possible practices for cultivating compassion in Appalachia. In the final section of this chapter, I discuss potential practices in more depth.

MOONSHINING AND OTHER DISCIPLINES OF COMPASSION

One vision of life in the Appalachian Mountains—a vision that has significant potential for cultivating an attentive, active relationship to the mountains—is expressed in the *Foxfire* series of books. The series began as a project in teacher Eliot Wigginton's high-school English class in rural Georgia. Beginning in 1966, Wigginton's students compiled materials ranging from folklore, recipes, and interviews to folk remedies for a class magazine. The magazines were published in a book, which was followed by twelve successive books, the most recent published in 2004. A quote from Maude Shope of North Carolina is illustrative of *Foxfire*'s distinctive approach to practices of place:

> When I first come to this creek, we broke up our land with a mule and a single-footed plow. We made plenty of corn t'do us all year long— never bought no corn when I first come t'this creek. Take what we called a single-footed plow, break up th'ground and then go and lay it off, cover it with a single foot-plow, drop it by hand. Now it's changed so that my grandchildren couldn't build a fire in that wood stove 'cause they don't know how. Well, I don't know how to drive a car, so I guess their way of doin' is just as good as mine. But I like my

way of doin' th'best. . . . Why, I wouldn't swap this little shack here for th'finest house in New York. I wouldn't do it. That's just the way I feel.[33]

This quote notwithstanding, *Foxfire* articles tend not to address abstract ideas like place or home, let alone morality. What stories are included tend to be simple with no clear point and certainly no obvious edifying value—stories of mystical fireballs or snakes with braided tails, for example. Most of the material is purely practical and steeped in minutiae. Readers learn how to churn butter, slaughter and butcher a hog, build a log cabin, or make an omelet from sheep sorrel. The first book opens with Aunt Arie, an elderly woman living in a log cabin in the mountains, inviting her interviewers to assist her in removing the eye from a pig's head to prepare souse meat, a kind of sausage.

I suggest, however, that it is precisely in this attention to detail and practical knowledge that *Foxfire* has real moral value. As Murdoch suggests, learning and practicing crafts of this sort shifts one's focus away from oneself enough to allow the other—in this case, the place—to speak for itself. Murdoch's self-forgetful pleasure in a place, reflected in sentiments like Maude Shope's devotion to her homeplace, may be expressed as fully in the details of old-time burials and corn shuckings as it is in Shope's reminiscences. As Murdoch and Berry make clear, compassion, the ability to know and love a place with particular sensitivity to its suffering is cultivated not in the abstract but through concrete interaction with a place. I am suggesting that practices of the sort described in *Foxfire* may have the capacity that Murdoch ascribes to art, an ability to draw individuals out of themselves and into a relationship of attention and care of "really seeing" a place. This is the intuition shared by Mary Garth in the introduction to this chapter: if it is possible to recover a kind of compassion for places that has been lost, the best place to begin may be by learning to make a basket. At the same time, clearly not any practice of interaction cultivates a compassionate relationship. As noted above, I am doubtful of the ability of a practice like mountaintop removal mining to do so. What sorts of practices are appropriate to this disciplined cultivation, then, and why?

One feature that characterizes virtually all of *Foxfire*'s stories, interviews, and other "affairs of plain livin'" is that they are inextricably bound to the requirements, rhythms, and resources of specific places. These accounts are irreducibly local. In some cases, the connection is obvious, such as a chapter on the uses of the various kinds of wood native to southern Appalachia: "Black birch, for example, was used seasoned for fiddles and guitars because of its curly grain. Sassafras was sometimes used seasoned for wheel hubs and ox yokes. Sourwood made fine canes and sled runners."[34] The various rules for determining when to plant and harvest crops based on the astrological signs—as well as when to gather and dry hay and to castrate hogs—are specific to the climate, seasons, crops, and skies of this region.[35] Even fanciful ghost stories are precisely situated: "There's a place over yonder at Jim Branch—they had people said they's seen balls of fire."[36] "Over there on Kelly's Creek up there where Jim Taylor lives . . . [a woman] said she'd seen a little baby out there that was flyin'—had wings."[37] Yet less obviously place-based practices also remain thoroughly placed, such as stories of midwives whose work was made more difficult and more necessary by unreliable roads and remote families or instructions for making a chair from wood that must be both appropriate to its purpose and locally plentiful.[38]

Perhaps the most direct connection human beings have to their place is through their food, and *Foxfire* is dominated by food practices: planting and harvesting, canning and pickling, hunting and dressing, cooking and moonshining. These practices, of course, developed in a culture that was necessarily local, and the techniques and wisdom expressed in them are marked by attention to growing seasons and local geography. For example, moonshining typically requires a location near the source of a stream, preferably "on the north side of a hill flowing west," often in the midst of a laurel thicket or under a large spruce.[39] Moonshine can be made in any season, but the process changes accordingly.[40] And distribution of moonshine, of course, requires knowing and trusting one's neighbors.[41] Like the other food practices described in *Foxfire*, and, indeed, in most of the stories and practices in the books, moonshining is inextricably connected with the plants, animals, seasons, and people of particular places.

There is a risk here, however. The picture painted by *Foxfire* is a romanticized, idealized vision of life in the mountains. While the books' covers describe their contents as "affairs of plain living," it is apparent that the topics are chosen for both their strangeness and their familiarity. We recognize characters like Maude Shope and Aunt Arie; these are our "contemporary ancestors," to borrow a phrase that was used to characterize Appalachians for much of the twentieth century. In descriptions of faith healings, ghost stories and, perhaps, most iconically, log cabins, we find images that are both exotic and comforting. These are the kinds of images and narratives that have typified descriptions of Appalachia since its "discovery" in the early twentieth century: a place that is part of the nation yet irremediably different. This characterization has allowed the region to be exploited and manipulated for a variety of purposes.[42]

Clearly, then, as a portrayal of life in the mountains *Foxfire* is incomplete at best. Thus I am not suggesting, as some have, that the way forward lies in a return to some fictitious past culture of simple harmony with nature. Yet as a resource for what we might call practices of moral cultivation—those crafts, in Murdoch's sense, that nurture a particular moral relationship with the place itself—it has great value. I suggest that by learning and, yes, practicing these crafts in the context of the mountains, persons and communities can work to develop the kind of loving relationship with place that can discern and respond to the mountains as expressing divine purposes. In other words we can, in this way, have compassion for the mountains.

CONCLUSION

In this chapter, I have defended a notion of compassion for places as places, in spite of the conceptual challenges such an application of compassion raises. I have suggested that this notion is important because it upholds both the integrity of places as such, rather than being simply an amalgamation of discrete components and their irreducible particularity as *this* place. The conceptual problems were addressed with reference to the theocentrism of H. Richard Niebuhr and James M. Gustafson, leading to a conception of compassion for places as one that discerns, especially in a place's suffering, something of that place's relationship to its creator and the source of its value and conforms to that relationship. I argued for a practical approach to this compassion, cultivating it through what Iris Murdoch calls crafts or *technai*, disciplined practices that draw attention away from ourselves and our interests to a more truthful perception of places. I then suggested that the practices described in the *Foxfire* series of books, as practices that express and enact a close connection to particular places, may be the kind of practices that can cultivate such compassion in an Appalachian context, giving real meaning to the popular notion of "loving the mountains."

It is no surprise that love for places or for land or for the earth is commonly invoked by writers and activists concerned with environmental issues. It is apparent that many contemporary attitudes regarding places are inadequate for addressing environmental problems, and the notion of compassion, with its long religious, philosophical, and spiritual pedigree, seems to suggest itself readily as an appropriate corrective. Yet if compassion for places is to have any real impact, it must move beyond an abstract notion to engage in concrete practices that give form to a disciplined, cultivated way of relating to places. This view of compassion is consistent with much traditional thought on compassion, where it is typically seen as a practiced response in both thought and deed to the suffering of another. The approach to compassion for places that I have described here, then, is an important step toward really protecting places, since, as Wendell Berry argues, it is difficult to see how we could care for something we do not truly love.

NOTES

1. Aldo Leopold, "The Land Ethic," in *Environmental Ethics: An Anthology*, ed. Andrew Light and Holmes Rolston, *Blackwell Philosophy Anthologies* 19 (Malden, MA: Blackwell Pub, 2003), 47.

2. Wendell Berry, *Our Only World: Ten Essays* (Berkeley, CA: Counterpoint, 2015), 51.

3. A complete discussion of the characteristics of "place" versus "space" is beyond the scope of this chapter. Here I follow philosopher Edward Casey in viewing space as abstract and place as referring to concrete, particular places. Edward S. Casey, *Getting Back into Place: Toward a Renewed Understanding of the Place-World* (Bloomington: Indiana University Press, 2009).

4. Leonardo Boff, *Cry of the Earth, Cry of the Poor* (Maryknoll, NY: Orbis Books, 1997), 112–113.

5. Catholic Bishops of Appalachia, *This Land Is Home to Me (1975) and At Home in the Web of Life (1995): Appalachian Pastoral Letters* (Martin, KY: Catholic Committee of Appalachia, 2007), 36, 10.

6. Catholic Bishops of Appalachia, *This Land Is Home to Me*, Ibid., 48.

7. Niebuhr and Gustafson's theocentrism is, of course, rooted in Christian theology, as is my general approach in this chapter. Nonetheless, even as he was conscious of this particularity, Niebuhr believed that theocentrism reflected more universal human concerns. Similarly, I will argue below that my approach does not depend on particular Christian commitments. See H. Richard Niebuhr, *Radical Monotheism and Western Culture: With Supplementary Essays*, Library of Theological Ethics (Louisville, KY: Westminster/John Knox Press, 1993).

8. Mary Garth, quoted in Eliot Wigginton, ed., *The Foxfire Book* (Garden City, NY: Anchor Books, 1972), 120.

9. H. Richard Niebuhr, *The Responsible Self: An Essay in Christian Moral Philosophy* (New York: Harper & Row, 1963), 109–26.

10. Niebuhr, *The Responsible Self*, 112.

11. Niebuhr, *The Responsible Self*, 122.

12. Niebuhr, *The Responsible Self*, 123.

13. Niebuhr, *Radical Monotheism*, 107.

14. Niebuhr, *Radical Monotheism*, 112.

15. Thomas James, "Responsibility Ethics and Postliberalism: Rereading H. Richard Niebuhr's The Meaning of Revelation," *Political Theology* 13, no. 1 (December 4, 2012): 46, doi:10.1558/poth.v13i1.37.

16. H. Richard Niebuhr, *The Meaning of Revelation* (Louisville, KY: Westminster/John Knox Press, 2006), xxxiv.

17. Niebuhr, *Responsible Self*, 126.

18. James M. Gustafson, *Ethics from a Theocentric Perspective, Volume 2: Ethics and Theology* (Chicago: University of Chicago Press, 1992), 153.

19. James M. Gustafson, *A Sense of the Divine: The Natural Environment from a Theocentric Perspective* (Cleveland, OH: Pilgrim Press, 1994), 148.

20. Gustafson, *A Sense of the Divine*, 26–27.

21. James M. Gustafson, *Ethics from a Theocentric Perspective, Volume 1: Theology and Ethics* (Chicago: University of Chicago Press, 1981), 84.

22. Niebuhr, *The Meaning of Revelation*, 55–60.

23. Iris Murdoch, *The Sovereignty of Good*, 2nd ed. (London: Routledge, 2001), 37.

24. Murdoch, *The Sovereignty of Good*, 68.

25. Murdoch, *The Sovereignty of Good*, 83.

26. Gustafson, *A Sense of the Divine*, 23.

27. Murdoch, *The Sovereignty of Good*, 86–89.

28. Wendell Berry, *The Art of the Commonplace: The Agrarian Essays of Wendell Berry*, ed. Norman Wirzba, (Emeryville, CA: Shoemaker and Hoard, 2002), 23.

29. Berry, *The Art of the Commonplace*, 299.

30. See, for example, Berry, *The Art of the Commonplace*, 188–89.

31. Berry, *The Art of the Commonplace*, 27.

32. Murdoch, *The Sovereignty of Good*, 83–87.

33. Eliot Wigginton, ed., *Foxfire 2* (Garden City, NY: Anchor Books, 1973), 25.

34. Wigginton, *The Foxfire Book*, 37.

35. Wigginton, *The Foxfire Book*, 212–27.

36. Wigginton, *The Foxfire Book 2*, 326.

37. Wigginton, *The Foxfire Book 2*, 339.
38. Wigginton, *The Foxfire Book 2*, 274–303; Wigginton, *The Foxfire Book*, 130.
39. Wigginton, *The Foxfire Book*, 307.
40. Wigginton, *The Foxfire Book*, 336.
41. Wigginton, *The Foxfire Book*, 343.
42. Rebecca R. Scott, *Removing Mountains: Extracting Nature and Identity in the Appalachian Coalfields* (Minneapolis: University Of Minnesota Press, 2010), 31.

REFERENCES

Berry, Wendell. *Our Only World: Ten Essays*. Berkeley, CA: Counterpoint, 2015.
———. *The Art of the Commonplace: The Agrarian Essays of Wendell Berry*. Edited by Norman Wirzba. Emeryville, CA: Shoemaker and Hoard, 2002.
Boff, Leonardo. *Cry of the Earth, Cry of the Poor*. Maryknoll, NY: Orbis Books, 1997.
Casey, Edward S. *Getting Back into Place: Toward a Renewed Understanding of the Place-World*. Bloomington: Indiana University Press, 2009.
Catholic Bishops of Appalachia. *This Land Is Home to Me (1975) and At Home in the Web of Life (1995): Appalachian Pastoral Letters*. Martin, KY: Catholic Committee of Appalachia, 2007.
Gustafson, James M. *A Sense of the Divine: The Natural Environment from a Theocentric Perspective*. Cleveland, OH: Pilgrim Press, 1994.
———. *Ethics from a Theocentric Perspective, Volume 1: Theology and Ethics*. Chicago: University of Chicago Press, 1981.
———. *Ethics from a Theocentric Perspective, Volume 2: Ethics and Theology*. Chicago: University of Chicago Press, 1992.
James, Thomas. "Responsibility Ethics and Postliberalism: Rereading H. Richard Niebuhr's The Meaning of Revelation." *Political Theology* 13, no. 1 (December 4, 2012): 37–59.
Leopold, Aldo. "The Land Ethic." In *Environmental Ethics: An Anthology*. Edited by Andrew Light and Holmes Rolston, 38–46. *Blackwell Philosophy Anthologies* 19. Malden, MA: Blackwell Pub, 2003.
Murdoch, Iris. *The Sovereignty of Good*. 2nd ed. New York: Routledge, 2001.
Niebuhr, H. Richard. *Radical Monotheism and Western Culture: With Supplementary Essays*. Library of Theological Ethics. Louisville, KY: Westminster/John Knox Press, 1993.
———. *The Meaning of Revelation*. Louisville, KY: Westminster/John Knox Press, 2006.
———. *The Responsible Self: An Essay in Christian Moral Philosophy*. 1st ed. New York: Harper & Row, 1963.
Scott, Rebecca R. *Removing Mountains: Extracting Nature and Identity in the Appalachian Coalfields*. Minneapolis: University Of Minnesota Press, 2010.
Wigginton, Eliot, ed. *Foxfire 2*. Garden City, NY: Anchor Books, 1973.
———, ed. *The Foxfire Book*. Garden City, NY: Anchor Books, 1972.

Chapter Six

An Ecotheology of Hunting

Perry Hodgkins Jones

In the southeast United States, the pervasiveness of hunting imagery and paraphernalia is hard to miss.[1] The popularity of camouflaged clothing and logos of arms or ammunition manufacturers are obvious even to those outside the hunting community. These emblems and accessories are found in nearly every gas station and on countless vehicles on the highway as well. As a frequent traveler, I have noticed that a specific symbol, affixed to the rear windows of pickup trucks and family cars along the highway, is overwhelmingly popular. At first, it looked to me like a kind of dancing figure doing a pirouette. It was only after asking a friend with this same sticker on his rear window that I was able to see the emblem for what it was: a bold lined buck with stylized antlers and the image of a doe as the negative space inside the line, the symbol of Browning Arms Company. I also have noticed another trend: this and other hunting symbols, frequently bucks or ducks, are commonly accompanied by Christian stickers like crosses, angels, scripture verses, denominational symbols, and so forth. As a student of theology, I began wonder whether these were expressions of contradictory identities or whether one can be both a hunter and a Christian.

Thus began my questions about the place of animals in Christian theology and whether a human acting as predator is something that can be condoned by the church as Christlike, especially in this era when hunting is not required for acquiring meat for the majority of the American population. If we are to widen our circle of theological consideration to include nonhuman animals, do they then fall under the commandment "thou shalt not kill," or do we enter into an alternative understanding with the role of hunter that is not only excusable but also perhaps even encouraged by the church? This chapter explores the theological and ethical considerations of contemporary hunting practices in the United States. By including animals, for example, in our understanding of incarnation and redemption, how then are we to treat them in a practical ethical manner?

Using the Christian ethical approach to animals as set up by Elizabeth Johnson's *Ask the Beasts: Darwin and the God of Love*[2] and David Clough's *On Animals: Volume 1: Systematic Theology*,[3] and an analysis of the relationship between hunters and conservation movements, this chapter attempts to provide a comprehensive ecological and theological ethic for hunting. The theocentric ethic given by Johnson and also by Clough informs this chapter's investigation of a Christian attitude toward animals as part of God's creation and as included in Christ's reconciliation of all things (for example, 2 Corinthians 5:19). Focusing on contemporary American hunting, I will analyze the effects hunting has on populations of animals, look at examples of different practices of hunting and the pain these practices may cause several species, and respond to the question of hunting as sport in an industrialized country, where meat is accessible in most grocery stores.

In the first place the tradition of environmental preservation in the hunting community may be surprising to many: conservation in the United States has been largely funded and supported by hunters and hunting outfitters who follow strict guidelines and restrictions for species type, season, quantity, and use; taxes on firearms, permits, and ammunition in North America fund many conservation movements; hunters are one of the most vocal and strongest lobbying groups for the responsible use of environments. Hunting, including fishing, has become less of a pastime and more of a relational and familial experience for individuals. And importantly, pursuing game animals as a part of a farm diet or as supplemental meat for a family table can be much more intimate than going to a supermarket that ships in meat from all over the country or world, likely from "farms" that are neither animal- nor environment-friendly. Hunting involves direct participation in the process from start to finish.

In search of a theological approach that includes animals, I found David Clough's most recently published volume *On Animals* had been released in time to offer substantial historic and theological background for this question. His second volume was not published at the time this chapter was written, but it will address practical ethical applications of this systematic theology on animals. Elizabeth Johnson also addresses the place of nonhuman animals in Christian theological terms. Both authors share the conclusion that humans must consider nonhuman animals in their theological schemes to determine appropriate action and interaction. Though Clough and Johnson differ in their ideas of redeemed living for predators, both take a comprehensive historical approach to ecotheology and present nonhuman animals as living in solidarity with humans as members of God's created order, being included in the redemption narrative of Christ and participating in a life of eschatological hope. Both Elizabeth Johnson and David Clough hold evolution as a widely accepted scientific theory and take issue with those who consider the theory theologically unnecessary.

David Clough presents a new consideration of animals both by reintroducing humans into the animal group and by expanding Christian theological categories of incarnation and redemption. By using a systematic theology that incorporates nonhuman animals, Clough insists on a revision of existing theologies that neglect to address all animals. Clough shows time and again how the Bible is "clear that other-than-human animals have a place in the purposes of their creator, that they are providentially sustained by God and respond to God in praise."[4] In his exploration of the theological implications of including animals into our theology of creation, incarnation, and reconciliation, Clough also reorients the human identity as a part of the greater animal order. In this animal-ness, humans are called to redefine neighbors and what it means to see Christ in one another.

Elizabeth Johnson also argues that instead of being exclusive of animals, theology should have space for and is actually quite inclusive of animals at the heart of the Trinitarian relationship. By comparing the seemingly sterile process of evolution with the loving God presented in the Nicene Creed, Johnson exposes the historic notion that the church and science have been classically understood as in conflict. In her new framework, she integrates the Holy Spirit with biological processes, such as mutation and natural selection, not in a causal role but as a connatural presence and indwelling. The suffering and pain that permeate the evolutionary history of the world are all redeemed when included in the cosmic reconciliation and redemption of Christ. By seeing all of creation as "groaning," Johnson introduces an ethic of consideration of animals as companions in a life of joy and pain. The ecological vocation to which all Christians are called is to include animals other than humans into our definition of neighbor, as fellow members of the *oikos*, or community/inhabited home in which we all live, and as

> the work of the Spirit of God who vivifies the community of creation from which we humans have also emerged. The ineffable holy mystery of Love creates, indwells, and empowers plants and animals, delights in their beautiful, wise and funny ways and grieves their sufferings. In the unexpected Christian view, the living God even chooses to become part of their story in Jesus Christ, a member of the community of life on this planet whose death and resurrection pledges a hopeful future for all.[5]

The possibility of ethical hunting raises two main questions. The first is whether or not killing of nonhuman animals is acceptable and the second is, assuming the first is satisfied, what the proper approach and methodology would be for hunting. As the second parameter of ethical hunting is dependent on the satisfaction of the first, we must first investigate the appropriateness of killing within the framework of implications that animals also live in eschatological hope.

Johnson introduces a notion of *deep incarnation*,[6] which presents Christ as sanctifying all matter through the incarnation, not just humans. Johnson and Clough each focus on the Greek word *sarx*, meaning flesh, earthly, or material, as the word used in John 1:14: "And the Word became flesh and lived among us."[7] That God became flesh and not exclusively human opens up the possibility of sanctification through incarnation for nonhuman animals. This inclusion also raises the question of eschatological life, which functions to guide and dictate earthly action. According to both Clough and Johnson, all animals have a place in the Eschaton; God's infinite nature has room for all that have been created, for if God had reason to create, God also has reason to redeem. David Clough highlights that when we consider the doctrine of redemption, we must remember that all are included regardless of time of death or species: "Just as we are accustomed to picturing human beings as being gathered up in Christ without regard to when they died, so we must become accustomed to think of other animals, too . . . being gathered up in the divine plan of redemption."[8] Therefore, when considering the resurrection of the body, one must ask whether all animals will maintain their essential nature or be transformed out of recognition in redeemed life. This is where Clough and Johnson seem to depart from one another. Elizabeth Johnson poses the question of redeemed form for predators with a sense of mystery and a strong notion of hope that the infinite can have space for even John Muir's bear.[9] Clough, on the other hand, prefers the "peaceable visions of Eden, Isaiah, Romans and Revelation"[10] and sees the promise of a Prince of Peace as meaning that the Kingdom of God will be a place without pain and therefore without predation. Both these approaches submit to the ultimate mystery of the Christian hope: we are unable to anticipate exactly what life will look like, but we expect both resurrection and transformation.

The different interpretations of redeemed living have profound effects on daily Christian practices. Clough concludes his volume by stating that human interaction and relation with animals "fall under the judgment of God and Christians therefore need to reconsider what account they can give of their actions."[11] If predation has a continuing place in the Reign of God, then we grant credence to Elizabeth Johnson's opinion of the sanctification of all predatory animals in their essences, which includes predatory instincts. In this image, the lion will be able to keep her hunting instincts and the predatory prowess that evolution has given her. If predation does not have a place in the Eschaton, then Clough's idea of complete transformation or peaceful living would be more correct. Clough understands redeemed living as perhaps maintaining the instinct of the predator but transformed as merely paying attention to would-be prey instead of maintaining true desire to kill or torture its subject. He sees a possible "perfect existence" for predatory animals in the Reign of God without causing pain and in which "they were freed from the burdens of having to kill to assure their continued existence." If Clough's image of redeemed living is correct and the Reign will be one in which "the lion will eat straw" (Isaiah 65:25), then what does this view imply for the meantime of life on earth?

Human predation in the form of ethical hunting may still be possible in the earthly realm if Clough's image of peaceful relationships in the Eschaton is not a command for this life but only the form into which all things will be transformed. If there is a command and a standard of not taking animal life to which all humans must adhere, then humans are exhorted to be total vegans or ovo-lactarian vegetarians with very strict parameters around husbandry. If there is not a command, then there exists the possibility that veganism is a form of eschatological vocation, of living into the image of redeemed life in the meantime, like celibacy is in many monastic traditions. As a "counsel of perfection," chastity, like poverty and obedience for other traditions, is not considered binding to all Christians or necessary for redemption. In the same way that celibacy does not condemn sexuality, veganism, as a sort of counsel of perfection for proper human relation with nonhuman animals, would not condemn omnivorous diets. And just as the alternative to celibacy is not promiscuity, the alternative to veganism is neither gluttony nor blood sport. There is a deep humility required in responsible sexuality through respectful monogamy, a humility that translates into the honoring of the alterity of an animal. In the same way ethical consumption of animals by omnivorous humans requires awareness of and participation in the process of acquiring meat. Hunting, then, offers the ethical eater the opportunity to observe, honor, and participate in the relationship of predator and prey. Ethical hunting in this manner would result not in a sense of power or machismo in the hunter but in awe and gratitude with an acknowledgment of the greater ecological context for that creature, its sacrifice, and the unavoidable creatureliness of all humans.

The Gospel teaches peaceful action, prayerful consideration, and forgiveness, which many see as contradictory to the predation involved in hunting, considered a violent and exploitative pastime in mainstream American culture. On the other hand, Christ never condemns consumption of other species and seems to assume a meat-eating culture. As an observant Jewish man in the first century, Jesus likely ate the Passover lamb each year. After his resurrection, Jesus requests food from his disciples and is given a "piece of broiled fish, and he took it and ate in their presence" (Luke 24:42–3). In the Gospel according to John, Jesus instructs his disciples on a better way to catch more fish than they could carry and is seen cooking fish over a charcoal fire to give to the disciples (John 21:9–14). As believers in the resurrection of the body, Christians must look to the image that the resurrected Christ posed to the disciples as an image of redeemed bodily life. In his presentation to the disciples, Jesus manifested as a material body with material needs, satisfying his hunger with fish. Is not this image, then, one of redeemed living from which we can extrapolate a general rule about what it means to have a resurrected body in the Reign of God?

It could be argued that in offering his body and blood in the Eucharist, not in flesh but in bread and wine, Jesus offered a vegan institution to replace the sacrificing of a lamb for Passover. This argument, however, would be in tension with his lesson that "it is not what goes into the mouth that defiles a person, but it is what comes out of the mouth that defiles" (Matthew 15:11). In the Beatitudes of Matthew, Jesus connects wrongful killing with anger, which could imply that the wrong attitude, one of retribution, punishment or power play in hunting could qualify it as unethical.

Now that the first question is answered, and we have satisfied that condition of possibility for the consumption of other animals to be sanctified, we must ask under what parameters hunters must operate in order to be ethical. David Clough argues strongly for the importance of reintroducing humans into the greater animal framework. As a part of a human identity, animalness also acknowledges a participation in a general food chain and predatory lifestyle. We must begin the conversation with an understanding that we are participating in the context of the modern American food industry. Though some may argue that it is not biologically necessary for humans to consume meat to survive, others see meat eating as part of a daily diet for the majority of Americans and many other cultures as well. The Department of Agriculture reported that in 2015 Americans consumed, on average, 211.1 pounds of poultry and livestock per person.[12] Our dietary choices and practices are also theological practices; how we treat creation, our bodies being a part of that creation, is very much a question of consumption and daily choice. The modern-day food industry treats animals as things, not with respect or even with acknowledgement as creatures, but as objects and economic units. Participating in this industry's profit and continuation by choice is a degrading and alienating process that has run our perception of animal dignity into the ground. This is a pervasive and unethical treatment of animals that should be condemned by humans with any sort of moral framework of animal rights.

Hunting, on the other hand, allows humans to participate in a natural predatory lifestyle, engaging the instincts of stalking, trapping, and chasing animals for subsistence and sport. Recreational hunting, unlike utilitarian hunting, does not have the end goal of the kill or the meat, per se, but rather kills and consumes the meat as a result of the pursuit—of the sport. Spanish philosopher José Ortega y Gasset's *Meditations on Hunting* explores the notion of the kill both ethically and existentially: "To the sportsman the death of the game is not what interests him; that is not his purpose. What interests him is everything he had to do to achieve that death—that is, the hunt. . . . Death is essential because without it there is no authentic hunting. . . . If one were to present a sportsman with the death of an animal as a gift he would refuse it."[13] Ortega y Gasset suggests that recreational hunting is not a blood sport, a pursuit of power over other animals, or an exercise in proving one's machismo or outdoor capabilities. The sport of hunting is about the pursuit, the technique, the reckoning between species, and the participation in the greater natural order of animal predation that has been lost by the majority of meat eaters in our world. The guns and other weaponry are in a sense incidental to the recreational hunter, who does not seek the death but the general experience or the passing down of wisdom from an older family member and the time spent quietly together in nature. By coming face to face with the animal that provides meat for food and witnessing it in its natural environment, the hunter becomes cognizant of the reality of the food chain and the source of nourishment for a large portion of our American diet. The reckoning between predator and prey can be a very spiritual and challenging experience; by forcing the human to acknowledge the life that is being sacrificed for his nourishment, he becomes immediately aware of his identity as simultaneously predator and animal. Ortega y Gasset comments on the participatory and natural experience that hunting can provide:

> a fascinating mystery of Nature is manifested in the universal fact of hunting: the inexorable hierarchy among living beings. Every animal is in relationship of superiority or inferiority with regard to every other. . . . Hunting submerges man deliberately in that formidable mystery and therefore contains something of religious rite and emotion in which homage is paid to what is divine, transcendent, in the laws of Nature.[14]

In maintaining that sense of hierarchy through his incarnation, Jesus Christ sanctified all flesh, including nonhuman animals, so the hunting community must operate carefully. Wasteful, trophy, and illegal hunting do not respect the dignity, nature, or integrity of nonhuman animals. Ethical hunting, therefore, requires careful attention to the repercussions of what may seem like minor details. Choice of firearms, for example, must be appropriate to the species one hunts and to the area in which one is hunting (rural versus hunting preserve); certain weapons that have crossed over from military grade to sporting gear and blurred the distinction are unquestionably inappropriate for the hunting of ducks and deer, though that is a separate topic altogether. A hunter must hone her skill to minimize risk of both human injury and unnecessary suffering for the targeted animal. Ammunition selection can help to reduce such risk as well, as there are bullets created for hunting specific species. A hunter must only kill and take what is needed for consumption in order to reduce or eliminate waste. When there is an excess of meat or hides from hunting, they should be prepared and donated to local food banks for future consumption or made use of in some other way. Wasteful or trophy hunting is not ethical; even if one hunts for recreation, the killed animal must be eaten and the parts that are unusable must be disposed of dutifully. Pursuing a specific size, color, or amount of a particular species for social recognition does not qualify as ethical hunting.

French twentieth-century philosopher Simone Weil identified respect for the autonomy of the other as the ideal form of relationship.[15] This concept that defines human relationships based on mutual distinctiveness must also be connected to human interaction with nonhuman animals. The animal pursued in the hunt must have a choice or opportunity to escape. The hunter that hones his skill and aim and who quietly and patiently observes the animal in its natural habitat with its natural habits has one chance at a kill shot, just as the animal has the chance to fly or run away. If a deer finds itself trapped at a fence or in some way restricted in its capacity to flee, then it doesn't have a sporting chance to live into its instincts as a prey species. Similarly, it would be unethical hunting to use explosives or poison. Respecting the natural context in which the animal's autonomy and evolved instincts are honored can lead to an even mystical experience.

The United States now finds itself in a situation in which, due to poor or ignorant wildlife management, hunting has become somewhat of a necessity to extirpate or decrease invasive or out-of-control populations in certain regions. The white-tailed deer, both the iconic target for hunters and an animal with a complex history in the United States, is a prime example of a species that has deleterious effects on environments and communities. Birth control options have proven to be largely ineffective in controlling this population in the United States, which went from around five hundred thousand nationwide in 1920 to almost thirty-five million today.[16] While some call the resurgence of the white-tailed deer a wildlife management success story for the United States, the lack of natural predators and the increase in suburban sprawl cause conditions that lead to hundreds of thousands of accidents in the country per year, the increase of diseases, and destruction of old-growth forests from large numbers of browsing deer.[17] Hunting has been proven to be the most cost- and result-effective method of wildlife management in terms of reduction of species due to mismanagement and habitat loss.

Commercial exploitation is extremely destructive to ecosystems and populations of animals, whereas private exploitation in the form of recreational hunting can be greatly beneficial to a population and greater ecosystems. Conservation biologists highlight the different effects of commercial versus recreational hunting, noting that "when a species is harvested commercially, the yield must be regulated by an organization whose existence and funding is independent of the economics of the industry that it regulates; otherwise it will necessarily endorse the quite rational economic decisions of the industry, which may well be to drive a stock to very low numbers and then switch to another stock." On the other hand, recreational hunting is "intrinsically safer than commercial hunting because sport hunters operate on an implicit discount rate of zero. Sport hunting, hence, has an enviable record of conserving hunted stocks. Instances of gross over-exploitation are rare but not unknown."[18] The common examples of blaming hunters for extirpating entire species like the carrier pigeon in the early twentieth century are grossly oversimplified and neglect to acknowledge the effects of other factors like industrialization, habitat loss, development, deforestation, and other forms of human encroachment.

Ethical hunting has also come to mean a greater contribution to the preservation and cultivation of wildlife and game species and their natural habitats. The historic relationship between hunters and conservation is storied and misunderstood. The modern mainstream nonhunting population may be surprised to learn how pervasive the conservation and even preservation movements by hunters have been in the past century, based on wildlife protection and population management and hunting territory wellness. The historic relationship between the hunting community and conservation is a complex one with surprising outcomes: people who hunt animals are also those who do the most to protect habitat and discourage behaviors that lead to species loss or endangerment. In the United States alone, organizations like Ducks Unlimited, The Theodore Roosevelt Conservation Partnership, The National Wild Turkey Federation, The Rocky Mountain Elk Foundation, The Wilderness Society, and dozens of others were founded by hunters who recognized how negatively habitat loss was affecting their hunting areas and the populations of animals. Today, hunters and anglers pay the highest fees for their recreational pursuits and contribute large sums of money to preservation, conservation, and wildlife management efforts.[19] The purchasing of permits and licenses, legal and taxed gear and firearms, etc. is therefore a necessary aspect of ethical hunting in modern-day America. The financial contributions of hunters to wildlife preservation in this manner has prevented further destruction and even helped to reverse habitat damage across the continent. Hunters have a much more intimate understanding of wildlife behavior, migration patterns, environmental needs, and the interdependence of species, whether on farms or in preserves. They thereby have a heightened awareness when environmental degradation occurs and a greater capacity to acknowledge and change it as a community through affiliations with groups like Ducks Unlimited.

If we are to see animals as included in God's beloved creation, incarnation, and redemption and humans as a part of the more general animal order, hunting must only be done when the prey is to be eaten and not wasted, the freedom of the animal is respected, and the tools with which one hunts must be carefully chosen to reduce risk and suffering. By widening the circle of consideration in theology, the exploitation of nonhuman animals becomes intolerable. Integrating all of creation into the Christian narrative of incarnation and redemption exposes Christ in the suffering of all nature throughout history in evolution and in the sacrifice of animals to each other through predation. It also insists on a deeper awareness of the conditions of creation and the responsibility to live honestly into our role as human animals: managing our environment responsibly and pastorally, changing for the better that which is in our power and reconciling our eating habits with our identity as predators living in eschatological hope. When respected, the relational, spiritual, and environmental experiences of hunting make it an honorable and worthwhile means of getting meat for an omnivorous country and can even have widespread conservation effects and benefits for ecosystems.

NOTES

1. Many ideas in this paper are results from conversations with the Rev. Dr. Robert Hughes in class and Dr. Gerald Smith in consultation. I am deeply grateful to them both for their contributions and guidance, but all mistakes in this chapter are mine alone.
2. Elizabeth A. Johnson, *Ask the Beasts: Darwin and the God of Love* (London: Bloomsbury Publishing, 2014).
3. David L. Clough, *On Animals: Volume 1: Systematic Theology* (London: T & T Clark, 2012).
4. Clough, *On Animals*, 173.
5. Johnson, *Ask the Beasts*, 285.
6. A term coined by Niels Henrik Gregersen in "The Cross of Christ in an Evolutionary World," *Dialog: A Journal of Theology* 40 (2001): 192–207.
7. All biblical references are from the New Revised Standard Version.
8. Clough, *On Animals*, 144.
9. Johnson, *Ask the Beasts*, 228.
10. Clough, *On Animals*, 159.
11. Clough, *On Animals*, 175.
12. With such a statistic, it is therefore safe to assume a meat-eating majority in the discussion of ethical eating and hunting. See United States Department of Agriculture, "Per Capita Consumption of Poultry and Livestock, 1965 to Estimated 2016, in Pounds," *National Chicken Council*, May 18, 2016, http://www.nationalchickencouncil.org/about-the-industry/statistics/per-capita-consumption-of-poultry-and-livestock-1965-to-estimated-2012-in-pounds/.
13. José Ortega y Gasset, *Meditations on Hunting*, trans. Howard B. Wescott (New York: Charles Scribner's Sons, 1972), 101.
14. Ortega y Gasset, *Meditations on Hunting*, 112.
15. Simone Weil, *Waiting for God,* New York: Harper Publications: 1951, 2009.
16. "None of the scientific studies demonstrated that reproductive control was effective in sharply reducing initial deer numbers. Other studies demonstrated that the typical cost for either reproductive control or surgical sterilization was approximately $1,000 in personnel and medical cost per deer." United States Congress, *The Science of How Hunting Assists Species Conservation and Management*, Hearing before the Subcommittee on Investigations and Oversight, Committee on Science, Space, and Technology, United States House of Representatives, 2nd Session, Serial no. 112–90, 112th, Cong. 5 (Washington, DC: U.S. Government Printing Office, 2012), https://www.gpo.gov/fdsys/pkg/CHRG-112hhrg74727/pdf/CHRG-112hhrg74727.pdf.
17. Lyme disease, anthrax, and bacterial diseases can be spread by deer and their external parasites. Greg K. Yarrow and Deborah T. Yarrow, *Managing Wildlife* (Birmingham, AL: Sweetwater Press, 1999), 110–11.
18. Anthony R. E. Sinclair, John M. Fryxell, and Graeme Caughley, *Wildlife Ecology, Conservation, and Management*, 2nd Ed. (Oxford: Blackwell Publishing, 2006), 317–18.

19. Malcolm Hunter, Jr. and James P. Gibbs, *Fundamentals of Conservation Biology* (Malden, MA: Blackwell Publishing, 2007), 50.

REFERENCES

Clough, David L. *On Animals: Volume 1: Systematic Theology*. London: T & T Clark, 2012.
Gregersen, Niels Henrik. "The Cross of Christ in an Evolutionary World." *Dialog: A Journal of Theology* 40 (2001): 192–207.
Hunter, Malcolm, Jr. and James P. Gibbs. *Fundamentals of Conservation Biology* (Malden, MA: Blackwell Publishing, 2007.
Johnson, Elizabeth A. *Ask the Beasts: Darwin and the God of Love*. London: Bloomsbury Publishing, 2014.
Ortega y Gasset, José. *Meditations on Hunting*. Translated by Howard B. Wescott. New York: Charles Scribner's Sons, 1972, 101.
Sinclair, Anthony R. E., John M. Fryxell, and Graeme Caughley. *Wildlife Ecology, Conservation, and Management*. 2nd ed. Oxford: Blackwell Publishing, 2006.
United States Congress. *The Science of How Hunting Assists Species Conservation and Management*. Hearing before the Subcommittee on Investigations and Oversight, Committee on Science, Space, and Technology, United States House of Representatives. 2nd Session. Serial no. 112–90. 112th Cong. 5. Washington, DC: U. S. Government Printing Office, 2012. https://www.gpo.gov/fdsys/pkg/CHRG-112hhrg74727/pdf/CHRG-112hhrg74727.pdf.
United States Department of Agriculture. "Per Capita Consumption of Poultry and Livestock, 1965 to Estimated 2016, in Pounds." *National Chicken Council*. May 18, 2016. http://www.nationalchickencouncil.org/about-the-industry/statistics/per-capita-consumption-of-poultry-and-livestock-1965-to-estimated-2012-in-pounds/.
Weil, Simone. *Waiting for God.* New York: Harper Publications: 1951, 2009.
Yarrow, Greg K. and Deborah T. Yarrow. *Managing Wildlife*. Birmingham, AL: Sweetwater Press, 1999.

Part III

Liturgical Practices and Hymnody

Chapter Seven

Singing to Subdue or to Sustain?

Looking for an Ethic of Conservation in Christian Liturgical Song and Hymnody

David Kendall

Hymns, chants, and songs are among the primary modes through which the Christian church has instructed, exhorted, and encouraged its congregants over much of the past millennium. From the simple devotional chanting of Psalms and biblical canticles in the early Christian era to settings for the immense quantities of liturgical texts of the mature church, music has played a central role in religious retention and evangelization. While there were many methods by which such evangelization and retention was accomplished, techniques from my own area of specialization illustrate their effectiveness. For example, colonial European powers used song as an effective method of conversion and catechism when seeking to convert newly encountered non-Christian populations. A common method was for missionary priests to enter a new region or village, learn the local language or dialect, and then teach the children to sing the basic doctrines and tenets of the faith. The children would then teach the adults, and the missionaries would thus have a foundation on which to build a new religious community.[1] Often, these community recitations would become an established local tradition with congregants meeting regularly to sing and recite.[2] From these early encounters, we can see that singing and chanting for corporate worship or for devotional purposes has remained a ubiquitous practice in Christianity until the present.

As hymn and chant repertories became standardized, they were often gathered into larger collections in choir books and hymnals. For ease of use, the musical materials were organized into separate books of related materials or different sections if the contents were bound in a single volume. In many cases, these materials were ordered according to liturgical function or followed the church year. In other cases, particularly those of the later Protestant traditions, they were organized by general subject material. There are numerous categories and organizational schema, such as the Power of God, Songs for the Home, Harvest Hymns, Wedding Songs, and Hymns for Christmas or Easter. These categories and the individual hymns populating them are often connected with common themes of Christianity and from specific passages in the Bible, generally passages that serve a specific spiritual lesson or pedagogical technique (such as memorization). But far less common, and consequently more difficult to find, are hymns that touch upon humankind's relationship with the earth, and, specifically, the nonhuman creation. The search for hymns of this kind is the subject of this chapter.

Among the reasons ecologically and environmentally focused hymns are rare in Christianity is the fact that biblical passages on the subject are themselves relatively infrequent, as is the general attitude of temporary pilgrimage found in much of Christian theology, emphasized in the following popular hymn text.

> This world is not my home,
> I'm just passing through.
> My treasures are laid up
> Somewhere beyond the blue.
> The angels beckon me
> From Heaven's open door
> And I can't feel at home
> In the world anymore.[3]

This song does not make any revolutionary statements or claims; rather, it resonates with sentiments found in parts of the New Testament. From the Pauline Epistles, we encounter them in the following passages: "But our citizenship is in heaven. And we eagerly await a Savior from there, the Lord Jesus Christ;"[4] "We are confident, I say, and would prefer to be away from the body and at home with the Lord."[5] The latter parts of the book of Revelation are full of imagery with ecological consequence up to and including a new heaven and a new earth.[6] While these passages and others like them can and have been interpreted allegorically, if taken to a logical conclusion, as often encountered in the hymnody, their message could be (quite literally) earth-shattering. If the world is not a permanent home, humanity does not have any particular mandate to care for it in a way that will ensure that it remains our home in the future, whether in our own lifetimes or for future generations. This outlook among many Christians, while positive in the sense that it often counters attitudes of rampant materialism[7] found outside (and too often, inside) the Church, is not very helpful for the earth when believers declare, "it's all going to burn anyway." While we may assert the dominance of this point of view, there are songs and hymns that illustrate both a recognition and a valuation of the earth. Among hymn texts that do exhibit a degree of ecological responsibility, we can detect three general categories, or ethics, at play. These include an Ethic of Acknowledgment, an Ethic of Subjugation, and an Ethic of Conservation.

I will explain each of the categories in turn, but what I am not including are simple references to the natural world or of nonhuman creatures that do not exist of their own selves, including references that are strictly symbolic or allegorical. The refrain of a recent hymn reads, "seed, scattered and sown, wheat, gathered and grown,"[8] but the references to seeds and wheat do not exist for the purpose or benefit of seeds and plants themselves but rather use them to symbolize the host of the communion sacrament. The common Latin liturgical hymn "Ave Maris Stella" ("Hail, Star of the Sea") refers specifically and exclusively to the Virgin Mary and not to stars or seas. Likewise, the countless settings of "Agnus Dei" ("Lamb of God") are not about lambs, neither are references to the Lion of Judah about lions or the Branch of Jesse about trees; all are explicitly personifications of Jesus Christ. Similarly, not included in the categories are comparisons or allegories between nonhuman creation and human and divine personages or of spiritual concepts. The commonly set passage from Psalm 42, "Sicut cervus desiderat ad fontes aquarum" ("As the deer longs for the streams of water") likens the soul's desire for God with the desire of a deer to quench its thirst. While the passage does acknowledge that deer exist and have physical needs, this acknowledgment is strictly anthropomorphic, having value only so far as it highlights and defines a purely human spiritual need.

AN ETHIC OF ACKNOWLEDGMENT

This category generally explains itself and is illustrated most easily through examples. A hymn that acts as a bridge between texts that I exclude from the three categories altogether, and one that fits into the first category, the Ethic of Acknowledgment, is "The Holly and the Ivy." This Gloucestershire folk carol, generally associated with the Christmas season, is an example of a setting that both acknowledges the existence of the nonhuman creation on its own merits and serves as a religious/pedagogical tool. These two facets exist in a delicate balance without one hindering the other. Most of the verses follow here; the last is the refrain.

> The holly and the ivy,
> When they are both full grown,
> Of all the trees that are in the wood,
> The holly bears the crown.
>
> The holly bears a blossom,

> As white as the lily flower,
> And Mary bore sweet Jesus Christ,
> To be our sweet Saviour.
>
> The holly bears a berry,
> As red as any blood,
> And Mary bore sweet Jesus Christ
> For to do us sinners good.
>
> The holly bears a prickle,
> As sharp as any thorn,
> And Mary bore sweet Jesus Christ
> On Christmas day in the morn.
>
> The holly bears a bark,
> As bitter as any gall,
> And Mary bore sweet Jesus Christ
> For to redeem us all.
>
> The rising of the sun
> And the running of the deer,
> The playing of the merry organ,
> Sweet singing in the choir.[9]

The descriptions of the holly tree are detailed and accurate and present it as an integral part of the natural world with few potentially anthropomorphic images, such as the red berry likened to (ostensibly human) blood. The holly tree is not presented as particularly *like* anything in the human realm. Indeed the holly blossom, as a nonhuman part of nature, is likened to another part of the nonhuman creation, the lily flower. The carol does not begin with the reference to growing things and later abandoning it to focus on issues of purely human interest but rather returns constantly to nature, presenting the human and nonhuman realms side by side, an equal billing that is rare in hymnody.[10]

Continuing on to what could be considered the mainstream of hymns created under the Ethic of Acknowledgment, I concede that there are very many such examples from outside the strictly Christian traditions of liturgy and hymnody.[11] However, the following hymn by Folliott Sandford Pierpoint illustrates the "classic" acknowledgment ethic.

> For the beauty of the earth,
> For the beauty of the skies,
> For the love which from our birth
> Over and around us lies:
> Christ, our God, to Thee we raise
> This our sacrifice of praise.

> For the beauty of each hour
> Of the day and of the night,
> Hill and vale, and tree and flower,
> Sun and moon and stars of light:
> Christ, our God, to Thee we raise
> This our sacrifice of praise. [12]

A similar sentiment is expressed in the following seventeenth-century German hymn by Paul Gerhart, later popularized in the early twentieth-century *English Hymnal* edited by Ralph Vaughan Williams.

> The duteous day now closeth,
> Each flower and tree reposeth,
> Shade creeps o'er wild and wood:
> Let us, as night is falling,
> On God our Maker calling,
> Give thanks to him, the Giver good.
>
> Now all the heavenly splendour
> Breaks forth the starlight tender
> From myriad worlds unknown;
> And man, the marvel seeing,
> Forgets his selfish being,
> For joy of beauty not his own. [13]

In these two hymns, the nonhuman created world exists, and it is glorious and beautiful; it causes humankind to praise the creator, and in the case of the Gerhart hymn, even causes man to forget his dominant position in the created hierarchy. While this is a relatively enlightened attitude, there is still nothing that defines the creation as valuable in itself and nothing that defines human responsibility or relationship to it except as reminder or prompt to praise God.

A number of hymns do go further than strict acknowledgment and describe God's special regard for the creation but with no further command or charge for humankind to display a similar regard and care. This hymn by Cecilia M. Caddell is characteristic of the type.

> Behold the lilies of the field,
> They neither toil nor sow;
> Yet God doth all things needful yield,
> That they may bud and blow.
>
> Not Solomon in glory shone
> Like one of these poor flowers,
> That look to God, and God alone,
> For sunshine and for showers. [14]

This hymn provides a potential lesson when read between the lines. The two verses above are settings of Matthew 6:28–9. The next verse (30) reads: "If that is how God clothes the grass of the field, which is here today and tomorrow is thrown into the fire, will he not much more clothe you—you of little faith?"[15] Implied within that passage is the fact that God clothes and cares for the flowers of the field despite the carelessness and capricious violence of mankind.

AN ETHIC OF SUBJUGATION

While the previous category of hymns recognizes the existence of the nonhuman creation on its own terms, it does not much connect with the human realm outside of a simple acknowledgment or as a reminder to humankind to look beyond its own limited sphere. The second category, an Ethic of Subjugation, does link the creation with humans and human activity and in a very specific way. In Genesis 1:28, humankind is commanded by God to multiply themselves and to subdue and have dominion over the earth and everything in it. The hymnody found in this category includes either echoes of the language of Genesis 1:28 or language that classifies creation as an object of value but for humankind alone. To put it another way, these hymns describe God's love for and control over the creation and the benefits received by humanity as a result, but no further command is given, overtly or implied, for mankind to express a concern for or perform any duty toward the creation other than so far as it benefits humanity directly. The following text by Isaac Watts, originally published in 1715, illustrates this reality in a very concentrated manner in the three verses commonly found in modern hymnals.

> I sing the almighty power of God,
> That made the mountains rise;
> That spread the flowing seas abroad,
> And built the lofty skies.
> I sing the wisdom that ordained
> The sun to rule the day;
> The moon shines full at his command,
> And all the stars obey.
>
> I sing the goodness of the Lord,
> That filled the earth with food;
> He formed the creatures with his word,
> And then pronounced them good.
> Lord, how thy wonders are displayed,
> Where'er I turn mine eye;
> If I survey the ground I tread,
> Or gaze upon the sky!
>
> There's not a plant or flower below,
> But makes thy glories known;

> And clouds arise, and tempests blow,
> By order from thy throne.
> Creatures (as numerous as they be)
> Are subject to thy care:
> There's not a place where we can flee,
> But God is present there.[16]

Much of the language of the hymn is similar to that found in texts in the first category, the Ethic of Acknowledgment. But here, we see hints of the subjugation ethic in the very Genesis-like passages of parts of the text as well as in the implication that the nonhuman creation is made for the express benefit of humanity ("that filled the earth with food"). The third verse includes the phrase "subject to thy care," referring to God, but it is revealing that humanity created in the image of God also claims the creatures as subjects through Genesis 1:28, but these creatures are generally not subject to humanity's care. That part is still left to God.

The following hymn, from a seventh-century Latin source, takes a similar path in including the language of acknowledgment together with language specific to subjugation, including the word "subdued." Humankind's status above that of the rest of creation is also specifically mentioned, implied through the discussion of "rank" through which "service" may be rendered.

> Maker of men, from Heaven Thy throne
> Who orderest all things, God alone;
> By Whose decree the teeming earth
> To reptile and to beast gave birth:
>
> The mighty forms that fill the land,
> Instinct with life at Thy command,
> Thou gav'st subdued to humankind
> For service in their rank assign'd.[17]

Similarly, the next hymn, originally intended for children,[18] values the creation (flowers in this case) strictly in terms of how they may benefit humanity: they brighten our hours, bring joy to our lives, and provide inspiration to our spiritual journeys. The significance of flowers is admitted but only in terms of physical and spiritual utility and benefit to humanity.

> God gives us the flow'rs, the radiant flow'rs;
> What joy to our life they bring!
> With gladness they crown our brightest hours,
> Inspiring hearts to sing.
>
> God gives us the flow'rs, the beautiful flow'rs,
> His wonderful love to show;
> And we may be flow'rs, His own bright flow'rs,
> If true to His word we grow.[19]

The following hymn is among the most expansive glosses on Genesis 1:28 I have yet encountered. In Isaac Watts's hymn above, mankind's dominant position is implied between the lines, as it were. Here, man's right to dominion over the earth is directly and unequivocally confirmed; it is secured by his proximity to God as the possessor of God's image with the nonhuman creation's sole purpose to provide for humanity's needs and wants.

> O Lord, our God! how great art thou!
> To whom all earthly Creatures bow;
> To thy unbounded Sway subjected:
> How great is through the World thy Fame!
> Oh! may thy ever glorious Name
> Be still, with Rev'rence due, respected.
>
> LORD, what is Man! surpris'd, I cry,
> That thou should'st thus his Wants supply,
> And take him under thy Protection!
> Or what his Offspring, prove so kind,
> To keep them ever in thy Mind,
> And guide them by thy sure Direction.
>
> Him cloth'd with Pow'r thou didst create,
> And crown'd with Dignity and State,
> In high exalted Station placed;
> Ev'n next to thy celestial Train;
> Thou gav'st him o'er all thy Works to reign.
>
> For him the lowing Oxen toil,
> To make the Earth with Plenty smile,
> And give their Labours uncomplaining:
> The bleating Sheep their Fleeces yield:
> He rules the Creatures of the Field,
> And those in desert Wilds remaining.
>
> To him thou hast in Mercy giv'n
> The Birds that mount the azure Heav'n,
> With out-stretch'd Wings the Air dividing:
> And all the Fish that thro' the Sea,
> Delight to cut their liquid Way,
> With glossy Fins for ever gliding.[20]

The actions of the earth and the nonhuman creatures are described in terms that sometimes imply enjoyment and, potentially, the capacity for self-awareness. The earth is made to "smile" with her plenty, and the fish of the sea "delight to cut their liquid way." However, in other places the language is strictly that of subjugation, where the oxen "toil" and the sheep "yield" their fleeces.

AN ETHIC OF CONSERVATION

While the previous categories acknowledge the existence of the nonhuman creation, or recognize its value for human needs, an Ethic of Conservation often admits of these prior classifications with some important additions. These additions include the confession that the members of the nonhuman created world each have value on their own terms and also that humanity has a responsibility to value and care for that nonhuman creation. This Ethic is by far the smallest of the categories found in hymns and songs and can be difficult to find, being often obscured by metaphors and rhetorical devices. The following hymn is similar in some respects to ones in the earlier categories. Like them, it places humans and the nonhuman creation side by side, as it were, in the text. Unlike texts belonging to the other categories, it admits the varied states of existence for the nonhuman creation, including their capacity to fade and die as a negative value unrelated to human consumption or need. More still, it presents the creation (flowers in this case) as possessing virtues and attributes worthy of human attention and imitation. While knowledge of these capacities and virtues still result in greater understanding and compassion within the *human* realm, it is a distinct step forward.

> We children, Lord, have come
> Into thy courts today,
> Bringing thee flowers from school and home,
> Glad with our offerings gay.
> Not for ourselves we bring
> This growth of sun and rain,
> But for thy children suffering
> Dark hours on beds of pain.
>
> Here is the deep red rose,
> Emblem of martyr's love;
> Here, too, are lilies white like those
> Who walk with Christ above.
> Sweet are they all, O Lord,
> And sweet to give our best;
> But sweeter still thy promised word
> To give the sufferers rest.
>
> Fair are these earthly flowers,
> Varied their bright array,
> Short is their term of sunny hours,
> Brief is their summer day.
> So must we too appear,
> As in thy light we stand,
> So short, so brief our sojourn here,
> So close the unknown land.[21]

Here there are some allegorical uses of plant life (i.e., the red rose emblematic of human martyrs), but also both a confession of the actual life of the flowers ("growth of sun and rain" and "short is their term") and the fact that they may be used for a higher purpose, albeit in this case for the purpose of alleviating human suffering. In the text, life, capacity for suffering, and ultimate fate of both humans and flowers are placed on the same plane in relatively equal positions.

This 1836 hymn by Joseph Anstice takes a similar tack:

> We cannot trust him as we should;
> So chafes weak nature's restless mood
> To cast its peace away;
> But birds and flowerets round us preach,
> All, all the present evil teach
> Sufficient for the day.
>
> Lord, make these anxious hearts of ours
> Such lessons learn from birds and flowers,
> Make them from self to cease;
> Leave all things to our Father's will,
> And taste, before him lying still,
> E'en in affliction, peace.[22]

While similar to others belonging to the Ethic of Acknowledgment, this hymn uses lessons gleaned from the nonhuman creation to teach human lessons. However, the birds and the flowers here are not only symbolic of attitudes humans should imitate; rather, they embody *actual* values that are innate to their own identities. In this sense, they are teaching humans to imitate that which humans themselves do not naturally possess. Implicit (but rather deeply buried) in that teaching is the need for humankind to value and cultivate these representatives of nonhuman creation in order that they may imitate them and improve their own lot.

We must move well into the twentieth and twenty-first centuries in order to find hymns with clear and direct commands to treat the nonhuman creation with respect and care. Even in the following, more enlightened text, humankind's power over the nonhuman creation is assumed and a "this world is not my home" sentiment is present, and the strongest exhortations are commands to avoid abusing the "toil" of other humans. Still, the hymn places humankind firmly in a kinship relationship with the rest of creation with the value of the natural world coupled with appeals to conserve and protect it.

> Lord, bring the day to pass
> When forest, rock and hill,
> The beasts, the birds, the grass,
> Will know your finished will:
> When we attain our destiny
> And nature lives in harmony.

> Forgive our careless use
> Of water, ore and soil—
> The plenty we abuse
> Supplied by others' toil:
> Save us from making self our creed,
> Turn us towards each other's need.
>
> Give us, when we release
> Creation's secret powers,
> To harness them for peace—
> Our children's peace and ours:
> Teach us the art of mastering
> In servant form, which draws death's sting.
>
> Creation groans, travails,
> Futile its present plight,
> Bound till the hour it hails
> God's children born of light,
> Who enter on their true estate.
> Come, Lord: new heavens and earth create. [23]

The last few decades have seen an increased interest in environmental themes in traditional hymnody. The following hymn is similar in many respects to the one above, but the exhortations are couched in the more modern and familiar terms of the environmental movement, and the balance of the exhortation is to avoid abuse of the creation itself and not only those things specifically detrimental to humanity.

> The earth is the Lord's and the fullness thereof.
> Creation reminds us, O God, of your love.
> By grace we are learning, as year leads to year,
> We're called to be stewards, your caretakers here.
>
> Your rainforests nurture the world that we share.
> Your wetlands give animals shelter and care.
> Your coral reefs cradle the life of the sea.
> You've shown us, in love, what your good world can be.
>
> Too often, O God, we abuse your good earth.
> We fail to remember its beauty and worth.
> We take from creation much more than we need,
> We threaten your world through indifference and greed.
>
> May we be good stewards of all that you give,
> Protecting creation wherever we live.
> May we be a church that renews and restores
> And lovingly cares for this earth that is yours. [24]

If hymns and songs continue to be a primary mode of instruction, exhortation, and encouragement for the Christian church, it is clear that ecological and environmental themes in such hymns and songs will expand as the church increases its focus in those directions. While there has been antagonism between many mainline Christian denominations and related organizations and the modern environmental movement, their stated goals and methods regarding environmental responsibility and stewardship are not fundamentally opposed. There is hope that the organized church will continue to recognize that the nonhuman creation has value and should be preserved and protected through concerted action, as well as through theology and pedagogy, including hymns and songs. The rate at which recognition and action can occur may depend on other social and political alliances existing within organized Christianity that have common cause with parts of the organized Church but that oppose the environmental movement.[25] In this context it may be that hymns and songs will become, as they have been many times in history, songs of protest and action as well as instruction and encouragement, meant to motivate and inspire, but in an oppositional manner. Challenging that common attitude in Christian hymnody, people may well sing: "This world *is* my home."

NOTES

1. For an example from the Philippines of this process, see Angel Martinez Cuesta, trans. Alfonso Felix, Jr. and Sor Caritas Sevilla, *History of Negros* (Manila: Historical Conservation Society, 1980), 87.

2. Pedro Chirino, S.J., trans. Ramón Echevarria, *Relacion de las Islas Filipinas: The Philippines in 1600* (Makati: Historical Conservation Society, 1969), 428.

3. Traditional. Unknown author.

4. Philippians 3:20 (New International Version).

5. 2 Corinthians 5:8 (New International Version).

6. Revelation 21:1 (New International Version).

7. Referring to those parts of the creation that can be exploited, monetized, coveted, or that have become objects of desire, lust, or avarice. Not all of the nonhuman creation is yet subject to these conditions though not for lack of trying on the part of humankind.

8. Dan Feiten (comp.), Eric Gunnison, R. J. Miller (arr.), "Seed, Scattered and Sown," *Ekklesia* (Bellingham, WA: Ekklesia Music, Inc., 1987), http://www.ekklesiamusic.com/track/323805/seed-scattered-and-sown?feature_id=48717.

9. Cecil J. Sharp, ed., *English Folk-Carols* (London: Novello & Co., 1911), 18.

10. Further research may show folk tunes to have this "equality of imagery" not found in hymns from more learned traditions or those primarily concerned with theological scholarship and doctrine.

11. Among the most well-known examples from the Western art music tradition are Antonio Vivaldi's four violin concertos known as *Le quattro stagioni* (The Four Seasons), published in 1725; Ludwig van Beethoven's Sixth Symphony (called the "Pastoral") from 1808; and Franz Josef Haydn's oratorios *Die Schöpfung* (The Creation, 1797–1798) and *Die Jahreszeiten* (The Seasons, 1801). The nineteenth century is crowded with many further examples.

12. Text by Folliott Sandford Pierpoint. First published in Rev. Orby Shipley, ed., *Lyra Eucharistica* (London: Longman, Green, Longman, Roberts, and Green, 1864), 340–41. The first two of eight total verses were used in the example.

13. From an original German text by Paul Gerhart, *Praxis Pietatis Melica*, 5th ed. (Berlin: Christoff Kunge, 1655). English translation in *The English Hymnal* (London: Oxford University Press, 1933), 399.

14. Text by Cecilia M. Caddell. *Catholic Hymns* (London: Burns and Lambert, 1853), 51.

15. Matthew 6:30 (New International Version).

16. Rev. Isaac Watts, *Divine and Moral Songs for Children* (London: T. Nelson and Sons, 1857), 6.

17. *The Day-Hours of the Church of England* (London: Joseph Masters, 1858), clxv.

18. I have often found that religious instruction to children is where our very worst theology, long abandoned by religious scholars, lives on in hiding.

19. Text by William W. Rock. *Elmhurst Hymnal* (St. Louis, MO: Eden Publishing House, 1921), 41.

20. *The Psalms of David with the Ten Commandments, Creed, Lord's Prayer, etc. in Metre* (New York: James Parker, 1767), 20–23.

21. Text by William Chatterton Dix. Hugh Blair and Albert Lister Peace, eds., *The Church Hymnal for the Christian Year* (London: Novello & Co., 1920), 91.

22. Text by Joseph Anstice. Roswell D. Hitchcock, Zachary Eddy, and Philip Schaff, eds., *Hymns and Songs of Praise for Public and Social Worship* (New York: A. S. Barnes & Co., 1874), 246.

23. Text by Ian Fraser. Stainer and Bell, Ltd., 1969 (copyright admin. Hope Publishing Co.). Used with permission.

24. Text by Carolyn Winfrey Gillette. 2001. Biblical References: Genesis 1–2, Psalms 8 and 24. Tune: Welsh Folk Hymn, Adapted in *Caniadau y Cyssegr*, 1839 ("Immortal, Invisible, God Only Wise"). Text: Copyright © 2001 by Carolyn Winfrey Gillette. All rights reserved. Used by permission. *Songs of Grace: New Hymns for God and Neighbor* by Carolyn Winfrey Gillette, Upper Room Books—Discipleship Resources, 2009. Email: bcgillette@comcast.net More hymns at www.carolynshymns.com.

25. Invoking Christ in one's political cause of choice is probably a technique nearly as old as Christianity itself and is partly what we are doing here in this volume. Among the more amusing political/social depictions of Christ, especially as juxtaposed with the common and traditional Christ as Shepherd portrayal, is Christ as Coal Miner, Christ as Corporate Executive, and Christ with a Rambo-style headband, twin bandoliers crossing his glistening, shirtless chest, gripping an AR-15 rifle.

REFERENCES

Anstice, Joseph, Roswell D. Hitchcock, Zachary Eddy, and Philip Schaff, eds. *Hymns and Songs of Praise for Public and Social Worship.* New York: A.S. Barnes & Co., 1874.

Catholic Hymns. London: Burns and Lambert, 1853.

Chirino, Pedro S. J. Translated by Ramón Echevarria, *Relacion de las Islas Filipinas: The Philippines in 1600.* Makati: Historical Conservation Society, 1969.

Cuesta, Angel Martinez. Translated by Alfonso Felix, Jr. and Sor Caritas Sevilla. *History of Negros.* Manila: Historical Conservation Society, 1980.

The Day-Hours of the Church of England. London: Joseph Masters, 1858.

Dix, William Chatterton, Hugh Blair, and Albert Lister Peace, eds. *The Church Hymnal for the Christian Year*. London: Novello & Co., 1920.

Feiten, Dan (comp.), Eric Gunnison, R. J. Miller (arr.). "Seed, Scattered and Sown." *Ekklesia.* Bellingham, WA: Ekklesia Music, Inc., 1987. http://www.ekklesiamusic.com/track/323805/seed-scattered-and-sown?feature_id=48717

Fraser, Ian. "Lord, bring the day to pass." London: Stainer and Bell, Ltd., 1969.

Gerhart, Paul. *Praxis Pietatis Melica.* 5th ed. Berlin: Christoff Kunge, 1655. Trans. in *The English Hymnal.* London: Oxford University Press, 1933.

Gillette, Carolyn Winfrey. "The Earth is the Lord's and the Fullness Thereof." *Songs of Grace: New Hymns for God and Neighbor.* Nashville: Discipleship Resources, 2009.

The Psalms of David with the Ten Commandments, Creed, Lord's Prayer, etc. in Metre. New York: James Parker, 1767.

Rock, William W. *Elmhurst Hymnal.* St. Louis, MO: Eden Publishing House, 1921.

Sharp, Cecil J., ed. *English Folk-Carols.* London: Novello & Co., 1911.

Shipley, Orby, ed. *Lyra Eucharistica.* London: Longman, Green, Longman, Roberts, and Green, 1864.

Watts, Isaac. *Divine and Moral Songs for Children.* London: T. Nelson and Sons, 1857.

Chapter Eight

Environmental Advocacy and the Absence of the Church

Jerry Cappel

Despite decades of hard work, stacks of data, and passionate pleas, the church seems barely moved by the injustices and spiritual disconnects the environmental crisis brings to its altars. "Green team" members trot out facts and figures and host documentaries created by those from the scientific and political battlefronts. They organize the use of fair trade coffee and washable dishes in efforts to raise awareness and align behavior. They make the case that good stewardship is wise and that environmental exploitation should be challenged by the church's prophetic voice.

Of course, much good work is being been accomplished here. Churches have long accepted the proper fit between its purpose and social justice and the long tradition of proper stewardship of God's gifts. Many books, teaching materials and programs have been created that inform and challenge church members to improve their stewardship, repent of consumerism and align their lifestyles.[1]

But environmental concerns remain relatively absent from the more central places in the church's life—its sacramental life of worship, practices of holiness, boundaries of fellowship, and messages of salvation. Environmental challenges often present as secular issues of material mismanagement rather than issues of soul and spirit. Clergy remain uninvolved in these issues they interpret as political, and bishops remain focused on more central and important "church matters." The sacramental and teaching life of the church remain unaffected, and the results appear shallow and disconnected to observers.

Willis Jenkins has noted this mismatch between the sacred and the secular even among environmental voices in religious circles. While secular environmental writers wax spiritual and poetic in their effort to express the beauty of the natural world and their sorrow over its destruction, religious writers deal in the factual and the scientific:

> Other cultural observers have noticed this spiritual creep in the environmental thought and trace religious valences in American environmentalism, sometimes with dismay. The veneration of nature, the feeling of prophetic alienation, the raptures and epiphanies, the sense of apocalyptic doom, the missional project of personal and cultural transformation—all this makes the environmental movement look religious. Meanwhile, the religious are beginning to look environmental.[2]

In the trenches of church work, this odd transposition of sacred and secular filters down into the daily work of environmental ministry. Creation Care teams are organized and promote activities for the buildings, grounds and hospitality committees, with occasional forays into education and an annual worship service, while the heart of church life remains unchallenged and unchanged. Its primary storytelling, expressed in music, preaching, and liturgy remains largely unaltered. These core sources of enculturation and formation remain largely unaffected.

These separations of heaven from earth not only separate the church from what is perhaps the single largest human issue in the world today, they also separate the church from the fullness of its own gospel of God's incarnation and salvation. Church members who feel the urgency of ecological concerns do not tend to feel confident challenging the church's liturgical and sacramental life. Clergy, teachers, and church members who focus upon things liturgical and sacramental do not connect them to ecological concerns. When the church's worship life is on the agenda, environmental concerns are absent. When environmental work is on the agenda, the church's worship life is absent.

This has spiritual consequences, separating not only the church from the fullness of its purpose, but also the Breath of God from clean air, Living Water from livable waters, the Bread of Life from daily bread, and the Body of Christ from creation's bodies. The result is a church uncertain of its own voice and a public uncertain of the church's relevance. Not just environmental ministry but also evangelism and spiritual formation suffer from these disconnects. The church needs help making the spiritual connections between what is happening with the natural ecosystems around her and within her own pews. These false dichotomies, perpetuated by false divisions of church ministry, lie at the root of the church's absence from environmental engagement.

TASK FOR REIMAGING THE EPISCOPAL CHURCH (TREC)

The challenge of this disconnect for environmental ministry can be illustrated by a recent process of listening conducted by The Episcopal Church's *Task Force for Reimaging The Episcopal Church* (TREC). In the final report to the General Council, they describe their process: "The Task Force spent two years in discussions with thousands of Episcopalians about their hopes, dreams, ideas, and concerns for the Church and about our collective mission to serve Christ."[3]

In those discussions, they asked participants to identify what they want the Church to maintain into the future and what they want to see changed. The list of items provided by the participants were then collated and rank ordered. In the Executive Summary, they summed up the responses to their questions, saying, "Taken together, all the responses suggest that what members value most about the Episcopal Church are the people, the sense of community and inclusion, and liturgical traditions."[4]

This should, of course, surprise no one. Most people engage church life for the community, not the work. They love the church primarily for its relationships, not its service. Works of service and acts of sacrifice play an important role, but they stem from being in community. As expected, then, when the researchers asked what things the church should hold onto for the future, items related to mission and service fell well behind items related to worship and fellowship. Similarly, when asked what would bring the most joy to them from the church in ten years, the answers were the same—people, community, love and inclusion. Service to the world and a sense of mission fell way down the list. In sum, the phrase that truly captured the hearts and minds of the faithful and hope for the future was "community of people."[5]

These Episcopal Church responses probably represent faith communities of all kinds. Thus they can illustrate why environmental concerns, when presented primarily as duties of advocacy and works of service, fail to capture the heart of the church. Such duty and work will always attract a few good souls who care deeply about the issues, but their numbers will remain low and their presence will remain marginal. Trying to move the church as a whole by depending upon calls to dutiful response to environmental facts is swimming upstream against the nature of religious communities, which are neither formed nor sustained around causes and concepts. They are formed around fellowship and sustained by the same. This cannot be beaten. It must be joined.

CELEBRATION, NOT OBLIGATION

It is neither gospel nor effective to go about wagging a green finger at the church and calling it to shame. What will engage each faith community at its center is not a louder call to duty but rather a call to celebration and fellowship. What will sustain engagement will not be cause but kinship. This is important because what the Senegalese poet and naturalist, Baba Dioum, said is true, "In the end, we will conserve only what we love. We will love only what we understand. We will understand only what we are taught."[6]

This can be adapted to say, *We will not save what we do not love, and we cannot love what we do not know.* We are kind to each other, care for each other and include each other, not because the other is a cause but because they are in some way family. And while much family making in the church is done in the trenches of common service, it is primarily located at the altar and in the fellowship hall, classrooms and homes. It cannot be the fruit of protest politics or self-denial (as important as those are in our day). It will be, rather, the work of inclusion and drawing near. And for this work, God's good creation needs to be more fully incorporated into parish life and the celebration of the gospel, which are the places where we learn to love each other.

In other words, at the heart of this work is to "familiarize" (make family) not just our human kin but the whole family of God's created order. And to create such an extended family within the church, the family story needs to be extended to include the nonhuman recipients of God's grace, who are also caught up in the unfolding work of God.

This need is explored in John Gatta's book, *The Transfiguration of Christ and Creation*, where he explains how integrating the theme of Christ's transfiguration into the theological and liturgical life of the church would serve to:

> Expand the ecological vision beyond the stewardship focus that has thus claimed almost exclusive attention among mainline churches . . . and enable her to respond in more integrally liturgical, contemplative and doxological terms, befitting her authentic charism as the church. For unless the church develops these latter gifts, she risks becoming, in her environmental witness, little more than a technically incompetent adjunct of the Sierra Club.[7]

Many leaders in environmental ministry learned their craft from the Sierra Club and similar groups and have naturally brought those methods to the churches in hopes of rallying the faithful to behavior change and social action. But at the same time, many clergy and other church leaders do not recognize the activity of the secular environmental movement as something "befitting the authentic charism [giftedness] of the church." To aid the recognition, authentic liturgical, contemplative, and doxological connections between the day's environmental realities and the regular life of the church need to be made. To fire the bones of the church, the realm of ecological wellbeing needs to be expanded beyond committee actions, material calculations, and life adjustments to include worship, holiness and salvation. Core Christian doctrines, such as the trinity and redemption, need to be revisited and reclaimed for their power to mediate such transformation. Gatta writes, "Participation in the interactive mystery of divine life points toward a model of earth ethics more profound than the 'stewardship' ideal now favored in religious circles, which suffers the liability of suggesting a commodity-based rather than a communitarian outlook."[8]

Gatta explores these connections and movements in his book and unpacks the Transfiguration as a central text. The key lies in how the transfiguration and other biblical stories can function within the life of the church to bring the whole creation onto the center stage of faith life. "The transfiguration points symbolically toward a doxological . . . rather than a resource-management model of apprehending our relationship to the natural world."[9]

A DISCONNECTED GOSPEL

Appeals to behavior change and advocacy are important as both entry points and basic obedience. But to function at the center of church life, environmental concerns need to connect with the central congregational stories that define a faith community's very identity as a called-out people living by the grace of God. Willis Jenkins identifies the heart of the matter, "Insofar as Christianity revolves around a story of persons healed, covenant restored, sinfulness redeemed, experience made holy, or the world reconciled, so far should environmental theologies seek soteriological roots."[10]

This is not a new suggestion. Joseph Sittler called for this in the early 1970s, and others have called for it since.[11] But it has not made its way into church practice. "Green" church members may organize recycling and present documentaries that call for ecocentric change, but they continue to pray and worship with words and symbols that marginalize creation. Any mention of creation in prayer or liturgy seldom rises above calls for gratitude and duty toward resources and objects of beauty. The story celebrated at the Eucharist may give creation honorable mention, but it then discounts its place in the story of graceful redemption. Thus, any deepened understandings about the relatedness of living systems and the role of human choices are then lost on the liturgy and diluted.

The church and creation need reconciliation, and as with all reconciliations, at its heart lies the question of relationship. As Willis Jenkins puts it, "The environmental crisis amounts to a crisis in the intimacies of God's salvation."[12] By "intimacies" he means fellowship: Who belongs and who does not? Who is loved and who is not? Who are players in our story and fellow pilgrims on our journey? By "salvation" he means celebration and hope for what God is doing in the world, but also where God is doing it: Within human persons? Among human communities? Throughout all creation? Is there hope for this body and this soil, or is there hope only for some other place and time? For what do we hope because God is active in the world?

The church is fairly experienced at debating these questions of intimacy and salvation in terms of human communities through issues of ethnicity, gender, class, and sexual orientation. Each version of the debate leads to questions of salvation and personhood. Each debate inevitably arrives at practical questions of fellowship—how is the church to relate to its kin, once named? Which voices are allowed? What care is taken? What roles are granted? And while these debates are far from settled, the environmental urgencies of the day are forcing an additional set of questions about intimacy and salvation in terms of nonhuman communities: the four legged, the finned, the winged, and the rooted. To what degree are they kin? Is their voice allowed? What care should be taken? What roles should be granted?

THE MARGINALIZATION OF CREATION

From early in its history, the Christian church developed language and concepts as a people separated from their own power and absent from their own land. They sought to find hope in a different day and a different place than the ground they presently failed to occupy. Their hope was based upon an inbreak of God's action from elsewhere to set things right somewhere else. From there the life of the church has gone on, as described by Jenkins, "Insofar as its notion of life with God could not live into the story of the land, the church read its scriptures, preached its sermons, planned its missions and baptized its members by landless, unsustainable theologies."[13]

This "landlessness" is deeply embedded in the modern church and acts as the very water in which it swims, making it difficult to recognize and even more difficult to change. This momentum of Christian history and tradition permeates the liturgy, music, polity, and teaching of the church. It can be described as the marginalization of creation within the Christian stories of our day. Some trajectories that perpetuate this marginalization have been compiled by Terence Fretheim, and it is illustrative to list them here:[14]

1. A focus on salvation history that places nature in the service of Israel's history;
2. Reading Jewish historic faithfulness as primarily competition with Near Eastern "nature religions;"
3. Relinquishing the study of nature to the scientists;

4. Theological perspectives that remove God from continuing life in the created order;
5. An existentialism that interprets all reality from human existence;
6. Political theologies that focus on the liberation of the human to the neglect of the nonhuman;
7. Preaching and sacraments that wholly focus on the salvation of the human;
8. Spiritualties that focus on the "otherworldly" to the neglect of the bodily and earthly;
9. End-of-world scenarios that celebrate God destroying the original creation;
10. The diminishment of the importance of the Old Testament in the preaching and teaching of the church;
11. A patriarchalism that emphasizes God's "mighty acts" of intervention over more feminine themes of nurture and blessing.

Fretheim's list is particularly challenging in that that it represents what many identify as the orthodox Christian faith rather than partial expressions subject to time and place. Those with an attunement to the day's larger web of life issues thus feel they have few options other than to turn away from Christianity altogether or keep silent within it. They may work to recruit the church's participation in environmental causes, but their challenge to the church's life of word and sacrament remains muted. On the other side of the aisle, those most committed to the church's life of faith and worship fail to see the relevance of environmental issues to the life of a church steeped in landless theologies. As long as environmental challenges are framed primarily as issues of environmental science, politics and economics, this division will continue. The need is to recognize what Norman Wirzba has so often called, "The destruction of the earth is, among other things, a theological catastrophe, and Christian apathy is a sign that theological reflection has lost its way."[15]

Thus, environmental ministry remains at the fringes of church life, and the church remains absent from these central issues of the day. An example of the core work needed within the church is to revisit and redo Fretheim's list of marginalizing trajectories in order to claim from the faith tradition trajectories that include the fullness of creation and the church's relationship to it:

1. A salvation history that begins with creation and ends with creation restored;
2. Reading Jewish historic faithfulness as centered on justice and trust in God;

3. Reclaiming a sacred role for the study of nature along with the scientists;
4. Theological perspectives that return God to a continued presence in the created order;
5. An ecological philosophy that interprets all reality from the whole web of life;
6. Political theologies that recognize how the liberation of the human depends upon the liberation of the nonhuman;
7. Preaching and sacraments that focus on the salvation of all creation;
8. Spiritualties that focus on the incarnational and sacramental presence of God in all creation;
9. End-of-world scenarios that celebrate God restoring the original creation;
10. The recovery of the importance of the Old Testament in the preaching and teaching of the church;
11. A relational view of creation that balances God's "mighty acts" of intervention with more feminine themes of nurture and blessing.

This is central, core church work that engages the church's traditional work of proclamation, fellowship, and celebration. This is work for clergy, teachers, musicians, and worship leaders. This is work for the lay leadership who abide at the heart of church matters, where priorities, purposes, and budgets are set. This is not work that can be done by only a few passionate members serving a cause at the edges of church life. This work requires the authority of those with a teaching office and access to the sacramental life of congregations.

This is also a tall order because its work lies at the heart of what a faith community loves, fears, and believes. It is a difficult task to challenge the core activities of being church, but the sheer relevancy of it, for both environmental and evangelical reasons, demands the church do so. To truly capture its commitment, the church will need to become more creation-inclusive in its understanding of salvation and redemption. To truly capture its heart, the church will need to expand its community of fellowship to include all of God's garden. To truly capture its imagination and soul, the church will need to incorporate these creation-inclusive trajectories into its hymnody, liturgy, art, and language. In so doing, creation care can become as natural as caring for other people—not as a cause, but as kin. Only then will the love for God's creation and participation in its health and well-being move from the fringes to the center of church life.

This challenge is concisely expressed by Larry Rasmussen (reflecting Joseph Sittler), "That the arc of creation does not match the arc of redemption is a big problem in Christianity."[16] It simply will not do to proclaim a gospel of God's work within a creation that cannot make sense of that gospel's "arc of redemption." It also will not do to perpetuate a gospel of God's work within a church that cannot make it fit the arc of creation. As long as this disconnect continues, people will adapt by either shutting down their Christian faith or shutting out the rest of creation. Both adaptations are evident within and without the church.[17] Church membership and participation declines as society fails to make sense of the Christian story within a 14.5 billion year-old evolving universe. Church engagement with the issues of creation remains stagnant as those in the church fail to make sense of a 14.5-billion-year-old evolving universe within their Christian story. Both conditions beg for a more holistic, creation-inclusive gospel.

Key to solving Rasmussen's problem is the work of drawing out from the Christian biblical witness expressions of the salvation of all creation as the work of Christ in the world (rather than simply as backdrop to the human salvation story). Claiming these expressions and establishing each as part of the foundational gospel story as told, celebrated, and lived within the church is essential to moving the issues of the day's environmental issues from the fringes of the faith community to the center pew. Then the church, in full embrace within its own gospel, can see its way to partner in God's unfolding salvation of all creation (rather than simply agenda items of justice and stewardship). David Horrell describes the depth of the work at hand, "Reading the Bible afresh in light of the environmental issues that face us involves reconfiguring the landscape, recasting the story, seeing the whole thing differently, and at the same time seeing ourselves and our world differently too."[18]

As with Fretheim's list of trajectories above, this work is not an exercise in inventing a new theology or salvation story but rather an exercise in aligning particular priorities of the day with existing (if muted) elements in the received Christian story. This is not some twisting of the tradition to meet modern demands. It is claiming and prioritizing biblical traditions in light of modern realities. It is not a rejection of orthodoxy or the Christian faith but is the same work the church has always done; as life on earth has presented various priorities and convictions in each day and time, "We are not simply claiming to read or present what the text 'says,' but are acknowledging that our reading of the Bible is a *construction*, shaped by certain priorities and convictions."[19]

Present-day environmental realities call for the particular hermeneutical work of revisiting and reinterpreting the place and purpose of the whole creation in God's love and work to discover what is misaligned and out of balance with the present day arc of creation. Particular themes within the whole Christian witness need to be valued while others are resisted. One list of necessary theological foundations for such rebalancing work can be drawn from Horrell's final chapter in his book, *The Bible and the Environment*:[20]

1. The goodness of all creation;
2. Humanity as part of the community of creation;
3. Interconnectedness in failure and flourishing;
4. The covenant with all creation;
5. Creation's calling to praise God;
6. Liberation and reconciliation for all things as a single work.

Each foundational item is a biblical part of the Christian witness but is not recognized as part of the modern popular religious witness. Each has also been muted within the milieu of Fretheim's trajectories listed above, such that the received popular Christian gospel proclaims that:

1. Creation's goodness is that of material gift to humankind;
2. Humanity is the pinnacle purpose of the community of creation;
3. Failure results from human sin while flourishing awaits transcendent intervention;
4. God's covenant is with humans with creation as backdrop;
5. Creation's praise of God is aesthetics but not fellowship or ethics;
6. Liberation and reconciliation of the human and nonhuman are separate spheres.

Making such a fundamental course correction within the church will require skill in recognizing how its gospelling has always been an act of both listening and selection. The church will need to be reminded that this is familiar work that has been done in other times and places and for other recent priorities: slavery, gender, race, and sexual orientation. Just as the bible, tradition and church practice continue to be revisited to find meaningful (and orthodox) alignment with these pressing issues, so it needs to be revisited to align with environmental issues. From within the very basic functions of life on earth, emerging priorities are raising challenges at the very juncture where the church names the place, purpose, and value of both the human animal and the larger web of life. To meet those challenges with a relevant gospel, the story of creation and the popular story of redemption need their own reconciliation.

Aligning the arc of redemption with the arc of creation is the heart of this work. If human beings are to thrive in a future environment, today's environmental behaviors need to change. If the church is to thrive in a future society, today's evangelical behaviors need to change as well. "Salvation is, after all, for the lost. Reclaiming our ecologies of grace can give us vocabularies of lament to name our sickened witness to prodigal powers defiling beauty, choking life, and wasting habitats."[21]

Such an aligned salvation story, in tune with biblical witness, needs to highlight the valued place of all God's good creation from beginning to end—the land, the trees, the animals, the stars, and the human community, all as one worshipping and suffering community, groaning together and looking together for the salvation of God, the redemption of all bodies and the renewal of the whole earth.[22] This is more than an opportunity for healing and wholeness throughout creation. This is opportunity for healing and wholeness within the church as well.

Such a course correction cannot succeed as an invented motivation to obtain church engagement with environmental issues. Nor can it be framed as work of the church for the sake of the earth. This is work of the church for the sake of the church as well. This is key. Making the connections between God's grace toward the human animal and God's grace toward all other animals is crucial for not only environmental motivation but for evangelistic motivation as well. For if the church cannot make sense of the world of creation, it will not be able to make sense of the human place in it either. If the church cannot provide a life-giving gospel story for the whole web of life, it will not be able to provide a life-giving gospel story for the human part of that web either.

Recruiting the church to the work of saving the earth is incomplete at best and misleading at worst. It is incomplete because it implies the earth has a problem but the church does not. It misleads because it frames the issue as a troubled earth in need of the church's repentance, rather than a troubled church in need of the church's repentance. The earth is indeed troubled, but so is the church, and the roots of both are intertwined. They both stem from fundamental misapprehensions of present-day realities along with gospel stories fundamentally insufficient to the task. Social myths of human progress that fail to account for ecological progress plague world politics and business practices. Christian gospels of human redemption that fail to account for the facts of the known universe or the biology, psychology, and sociology of the human animal plague the church. In both church and state, this leads to compartmentalization of issues, paralysis of motivation, and denial of truth in experience.

Making these connections brings an additional invitation to the church to move beyond the timidity and poverty of spirit called out by Teilhard de Chardin's *Mass on the World*, "Shatter, my God, through the daring of your revelation the childishly timid outlook that can conceive of nothing greater or more vital in the world than the pitiable perfection of our human organism."[23] Emerging environmental realities challenge the church to look and see whether it is indeed proclaiming little more than the "pitiable perfection" of the human enterprise, isolated somehow from the rest of creation (as if such were even possible). Such a challenge reaches to the church's understanding of God's work, love, and purpose and the human response to it. But making such challenges has always been a natural and core work of the church's prophetic voice.

The church will never find the heart to align its mission and purpose with the larger web of life as long as that web is missing from its celebration of God's work. Motivated members of the green team will always find themselves at the fringe of church life as long as the church's celebrated arc of redemption tells a story of human-only salvation separate from a web of life. The church's voice about ecological issues will always be muted as long as the book of life contains only the names of Homo sapiens.

A LIFE OF GRACE FOR ALL CREATION

The real work in the church, then, is not so much the science, but the Bible and tradition; not economics, but faith and faithfulness. The scientific realities of climate change, extinctions, and pollutions are but pointers that expose a misfit faith. The facts and figures of consumerism and eco-injustice expose the same. They extend an invitation to the church to respond not only to the troubling social issues brought to her doors but also to revisit her role in perpetuating the attitudes, worldviews, and habits that generate them. But it does not stop there. They also extend an invitation to the church to revisit her bounds of fellowship and message of salvation.

Just as faith communities continue to recognize and modify the places of gender or racial misalignment in its language and practices, the present day calls for the further work of recognizing and modifying the anthropocentrism that so permeates the language and practices of church life. To rightly understand and name the established trajectories that perpetuate a misaligned faith, church leaders will need to identify the many places in church life where such misalignments are proclaimed, celebrated, and taught. These are not simply the words of catechisms, sermons, and theology texts but also include the many places in church life where God's presence is set to music, ritualized, and danced. They include the places where gospel is more enculturated and absorbed than spelled out and spoken. Since these are the places where values and fellowship are formed, they are the places where the circle of fellowship needs thoughtful and deliberate expansion.

Such realignment cannot be accomplished through only seasonal lessons for children or occasional accommodations to nature lovers and environmental activists. To be core work at the center of church life, such realignment needs to be defined as the right engagement in the mission of God's whole gospel of salvation, which, as Paul writes in Colossians, chapter 1, "was proclaimed to every creature under heaven" and all of which, as he writes in Romans 8, along with us, "groan inwardly while we wait for adoption, the redemption of our bodies." Taking the opportunity to align in word and practice a gospel of salvation that encompasses the environmental realities of the present-day world would create an integrity and relevance that will connect to those within the church and those without.

Aligning word and practice is the appropriate domain of the church, whose work is to open human eyes to the truth of God's presence and work in the world and the right relationship to it. While the sciences can point to the way of things, faith must point to the value of things. This work truly befits the charism of the church, a work whose end is not to save the planet but rather to live rightly, as the Creator intended, and join in the celebration of a gospel of salvation that proclaims the reconciliation of all things in heaven and on earth.

NOTES

1. Compiled lists of resources are many. Two examples are GreenFaith's resource collection at http://greenfaith.org/resource-center and the National Council of Churches Eco-Justice resource page at http://www.creationjustice.org/educational-resources.html.

2. Willis Jenkins, *Ecologies of Grace: Environmental Ethics and Christian Theology* (New York: Oxford University Press, 2008), 9.

3. "Final Report of the Task Force for Reimaging The Episcopal Church," December 15, 2014, http://reimaginetec.org/TREC_Report.pdf. Their listening process was conducted from February 2013 through December 2014.

4. Ibid., 26.

5. Ibid., 39. The hopes and dreams of the Episcopal faith community are summed up in one phrase: community of people. Expressions of "care for the world" are about a world of people, not other creatures. Expressions of care and hope for the nonhuman world are practically nonexistent.

6. Baba Dioum, from a speech made in New Delhi, India to the general assembly of the International Union for Conservation of Nature, 1968.

7. John Gatta, *The Transfiguration of Christ and Creation* (Eugene, OR: Wipf & Stock, 2011), 73.

8. Gatta, *The Transfiguration of Christ and Creation*, 117.

9. Gatta, *The Transfiguration of Christ and Creation*, xx.

10. Jenkins, *Ecologies of Grace*, 17.

11. Joseph Sittler, "Called to Unity," in *Evocations of Grace: The Writings of Jospeh Sittler on Ecology, Theology, and Ethics*, ed. Steven Bouma-Prediger and Peter W. Bakken (Grand Rapids, MI: Eerdmans, 2000), 45–46.

12. Jenkins, *Ecologies of Grace*, 17.

13. Jenkins, *Ecologies of Grace*, 26. Even in times and places where Christianity became part of the economic establishment, a landless theology was a handy tool to evangelize and manage the landless classes.

14. Terence E. Fretheim, *God and World in the Old Testament* (Nashville: Abingdon Press, 2005), x–xi.

15. Norman Wirzba, "All Creatures: Ecology and the Eyes of Faith," *The Christian Century*, July 22, 2015, 26. http://www.christiancentury.org/article/2015-07/all-creatures.

16. Larry Rasmussen, "The Sacred 'neath Your Sole" in a speech delivered at the Festival of Faiths, Louisville, Kentucky, 2010. See Joseph Sittler, *Essays on Nature and Grace* (Philadelphia: Fortress Press, 1972), 18. See also Larry Rasmussen, *Earth Honoring Faith: Religious Ethics in a New Key* (New York: Oxford Press, 2013), 103.

17. This disconnect between how the Christian salvation story is commonly told and more recent understandings of our 14.5-billion-year-old universe is a problem not just for the environment but also underlies such controversies as the creationism/evolution debate, millennialism and many other issues.

18. David G. Horrell, *The Bible and the Environment: Towards a Critical Ecological Biblical Theology* (London: Equinox, 2010), 128.
19. Horrell, *The Bible and the Environment*, 122–23.
20. Horrell, *The Bible and the Environment*, 129–44.
21. Jenkins, *Ecologies of Grace*, 229.
22. See William P. Brown, *The Ethos of the Cosmos* (Grand Rapids, MI: William B. Eerdman's, 1999), 396–405. See also Denis Edwards, *Ecology at the Heart of Faith* (Maryknoll, NY: Orbis Books, 2006), 34–39.
23. Pierre Teilhard de Chardin, "The Mass on the World," in *Hymn of the Universe* (London: William Collins Sons; New York, Harper & Row, 1965), 25.

REFERENCES

Brown, William P. *The Ethos of the Cosmos.* Grand Rapids, MI: William B. Eerdman's, 1999.
Teilhard de Chardin, Pierre. *Hymn of the Universe.* London: William Collins Sons; New York: Harper & Row, 1965.
Edwards, Denis. *Ecology at the Heart of Faith.* Maryknoll, NY: Orbis Books, 2006.
The Episcopal Church. "Final Report of the Task Force for Reimaging The Episcopal Church." December 15, 2014. http://reimaginetec.org/TREC_Report.pdf.
Fretheim, Terence E. *God and World in the Old Testament: A Relational Theology of Creation.* Nashville: Abingdon Press, 2005.
Gatta, John. *The Transfiguration of Christ and Creation.* Eugene, OR: Wipf & Stock, 2011.
Horrell, David G. *The Bible and the Environment: Towards a Critical Ecological Biblical Theology.* London: Equinox, 2010.
Jenkins, Willis. *Ecologies of Grace: Environmental Ethics and Christian Theology.* New York: Oxford University Press, 2008.
Rasmussen, Larry. *Earth Honoring Faith: Religious Ethics in a New Key.* New York: Oxford Press, 2013.
Sittler, Joseph. "Called to Unity." In *Evocations of Grace: The Writings of Jospeh Sittler on Ecology, Theology, and Ethics.* Edited by Steven Bouma-Prediger and Peter W. Bakken, 45–46. Grand Rapids, MI: Eerdmans, 2000.
———. *Essays on Nature and Grace.* Philadelphia: Fortress Press, 1972.
Wirzba, Norman. "All Creatures: Ecology and the Eyes of Faith." *The Christian Century.* July 22, 2015. http://www.christiancentury.org/article/2015–07/all-creatures.

Part IV

Catholic Perspectives

Chapter Nine

Efficacious Ethics: The Trinity, Environment, and Green Design

Robert Robin Gottfried

> Not everyone who says to me, "Lord, Lord,"
>   will enter the kingdom of heaven,
>   but only the one who does the will of my Father in heaven.
> On that day many will say to me,
>   "Lord, Lord, did we not speak out against toxic waste,
>   lie down before the bulldozers destroying your creation,
>   and promote solar panels and wind power?"
> Then I will declare to them,
>   "I never knew you;
>   go away from me, you evildoers."
>   —Matthews 7: 21–23 (with apologies to Matthew)

Most of us concerned about ethics care about them because we hope to make a difference in the world; however, a boogie-woogies from 1939 offers us a word of caution:

> TAIN'T WHAT YOU DO, it's the way that cha do it,
> Tain't what you say, it's the way that cha say it,
> [...]
> That's what gets results.[1]

Reading these lines quickly leads one to ask, "What *is* the way that ultimately gets results? How do people make a difference?" This chapter explores this question from the perspective of the importance of relationships in the economy of God. As such, this exploration leads to the interconnectivity of all creation and humanity's role within the plan of a God who is alive and actively engaged with the world. The chapter's final section discusses the implications of these ideas for selecting the types of technologies humans use to interface with the material world about them.

THE CENTRALITY OF RELATIONSHIPS

When we go to the art museum, without looking at the little card on the wall we often can identify a Matisse or Degas just by looking at the painting. We can do so because the artist reveals something of him or herself in their works. Similarly, when we look at the world around us, we see all kinds of systems: social systems, ecosystems, nutrient cycles, water cycles, and so forth. So, when we look at the "work of God's hands," we can infer that God must like systems. Systems somehow must reflect something of the nature of God.

Of course, Christians believe that God is a system—a three-person community or, as the church fathers have said for so long, a three-person dance—the Trinity. More recently Robert Jenson, a Lutheran theologian, describes the Trinity as a "fugued melody," one played in three variations that so skillfully intertwine that they sound like one entity, not three.

We might best understand the Trinity as three relators, or even as three relationships, as opposed to three individuals who relate to one another. When we think about the Trinity, we emphasize the relating between the three persons as opposed to the three persons themselves. This is because each person relates totally to the other two by wholeheartedly giving itself to the other two, holding nothing back. Each person also responds with total abandon to the others. This is why we think of God as Love. It's in God's nature to give fully to others and to respond totally to them. We might think of God as a Mad Lover or as Perfectly Harmonious Relationship.

So, Matthew (see above) and Paul (1Cor 13) make the point that just doing the right thing, just earning enough merit badges, does not get one into the kingdom of God. If one does these things without love, one does not fulfill the purpose for which we were created: to be in relationship with God. For our good actions to "do us any good" they should flow out of our intimate love of others, indicating our love affair with God. God, perfect relationship itself, longs for that sort of relationship with us. Once in that relationship we naturally treat others in the same way, naturally doing the right thing.

However, in this author's opinion we often do not go far enough when we think about these texts. Not only does doing the right things without love fail to gain us entry into the kingdom of God, but even those good things we do may not produce the hoped-for results in the world.

Consider an automated orphanage where machines bathe, feed, educate, and put the children to bed. To the observer the children appear well-fed and, by all objective standards, well cared for. However, most of us probably recoil from the idea of automated orphanages. Why? Because for children to flourish they require loving care from other humans. Automated orphanages lack the most important thing for children to thrive: loving relationships with adults committed to their care. For children love is the key. Focusing only on children's physical needs fails to address the root problem they face–the lack of loving, committed relationships with adults.

How does this relate to the environment? It does not at all if the world is a clock. If the only components of the world worth relating to are the humans living in it, then we need only love humans. Although a thorough examination of a biblical view of humanity's relationship to nonhuman creation lies beyond the scope of what we can explore here, allow me to suggest a few points from Genesis 2 that suggest that God sees creation as far more than a machine.

First, we see that God, the ultimate gardener, gets his hands dirty. He fashions the first human out of dirt and breathes the breath of life into him. This is no distant God but one who gets intimately involved with the creature he makes.

Second, he gives Adam the authority to name the other creatures God makes. In this context this implies giving each creature a name that captures the essence of its being. This requires Adam to intimately know each creature so that he can devise a name that truly reflects the nature of the creature. God's allowing Adam to name each creature while God looks on implies total confidence in Adam, confidence that he is in a loving, intimate relationship with them.

Finally, God places Adam in the garden of Eden to "till and to keep it." The Hebrew words here that describe Adam's vocation consist of *abad* and *shamar*. The former means "to serve," even to the point of being a slave. The latter not only means "to keep," but also "to watch or preserve." God puts Adam (and Eve) in the Garden to slavishly care for and preserve it.[2] So, not only does God want humans to have an intimate relationship with all nonhuman creation, God wants them to give themselves totally to it just as God gives Godself totally to humans. Humans serve as God's image on earth (Gen 1: 26) by mirroring God's kenosis, or total self-giving.[3]

EFFICACY AND GOD'S ECOLOGICAL INTERVENTION

All this suggests that just as automated orphanages that take care of children without providing them the love they need fail to produce vibrant children, humans who eat organic food and install solar panels out of a sense of duty or of avoiding environmental calamity miss the boat. Despite their good intentions, they ultimately will fail to produce the environmental benefits they anticipate.

Understanding why this is so requires an understanding of God's ecological intervention, of God's plan for healing creation. This intervention involves three stages: the Incarnation, Jesus's death and resurrection, and Pentecost.

As humans, we tend to interpret the Incarnation as The Word becoming human, which, of course, did occur. However, the scriptures point to a much larger reality—that the Word became "flesh" (John 1:14); i.e., that It became part of the created order, became matter. God became, therefore, part of the entire created order, not just part of humanity.

One might ask, therefore, why God chose to become human and not a beaver or a rock. As one might expect, there are many ways to approach that question. However, one way to address it is to examine the biblical role of priest, head of household, or king in the Hebrew scriptures. The king, priest, and heads of households all possessed the power to bless those in their care. This blessing consisted of God's sustaining and nourishing power flowing through the intermediary to the creation he or she cared for. Notably, when the king (and Israel as a whole) was virtuous, the community of creation (the people and the land) flourished. However, when the king and his people strayed from their relationship with their God, they and their land languished. For The Blessing to flow, the head of the household, priest, or king needed to listen to and to obey God.

Humans, as the priest of creation or its head, in a similar fashion need to be in a close, intimate relationship with God, who they come to know through the created order. When they get out of touch with creation, they get out of touch with God, and The Blessing ceases to flow. Creation then suffers. As a result, it eagerly awaits the "revelation of the sons of God" (Rom 8:19) so that The Blessing once again may flow and all may prosper.[4]

As the priests of creation God also intended for humans to give voice to creation's silent praise of God, to provide creation its full meaning within a life of intimate communion with God.[5]

Unfortunately, humans also constitute the weak link in creation. While full of potential, they stray easily from the purpose for which God made them, thereby threatening all of creation by failing to bring the Blessing to it. So, the Word became human to enable us to perform humanity's priestly function within creation.

By going through creation's process of birth, suffering and death, God changed the world order in a dramatic way. Whereas up to this point death meant the end of life, death now brings a *renewed* life. God transformed the very nature of the world order so that Jesus is the firstborn of a *new* creation (Col 1:15). Something new emerged—the advent of the Peaceable Kingdom of Isaiah, the breaking forth of *shalom*. Whereas the Incarnation and the death and resurrection of Jesus ushered in the possibility of a transformed, or *transfigured*, creation, the coming of the Holy Spirit at Pentecost provided the fuel, making it possible for humans to grow into their role as mediators of God's blessing to creation.

Why did God go to all this trouble? John tells us: "For God so loved the world that he gave his only son" (John 3:16). Again, we tend to anthropomorphize that phrase. Once more "world" signifies more than humanity. The Greek word here is *cosmos*, which means the entire created order, including its processes and order. It also means Beauty.[6] God loves all components of God's creation and the way they relate to one another. God finds it good and beautiful, something expressing God's love through and in it. By becoming one with it, including its pain and death, God reconciles all things unto Godself so that God might be "all in all."[7] The transfiguration gives us a glimpse of the new creation, as does Jesus's appearances after the Resurrection.

How can we love an ineffable God if we do not love God in the world in which God dwells?[8] Similarly, how can we claim to follow the person of Jesus if we do not recognize him in the many ways he presents himself to us? Do we run the risk of Jesus telling us at some point, "Get away from me you evildoers—I do not know you?"

True social and environmental progress requires the guidance of the Holy Spirit, whereby our society and we individuals are transformed into a people that intimately know and love all. To become Godlike requires us to learn to give ourselves totally to one another and to all creation and to respond wholeheartedly to God's world. Without transformation we cannot follow the Holy Spirit and effectively work for the nascent kingdom of God. For, "unless the Lord build the house, the builder toils in vain." We need intimate, loving knowledge of the world so that we can learn to cooperate with its processes, respect its nature, and collaboratively make God manifest in the works of our hands. We need wisdom. And, as Kallistos Ware cautions us,

> Let us not for one moment imagine that the ecological crisis can be resolved simply through sentimental expressions of regret. What is asked from us is costly self-discipline, sacrificial forbearance, and inner martyrdom—in a word, Cross-bearing.[9]

WISDOM AS VIRTUOUS DESIGN[10]

The process of actively engaging with creation under the guidance of the Holy Spirit through work and prayer leads us to grow in wisdom, an understanding of how things work and how God intends us to work with it.[11] We learn about natural processes and the nature of things and how to cooperate lovingly with them. This involves more than technical or scientific knowledge. It implies an intimate "knowing" of God's creatures, of living in a vibrant ongoing relationship with all around us and of understanding God's will for it.[12] We work and live amidst all beings not just to earn a living and to enjoy responsibly the fruits of creation, but to reveal through our loving altering of creation the hand of God. This level of intimacy and knowledge transcends facts (while including them), moving us to maximize meaning and Beauty in the world rather than narrowly-defined profit or even broadly-construed social (human) benefit.[13]

If we manifest God working through us, then we will choose to do those things that bring life to all of creation. To get the results we are hoping for—the healing of creation—we cannot seek just to do the right things. Instead we must cooperate with the Holy Spirit to transform the way we interact with nonhuman creation. The ultimate solution to environmental problems lies in restoring our relationships with all of creation, so that when we do the right things, we do them out of love and compassion.

At the same time our love for creation must stem from an intimate knowledge of the components of creation and its interrelationships. We must learn to love and understand particular ecosystems and landscapes as well as particular places. "Love for the environment" in general or in theory will not suffice. When we love particular corners of creation and have been transformed by them, we then have the possibility of empathizing with its other parts. This wisdom, or intimate knowledge of creation both in love and in understanding, can help us avoid well-intentioned disasters. As a forester colleague once cautioned me, "Love is fine. But you can love a tree to death."

"The world is not only a gift but a task."[14] As God's creature most able to alter its environment in a short amount of time, we face the task of having to choose *how* we wish to alter creation. All creation alters its environment—beavers create lakes, wolves reduce the presence of elk, elk affect the populations of plants along rivers. The very act of breathing changes the atmosphere, and flowing water erodes rock and riverbanks. So, we will change our environment. The question is how will we do so?

How we choose to interact with the rest of creation is a question of design. Van der Ryn and Cowan define *design* as "the intentional shaping of matter, energy, and process to meet a perceived need or desire."[15] As a species chosen to image God to the world, we bear a special responsibility to design appropriately. If we are a people through whom God's beauty and glory shine forth, then we would hope that the works of our hands would make God manifest to all creation. Just as God's works speak about God, so do our works speak about us. Our works, like God's, must be virtuous. So, what might virtuous design look like?

We might start by asking what sort of design seems to dominate today. Imagine scenes of badly denuded hillsides, shore or water birds dripping with oil, polluted streams filled with trash, mountain tops blasted off for their coal, urban slums, strip malls, children with bloated bellies. How do they make you feel? You might respond to them, as others have told me, by saying that you feel defiled, dirty, ill, anxious, angry, sad, depressed, discouraged, grief-filled, despairing.

These reactions to the work of our hands reveal certain attitudes: an acceptance of waste as a fact of life, whether of human life, energy, materials or other creatures;[16] a willingness to degrade and foul other people or living systems as long as we ourselves benefit; an embrace of using things that are toxic to life, whether human or nonhuman; a love of superficial novelty. We experience a creator, humanity, who evidences little regard for life, human or nonhuman. This creator loves little and ignores the impacts of its actions. This creator does not respond selflessly to the world around it and holds back its very self from it. Objectifying creation, both human and nonhuman, we manipulate the world to satisfy our desires. Rather than cooperate with the rest of creation, humans today all too often seek to dominate and tame it. Our experience in our human-influenced world all too often speaks of greed, desire for control, and pride.

The works of our hands reveal who we are. They embody, or incarnate, our values. Take a disposable ballpoint pen, for example. Made largely of petroleum-derived plastic, the pen declares that society believes that it is acceptable, and perhaps preferable, to use a nonrenewable resource once and then discard it. Convenience matters most. The pen declares as acceptable, or inevitable, the energy usage, carbon emission, and associated pollution from drilling, transporting, and refining oil, the manufacture of the plastic and then the pen, and finally the transportation of the pen into the retail establishment that required the use of resources to build (and continues to require resources to maintain). If workers toiling under inhumane labor conditions produced the pen, it also declares this practice as acceptable. Finally, we rate the convenience of the pen as worth the costs to people and to the land of disposing of it. These attitudes tend to reveal disrespect for life in all its forms, love for power and control, greed, pride (at the human, social, and species levels), and alienation from the rest of creation and humans.

What might virtuous design look like? Once again, imagine that you are viewing mountain vistas, close-ups of flowers, children playing, picturesque farmsteads, otters, tigers and scenes of vibrant urban social life and people dancing. How do you feel upon seeing these things? If you were to do this in a retreat setting or other situations where you feel open to God's presence, you might say, as many others have, that you feel peaceful, loved, nurtured, forgiven, joyful, nourished, alive, hopeful, awed, filled with mystery, one with all things.

These reactions clearly reflect the impacts of encountering a Creator who loves creation. They speak of God's mercy, forgiveness and healing, of God's delight in creation. We sense God's welcoming call to us and to all things. We also may experience God's immense power, a power always humble and intimate or a stirring call to change. Beauty speaks to us of an immense Other who seeks our companionship and well-being.

If we design as transparent instruments of God's ongoing creativity and love, then we need to find ways of doing so that incarnate the same values that God manifests in God's interactions with creation. God creates using a certain stance or approach. This approach involves total, intimate involvement with and profound respect and love for the community of life. As a result God works within its natural processes, according all of creation (whether one lion or an ecosystem) freedom to act according to its nature. God respects all things. God does not waste—all things have meaning and purpose whether or not we can perceive it. God never takes without giving back many fold. Because of God's great love, God always creates with the good of creation in mind. God cooperates with it, knows it intimately, and works with it. God does not stand apart from it, creating at a distance. Rather, God constantly supports and interacts with it.

What does this mean in practice? Fortunately for us there exists today a discipline that embodies many of these same principles: ecological design. Van der Ryn and Cowan define *ecological design* as "any form of design that minimizes environmentally destructive impacts by integrating itself with living processes."[17] Proponents of ecological design share many of the same goals as virtuous design, as evidenced by the following quotes from some of its foremost proponents.

> Ecological design is the art that reconnects us as sensuous creatures evolved over millions of years to a beautiful world. That world does not need to be remade but rather revealed. To do that, we do not need research as much as the rediscovery of old and forgotten things. We do not need more economic growth as much as we need to relearn the ancient lesson of generosity, as trustees for a moment between those who preceded us and those who will follow. Our greatest needs have nothing to do with the possession of things but rather with heart, wisdom, thankfulness, and generosity of spirit. And these virtues are part of larger ecologies that embrace spirit, body, and mind—the beginning of design.[18]

We hope to serve a rapidly growing network of people in the world who see the world as it can be, not merely as it is. Wendell Berry writes in his *Recollected Essays*:

> We have lived by the assumption that what was good for us would be good for the world. We have been wrong. We must change our lives, so that it will be

possible to live by the contrary assumption that what is good for the world will be good for us. And that requires that we make the effort to know the world and to learn what is good for it. We must learn to cooperate in its processes, and to yield to its limits. But even more important, we must learn to acknowledge that the creation is full of mystery; we will never clearly understand it. We must abandon arrogance and stand in awe. We must recover the sense of the majesty of the creation, and the ability to be worshipful in its presence. For it is only on the condition of humility and reverence before the world that our species will be able to remain in it.[19]

Various designers have offered statements of ecological design principles. We might summarize them along the following lines:

- Design with nature—all creation should prosper; integrate living processes into the design;
- Replenish, restore, and nourish the rest of creation instead of merely minimizing environmental impact;
- Recognize the interdependence of humans and nature;
- Respect the spiritual aspect of the material world;
- Design for and with the local area and region;
- Mimic nature's processes;
- Rely on natural energy flows;
- Eliminate the concept of waste;
- Allow the design to coevolve with the natural world;
- Seek social and biological equity;
- Involve all the stakeholders in a participatory process;
- Consider all the costs and benefits (economic, social, and ecological) of a design.[20]

The above principles suggest more than a utilitarian appreciation of what nature can do for humans. Rather, it exhibits a love for nature itself and an appreciation of its numinous (spirit-filled) character and beauty. Ecological design takes a systems approach that includes both human and nonhuman creation and that works to benefit all parts of the system. At the same time it recognizes the individuality of a particular place, both socially and ecologically. In recognizing the importance of individuals and of community, ecological design stresses the importance of equity for all, including future generations, and of including all parties at the table. Ecological design, thus, excludes no one. Accepting that change is part of life; it also designs for change.[21]

These values that underlie ecological design remarkably resemble the principles derived from our understanding of the way that God interacts with and designs God's world. This is not surprising given that the espoused vision of an ecologically designed world sounds a lot like *shalom*, where all things prosper and contribute to the well-being of one another.[22] By choosing to cooperate with the way God's creation works and to respect the interrelationships in a creation that harbors a spiritual presence, ecological design appears to offer us an approach that might aid us in seeking Truth, choosing Good, and manifesting Beauty.

THE PRACTICALITY OF WISDOM

But do these principles work? They do on many levels though their success, of course, depends upon the skill and knowledge we bring to their application as well as upon the cultural, political, and policy environment within which they are applied. However, numerous examples attest to the power of this new approach to designing our world.[23]

One area where much practical experience has accumulated is green building. In the United States buildings use 13.6 percent of all potable water and 40 percent of all raw materials while generating over a third of all waste.[24] Efforts to change building practices, therefore, can have a huge environmental impact.

Green building appears to be here to stay. A 2008 U.S. General Services Administration (GSA) study comparing the performance of twelve of its sustainably designed buildings found that they experienced 26 percent less energy use, 13 percent lower aggregate maintenance costs, 27 percent higher occupant satisfaction, and 33 percent fewer CO_2 emissions compared to national averages. The GSA's gold LEED buildings, which took a fully integrated approach to sustainable design, achieved the best overall performance.[25] Similarly, by positioning the building to admit the most daylight and the least heat, and by using double-glazed windows, extra insulation, and a highly reflective "cool roof" with photovoltaic cells mounted on it, Toyota's 724,000-square-foot office in Torrance, California, for 2,500 employees used 42 percent less energy than that allowed by California's very strict building code. Overall it saved 60 percent on energy costs over a comparable conventional building built to the same code.[26] These LEED buildings emphasized using natural energy flows and reducing energy waste. This implied considering not only up-front construction costs (typically the only consideration) but also the costs and benefits of the new building over its lifetime, a much more inclusive approach that takes into account nature's contributions to the building's operation.

Benefits go beyond energy savings. Studies on using day lighting instead of artificial light consistently demonstrate health benefits such as increased student learning rates and decreased worker sick days. Improvements in indoor air quality improve worker health and productivity.[27] As a result green buildings experience higher rents, greater occupancy rates, higher returns on investment, higher sales prices, and lower operating costs.[28]

All this occurs "free of charge." While a 2003 article found that green building tended to cost about 2 percent more than conventional homes, more recent studies find no empirical evidence for any cost premium.[29] Considering that one can receive the above benefits at little or no increase in cost, green building makes economic sense. These benefits have caused such a huge demand for green buildings that the *Harvard Business Review* states, "owners of standard buildings face massive obsolescence. They must act now to protect their investments."[30]

The implications of green design go far beyond the construction industry. Ecological agriculture attempts to work with ecological processes to lower costs and maximize the amount of food that can be produced in a sustained manner over time with minimal use of fossil fuels and purchased inputs.

Sustainable forestry, or natural forest management, takes a similar approach by mimicking natural forest processes. The field of biomimicry imitates the "models, systems, and elements of nature for the purpose of solving complex human problems," ranging from agriculture to renewable energy technology and architecture.[31] For example, John Todd's "Living Machine" treats wastewater efficiently and cost-effectively by using a series of indoor constructed wetlands, thereby substituting solar energy and biological processes for fossil fuel and industrial processes.[32] Low-cost composting toilets in Malawi, another example of green design, create valuable odor-free compost, making them popular with farmers who can substitute this manure for expensive purchased fertilizer.[33]

Green design can occur at a level incorporating multiple technologies. Interface Carpet, the largest commercial carpet company in the world, and perhaps the greenest United States corporation, is on the road to achieving its goal of obtaining 100 percent of its energy needs from renewable sources by 2020. Its website reported the following manufacturing results for 2014:

- The carbon footprint of our carpet is down 22 percent on average since 2008.
- Our energy use per unit of production is down 40 percent since 1996.
- 45 percent of the energy we use is from renewable sources.
- Our GHG emissions per unit of production are down 73 percent since 1996.
- 50 percent of our total raw materials are recycled or biobased.
- Our water intake per unit of production is down 87 percent since 1996.
- Our waste sent to landfill per unit of production is down 91 percent since 1996.
- We have diverted more than 309 million pounds of material from landfills since our ReEntry program began in 1995.
- Our safety performance has improved with our Total Reportable Accident Frequency Rate down 67 percent since 1999.[34]

Because of its drive for sustainability, Interface has the least vulnerability to the volatility of the oil market of any carpet company. Interface's founder, the late Ray Anderson, believed that this strategy not only has saved the company millions of dollars but also has enabled it to gain and hold market share.[35]

This result is not surprising. A report from Goldman Sachs found that stocks of companies considered leaders in environmental, social, and governance policies outperformed other firms by an average of 25 percent. Compared to their industry peers, 72 percent of these companies performed better. Michael Porter of the Harvard Business School states, "Our central message is that . . . managers must start to recognize environmental improvement as an economic and competitive opportunity . . . it is time to build on the underlying economic logic that links the environment, resource productivity, innovation, and competitiveness."[36] Similarly, a 2009 *Harvard Business Review* article states,

> Sustainability isn't the burden on bottom lines that many executives believe it to be. In fact, becoming environment-friendly can lower your costs and increase your revenues. That's why sustainability should be a touchstone for all innovation. In the future, only companies that make sustainability a goal will achieve competitive advantage. That means rethinking business models as well as products, technologies and processes.[37]

SUMMARY AND CONCLUSION

We have seen that the root of the environmental crises we experience today lies in our spiritual poverty and the social problems stemming from it, as well as in our lack of wisdom as to how best to alter, or "garden," the world in which we live. Intimate knowing also implies close observation, so that we come to know how the rest of our created community functions and how it responds to our actions. Only by lovingly and wisely interacting with creation can we hope to act in ways that help bring about *shalom*, the peaceable kingdom where all creation rejoices and prospers.

Loving and wise interaction with nonhuman creation implies that we carefully and intentionally design, that we design in ways that mirror God's relationship with God's creation—i.e., that we design virtuously. Green design principles reflect these values and offer us a practical approach to implementing virtuous design, an approach that increasingly appears not only to offer innovative solutions to complex problems, but ones also that are socially and economically viable.

If we wish to "proclaim the gospel to all creatures" and to "reveal the sons of God" to a groaning creation, we would do well to return to the basics:

returning to a spiritual life that reconnects us to our world and rethinking what it means to be human in a world loved dearly by its creator.

NOTES

1. Sy Oliver and James "Trummie" Young, *Boogie Woogie Juke Box: A Collection of All-Time Boogie Woogie Song Hits* (Radio City, NY: Leeds Music Corporation, 1945), 11–12. The song was first copyrighted in 1939.

2. Walter Brueggemann, *Interpretation: Genesis* (Atlanta: John Knox Press, 1983), 32–33; Wesley Granberg-Michaelson, *A Worldly Spirituality: The Call to Redeem Life on Earth* (San Francisco: Harper & Row, 1984), 65.

3. Eugene H. Maly, "Genesis," 11; Brueggemann, in *The Jerome Biblical Commentary*, eds. Raymond E. Brown, Joseph A. Fitzmyer, and Ronald E. Murphy (Englewood Cliffs, NJ: Prentice-Hall, 1968), 11; Brueggermann, Interpretatim: Genesis, 31–32; Douglas John Hall, *Imaging God: Dominion as Stewardship* (Grand Rapids:, MI: W. W. Eerdmans, 1986), 132. For a more thorough examination of a biblical perspective on the relationship between God, humans and nonhuman creation see Robert R. Gottfried, *Economics, Ecology, and the Roots of Western Faith: Perspectives from the Garden* (Lanham, MD: Rowman & Littlefield, 1995), chapters 3 and 4.

4. For a more thorough discussion of The Blessing see Robert R. Gottfried, *Economics, Ecology, and the Roots of Western Faith: Perspectives from the Garden* (Lanham, MD: Rowman & Littlefield, 1995), 39-42.

5. Ware, "Through Creation to the Creator," 101.

6. John Anthony McGuckin, "The Beauty of the World and Its Significance in St. Gregory the Theologian," in *Toward an Ecology of Transfiguration: Orthodox Christian Perspectives on Environment, Nature, and Creation*, ed. John Chryssavgis and Bruce V. Foltz (New York: Fordham University Press, 2013), 36.

7. Pope Francis, *Laudato Si': On Care for Our Common Home*, (Vatican City, Rome: Holy See Press Office, 2015), n 48, 83, 89, The Holy See, accessed October 1, 2016, http://w2.vatican.va/content/francesco/en/encyclicals/documents/papa-frances-co_20150524_enciclica_laudato-si.html.

8. cf. 1 John 4:20: ". . . those who do not love a brother or sister whom they have seen, cannot love God whom they have not seen."

9. Ware, "Through Creation to the Creator," 103.

10. This section draws on material from Gottfried, "Beauty by Design."

11. Robert K. Johnston, "Wisdom Literature and its Contribution to a Biblical Environmental Ethic," in *Tending the Garden: Essays on the Gospel and the Earth*, ed. Wesley Granberg-Michaelson (Grand Rapids, MI: Eerdmans, 1987); Claus Westermann, *Elements of Old Testament Theology*, trans. Douglas W. Scott (Atlanta: John Knox Press, 1982), 98–100.

12. For an intriguing example of a modern scientist adept at wisdom, see Glenn Clark, *The Man Who Talks with the Flowers: The Life Story of Dr. George Washington Carver* (St. Paul, MN: MacAlester Park, 1976).

13. For a thorough discussion of these thoughts see Francis, "Laudato Si': On Care for Our Common Home," http://w2.vatican.va/content/francesco/en/encyclicals/documents/papa-francesco_20150524_enciclica-laudato-si.html.

14. Ware, "Through Creation to the Creator," 101.

15. Sim Van der Ryn and Stuart Cowan, *Ecological Design* (Washington, DC: Island Press, 1996), 8; Ibid.

16. Note that producing with no waste is not a pipe dream. The ideas of continuous quality improvement, avoiding *muda* (a term coined by the founder of Toyota for any sort of purposeless use of resources), and industrial ecology all have to do with the elimination of waste. After all, why pay for an input only to throw it away? See Paul Hawken, Amory Lovins, and L. Hunter Lovins, *Natural Capitalism: Creating the Next Industrial Revolution* (New York: Little, Brown & Company, 1999) for an excellent primer.

17. Van der Ryn and Cowan, *Ecological Design*, 8 & 18.
18. David W. Orr, *The Nature of Design: Ecology, Culture, and Human Intention* (New York: Oxford University Press, 2002), 32.
19. Hawken, Amory Lovins, and L. Hunter Lovins, *Natural Capitalism: Creating the Next Industrial Revolution*, xiv.
20. These points are a compendium of points drawn from a variety of design statements summarized in Andres R. Edwards, *The Sustainability Revolution: Portrait of a Paradigm Shift* (Gabriola Island, BC, Canada: New Society, 2005).
21. For an excellent example of this type of thinking, explore William McDonough's architectural firm's website: http://www.mcdonoughpartners.com.
22. For a discussion of *shalom* see Gottfried, *Economics, Ecology, and the Roots of Western Faith: Perspectives from the Garden*, 47–49.
23. The field of green design is large. Two examples in addition to those discussed in more depth in the text provide some sense of its scope. *Agroecology*, the ecological approach to agriculture, offers another example of green design. For a quick introduction to this field see Olivier De Schutter and Gaëtan Vanloqueren, "The New Green Revolution: How Twenty-First-Century Science Can Feed the World," *Solutions* 2, no. 4 (2011). Available online at http://www.thesolutionsjournal.com/node/971. Industrial ecology attempts to mimic ecosystems, which recycle and reuse nutrients by using the waste of one component to nourish the next component. For an introduction see T. E. H. Graedel and Braden R. Allenby, *Industrial Ecology and Sustainable Engineering* (Upper Saddle River, NJ: Prentice Hall, 2009).
24. L. Hunter Lovins and Boyd Cohen, *Climate Capitalism: Capitalism in the Age of Climate Change* (New York: Hill & Wang, 2011), 329, footnote 4.
25. "Assessing Green Building Performance: A Post Occupancy Evaluation of 12 GSA Buildings," (Washington, DC: U.S. General Services Administration, 2008). Available at http://www.gsa.gov/graphics/pbs/GSA_AssessGreen_white_paper.pdf.
26. Lovins and Cohen, *Climate Capitalism: Capitalism in the Age of Climate Change*, 89.
27. A study of a chain of West Coast franchise stores found that those stores that were well-daylit experienced 40 percent higher sales and that employees much preferred working there compared to conventional franchise stores (Heschong Mahone Group, "Windows and Offices: A Study of Office Worker Performance and the Indoor Environment," Technical Report of the California Energy Commission," 2003, http://www.h-mg.com/projects/daylighting/summaries%20on%20daylighting.htm.

When energy-efficient lighting, efforts to increase indoor air quality, and strategies to address building acoustics and thermal qualities are combined, these can increase employee productivity 3 to 5 percent, dwarfing the money saved on energy savings. See Greg Kats, *Greening Our Built World: Costs, Benefits, and Strategies* (Washington, DC: Island Press, 2009), quoted in Amory Lovins and Rocky Mountain Institute, *Reinventing Fire: Bold Business Solutions for the New Energy Era* (White River Junction, VT: Chelsea Green, 2011), 102.
28. An analysis of buildings built under the LEED or Energy Star programs found that these buildings received 3 percent higher rent, experienced greater occupancy rates, and sold for 13 percent more than comparable properties. See Nadav Malin, "Non-Green Office Buildings Sacrifice 8% in Rent Revenues," Building Green.com, http://www.buildinggreen.com/auth/article.cfm/2010/11/9/Non-Green-Office-Buildings-Sacrifice-8-in-Rent-Revenues/, quoted in Lovins and Rocky Mountain Institute, *Reinventing Fire: Bold Business Solutions for the New Energy Era*, 103. Another study of green buildings found similar results: operating costs decreased 8 to 9 percent, occupancy rates increased by more than 4%, rents increased 3%, and return on investment rose by more than 6 percent. See Lovins and Cohen, *Climate Capitalism: Capitalism in the Age of Climate Change*, footnote 7.
29. Greg Kats et al., "The Costs and Financial Benefits of Green Buildings" (Sustainable Building Task Force, 2003); Lovins and Cohen, *Climate Capitalism: Capitalism in the Age of Climate Change*; Lisa Fay Matthiessen and Peter Morris, *The Cost of Green Revisited* (Seattle: Davis Langdon, 2007); James D. Qualk and Paul McCown, "The Cost-Effectiveness of Building Green," HPAC Engineering, http://hpac.com/green/cost-effectiveness-building-green-1009.

30. L. Hunter Lovins, "Entreprenouring the Solutions: Key to Competitiveness and Prosperity," PowerPoint presentation at Sewanee, The University of the South, March 24, 2008. Available upon request from the author of this chapter. The *Wall Street Journal* predicted in 2010 that half of all nonresidential buildings would be green by 2015. While only 2 percent of the nonresidential construction starts were green in 2005, McGraw-Hill Construction reported that they rose by 2008 to 10 to 12 percent and predicted that they would grow to 20 to 25 percent by 2013. See Lovins and Cohen, *Climate Capitalism: Capitalism in the Age of Climate Change*, 103 footnote 36.

31. Biomimicry Institute, accessed May 29, 2016, http://biomimicry.org/what-is-biomimicry/.

32. John Todd, *Ecological Design*. Cyberpress, accessed May 29, 2016, http://www.toddecological.com.

33. Peter Morgan, "Lessons from a Low-Cost Ecological Approach to Sanitation in Malawi" (Washington, DC: The World Bank, 2007). http://my.ewb-usa.org/theme/library/myewb-usa/project-resources/technical/LessonsFromLowcostMalawiToilet.pdf.

34. Interface Carpet, accessed May 29, 2016,http://www.interfaceglobal.com/Sustainability/Our-Progress/AllMetrics.aspx.

35. Lovins and Rocky Mountain Institute, *Reinventing Fire: Bold Business Solutions for the New Energy Era*, 162.

36. Lovins, "Entreprenouring the Solutions: Key to Competitiveness and Prosperity."

37. Lovins and Cohen, *Climate Capitalism: Capitalism in the Age of Climate Change*, 27, n 94. Similarly, Hunter Lovins states that a 2005 Price Waterhouse Cooper survey of CEOs from forty-three countries found that 83 percent believed that environmental sustainability was an important factor in determining their profits, up from 79 percent in 2004 and 69 percent in 2003. She also cites a Davos CEO survey's findings that 90 percent believed that going beyond merely obeying environmental laws enhanced their reputation, 75 percent believed it provided competitive advantages, and 73 percent believed it led to cost savings. See Lovins, "Entreprenouring the Solutions: Key to Competitiveness and Prosperity."

REFERENCES

"Assessing Green Building Performance: A Post Occupancy Evaluation of 12 GSA Buildings." Washington, DC: U.S. General Services Administration, 2008. http://www.gsa.gov/graphics/pbs/GSA_AssessGreen_white_paper.pdf.
Biomimicry Institute. Accessed May 29, 2016. http://biomimicry.org/what-is-biomimicry/.
Brueggemann, Walter. *Interpretation: Genesis*. Atlanta: John Knox Press, 1983.
Clark, Glenn. *The Man Who Talks with the Flowers: The Life Story of Dr. George Washington Carver*. St. Paul, MN: MacAlester Park, 1976.
De Schutter, Olivier and Gaëtan Vanloqueren. "The New Green Revolution: How Twenty-First-Century Science Can Feed the World." *Solutions* 2, no. 4 (2011).
Edwards, Andres R. *The Sustainability Revolution: Portrait of a Paradigm Shift*. Gabriola Island, BC, Canada: New Society, 2005.
Gottfried, Robert. "Beauty by Design." *Sewanee Theological Review*, December (2015).
———. *Economics, Ecology, and the Roots of Western Faith: Perspectives from the Garden*. Lanham, MD: Rowman & Littlefield, 1995.
Graedel, T. E. H. and Braden R. Allenby. *Industrial Ecology and Sustainable Engineering*. Upper Saddle River, NJ: Prentice Hall, 2009.
Granberg-Michaelson, Wesley. *A Worldly Spirituality: The Call to Redeem Life on Earth*. San Francisco: Harper & Row, 1984.
Hall, Douglas John. *Imaging God: Dominion as Stewardship*. Grand Rapids, MI: W. W. Eerdmans, 1986.
Hawken, Paul, Amory Lovins, and L. Hunter Lovins. *Natural Capitalism: Creating the Next Industrial Revolution*. New York: Little, Brown & Company, 1999.

Heschong Mahone Group. "Windows and Offices: A Study of Office Worker Performance and the Indoor Environment." Technical Report of the California Energy Commission, 2003. http://www.h-mg.com/projects/daylighting/summaries%20on%20daylighting.htm.

Interface Carpet. Accessed May 29, 2016. http://www.interfaceglobal.com/Sustainability/Our-Progress/AllMetrics.aspx.

Irenaeus. *Against Heresies*. Book II, Chapter 9.1. Ante-Nicene Christian Library: Translation of the Writings of the Fathers. Edinburgh: T & T Clark, 1865.

Johnston, Robert K. "Wisdom Literature and Its Contribution to a Biblical Environmental Ethic." In *Tending the Garden: Essays on the Gospel and the Earth*. Edited by Wesley Granberg-Michaelson. Grand Rapids, MI: Eerdmans, 1987.

Kats, Greg. *Greening Our Built World: Costs, Benefits, and Strategies*. Washington, DC: Island Press, 2009. Quoted in Amory Lovins and Rocky Mountain Institute. *Reinventing Fire: Bold Business Solutions for the New Energy Era*. White River Junction, VT: Chelsea Green, 2011, 102.

Kats, Greg, Leon Alevantis, Adam Berman, Evan Mills, and Jeff Perlman. "The Costs and Financial Benefits of Green Buildings: A Report to California's Sustainable Building Task Force." PDF. Capital E and the United States Building Council, 2003.

Pope Francis. *Laudato Si': On Care for Our Common Home*. Vatican City, Rome: Holy See Press Office, 2015. *The Holy See*. Accessed July 30, 2016. http://w2.vatican.va/content/francesco/en/encyclicals/documents/papa-francesco_20150524_enciclica-laudato-si.html.

Lovins and Rocky Mountain Institute, *Reinventing Fire: Bold Business Solutions for the New Energy Era*, 162.

Lovins, L. Hunter. "Entreprenouring the Solutions: Key to Competitiveness and Prosperity." PowerPoint presentation at Sewanee, The University of the South, March 24, 2008.

Lovins, L. Hunter and Boyd Cohen. *Climate Capitalism: Capitalism in the Age of Climate Change*. New York: Hill & Wang, 2011.

Malin, Nadav. "Non-Green Office Buildings Sacrifice 8% in Rent Revenues." Building Green.com. http://www.buildinggreen.com/auth/article.cfm/2010/11/9/Non-Green-Office-Buildings-Sacrifice-8-in-Rent-Revenues/. Quoted in Lovins and Rocky Mountain Institute. *Reinventing Fire: Bold Business Solutions for the New Energy Era*, 103.

Maly, Eugene H. "Genesis." In *The Jerome Biblical Commentary*. Edited by Raymond E. Brown, Joseph A. Fitzmyer, and Roland E. Murphy. Englewood Cliffs, NJ: Prentice-Hall, 1968.

Matthiessen, Lisa Fay and Peter Morris. *The Cost of Green Revisited*. Seattle: Davis Langdon, 2007.

McGuckin, John Anthony. "The Beauty of the World and Its Significance in St. Gregory the Theologian." In *Toward an Ecology of Transfiguration: Orthodox Christian Perspectives on Environment, Nature, and Creation*. Edited by John Chryssavgis and Bruce V. Foltz. New York: Fordham University Press, 2013.

Morgan, Peter. "Lessons from a Low-Cost Ecological Approach to Sanitation in Malawi." Washington, DC: The World Bank, 2007. *Water and Sanitation Program Field Note*. PDF. June, 2007. Accessed May 27, 2016. http://my.ewb-usa.org/theme/library/myewb-usa/project-resources/technical/LessonsFromLowcostMalawiToilet.pdf.

Oliver, Sy and James "Trummie" Young. *Boogie Woogie Juke Box: A Collection of All-Time Boogie Woogie Song Hits*. Radio City, NY: Leeds Music Corporation, 1945.

Orr, David W. *The Nature of Design: Ecology, Culture, and Human Intention*. New York: Oxford University Press, 2002.

Qualk, James D. and Paul McCown. "The Cost-Effectiveness of Building Green." HPAC Engineering. http://hpac.com/green/cost-effectiveness-building-green-1009.

Todd, John. *Ecological Design*. Cyberpress, accessed May 29, 2016, http://www.toddecological.com.

Van der Ryn, Sim and Stuart Cowan. *Ecological Design*. Washington, DC: Island Press, 1996.

Ware, Kallistos. "Through Creation to the Creator." In *Toward an Ecology of Transfiguration: Orthodox Christian Perspectives on Environment, Nature, and Creation*. Edited by John Chryssavgis and Bruce V. Foltz. New York: Fordham University Press, 2013.

Westermann, Claus. *Elements of Old Testament Theology*. Trans. Douglas W. Scott. Atlanta: John Knox Press, 1982.

Chapter Ten

Care and Compassion

The Need for an Integral Ecology

Cristina Vanin

Cultural historian and long-time advocate for a transformation of human relationship to the natural world, Thomas Berry, says we do not choose the time in which we are born, the particular moment of history in which we find ourselves. Yet, the meaning of our lives depends on how we understand and fulfill our role.

> Our own special role, which we will hand on to our children, is that of managing the arduous transition from the terminal Cenozoic to the emerging Ecozoic Era, the period when humans will be present to the planet as participating members of the comprehensive Earth community. This is our Great Work and the work of our children.[1]

At its core, the fulfillment of our human role in the life of the Earth community regards a transformation of our understanding of our human subjectivity and our relationship to other-than-human beings.

In this chapter, I will consider the developments that have taken place over the past fifty years in Catholic thinking about care for the natural world. I will indicate four areas in which the social encyclical letter, *Laudato Si': On Care for Our Common Home*, is a significant development of Catholic social teaching. This 2015 document brought the Roman Catholic church more directly into the international discussion about humanity's relationship and responsibility to other-than-human beings. In particular, I will indicate that *Laudato Si'*'s discussion of the need for an integral ecology, set within the context of the life and thought of St. Francis of Assisi, is a critical contribution to the creation of a community of compassion.

THE CONTEXT OF CATHOLIC SOCIAL TEACHING

The contemporary Catholic conversation about ecology emerges out of a long tradition of engagement in issues of social justice, especially justice for the poorest, most oppressed persons of the world. Catholic teaching on society begins with a foundational principle regarding the dignity of human persons. This dignity originates from God because human beings are made in God's own image and likeness (Genesis 1:27). Consequently, human life is considered sacred because human persons are seen to be the clearest reflection of God's presence among us. This human dignity is inalienable which means that it is integral to our human nature. The Second Vatican Council affirmed:

> There is a growing awareness of the sublime dignity of human persons, who stand above all things and whose rights and duties are universal and inviolable. They ought, therefore, to have ready access to all that is necessary for living a genuinely human life: for example, food, clothing, housing . . . the right to education, and work.[2]

We are to order society according to the intrinsic worth, freedom, and dignity of every human person. Therefore, the Second Vatican Council went on to say:

> Whatever insults human dignity, such as subhuman living conditions, arbitrary imprisonment, deportation, slavery, prostitution, the selling of women and children; as well as disgraceful working conditions, where [people] are treated as mere tools for profit, rather than as free and responsible persons; all these things and others of their like are infamies indeed. . . . They poison human society.[3]

Catholic social teaching also repeatedly makes the claim that human beings are fundamentally social creatures. "It is in interrelationships on many levels that a person lives, and that society becomes more 'personalized.' . . .Today, the church's social doctrine focuses especially on [human persons as they are] involved in a complex network of relationships within modern society."[4] We are constituted by our relationships; who we are is, in large part, the result of all of our lifetime relationships.

This anthropological perspective is contrasted with the political and economic thinking in Western culture, which tends to present the autonomous individual as the basic social unit. Within this perspective, social relationships are the result of "contracts" that we make with each other because it is in our personal best interests to do so. However, Catholic social teaching argues that human beings are created in the image of God whose very nature is relationship; God is Trinitarian. Consequently, if human beings are made in the image of God, then we are also made of relationships and for relationships.

If we are social in nature, then we have social obligations. This is why the social teaching of the Catholic church emphasizes working together for the common good.

> [In] a world divided and beset by every type of conflict, the conviction is growing of a radical interdependence. . . . When interdependence becomes recognized in this way, the correlative response as a moral and social attitude, as a "virtue," is solidarity. This then is not a feeling of vague compassion or shallow distress at the misfortunes of so many people, both near and far. On the contrary, it is a firm and persevering determination to commit oneself to the common good.[5]

From the Catholic church's perspective, the claim that human persons are social in nature is to say that this is the way things are at their most fundamental level (ontology), and that this is the way things ought to be (ethics). If we are social by nature, then we have an obligation and responsibility not simply to ourselves as individuals but also to society; we are interdependent. St. Pope John Paul II was instrumental in talking about this obligation with the language of solidarity, another key principle of Catholic social teaching. For him, interdependence means relationships in all spheres—economic, cultural, political, and religious. That is why interdependence leads to the obligation to work for the common good, another key principle of Catholic social teaching.

In 1961, St. Pope John XXIII described the common good as "all those social conditions which favour the full development of human personality."[6] The human person who is made in God's image is a social being, who can only flourish in community, whose rights and duties are realized in community. This is why the good of each individual person in society is closely connected to the good of the wider society. The principle of the common good suggests that human beings achieve their dignity in communities, not in isolation. It requires a foundation of basic rights as minimum standards for life, and it is concerned that all persons participate and share in society's advances.

THE DEVELOPMENT OF A CATHOLIC RESPONSE

> In our day, there is a growing awareness that world peace is threatened not only by the arms race, regional conflicts and continued injustices among peoples and nations, but also by a lack of *due respect for nature*, by the plundering of natural resources and by a progressive decline in the quality of life. . . . Faced with widespread destruction of the environment, people everywhere

understand that we cannot continue to use the goods of the earth as we have in the past . . . [A] new *ecological awareness* is beginning to emerge.[7]

John Paul II's 1990 World Day of Peace message, "Peace with God the Creator, Peace with all of Creation," is regarded as the time when the leadership of the Roman Catholic church started to dedicate whole documents to ecological issues. In this same message, he describes the core of the ecological crisis: "It is manifestly unjust that a privileged few should continue to accumulate excess goods, squandering available resources, while masses of people are living in the conditions of misery at the very lowest level of subsistence."[8] Our waste is dumped where the poor live. We build incinerators to deal with our garbage in the backyards of the poorest people. Too many of us consume at such a rate that land is taken over by corporations for the exporting of crops. This means that Indigenous peoples all over the world cannot grow their own food and feed their families. They are forced to move to cities in the hope of finding work that does not usually exist. They have to look for food wherever they can, even in garbage dumps. What we are doing to the planet has the greatest human impact on the poorest people of the planet.

The ecological awareness that was emerging in the 1980s saw connections between the suffering that human beings are experiencing and the damage that is being caused to the planet. A healthy planet starts to be understood as another condition for fulfillment and the achievement of the common good, not just for human persons but also for all other-than-human beings. In 2001, the Canadian Conference of Catholic Bishops spoke about an expanded notion of the common good:

> The principle of the common good should lead to increased care for creation, understood as the sustenance and flourishing of life for all beings and for future generations. . . . With one in 10 species of birds, one in four species of mammals and over half of all species of primates on the planet threatened with extinction, the "common good" takes on an entirely new meaning. Since current production and consumption are so highly concentrated among the wealthy, the present model of development not only excludes the majority of this and future generations, but is exploitative and destructive of many forms of life on earth. . . . The principle of the common good must today be enlarged not only to accept the stewardship of the earth, but to include all forms of creation.[9]

This statement is suggesting a number of significant things. If the common good has to do with having access to whatever conditions are necessary for fulfillment, and if the common good now needs to include all forms of creation, this means that, as we order society, we have to be asking whether all forms of life have access to the conditions that are necessary for their fulfillment. For example, we have to ask about the need of other species for adequate habitats and comprehensive ecosystems as we decide on development projects. We have to take all forms of creation into consideration as we make decisions about what is good for all.

On October 4, 2003, the feast of St. Francis of Assisi, the patron saint of ecology, the Canadian bishops issued a pastoral letter on what they called, the "Christian Ecological Imperative." Then, in 2008, the United Nations International Year of Planet Earth, they issued another letter called "Our Relationship with the Environment: The Need for Conversion." In both, the bishops say that serious responses to the ecological crisis demand "that human beings change our thinking, relationships and behaviours in order to recognize the interconnectedness of all creation."[10] In other words, the only way to meet this crisis is with conversion. In the 2008 document, the bishops speak of this crisis as moral and spiritual, which means that the conversion also needs to be moral and spiritual: "A moral crisis must be met with conversion, which is a change in perspective, attitudes and behaviour."[11] What the Canadian bishops state is reflective of statements made by other conferences of bishops, John Paul II, and the Ecumenical Patriarchate Bartholomew I. The notion of ecological conversion is also central to Pope Francis's recent encyclical on the environment.

LAUDATO SI': ON CARE FOR OUR COMMON HOME

At the heart of *Laudato Si'* is this question: "What kind of world do we want to leave to those who come after us, to children who are now growing up?"[12] What this question does, Pope Francis suggests, is push us to ask about the meaning of existence and the values at the basis of social life, for only an honest struggle with these deeper issues will produce significant ecological results. He suggests that we will find ourselves needing to ask: "What is the purpose of our life in this world? Why are we here? What is the goal of our work and all our efforts? What need does the earth have of us?"[13] Pope Francis thinks that what is at stake in this serious endeavor is our own dignity. This same sentiment is expressed by cultural historian, Thomas Berry: "The Great Work before us, the task of moving modern industrial civilization from its present devastating influence on the Earth to a more benign mode of presence, is not a role that we have chosen. It is a role given to us. . . . The nobility of our lives . . . depends upon the manner in which we come to understand and fulfill our assigned role."[14]

Against any who might argue that a papal encyclical on the environment does not have any real authority, Pope Francis explicitly states at the outset that *Laudato Si'* is now part of the body of the Church's social teaching. He hopes that it can help us deal with the immensity and urgency of the challenges before us. This encyclical continues the kind of reflection on society that began with Pope Leo XIII's *Rerum Novarum*, published in 1891, on the impact of industrialization and the rights of workers.

Pope Francis uses some of the traditional foundations of Catholic social teaching, particularly the ideas of human dignity, solidarity, a preferential option for the poor, and the "common good," to frame his discussion. As with previous writings on social issues, Pope Francis combines the riches of the church's theology with the findings of experts in a variety of fields as he reflects on this particular problem of our times. What is new here is that Pope Francis says that concern and care for the earth is not optional. It is now, definitely, an integral part of the church's teaching on social justice.

This is the first encyclical letter that is dealing, in its entirety, with environmental issues. It takes its name, *Laudato Si'*, from the invocation that St. Francis of Assisi uses in his *Canticle of the Creatures*, "Praise be you, my Lord." This earth, our common home, "is like a sister with whom we share our life and a beautiful mother who opens her arms to embrace us."[15] But Pope Francis challenges us with the fact that "This sister now cries out to us because of the harm we have inflicted on her by our irresponsible use and abuse of the goods with which God has endowed her."[16] Because human beings regard themselves as masters of the earth, "the earth herself, burdened and laid waste, is among the most abandoned and maltreated of our poor."[17] We maltreat the earth because we have forgotten who we really are, that we are dust of the earth as the book of Genesis says, that the elements of our bodies are the elements of the earth and the stars, that we breathe the air of the earth, that we receive life and refreshment from the waters of the earth. The earth is lamenting; today, the groans of the earth join the groans of all those persons who are forsaken.

Like John XXIII's 1963 document, *Pacem in Terris*,—a document on violence, cold war, nuclear weapons—*Laudato Si'* is addressed not just to Catholics or Christians but to all people: "I wish to address every person living on this planet."[18] Pope Francis points to his predecessors, Paul VI, John Paul II, and Benedict XVI, to indicate that this authoritative text is in continuity with what has come before. Pope Francis also refers to other churches, Christian communities, and other religions—many of which have expressed deep concern about the earth and which he considers to offer valuable reflections on ecology.

Pope Francis especially highlights the contributions of the Ecumenical Patriarch Bartholomew, whose writings challenge our comfortable lifestyles and our disregard for our common home. He quotes a 1997 address given by Patriarch Bartholomew in which he said, "For human beings to cause species to become extinct and to destroy the biological diversity of God's creation; for human beings to degrade the integrity of Earth by causing changes in its climate, by stripping the Earth of its natural forests, or destroying its wetlands; for humans to contaminate the Earth's water, its land, its air, and its life, with poisonous substances—these are sins."[19]

With this encyclical, the language of faith enters the discussion on the environment in a very clear and decisive way. Pope Francis firmly grounds the discussion in a spiritual perspective and invites others to listen and to dialogue with a religious point of view. It is a groundbreaking document that expands the conversation by inviting believers into the dialogue and by providing fresh insights for those already involved with the issues. In a spirit of hope and joy, he asks for all human beings to come together "to seek a sustainable and integral development, for we know that things can change."[20] The responsibility for care of our common home belongs to all of us, and so each of us has to look at how we contribute to what is happening. We are culpable for our indifference; we cannot just sit by and let things go on as they are. We not only ask forgiveness for what we have done but also for what we have failed to do, as the Lord's prayer suggests.

Since we are all complicit in some way, and we are all responsible, Pope Francis appeals for dialogue about how, together, we want to shape the future of the planet. "We need a conversation which includes everyone, since the environmental challenge we are undergoing, and its human roots, concern and affect us all."[21] Everyone needs to be included in this conversation because the environmental challenges affect every being of the earth. This encyclical is a call for a new solidarity: with those who suffer the most immediate consequences of environmental damage; with other-than-human creatures; with future generations. In other words, this is a call for an intergenerational solidarity. As we dialogue with each other, we will need to overcome our indifference and face what is happening to our common home. That is what Pope Francis does in chapter 1, entitled "What is Happening to Our Common Home?"[22]

This question is not arbitrary. It has its roots in the Second Vatican Council and in the document on the Church in the modern world, *Gaudium et spes*, which says: "The Church has always had the duty of scrutinizing the signs of the times and of interpreting them in the light of the gospel."[23] Pope Francis takes up this mandate from the council and speaks to this critical set of issues in our time. His goal "is not to amass information or to satisfy curiosity, but rather to become painfully aware, to dare to turn what is happening to the world into our own suffering . . . and thus to discover what each of us can do about it."[24]

Like all the problems that Pope Francis addresses in the first chapter—pollution, waste, the issue of water, the loss of biodiversity, decline in the quality of life and the breakdown of society—climate change is understood to be a global problem. It has environmental, social, economic, and political implications, and it affects the distribution of goods. Pope Francis indicates clearly that we are to think of the climate as "a common good, belonging to all and meant for all."[25] Pope Francis also accepts the current scientific data: "A very solid scientific consensus indicates that we are presently witnessing a disturbing warming of the climatic system."[26] Furthermore, in order to avoid any further warming of the climate, "[h]umanity is called to recognize the need for changes of lifestyle, production and consumption, in order to combat this warming or at least the human causes which produce or aggravate it."[27]

Throughout the encyclical, Pope Francis indicates that the poor are disproportionately affected by climate change. This is not simply the result of the power of the rich to make decisions that do not take the poor into account, but it is because the poor themselves have fewer financial resources that enable them to adapt to climate change. Pope Francis continually condemns the culture of indifference, which does not respond to the needs of the poorest people nor of the suffering earth. In the world of this encyclical, there is no room for selfishness or indifference.[28] One cannot care for the rest of nature, Pope Francis says, "if our hearts lack tenderness, compassion and concern for our fellow human beings."[29] The intimate relationship between the poor and the fragility of the planet is one of the central themes that runs through the entire document and is looked at from a variety of perspectives.

What is to be done to respond adequately, effectively, and for future generations, to the suffering of the earth and the poor? I will highlight four areas that Pope Francis deals with throughout the encyclical: ecological conversion, developing ecological virtues, creating an ecological culture, nurturing an ecological spirituality.[30]

ECOLOGICAL CONVERSION

To begin to face our current ecological problems, Pope Francis turns in the second chapter to certain Biblical accounts, offering a comprehensive view that comes from the Judeo-Christian tradition. While the encyclical is addressed to everyone, Pope Francis also says that it is worthwhile to look at the convictions of people of faith. Quoting John Paul II, the encyclical states: "Christians in their turn, 'realize that their responsibility within creation, and their duty towards nature and the Creator, are an essential part of their faith.'"[31] Pope Francis talks about the "tremendous responsibility" of humankind for creation, the intimate connection among all creatures, and the fact that "[t]he natural environment is a collective good, the patrimony of all humanity and responsibility of everyone."[32]

In the Bible, he says, "the God who liberates and saves is the same God who created the universe, and these two divine ways of acting are intimately and inseparably connected."[33] The stories of creation are central for reflecting on the relationship between human beings and other creatures and on how sin breaks the equilibrium of all creation in its entirety. "They suggest that human life is grounded in three fundamental and closely intertwined relationships: with God, with our neighbour and with the earth itself. According to the Bible, these three vital relationships have been broken, both outwardly and within us. This rupture is sin."[34]

Consequently, Pope Francis speaks strongly and directly about incorrect interpretations of these accounts that must be rejected. Even if "we Christians have at times incorrectly interpreted the Scriptures, nowadays we must forcefully reject the notion that our being created in God's image and given dominion over the earth justifies absolute domination over other creatures."[35] Instead of dominion, human beings have the responsibility to "till and keep" the garden that is our common home,[36] knowing that the "ultimate purpose of other creatures is not to be found in us. Rather, all creatures are moving forward with us and through us towards a common point of arrival, which is God."[37]

Pope Francis's presentation of the Judeo-Christian witness, leads him to speak again of another of the central themes of the encyclical—everything is interconnected; or, put another way, there is a universal communion among all created beings. "All of us are called into being by one Father. All of us are linked by unseen bonds and together form a kind of universal family, a sublime communion which fills us with a sacred, affectionate and humble respect."[38] In ecological conversion, with awareness of universal communion, we are called to recognize that other living beings have a value of their own in God's eyes. Other creatures are not completely subordinated to the good of human beings, as if they have no worth in themselves and can be treated and used as we wish. There is no separation between the genuine care for our own lives and our relationships with the natural world. This idea of universal communion is connected to a sense of other beings as my sisters and brothers, to justice and solidarity with all creation, and to faithfulness in my relationships with others, human and other-than-human, alike.

DEVELOPING ECOLOGICAL VIRTUES

The Judeo-Christian tradition affirms that creation is a holy and precious gift from God; it is a gift given out of love. Pope Francis refers to the book of Wisdom: "For you love all things that exist, and detest none of the things that you have made; for you would not have made anything if you had hated it." (Wisdom 11:24). God loves all that exists, every single thing that exists, in its individuality and in its contribution to the whole of creation. In their 2003 pastoral letter on the environment, the Canadian bishops used this verse from Wisdom as part of the title of their letter. It indicates clearly that if God loves all that exists, we are called to do the same, to love to the fullness and to the degree that God loves. Truly acknowledging the value of the natural world should have an impact on how we live our individual lives and the way we order and structure our society.

Pope Francis has hope and trust that human beings can undergo the needed ecological conversion. The encyclical invites everyone to ecological conversion with the conviction that such conversion should result in a change of our hearts, minds, and our living. But, in Pope Francis's mind, the roots of the cultural crisis of our time are quite deep; it is extremely difficult to reshape deeply ingrained, and very comfortable, habits and behaviors. It is especially not easy within the context of the current global market system, which is primarily concerned with its bottom line. That bottom line will grow only if you and I consume as much as possible.

Pope Francis takes aim against what he calls the "techno-economic paradigm" in which technology is seen as the "principal key" to human existence.[39] This is not a blanket rejection of technology. Instead, Pope Francis critiques our unthinking reliance on market forces that embrace every technological, scientific or industrial advancement before considering how they will affect the environment and "without concern for its potentially negative impact on human beings."[40]

Pope Francis also critiques the society of "extreme consumerism" that has emerged alongside this techno-economic paradigm. People are unable to resist what the market places before them. But, as a result of this extreme consumerism, the earth is despoiled and billions of human persons are left impoverished.[41] That is why a true ecological conversion should manifest itself in a change of lifestyle. It is time, Pope Francis says, to accept "decreased growth in some parts of the world, in order to provide recourse for other places to experience healthy growth."[42] In contrast with the consumerist mindset, "Christian spirituality proposes a growth marked by moderation and the capacity to be happy with little."[43]

What Pope Francis is talking about is nothing less than a redefinition of our notion of progress. The starting point is "to aim for a new lifestyle" that would open up the possibility of bringing "healthy pressure to bear on those who wield the political, economic, and social power" in our world.[44] Pope Francis highlights and praises the good things that are going on, the efforts that people are making to care for our common home. He truly believes that we are able to change "the way businesses operate, forcing them to consider their environmental footprint and their patterns of production."[45] He references Benedict XVI, who said: "Purchasing is always a moral—and not simply economic—act."[46] And he points to actions like boycotts when human beings have pushed companies to change their patterns of production.

What are the values that Pope Francis wants the market to pay attention to? What are the values that will guide our own personal consuming? Will we think, for example, of the question with which we started: what kind of world do we want to leave for our human and other-than-human grandchildren? This is why Pope Francis says that we cannot overstate the importance of ecological education. This is the kind of education that can help us understand the nature of the universe and raise our consciousness. Even moreso, ecological education can help to open our eyes to the myths of our modern culture: individualism, unlimited progress, competition, consumerism, and an unregulated market. Ecological education can help us to reestablish just and loving relationships with ourselves, with other human persons, with the natural world and other living creatures, and with God.

Ecological education is also able to affect our actions and daily habits. For Pope Francis, developing ecological virtues is key to the transformation of our world. We develop these virtues by what we do every single day. There is a nobility, Pope Francis says, in the duty to care for creation through all of our small daily actions.[47] It is striking that he talks about some of the small things that we do every day that can make a real difference such as: "avoiding the use of plastic and paper, reducing water consumption, separating refuse, cooking only what can reasonably be consumed, showing care for other living beings, using public transit or car-pooling, planting trees, turning off unnecessary lights, or any number of other practices."[48]

Pope Francis recognizes how beneficial these actions are to society but also to our own sense of ourselves: to our nobility, self-esteem, and a real sense of living as people of dignity. "An integral ecology is . . . made up of simple daily gestures which break with the logic of violence, exploitation and selfishness, which can help to create a culture in which life is shared and all beings are respected."[49] Furthermore, "[w]e must regain the conviction that we need one another, that we have a shared responsibility for others and the world, and that being good and decent are worth it."[50]

CREATING AN ECOLOGICAL CULTURE

The heart of the encyclical's proposals for responding to the devastation of our common home is an integral ecology. As Pope Francis presents it, the notion of an integral ecology is a new paradigm of justice, an ecology "which respects our unique place as human beings in this world and our relationship to our surroundings."[51] The word *environment* itself needs to be understood as having to do with a relationship between the natural world and human persons. "Nature cannot be regarded as something separate from ourselves or as a mere setting in which we live."[52] As Pope Francis says many times in *Laudato Si'*, ecological conversion helps us understand that "[w]e are part of nature, included in nature, in constant interaction with it."[53] It confirms that everything is interconnected. An integral ecology is not simply a religious notion but, rather, it applies to all aspects of human society: economics and politics, in different cultures, particularly in those most threatened, and even in every moment of our daily lives. An integral perspective brings the ecology of institutions into play: "[i]f everything is related, then the health of a society's institutions has consequences for the environment and the quality of human life."[54]

Since the crisis is social and environmental, the strategies that we develop to respond to the crisis have to be social and environmental. With many concrete examples, Pope Francis confirms his thinking that "the analysis of environmental problems cannot be separated from the analysis of human, family, work-related and urban contexts, nor from how individuals relate to themselves."[55]

So many of our problems, Pope Francis says, stem from the centrality and pervasiveness of the technological paradigm. It shapes every aspect of our lives. The technocratic paradigm dominates not only our social lives but our economic and political lives as well. Profit governs economics and politics. As a consequence, we become primarily concerned about the economy but the economy as understood within this technocratic paradigm.

Pope Francis reiterates the teaching of Benedict XVI, who reminded us in his encyclical, *Caritas in Veritate*, that, "by itself, the market cannot guarantee integral human development and social inclusion."[56] What we need is a new way of looking at our culture; we need a new way of thinking; we need new policies, a new education, a new lifestyle, and a new spirituality, which resists the dominant technocratic paradigm. A significant problem for us is that this paradigm is so pervasive and extensive that we cannot imagine a different way of understanding the world. Furthermore, the mindset is so dominant that it would be difficult for us to operate without all of its benefits and resources. And, when we use those resources, we cannot avoid being pulled into the logic that governs the use of the resources.

Yet, in the face of these significant cultural and personal challenges, Pope Francis raises again his voice of hope: "An authentic humanity, calling for a new synthesis, seems to dwell in the midst of our technological culture, almost unnoticed, like a mist seeping gently beneath a closed door."[57] Still, despite the hope, the question remains: can this new authentic ecological culture continue to overcome the inevitable resistance to change? We continually hear that there is no other way to order our society, that the way our economy works is the only option; that, at best, we simply need to make some adjustments to the current paradigm so that it works better for more people and for the environment.

Pope Francis has hope that we can continue to move forward with a cultural revolution. But to do so we will have to eliminate the excessive anthropocentrism that is part of our technocratic culture. This distorted anthropocentrism works really well with a paradigm that "sees the natural world as an insensate order, as a cold body of facts, as a mere 'given,' as an object of utility, as raw material to be hammered into useful shape."[58] Quoting one of his favorite authors, Romano Guardini and his book *The End of the Modern World*, Pope Francis states that the technological mind "views the cosmos . . . as a mere 'space' into which objects can be thrown with complete indifference."[59]

This excessive or distorted anthropocentrism compromises the intrinsic dignity of the world. It indicates what Pope Francis states at the outset, that we do not understand who we truly are; we end up acting against ourselves.

> The culture of relativism is the same disorder which drives one person to take advantage of another, to treat others as mere objects, imposing forced labour on them or enslaving them to pay their debts. The same kind of thinking leads to the sexual exploitation of children and abandonment of the elderly who no longer serve our interests. . . . This same 'use and throw away' logic generates so much waste, because of the disordered desire to consume more than what is really necessary.[60]

The throwaway dimension of our culture is another consistent and central theme for Pope Francis. In order to develop an ecological culture, we need to stop operating out of the model of dominion—dominion of human beings, and dominion of the natural world. We need, instead, to develop a proper sense of stewardship or care for the world.

NURTURING AN ECOLOGICAL SPIRITUALITY

For Pope Francis, the development of responsible stewardship is helped by nurturing an ecological spirituality. And the guide that Pope Francis turns to is St. Francis of Assisi: he is "the example par excellence of care for the vulnerable and of an integral ecology that is lived out joyfully and authentically."[61] He is the model of "just how inseparable the bond is between concern for nature, justice for the poor, commitment to society, and interior peace."[62]

St. Francis shows that an integral ecology and spirituality opens us to categories that can get to "the heart of what it is to be human."[63] Pope Francis reminds us of St. Francis's relationship to the natural world: "just as happens when we fall in love with someone, whenever [Francis] would gaze at the sun, the moon or the smallest of animals, he burst into song, drawing all other creatures into his praise. He communed with all creation, even preaching to the flowers."[64] For St. Francis, "each and every creature was a sister united to him by bonds of affection."[65]

What St. Francis models is not naïve romanticism. Rather, it reflects a kinship model of relationship to the rest of creation. It starts from the fundamental notion that we human beings, all of us, are part of creation. We are not aliens on this earth but an integral part of creation. We are made of the same elements, part of the same family, sharing DNA with most of the rest of creation. This model of relationships affects all aspects of our behavior.

> If we approach nature and the environment without this openness to awe and wonder, if we no longer speak the language of fraternity and beauty in our relationship with the world, our attitude will be that of masters, consumers, ruthless exploiters, unable to set limits on their immediate needs. By contrast, if we feel intimately united with all that exists, then sobriety and care will well up spontaneously. The poverty and austerity of Saint Francis were no mere veneer of asceticism, but something much more radical: a refusal to turn reality into an object simply to be used and controlled.[66]

St. Francis is an example of how to feel intimately united with all that exists. As Pope Francis says in his 2013 apostolic exhortation, *Evangelii Gaudium*: "God has joined us so closely to the world around us that we can feel the desertification of the soil almost as a physical ailment, and the extinction of a species as a painful disfigurement."[67] This is the depth of intimacy that St. Francis models. It is the depth of intimacy that an ecological spirituality can nurture in us.

Pope Francis is convinced that we are capable of undergoing the depth of transformation that is needed in our relationship to our common home: "Yet all is not lost. Human beings, while capable of the worst, are also capable of rising above themselves, choosing again what is good, and making a new start."[68] When we start from the perspective of being an intimate part of the family of creation, then we begin to know that our care for our common home is fundamentally about love. And such deep love and care for the gift of God's creation leads us to praise God as St. Francis did in his *Canticle of the Creatures*[69] and to live with compassion and justice as members of this beautiful and comprehensive Earth community.

NOTES

1. Thomas Berry, *The Great Work: Our Way Into the Future* (New York: Bell Tower, 1999), 7–8.

2. Paul VI, *Gaudium et spes [Pastoral Constitution on the Church in the Modern World]* (Vatican City, Rome: Holy See Press Office, 1965), n. 26, *The Holy See*, accessed June 25, 2016, http://www.vatican.va/archive/hist_councils/ii_vatican_council/documents/vat-ii_const_19651207_gaudium-et-spes_en.html. For more on Catholic social teaching, see Thomas Massaro, S.J., *Living Justice: Catholic Social Teaching in Action*, Second Classroom Edition (Lanham, MD: Rowman & Littlefield Publishers, 2012); Donal Dorr, *Option for the Poor and for the Earth: Catholic Social Teaching*. (Maryknoll, NY: Orbis Books, 2012); Daniel G. Groody, *Globalization, Spirituality, and Justice*. (Maryknoll, NY: Orbis Books, 2007).

3. Ibid., 27. For more on the Second Vatican Council, see Timothy G. McCarthy, *The Catholic Tradition: The Church in the Twentieth Century*, Second Edition (Chicago: Loyola Press, 1998); Giuseppe Alberigo, *A Brief History of Vatican II* (Maryknoll, NY: Orbis Books, 2006); Richard R. Gaillardetz and Catherine E. Clifford, *Keys to the Council: Unlocking the*

Teaching of Vatican II. (Collegeville, MN: Liturgical Press, 2012); John W. O'Malley, *What Happened at Vatican II.* (Cambridge, MA: Belknap Press of Harvard University Press, 2008); Austin Flannery, O.P., general editor, *Vatican Council,* Ibid., n. 8.II: *Volume 1, The Conciliar and Post Conciliar Documents,* New Revised Edition (Northport, NY: Costello Publishing Company, 2004).

4. John Paul II, *Centesimus Annus* [Encyclical Letter on The Hundredth Anniversary of *Rerum Novarum*] (Vatican City, Rome: Holy See Press Office, 1991), nn. 49, 54, *The Holy See,* accessed June 24, 2016, http://w2.vatican.va/content/john-paul-ii/en/encyclicals/documents/hf_jp-ii_enc_01051991_centesimus-annus.html.

5. John Paul II, *Sollicitudo rei socialis* [Encyclical Letter on the twentieth anniversary of *Populorum Progressio*] (Vatican City: Holy See Press Office, 1987), nn.26, 38, *The Holy See,* accessed June 24, 2016, http://w2.vatican.va/content/john-paul-ii/en/encyclicals/documents/hf_jp-ii_enc_30121987_sollicitudo-rei-socialis.html.

6. John XXIII, *Mater et magistra* [Encyclical Letter On Christianity and Social Progress] (Vatican City, Rome: Holy See Press Office, 1961), n. 65, *The Holy See,* accessed June 24, 2016, http://w2.vatican.va/content/john-xxiii/en/encyclicals/documents/hf_j-xxiii_enc_15051961_mater.html.

7. John Paul II, *Peace with God the Creator, Peace with all of Creation* [1990 World Day of Peace Message] (Vatican City, Rome: Holy See Press Office, 1990), n. 1, *The Holy See,* accessed June 24, 2016, https://w2.vatican.va/content/john-paul-ii/en/messages/peace/documents/hf_jp-ii_mes_19891208_xxiii-world-day-for-peace.html.

8. John Paul II, *Peace with God the Creator, Peace with all of Creation* [1990 World Day of Peace Message], 8.

9. Canadian Conference of Catholic Bishops, *The Common Good or Exclusion: A Choice for Canadians,* [Public Statement], n. 12, accessed June 24, 2016, https://w2.vatican.va/content/john-paul-ii/en/messages/peace/documents/hf_jp-ii_mes_19891208_xxiii-world-day-for-peace.html.

10. Canadian Conference of Catholic Bishops, Social Affairs Commission, *A Pastoral Letter on the Christian Ecological Imperative,* n. 14, accessed June 24, 2016, http://www.cccb.ca/site/Files/pastoralenvironment.html.

11. Canadian Conference of Catholic Bishops, Social Affairs Commission, *Our Relationship with the Environment: The Need for Conversion,* accessed June 24, 2016, http://www.cccb.ca/site/images/stories/pdf/enviro_eng.pdf.

12. Francis, *Laudato Si'* [Encyclical Letter On Care for Our Common Home] (Vatican City, Rome: Holy See Press Office, 2015), n. 160, *The Holy See,* accessed June 24, 2016, http://w2.vatican.va/content/francesco/en/encyclicals/documents/papa-francesco_20150524_enciclica-laudato-si.html. The author has been granted permission from the Libreria Editrice Vaticana for nonexclusive use of © *Laudato Si'* for this publication.

13. Francis, *Laudato Si'* [Encyclical Letter On Care for Our Common Home].
14. Thomas Berry, *The Great Work,* 7.
15. Pope Francis, *Laudato Si',* n. 1.
16. Pope Francis, *Laudato Si',* 2.
17. Pope Francis, *Laudato Si',* 2.
18. Pope Francis, *Laudato Si',* 3.
19. Ecumenical Patriarch Bartholomew, *Environmental Symposium,* Santa Barbara, November 8, 1997, accessed July 4, 2016, https://www.orthodoxcouncil.org/addresses-and-texts/-/asset_publisher/fNvoWrMe3Xst/content/address-of-ecumenical-patriarch-bartholomew-at-the-environmental-symposium-saint-barbara-greek-orthodox-church-santa-barbara-california/32008, quoted in Francis, *Laudato Si',* n. 8.

20. Francis, *Laudato Si',* 13.
21. Francis, *Laudato Si',* 14.
22. Francis, *Laudato Si',* 17–63. The remaining chapters are entitled: "The Gospel of Creation;" "The Human Roots of the Ecological Crisis;" "Integral Ecology;" "Lines of Approach and Action;" "Ecological Education and Spirituality."
23. Pope Paul VI, *Gaudium et spes,* n. 4.
24. *Laudato Si',* n. 19.

25. Francis, *Laudato Si'*, 23.
26. Francis, *Laudato Si'*, 23.
27. Francis, *Laudato Si'*, 23.
28. Francis, *Laudato Si'*, 25.
29. Francis, *Laudato Si'*, 91.
30. This framework is used with permission from Neil Ormerod, Australian Catholic University.
31. Francis, *Laudato Si'*, 64.
32. Francis, *Laudato Si'*, 95.
33. Francis, *Laudato Si'*, 73.
34. Francis, *Laudato Si'*, 66.
35. Francis, *Laudato Si'*, 67.
36. Francis, *Laudato Si'*, 67.
37. Francis, *Laudato Si'*, 83.
38. Francis, *Laudato Si'*, 89.
39. Francis, *Laudato Si'*, 110.
40. Francis, *Laudato Si'*, 109.
41. Francis, *Laudato Si'*, 203.
42. Francis, *Laudato Si'*, n. 193.
43. Francis, *Laudato Si'*, 222.
44. Francis, *Laudato Si'*, 206.
45. Francis, *Laudato Si'*, 206.
46. Francis, *Laudato Si'*, 206.
47. Francis, *Laudato Si'*, 211.
48. Francis, *Laudato Si'*, 211.
49. Francis, *Laudato Si'*, 230.
50. Francis, *Laudato Si'*, 229.
51. Francis, *Laudato Si'*, 15.
52. Francis, *Laudato Si'*, 139.
53. Francis, *Laudato Si'*, 139.
54. Francis, *Laudato Si'*, 142.
55. Francis, *Laudato Si'*, 141.
56. Francis, *Laudato Si'*, 109.
57. Francis, *Laudato Si'*, 112.
58. Francis, *Laudato Si'*, 115.
59. Francis, *Laudato Si'*, 115.
60. Francis, *Laudato Si'*, 123.
61. Francis, *Laudato Si'*, 10.
62. Francis, *Laudato Si'*, 10.
63. Francis, *Laudato Si'*, 11.
64. Francis, *Laudato Si'*, 11.
65. Francis, *Laudato Si'*, 11.
66. Francis, *Laudato Si'*, 11.
67. Francis, *Laudato Si'*, 89.
68. Francis, *Laudato Si'*, 205.
69. Francis, *Laudato Si'*, 87.

REFERENCES

Berry, Thomas. *The Great Work: Our Way into the Future.* New York: Bell Tower, 1999.
Bartholomew, Ecumenical Patriarch. *Environmental Symposium.* Santa Barbara, CA. November 8, 1997. Accessed July 4, 2016. https://www.orthodoxcouncil.org/addresses-and-texts/-/asset_publisher/fNvoWrMe3Xst/content/address-of-ecumenical-patriarch-bartholomew-at-the-environmental-symposium-saint-barbara-greek-orthodox-church-santa-barbara-california/32008. Quoted in Francis, "Laudato Si'" (Vatican City, Rome: Holy See Press Office,

2015), n. 8, *The Holy See*. Accessed June 24, 2016. http://w2.vatican.va/content/francesco/en/encyclicals/documents/papa-francesco_20150524_enciclica-laudato-si.html.

Canadian Conference of Catholic Bishops. *The Common Good or Exclusion: A Choice for Canadians* [Public Statement]. Accessed June 24, 2016. https://w2.vatican.va/content/john-paul-ii/en/messages/peace/documents/hf_jp-ii_mes_19891208_xxiii-world-day-for-peace.html.

———, Social Affairs Commission. *A Pastoral Letter on the Christian Ecological Imperative*. Accessed June 24, 2016. http://www.cccb.ca/site/Files/pastoralenvironment.html.

———, Social Affairs Commission. *Our Relationship with the Environment: The Need for Conversion*. Accessed June 24, 2016. http://www.cccb.ca/site/images/stories/pdf/enviro_eng.pdf.

Dorr, Donal. *Option for the Poor and for the Earth: Catholic Social Teaching*. Maryknoll, NY: Orbis Books, 2012.

Francis. "Laudato Si' : On Care for Our Common Home." Vatican City, Rome: Holy See Press Office, 2015. *The Holy See*. Accessed June 24, 2016. http://w2.vatican.va/content/francesco/en/encyclicals/documents/papa-francesco_20150524_enciclica-laudato-si.html.

Groody, Daniel G. *Globalization, Spirituality, and Justice*. Maryknoll, NY: Orbis Books, 2007.

John XXIII. *Mater et magistra: On Christianity and Social Progress*. Vatican City, Rome: Holy See Press Office, 1961. *The Holy See*. Accessed June 24, 2016. http://w2.vatican.va/content/john-xxiii/en/encyclicals/documents/hf_j-xxiii.enc_15051961.

John Paul II. *Sollicitudo rei socialis*. Vatican City, Rome: Holy See Press Office, 1987. *The Holy See*. Accessed June 24, 2016. http://w2.vatican.va/content/john-paul-ii/en/encyclicals/documents/hf_jp-ii_enc_30121987_sollicitudo-rei-socialis.html.

———. *Peace with God the Creator, Peace with all of Creation*. Vatican City, Rome: Holy See Press Office, 1990. *The Holy See*. Accessed June 24, 2016. http://w2.vatican.va/content/john-paul-ii/en/messages/peace/documents/hf_jp-ii_19891208-world-day-for-peace.html.

———. *Centesimus Annus*. Vatican City, Rome: Holy See Press Office, 1991. *The Holy See*. Accessed June 24, 2016. http://w2.vatican.va/content/john-paul-ii/en/encyclicals/documents/hf_jp-ii_enc_01051991_centesimus-annus.html.

Massaro, Thomas, S. J. *Living Justice: Catholic Social Teaching in Action*, Second Classroom Edition. Lanham, MD: Rowman & Littlefield Publishers, 2012.

Paul VI. *Gaudium et spes*. Vatican City, Rome: Holy See Press Office, 1965. *The Holy See*. Accessed June 25, 2016. http://www.vatican.va/archive/hist_councils/ii_vatican_council/documents/vat-ii_const_19651207_gaudium-et-spes_en.html.

Part V

Jesus and the Animals in the Gospel of Mark

Chapter Eleven

Liberating Legion

An Ecocritical, Postcolonial reading of Mark 5:1–20

Kendra Haloviak Valentine

The story of the demoniac named Legion in the Gospel of Mark (5:1–20) raises many questions for readers today. First, the story makes Jesus responsible for the destruction of two thousand pigs. In addition, it causes us to ask why the demons, when confronted, want to remain in the land? Why does Jesus negotiate with them? Why do the demons, once they get what they want, seem to commit suicide? Upon seeing a restored man, why do the locals become deeply afraid (rather than angry) at their financial loss? Some interpretations dismiss the ethical question of Jesus's destruction of nonhuman life as "missing the point," suggesting instead that it is fitting that he sends unclean spirits into unclean animals and that the "story of the deliverance of a man becomes the story of the deliverance of a land."[1] But is such an interpretation superficial and inadequate since it seems to avoid so many of the other questions? Or does such an interpretation offer insights at a more profound level than previously thought?

This study attempts to understand this problematic story from within the framework of an ecocritical and postcolonial hermeneutic in order to explore what insights these particular approaches can offer that other approaches miss. This hermeneutical approach reads literary texts with a more acute awareness of the importance and significance of land in the ecologically sensitive, anti-imperial imagination.[2] Reading the story of Legion with careful attention to the depiction of land and nature provides new interpretative possibilities for this strange and difficult story. Such a reading also provides biblical support for ecotheological reflections on nature, sustainability, nonhuman life and human ethical responsibility. Reading Mark 5 through the lens of ecocriticism also keeps readers from collapsing Mark's depiction of land to a simplistic understanding of the passage as merely reflecting Jewish abhorrence of Gentile territory. Instead, the land is understood as "unclean"—hazardous and dangerous—through the narrative's emphasis on the threat to its ecological sustainability.[3]

Attending carefully to the depiction of land and nature leads to the observation that the story of the possessed Legion character is not simply a story of spiritual slavery. His possession is also political. A postcolonial lens allows the reader to see Legion as the embodiment of the violence used by imperial powers to control populations. In resistance to imperialism, postcolonial ecological texts reimagine the environment restored and people able to return to their place.

Following an English translation of Mark 5:1–20, the first part of this chapter, "Hazardous Land," considers Legion's story with careful attention to the descriptions of landscape through ecocritical observations. The story of Legion will be considered with the help of anthropologist Mary Douglas's groundbreaking contributions to understanding purity and pollution in the ordering of societies and with Roland Boer's recent work on the economics of ancient cultures. Various aspects of the story highlight Legion's land as hazardous.

The second part of this chapter, "Occupied Habitats," explores the story's environmental backdrop through postcolonial critical observations. Legion's land was occupied by Roman soldiers at the time of Mark's writing. Fields cultivated to provide food for surrounding villages had been occupied by Rome's military forces with obvious economic implications for the local farmers. Given the descriptions in Mark, many people had been displaced.[4] The political situation in this story legitimizes a postcolonial ecocritical interpretation since "one vital aspect of postcolonial ecology is to reimagine this displacement between people and place through poetics."[5] In this chapter I argue that Mark's story is doing just that: he is reimagining the displacement of people from their place through the exorcism story of Legion. The presence of two thousand pigs tells Mark's readers that the poor have been slaughtered or are starving, but once the pigs and the Roman legion are gone, oppressed people are able to return home. Therefore, the destruction of nonhuman life can be seen as a resistance story against the earlier violence on people and their land.

This exorcism story, the longest single episode in Mark's gospel,[6] occurs on the first occasion Jesus travels into Gentile territory and is typically interpreted as Jesus expanding his ministry beyond the borders of Judaism.[7] However, the depictions of a threatened environment along with the language of Roman colonial oppression redefine "unclean land" beyond ethnic categories. This story shows a major shift in thinking within Mark's narrative. By the time this scene ends, the land is unclean not only because it is Gentile land but also because of Roman invaders and the political decision by local elites to align with them in order to maintain economic privilege and to keep the colonized controlled. As well, by the end of this scene, "unclean spirits" are not only spiritual phenomena but also colonial systems that keep people oppressed.

Mark 5:1–20 may thus be understood as a protest against the oppression of the poor, an oppression caused by the Roman colonizing army and the local elites.

The nuanced description of various forms of life in this story tells of the discrepancy between the powerful and the vulnerable. An ecocritical, postcolonial reading of this text helps readers see the tightly woven relationship between Mark's environmental message and the mission of Jesus, a mission that challenges demonic colonial forces in order to liberate Legion.

MARK 5:1–20

> 1 They came to the other side of the sea to the land of the Gerasenes. 2 When he [Jesus] had come out of the boat, immediately out of the tombs there met him a man with an unclean spirit 3 who lived in the tombs, and no one and nothing could any longer bind him, not even with a chain; 4 for often he had been bound with shackles and with chains, but he had been able to wrench apart the chains, and he had crushed the shackles, and no one was strong enough to restrain him. 5 Through every night and day in the tombs and in the mountains he was crying out and cutting himself with stones. 6 When he saw Jesus from afar, he ran and fell down to worship him. 7 Crying out with a loud voice, he said: "What have you to do with me, Jesus, son of the most high God? I adjure you by God do not torture me." 8 For he was saying to him: "Unclean spirit, come out of the man." 9 He asked him, "What is your name?" And he said to him, "Legion is my name, for we are many." 10 He repeatedly begged him that he not send them out of the land. 11 Now there was on the mountain a large herd of pigs feeding. 12 They begged him, saying: "Send us into the pigs so that we might enter them." 13 And he dismissed them. And going out, the unclean spirits entered into the pigs and the herd, about 2,000, charged down the steep bank into the sea and drowned in the sea. 14 The ones who grazed them fled and reported in the city and in the country. And they came to see what had happened. 15 And they came to Jesus and saw the demon-possessed man sitting clothed and in a right mind, the one who had had the legion, and they were afraid. 16 The ones who had seen described to them what had happened to the demon-possessed man and concerning the pigs. 17 And they began to beg him to go away from their domain. 18 And, as he was getting into the boat, the demon-possessed man begged him that he might be with him. 19 He did not allow him but said to him, "Go away to your home to your people and report to them all that the Lord has done, how he has shown mercy to you." 20 And he departed and began to proclaim in the Decapolis all that Jesus had done for him, and everyone marveled. [8]

HAZARDOUS LAND

Mark's telling of Jesus's first sojourn in Gentile territory is full of textual clues highlighting location, natural environment, and people relegated to particular places.[9] The scene begins when Jesus crosses the lake known at this time as the Sea of Galilee. This body of water was a natural barrier between Jewish villages on the western shore and Gentile (primarily Hellenistic) territory on the eastern side of the sea. Having crossed over the sea (4:35–41), Jesus gets out of the boat at "the land of the Gerasenes" (5:1). This "land" (*chora* in Greek) probably refers to the countryside that surrounded one or more of the major cities of the Decapolis (a loose network of cities mostly on the eastern side of the sea of Galilee and the Jordan River).[10] Jews of Mark's day would not have given such nuanced descriptions to this region. They would have understood all the land on the "other side" as outside the land of Israel, far from the temple in Jerusalem. It was Gentile land and therefore unclean land. However, for the locals, *chora* probably referred to the areas where farming and animal husbandry occurred, regions around towns where land could be cultivated. More contemporary expressions would contrast the *chora* or rural "fields" with more urban areas, where people lived.[11] And so this story starts with different understandings of the "land" that provide the setting for this story. Is the land the vast, inclusive land on the "other side" of the sea, making the Jewish side normative and the "other" and its "others" unclean? Or is the land defined by what can be cultivated in order to provide food for its surrounding villages?

A Jewish person reading Mark's gospel would notice how almost everything described at the story's beginning is unclean. The man is unclean and contains many unclean spirits. He lives in tombs, which are unclean places[12] and in an unclean land. To top it off, two thousand unclean pigs feed nearby.[13] As one commentator summarizes the story, "Nothing about it is kosher."[14] One imagines the Jewish (Christian) reader shuddering at even the thought of Jesus spending any time in such a place.

But a Gentile reader, though perhaps for other reasons, might not respond much differently. The classic anthropological study by Mary Douglas, *Purity and Danger*, suggests that ancient social order was maintained by adherence to social boundaries.[15] What is pure and clean are those events, people and objects that easily fit into socially accepted categories with clear boundaries. The dirty and therefore dangerous are those things that are ambiguous (with no clear category) or out of place. Mark's description of the man calling himself "Legion" is one who acts more beastlike than human. He is living in the tombs (not a place for a living human), he howls on the mountains day and night, and he cuts himself with stones.[16] The description in Mark 5:3–4 underscores the efforts that had failed to contain Legion: "no one and nothing could any longer bind him, not even with a chain." In the Greek the quick list of negative nouns and adverbs carry this meaning even more clearly: "no one," "nothing," "no longer," and "not even." The description continues by mentioning shackles and chains that Legion can wrench apart and crush. The description goes well beyond him being merely "out of place." Legion is downright terrifying—he cannot be contained at all.

When Legion comes out of the tombs to meet a Jewish visitor coming out of a boat, the scene would have both Jew and Gentile reader on the alert, uncomfortable and anxious. Legion and his Gentile land threaten the ability of Jesus the Jew to maintain ritual purity. In addition, Legion's dangerous boundary-breaking behavior threatens social order in the Decapolis. He should be chained up and kept out of sight. Legion should *not* be the Gerasene welcoming committee. This is indeed hazardous land.

But the description of Legion is not the only hint at the hazards in Gerasa. Although the portrayal of a large herd of pigs feeding on a nearby mountain may give contemporary readers a sense of idyllic rural life, in actuality such a description suggests an extraction (state-estate) economy, where elite land owners valued luxury animal husbandry over the public health of the tenant farmers in the region. Mark's world was a time when locations such as that of the Gerasenes were shifting from land-share villages to estates owned by the very few. "Evidence for aristocratic control of major portions of arable land is most abundant for the period following the Jewish War."[17]

Roland Boer's recent work *The Sacred Economy of Ancient Israel* argues that in regions like that of the Gerasenes, villages were constantly responding to the tensions between allocation and extraction economies.[18] Allocation economies functioned as kinship communities allocating labor as well as the fruits of one's labor to members of the village. A village typically consisted of seventy-five to one hundred and fifty people, who "all belonged to the collective" and participated in subsistence agriculture. Work on the land was regularly reallocated, and surplus (crops as well as animal supply) was avoided since the villages were self-sufficient (no major trading with outsiders) and were nomadic (would relocate as needed).[19] In contrast, extractive economies were established in order to provide for nonlaborers (priests, elite), making large amounts of surplus both essential and compulsory.[20]

Allocation economies operating as self-sufficient tended to avoid grazing animals that required large pasturage and dependable water supplies with minimum benefit beyond meat. Since sheep and goats produce meat, milk, and fiber (wool or hair) and are "versatile eaters," able to "recover quickly after water shortage,"[21] they were chosen over cows and pigs.[22] Pigs, in particular, while providing "good quality meat," have other disadvantages: "They fare ill under temperature extremes, require relatively high levels of water, and do not provide fiber or milk for human consumption."[23]

Anthropologist Marvin Harris further notes, "the world zones of pastoral nomadism correspond to unforested plains and hills that are too arid for rainfall agriculture and that cannot easily be irrigated. The domestic animals best adapted to these zones are the ruminants—cattle, sheep, and goats. [. . .] The pig, however, is primarily a creature of forests and shaded riverbanks." Harris suggests that the Israelite prohibition against eating pigs was a "sound ecological strategy."[24]

Harris goes on to argue that pigs compete with humans for nourishment (nuts, fruits, tubers, grain). They do not produce milk. They are "difficult to herd over long distances," and "nowhere in the world do fully nomadic pastoralists raise significant numbers of pigs."[25] He concludes that in regions similar to Gerasa, pork was "an ecological and economic luxury."[26]

So why would the hills in the land of the Gerasenes have a herd of two thousand pigs feeding? Where were the sheep and goats that provided milk and meat and wool for local villagers? What happened to the former crops now taken over as the land was converted into grazing areas for the pigs? What water supplies had been rerouted in order to meet the demands of the pigs? Does Legion greet Jesus at the shore because the majority of the population, without land or resources, had moved on?[27]

Boer suggests that when extraction economies displace allocation economies, laborers spend the majority of their time providing surplus for the few nonlaborers whose needs are never satisfied. The social fabric of the villages begins to unravel as provision of surplus luxury goods take the place of self-sufficiency values and subsistence agriculture. Rather than the "optimal engagement with nature" of allocation economies preferring "animals that have minimal impact on their environment," maximal engagement with nature is the mode of operation for extraction economies along with animals "which suck up water and fodder as though they were nothing."[28]

If we were reading Mark 5 with the eyes of a first-century reader aware of common agricultural practices, we might be astonished at any pig husbandry at all and especially at this unusually large herd of pigs. We would quickly surmise that it is a huge excess of luxury animals unsuited for the environment and an inefficient use of valuable resources. Far more shocking would be the realization, beyond the dietary prohibition associated with them, that the pigs required such a vast amount of land and other resources (grain and water). Put simply, the land and grain and water had been taken from people and given to the pigs. Within this cultural context, the "unclean land" of the Gerasenes was not as much about ethnicity as it was about ecological unsustainability. Some coercive power must be behind this inefficient and deadly agricultural decision. Who was responsible for this economic and environmental disaster?

OCCUPIED HABITATS

In the story of Legion, Mark gives several textual clues that clearly place the responsibility upon the Roman invading army. Rome was the coercive power that threatened the economic and environmental survival of the land of the Gerasenes. At the time Mark was writing his gospel, the Decapolis was the eastern frontier of the Roman Empire. Many veterans in the army had been given the "conquered lands as payment for their service."[29] Given the instability of the war years (66–70 CE), huge numbers of Roman troops were located in this region in order to quickly eliminate any insurrections against the colonial power or any advances from enemies to the east of the empire.

One of the cities of the Decapolis, Gadara (one of the possible locations for Mark's story), fell to the Roman military leader Vespasian in 67 or 68, who then ordered that all the youth be killed by the sword and the villages around Gadara burned. Josephus notes that after the armies carried out Vespasian's orders, some villages "were quite destitute of inhabitants."[30] In an account that occurs during these same years and not far from Gadara, another slaughter of local villagers by Rome is described. Josephus says that Placidus, one of Vespasian's generals, instigates a revenge killing that leaves thousands drowned in the Jordan River:

> But Placidus, relying much upon his horsemen, and his former good success, followed them, and slew all that he overtook, as far as Jordan; and when he had driven the whole multitude to the river-side, where they were stopped by the current (for it had been augmented lately by rains, and was not fordable) he put his soldiers in array over-against them; so the necessity the others were in, provoked them to hazard a battle, because there was no place whither they could flee. They then extended themselves a very great way along the banks of the river, and sustained the darts that were thrown at them as well as the attacks of the horsemen who beat many of them, and pushed them into the current. At which fight, hand to hand, fifteen thousand of them were slain, while the number of those that were unwillingly forced to leap into Jordan was prodigious. There were besides two thousand and two hundred taken prisoners.[31]

Josephus concludes the episode by saying that the "Jordan could not be passed over, by reason of the dead bodies that were in it."[32] But the region would see still further slaughter. In Gerasa (another city of the Decapolis and also a potential location for Mark's story), Vespasian set up a fortification after killing one thousand young men of the region, plundering their families and setting fire to their villages. Josephus says that "the men of power fled away, and the weaker part were destroyed, and what was remaining was all burnt down." War had gone through "all the mountainous country, and all the plain country also."[33]

Mark remembers and resists this human and environmental devastation by the Roman invading army. He does so by describing a man who embodies the uncontrollable power of Rome and is one of its victims—Legion. But when Jesus gets out of the boat, that power is now being subjected to a "stronger one."[34] For Mark, "the alien demonic forces that are wreaking such violence among the people are clearly identified as the instruments and effects of Roman rule."[35] But Jesus is able to cast them out of the man.

Mark, after mentioning the unpredictable nature of the man who lives among the tombs, describes him as "worshiping" Jesus and calling him "Son of the Most High God" (5:7).[36] Legion pleads to not be tormented by Jesus (5:8), and then Jesus exposes his name.[37] Typically in Mark's gospel it is the demon who exposes Jesus's identity.[38] But here the tables are turned. Manifesting a power associated with knowing someone's name, Jesus immediately gets a response: "My name is Legion; for we are many" (5:9). *Legion* is a Latin word brought into the Greek language (and now English). This word "had only one meaning in Mark's social world: a division of Roman soldiers."[39] And "legions were military units meant to enforce through overwhelming power."[40] When Jesus "ordered the demon to come out of the man and elicits its name, it is evident that the struggle is really against Roman imperial Rule."[41]

In sending the invasive spirits out of Legion, Jesus grants their request to take possession of the pigs. Connections between a legion of Roman soldiers and pigs not only include the fact that pork was the most popular meat among the Romans[42] but also the fact that pigs were a type of mascot. "Caesar's tenth legion (Legio X *Fretensis*) had, among other things, the image of a boar on its standards and seals."[43] Additional textual clues include the use of "herd" (*agelē*) to describe the pigs, an atypical word for a group of pigs and more commonly used to describe a band of military recruits. Also the verb translated as "he dismissed them" (*epetrepsen*) is a military command, and the word describing the pigs "charging" (*ōrmēsen*) into the sea was a way to describe military forces going into battle.[44] Is the "sea" a reminder of how the Romans had come to their territory by crossing the Mediterranean Sea, and then, led by Placidus, had drowned thousands of local fighters so that the Jordan "could not be passed over" for all "the dead bodies that were in it"?[45] Perhaps Mark is even drawing on echoes from the Exodus story when Pharaoh's army is defeated and "horse and rider" are "thrown into the sea."[46] Is this story suggesting that Jesus is a first-century anti-imperialist who challenges the presence of Roman colonizers by symbolically ridding the area of "Legion," first by casting demons out of a man and then finishing the job by ridding the land of "pigs?"

Some commentators have even seen the pleading of the legion/demons to not leave the land as suggesting the Roman army's desire to stay in the region. To "remain in the country" is "precisely what the Romans also want."⁴⁷ First the demons plead (*parekalei auton*) with Jesus not to send them out of the land (5:10), and then the locals plead (*parekalein auton*) with him to leave their region (5:17). Are the locals afraid of Roman retaliation?⁴⁸ The very name of their city "Gerasa" means "to drive away" or "to banish."⁴⁹ Is this story primarily about a legion of demons being banished? Or is it imagining the Roman legion driven away? If Mark's gospel is only about spiritual healing, why would the author so blatantly associate demons with legion?

Perhaps the accounts of Rome's acts of violence are reason enough to equate the Roman military machine with demonic forces. Postcolonial criticism asks us to further reflect on this story and the far-reaching implications of the banishing of Legion. Why is it that when the demons are sent away, the man remains? No longer called "Legion," he continues to be referred to in light of his past: he is called the "demon-possessed" (5:15, 16) and "the one who had been demon-possessed" (5:18).⁵⁰ Even though he is free of demons, he remains nameless through the rest of the story.

Several scholars have explored the character of Legion as an example of the dehumanizing oppression experienced by colonized people as others take their land. Drawing on Franz Fanon's *The Wretched of the Earth*, Paul Hollenbach explores the story of Legion as one whose oppression has caused madness. He has witnessed the slaughter of family and neighbors. As argued in the first section of this study, the land previously used for cultivating crops now feeds pigs used to feed the invading Roman army. Legion's screams fill the air as protests against all that is wrong in his land. Yet, even in protest, he is named by his tormentors; the colonizers have him trapped. Legion's life is a "living death."⁵¹ He is described as "the most dehumanized and wretched individual whom Jesus has yet encountered."⁵² Mark's description of Legion makes a mere spiritual interpretation insufficient. It points to something larger. This is a political, anti-imperial story offering a "symbolic portrait of how Roman imperialism was destroying the hearts and minds of a colonized people."⁵³

It is even possible that the demons represent the restless dead who were violently slaughtered. "The association with tombs may indicate that the man is possessed by the spirits of those who have died untimely or violent deaths."⁵⁴ Using two different Greek words (*mnemeion, mnema*), Mark causes his readers to hear that Legion lives among the "tombs" (monument or memorial, a place of remembrance).⁵⁵ How is Legion's life a testimony to remembering? How does his name expose his oppressors? Legion's

> very madness permitted him to do in a socially acceptable manner what he could not do while sane, namely, express his total hostility to the Romans; he did this by identifying the Roman legions with demons. His possession was

thus at once both the result of oppression and an expression of his resistance to it."[56]

The reaction of the townspeople to Legion's freedom from demons is a hint that they are most likely the elite pig owners who have benefitted from Rome's presence and clientele. When they see Legion sane and dressed and acting like a human, they are terrified.[57] Like the Roman army, these collaborators have been exposed. The pigs are gone. If the Roman army is also banished, who will provide their security? Jesus's healing of Legion challenges Rome's power structure so that the whole social system is in jeopardy. Legion was created because of an oppressive system. Kept in the tombs and with the howling animals, his protest was kept in check. But what to do when he is restored? How to keep him separate from society now? Jesus is a terrible threat to those who have adjusted to and benefited from the occupation. In the story, these elite pig owners from the town resist Jesus's ethic and banish him from their domain. But their absence from the rest of the narrative leaves open a question for contemporary readers of Mark: How will we care for our ecological resources? What human and nonhuman life will occupy the land after the luxury foods and invading armies are gone? Which ethical principles will guide those who remain?

As many have noted, this is the first time in Mark that Jesus walks on Gentile land and heals a demon-possessed man outside Jewish territory.[58] However, this study notes the way Mark redefines the unclean land of the Gerasenes, not with racial categories but with the ecological descriptions of unsustainability—luxury foods (pigs) consumed and depleted ecological resources. In addition, Legion's demons are not merely spiritual but also are symbolic of how he is a political victim of imperial violence

Jesus challenges the Roman army's oppression of Gentile indigenous people. The story concludes with the formerly possessed man going to his "home and people" (5:19), something not previously possible. He is no longer forced to live among the dead. Instead, he can go to the place where the demons wished to remain (5:10). But since Jesus has "banished" them, making Gerasa a place for people again and not just for pigs, sustainable life is restored to the region through Mark's imagination.

CONCLUSION: LIBERATING LEGION AND THE LAND

This chapter began with an apprehension that an apparently superficial approach too easily dismisses the ethical questions about Jesus's destruction of nonhuman life. Some commentaries say that such questions "miss the point" of the story, which emphasizes Jesus's ability to both clean an unclean man and to trick demons into self-destructing so that Jesus also cleans up unclean land: "The story of the deliverance of a man becomes the story of the deliverance of a land."[59] This study leads to the proposal of an acceptance of this interpretation but at a more profound level and with a far more nuanced understanding. Yes, the deliverance of a man is also the deliverance of a land since Legion's liberation means that countless other men, women, children and animals will live.[60]

This ecocritical, postcolonial study first argues that the assumption that "unclean" land merely refers to Gentile land is insufficient. Rather, the land is "unclean"—hazardous and dangerous—due to its ecological unsustainability. The land is depicted as taken over by an extraction economy. Retainers rule and any farmers left create crops for pigs to graze while all other life withers, dies, or goes mad. Second, when one explores what made the lands hazardous, one learns that they are recently occupied habitats being manipulated by colonial oppressors whom Mark labels as "demonic." Thus, demon possession is not merely a spiritual condition, it is also a political one. The violence of imperialism destroys various forms of life, relegating humans to "living among the tombs."

From an ecocritical and postcolonial perspective Mark 5:1–20 can be read as reimagining the land of Gerasa without pigs (and their elite owners) and without invading (demonic) armies controlling the local economy and ecology. Such reimagining means liberation for Legion, who is finally able to return home.

NOTES

1. Robert A. Guelich, *Mark 1–8:26*. Word Biblical Commentary, vol. 34a (Dallas: Word Books, 1989), 283. Ben Witherington, *The Gospel of Mark: A Socio-Rhetorical Commentary* (Grand Rapids, MI: Eerdmans, 2001), 182, even states: "It is possible that originally this story was meant to be humorous—unclean spirits destroy unclean animals!" I find this interpretation problematic in its callousness to nonhuman life.

2. Edward Said, *Culture and Imperialism* (New York: Vintage Books, 1993), 77; Elizabeth DeLoughrey and George B. Handley, "Introduction: Toward an Aesthetics of the Earth," in *Postcolonial Ecologies: Literatures of the Environment* (New York: Oxford University Press, 2011), DeLoughrey and Handley, eds., 3–5. DeLoughrey and Handley, 5, argue for merging postcolonial studies and ecocritical studies. Their preferred phrase, postcolonial ecology, pays "heed to the histories of colonial violence embedded in the earth."

3. Robert Kern, "Ecocriticism: What Is It Good For?" in *The ISLE Reader: Ecocriticism, 1993–2003*, Michael P. Branch and Scott Slovic, eds. (Athens: University of Georgia Press, 2003), 260, states: "ecocriticism becomes most interesting and useful . . . when it aims to recover the environmental character or orientation of works whose conscious or foregrounded interests lie elsewhere." Walter Brueggemann, *The Land: Place as Gift, Promise, and Challenge in Biblical Faith*, 2nd edition (Minneapolis, MN: Fortress Press, 2002), 197, states: "if land is indeed a prism through which biblical faith can be understood, not only will specific texts take on different nuances and tones, but we shall find that the Bible in its entirety is about another agenda that calls into question our conventional presuppositions and our settled conclusions."

4. DeLoughrey and Handley, 13, "To speak of postcolonial ecology is to foreground the historical process of nature's mobility, transplantation, and consumption."

5. DeLoughrey and Handley, 13.

6. Brendan Byrne, *A Costly Freedom: A Theological Reading of Mark's Gospel* (Collegeville, MN: Liturgical Press, 2008), 95. John R. Donahue and Daniel J. Harrington, *The Gospel of Mark*, Sacra Pagina Series, Vol. 2 (Collegeville, MN: Liturgical Press, 2002), 169, see it as a perplexing story: "This narrative is by far the most elaborate and enigmatic gospel miracle story," in the Markan narrative.

7. In Jewish thought, a land occupied by "unclean people," i.e., Gentiles, made the land itself unclean.

8. While influenced by many commentaries which seek to arrive at the correct rendering of specific phrases in this story, this translation from Koine Greek to English is my own. Analyses are based on the Greek text.

9. An earlier version of this study was presented at the 2016 *Natures* Conference: "Environmental Humanities: Habitats and Hazards," La Sierra University, Riverside, California, February 19, 2016.

10. The location of this episode in the Synoptic Gospels is problematic. Mark and Luke refer to the land of the Gerasenes, suggesting residents of Gerasa (modern Jerash), a city which was part of the Decapolis but located 37 miles southeast of the shores of the Sea of Galilee (Mark 5:1–20; Luke 8:26–39). Matthew mentions the land of the Gadarenes with reference to residents of Gadara (modern Um Qeis), another city of the Decapolis much closer to the sea but still five miles southeast from it (Matthew 8:28–34). Origen (third century) suggested the town should be understood as Gergesa (modern El Kursi), a coastal village. Archaeological evidence shows that a monastery and church were built in Gergesa by the fifth century, suggesting the location of a significant event in the Jesus movement. However, no extant textual evidence supports this location. The important issue for this study's argument is that the Greek word *chora* ("land") is probably best understood as referring to the rural land around a village (country as distinct from town), or dry land as opposed to the sea. See Joel Marcus, *Mark 1–8*, Anchor Bible (New York: Doubleday, 2000), 345.

11. Douglas W. Geyer, "Mark 5:1–20: A Demoniac Legion," in *Fear, Anomaly, and Uncertainty in the Gospel of Mark* (Lanham, MD: Scarecrow Press, 2002), 125.

12. Guelich, 278, considers tombs a place for demons. It is interesting to note that both the word used for "tomb" in verse 2, as well as the word used for "tomb" or "sign of remembrance" in verses 3 and 5 are found at the end of Mark's narrative (15:46). See also Adela Yarbro Collins, *Mark*, Hermeneia (Minneapolis, MN: Fortress, 2007), 267.

13. Jewish sacred scripture declared: "The pig, for even though it has divided hoofs and is cleft-footed, it does not chew the cud; it is unclean for you. Of their flesh you shall not eat, and their carcasses you shall not touch; they are unclean for you" (Leviticus 11:7–8); See also Deuteronomy 14:8. Given this story, Isaiah 65:3–4 is also interesting in its description of a rebellious people from the perspective of God the speaker: "a people who provoke me to my face continually, sacrificing in gardens and offering incense on bricks; who sit inside tombs, and spend the night in secret places; who eat swine's flesh, with broth of abominable things in their vessels." Guelich, 281, adds: "Mishnaic law strictly forbade the Jews from raising pigs (*m. B. Qam.* 7:7)."

14. Lamar Williamson, Jr. *Mark*. Interpretation (Louisville, KY: Westminster/John Knox Press, 2009), 104.

15. Mary Douglas, *Purity and Danger: An Analysis of the Concepts of Pollution and Taboo* (New York: Routledge, 1966), argues that contemporary western social order follows similar rules. Douglas, 4, states: "For I believe that ideas about separating, purifying, demarcating and punishing transgressions have as their main function to impose system on an inherently untidy experience. It is only by exaggerating the difference between within and without, above and below, male and female, with and against, that a semblance of order is created." In a fascinating contemporary reflection on the psychology of disgust, Richard Beck, *Unclean: Meditations on Purity, Hospitality, and Mortality* (Eugene, OR: Cascade Books, 2011), explores the use of purity categories in communities of faith.

16. Bruce J. Malina and Richard L. Rohrbaugh, *Social-Science Commentary on the Synoptic Gospels* (Minneapolis, MN: Fortress Press, 1992), 208, discuss a Jewish document that considers the following as proof of madness: (1) spending the night in a tomb; (2) tearing one's clothes; (3) walking around at night; (4) destroying things received from others. They con-

clude: "All are present in this case. Abnormal behavior was frequently attributed to involvement in abnormal relationships—in this case with unclean spirits."

17. Richard L. Rohrbaugh, "The Social Location of the Markan Audience," in *Gospel Interpretation: Narrative-Critical & Social-Scientific Approaches*, edited by Jack Dean Kingsbury (Harrisburg, PA: Trinity Press International, 1997), 115. The Jewish war with Rome took place between 66–70 CE. Most Markan scholars place the creation of the gospel during or immediately after the war.

18. Roland Boer, *The Sacred Economy of Ancient Israel* (Louisville, KY: Westminster/John Knox Press, 2015), see especially chapter 2, "Of Bread, Beer, and Four-Legged Friends," 53–81, and chapter 4, "Feeding the Nonproducers, or, (E)states," 110–45.

19. Boer, *The Sacred Economy of Ancient Israel*, 66, "small surpluses was a necessary feature of survival." Boer defines "self-sufficiency" as when a village "produces all that is needed, and in which need is minimal" (76).

20. Boer, *The Sacred Economy of Ancient Israel*, 120–21, "it was ultimately in the interest of the ruling class to drag subsistence laborers into an estate system, to lengthen the periods of service, to make permanent the indenture of as many as possible, and to expand the land tilled in the estates."

21. Boer, *The Sacred Economy of Ancient Israel*, 60–61.

22. Allocation economies avoided grazing cows because of the larger pasture and water sources required. Studies have shown that it was the occupants of more luxurious estates who ate cow meat and "such consumption is a distinct mark of ruling class identity" (63, footnote 25). States Boer, 63: "Herds of bovines would have put stress on precisely these resources [pasture and water] and thereby threatened the survival of all."

23. Boer, *The Sacred Economy of Ancient Israel*, 65–66.

24. Marvin Harris, "Pig Lovers and Pig Haters," in *Cows, Pigs, Wars, and Witches: The Riddles of Culture* (New York: Vintage Books, 1974), 41.

25. Harris, "Pig Lovers and Pig Haters," 42. Global Invasive Species Database, http://issg.org/publications.htm#worst100, includes pigs among the one hundred worst invasive species: "Rooting pigs dig up large areas of native vegetation and spread weeds, disrupting ecological processes such as succession and species composition."

26. Harris, "Pig Lovers and Pig Haters," 44. See Jean-Bertrand Aristide, *Eyes of the Heart: Seeking a Path for the Poor in the Age of Globalization* (Monroe, ME: Common Courage Press, 2000), 13–15, 79, for a more recent example where raising Haitian Creole pigs "well adapted to Haiti's climate and conditions" were replaced by pigs from Iowa in 1982 by international agencies. The new pigs required food and water that cost Haitian peasants $600 million dollars.

27. Stephen D. Moore, "Mimicry and Monstrosity," in *Untold Tales from the Book of Revelation: Sex and Gender, Empire and Ecology* (Atlanta: Society of Biblical Literature, 2014): 17, "Settler colonies" are "those in which the indigenous population is decimated and uprooted, eventually becoming a minority in relation to the majority settler-invader population."

28. Boer, *The Sacred Economy of Ancient Israel*, 220. Brian Hesse, "Pig Lovers and Pig Haters: Patterns of Palestinian Pork Production," in *Journal of Ethnobiology* 10:2 (Winter 1990): 199, confirms that "Because of the particular requirements demanded by the physiology and behavior of pigs, these animals are missing from the larders of those who occupy hot, dry climates and from the herds of those whose lifestyle is migratory or nomadic. . . . He later quotes Pamela Crabtree,"Sheep, Horses, Swine and Kine: A Zooarchaeological Perspective on the Anglo-Saxon Settlement of England," *Journal of Field Archaeology* 16 no. 2 (1989): 205-213, saying "they are ideal animals for colonizers." Eliezer Diamond, "Jewish Perspectives on Limiting consumption," in *Ecology and the Jewish Spirit*, Ellen Bernstein, ed. (Woodstock, VT: Jewish Lights Publishing, 2008), 80, says: "when we take more than we give back, when we consume excessively, we deplete and potentially ruin the system that provides for us."

29. Ched Myers, et al., *"Say to This Mountain": Mark's Story of Discipleship*, ed. Karen Lattea (Maryknoll, NY: Orbis Books, 1997), 58.

30. Flavius Josephus, *The Wars of the Jews* Book III:7:1, in *The Works of Flavius Josephus*, Vol. 1, trans. William Whiston (Grand Rapids, MI: Baker Book House, 1979), 236.

31. Josephus, *Wars of the Jews*, Book IV:7:5.
32. Josephus, *Wars of the Jews*, Book IV:7:6.
33. Josephus, *Wars of the Jews*, Book IV:9:1.
34. Some see this as a motif in Mark. As early as chapter 1, John the Baptist anticipates the "one who is stronger" (1:7), and later in a parable, Jesus talks about "binding the strong man," (3:26–27), which is only possible by one who is stronger.
35. Richard A. Horsley, *Hearing the Whole Story: The Politics of Plot in Mark's Gospel* (Louisville, KY: Westminster/John Knox, 2001), 141.
36. This phrase is typically used by those outside Israel to refer to God and in reference to God's reign over all of the earth. See 2 Samuel 22:14, 18; Marcus, 344. R. Alan Culpepper, *Mark*, Smyth & Helwys Bible Commentary (Macon, GA: Smyth & Helwys Publishing, 2007), 166, wonders if even at the start of the story, readers are to understand the power of this region as falling at the feet of Jesus since to "fall on one's face before one who has just stepped on your shores would be an appropriate way to welcome a conqueror." This becomes even more powerful when we learn that the man bowing before Jesus is Legion.
37. There is an interesting scene in *Testament of Solomon* 11:5 in which Solomon asks a demon his name and the demon responds: "If I tell you his name, I place not only myself in chains, but also the legion of demons under me." See also *Testament of Solomon* 5:1–3; 13:1–7. See discussion in Yarbro Collins, 268–69.
38. See Mark 1:24, 34.
39. Ched Myers, *Binding the Strong Man: A Political Reading of Mark's Story of Jesus* (Maryknoll, NY: Orbis Books, 1988), 191. Yarbro Collins, 269, notes that a Roman legion consisted of 5,400 army troops accompanied by 120 cavalry.
40. Geyer, "Mark 5:1–20: A Demoniac Legion," 137.
41. Horsley, *Hearing the Whole Story*, 147.
42. Maguelonne Toussaint-Samat, *A History of Food* (Hoboken, NJ: John Wiley & Sons, 2009), 93.
43. Yarbro Collins, 269. Yarbro Collins continues, "This legion was stationed in Cyrrhus, a city of northwestern Syria, from 17 CE to 66 CE . . . it took part in the first Jewish war and was subsequently stationed in Jerusalem."
44. Myers, *Binding the Strong Man*, 191; see also Horsley, *Hearing the Whole Story*, 140–41.
45. Josephus, *Wars*, Book IV:7:6.
46. Exodus 15:21; see also Exodus 15:1–10 where the "Song of Moses" contains the verse: "You blew with your wind, the sea covered them; they sank like lead in the mighty waters." For further connections between the gospel of Mark and Exodus imagery, see Rikki E. Watts, *Isaiah's New Exodus in Mark* (Grand Rapids, MI: Baker Academic, 1997).
47. Gerd Theissen, *The Miracle Stories of the Early Christian Tradition*, ed. John Riches, trans. Francis McDonagh (London: T & T Clark, 1983), 255.
48. Myers, *Binding the Strong Man*, 191. At least one commentator, Joel Marcus, *Mark 1-8*, 345, wonders if the plea of the demons to be able to "enter into" the swine (5:12) is a veiled reference to the practice of Roman military on the battlefield to rape their conquered enemies.
49. Myers, *Binding the Strong Man*, 342.
50. Malina and Rohrbaugh, 182–83, clarify that since Jews referred to possession as having an "unclean spirit" and Greeks as having a "demon," it makes sense that this man is called a "demoniac" after he is no longer Legion. But why not a new name altogether?
51. Herman C. Waetjen, *A Reordering of Power: A Socio-Political Reading of Mark's Gospel* (Eugene, OR: Wipf & Stock, 1989), 115.
52. Waetjen, *A Reordering of Power*, 114. Paul W. Hollenbach, "Jesus, Demoniacs, and Public Authorities: A Socio-Historical Study," in *The Journal of the American Academy of Religion* 49:4 (1981), 575, says: "The main point here, then, is that the colonial situation of domination and revolution nourishes mental illness in extraordinary numbers of the population."
53. Ched Myers, et al., 59.
54. Yarbro Collins, 267. Sejong Chun, "Exorcism or Healing? A Korean Preacher's Rereading of Mark 5:1–20," in *Mark*, eds, Nicole Wilkinson Duran, Teresa Okure and Daniel M. Patte

(Minneapolis, MN: Fortress, 2011), 15–33 considers the Korean understanding of *han* (dying without closure and so remaining restless) alongside the story of Legion. Chun, 30, says that "the unclean spirits are the souls of the colonized who suffered from the brutal violence of the Roman imperial force, Legion. Their name, Legion, refers to the cause of their death: they could have been abused and murdered by the Roman army, Legion." Sarah Iles Johnston, "The Unavenged: Dealing with Those Who Die Violently," in *Restless Dead: Encounters Between the Living and the Dead in Ancient Greece* (Berkeley: University of California Press, 1999), 127–60, call those who die a violent death the "*biaiothanatoi.*" Adding the weight of the victimizer as well as victims to the possessed, Robert G. Hamerton-Kelly, *The Gospel & the Sacred: Poetics of Violence in Mark* (Minneapolis, MN: Fortress Press, 1994), 93, states that Legion "carries his persecutors inside himself in the classic mode of the victim who internalizes his tormentors." Geyer, 132, considers the possibility that demons are "the disembodied presences of the deceased," who had suffered violently and required vengeance.

55. Both words will be used again at the cross scene. See Mark 15:46.
56. Hollenbach, 581.
57. Moore, 18, explains: "The concept of hegemony usefully illuminates the situation of Roman Asia.... Like any Roman province, the routine governance of Asia depended on the active cooperation and participation of the local urban elites. The administrative infrastructure consisted of a loose coalition of self-governing cities, each having responsibility for the territorial hinterland attached to it."
58. Francis Moloney, *The Gospel of Mark: A Commentary* (Grand Rapids, MI: Baker Academic, 2002), 106, states: "the good news is preached in a Gentile land for the first time in the Gospel of Mark." D. E. Nineham, *Saint Mark* (New York: Penguin Books, 1963), 151, says that Jesus's presence "banishes uncleanness" and "the land is cleansed by his coming, and the way prepared for its Christianizing."
59. Guelich, 283.
60. Richard Bauckham, in his chapter "Jesus and Animals" in *Living with Other Creatures: Green Exegesis and Theology* (Waco, TX: Baylor University Press, 2011), 79–110, finds this story in conflict with the typical way Jesus treats animals, which he shows is with compassion, while emphasizing God's provision and care for all creatures. Bauckham begrudgingly concludes, 98: "There is no reason at all to suppose that he [Jesus] sets no value on the life of the pigs or values it only for the sake of human beings. But the destruction of the pigs is preferable to the destruction of a human personality. The principle that human beings are of more value than other animals here operates to the detriment of the latter, in a case, unique within the Gospels, where a choice has to be made." The present study suggests that the pigs reflect an economic system that threatens both human and nonhuman life in the land of the Gerasenes. Jesus acts to restore a human personality and a whole community, including the land and other nonhuman life. Thus, this study provides an alternative interpretation to Bauckham's.

REFERENCES

Aristide, Jean-Bertrand. *Eyes of the Heart: Seeking a Path for the Poor in the Age of Globalization*. Monroe, ME: Common Courage Press, 2000.
Bauckham, Richard. *Living with Other Creatures: Green Exegesis and Theology*. Waco, TX: Baylor University Press, 2011.
Beck, Richard. *Unclean: Meditations on Purity, Hospitality, and Mortality*. Eugene, OR: Cascade Books, 2011.
Boer, Roland. *The Sacred Economy of Ancient Israel*. Louisville, KY: Westminster/John Knox Press, 2015.
Brueggemann, Walter. *The Land: Place as Gift, Promise, and Challenge in Biblical Faith*, 2nd ed. Minneapolis, MN: Fortress Press, 2002.
Byrne, Brendan. *A Costly Freedom: A Theological Reading of Mark's Gospel*. Collegeville, MN: Liturgical Press, 2008.

Chun, Sejong. "Exorcism or Healing? A Korean Preacher's Rereading of Mark 5:1–20." In *Mark, Texts @ Contexts.* Edited by Nicole Wilkinson Duran, Teresa Okure and Daniel M. Patte, 15–33. Minneapolis, MN: Fortress, 2011.

Crabtree, Pamela. "Sheep, Horses, Swine and Kine: A Zooarchaeological Perspective on the Anglo-Saxon Settlement of England." *Journal of Field Archaeology* 16 no. 2 (1989): 205-213. Quoted in Brian Hesse. "Pig Lovers and Pig Haters: Patterns of Palestinian Pork Production." *Journal of Ethnobiology* 10, no. 2 (Winter 1990): 195–225.

Culpepper, R. Alan. *Mark.* Smyth & Helwys Bible Commentary. Macon, GA: Smyth & Helwys Publishing, 2007.

DeLoughrey, Elizabeth and George B. Handley. "Introduction: Toward an Aesthetics of the Earth." In *Postcolonial Ecologies: Literatures of the Environment.* Edited by Elizabeth DeLoughrey and George B. Handley, 3–39. New York: Oxford University Press, 2011.

Diamond, Eliezer. "Jewish Perspectives on Limiting Consumption." In *Ecology and the Jewish Spirit.* Edited by Ellen Bernstein, 80–87. Woodstock, VT: Jewish Lights Publishing, 2008.

Donahue, John R. and Daniel J. Harrington. *The Gospel of Mark.* Sacra Pagina Series. vol. 2. Edited by Daniel J. Harrington. Collegeville, MN: Liturgical Press, 2002.

Douglas, Mary. *Purity and Danger: An Analysis of the Concepts of Pollution and Taboo.* New York: Routledge, 1966.

Fanon, Frantz. *The Wretched of the Earth.* Translated by Richard Philcox. Paris: F. Maspero, 1961. Reprint, New York: Grove Press, 2004.

Geyer, Douglas W. "Mark 5:1–20: A Demoniac Legion." In *Fear, Anomaly, and Uncertainty in the Gospel of Mark*, by Douglas W. Geyer. 125–60. Lanham, MD: Scarecrow Press, 2002.

Global Invasive Species Database. Accessed May 22, 2016, http://issg.org/publications.htm#worst100.

Guelich, Robert A. *Mark 1–8:26.* Word Biblical Commentary. vol. 34a. Dallas: Word Books, 1989.

Hamerton-Kelly, Robert G. *The Gospel & the Sacred: Poetics of Violence in Mark.* Minneapolis, MN: Fortress Press, 1994.

Harris, Marvin. *Cows, Pigs, Wars, and Witches: The Riddles of Culture.* New York: Vintage Books, 1974.

Hesse, Brian. "Pig Lovers and Pig Haters: Patterns of Palestinian Pork Production." *Journal of Ethnobiology* 10, no. 2 (1990): 195–225.

Hollenbach, Paul W. "Jesus, Demoniacs, and Public Authorities: A Socio-Historical Study." *The Journal of the American Academy of Religion* 49, no. 4 (1981): 567–88.

Horsley, Richard A. *Hearing the Whole Story: The Politics of Plot in Mark's Gospel.* Louisville, KY: Westminster/John Knox, 2001.

Johnston, Sarah Iles. "The Unavenged: Dealing with Those Who Die Violently." In *Restless Dead: Encounters Between the Living and the Dead in Ancient Greece,* by Sarah Iles Johnston. 127–60. Berkeley: University of California Press, 1999.

Josephus, Flavius. *The Works of Flavius Josephus.* Vol. 1. Translated by William Whiston. Grand Rapids, MI: Baker Book House, 1979.

Kern, Robert. "Ecocriticism: What Is It Good For?" In *The ISLE Reader: Ecocriticism, 1993–2003.* Edited by Michael P. Branch and Scott Slovic, 258–81. Athens: University of Georgia Press, 2003.

Malina, Bruce J. and Richard L. Rohrbaugh. *Social-Science Commentary on the Synoptic Gospels.* Minneapolis, MN: Fortress Press, 1992.

Marcus, Joel. *Mark 1–8.* Anchor Bible. New York: Doubleday, 2000.

Moloney, Francis. *The Gospel of Mark: A Commentary.* Grand Rapids, MI: Baker Academic, 2002.

Moore, Stephen D. "Mimicry and Monstrosity." In *Untold Tales from the Book of Revelation: Sex and Gender, Empire and Ecology,* by Stephen D. Moore. 13–37. Atlanta: Society of Biblical Literature, 2014.

Myers, Ched. *Binding the Strong Man: A Political Reading of Mark's Story of Jesus.* Maryknoll, NY: Orbis Books, 1988.

Myers, Ched, Marie Dennis, Joseph Nangle, Cynthia Moe-Lobeda, and Stuart Taylor. *"Say to This Mountain": Mark's Story of Discipleship*. Edited by Karen Lattea. Maryknoll, NY: Orbis Books, 1997.
Nineham, D. E. *Saint Mark*. New York: Penguin Books, 1963.
Rohrbaugh, Richard L. "The Social Location of the Markan Audience." In *Gospel Interpretation: Narrative-Critical & Social-Scientific Approaches*. Edited by Jack Dean Kingsbury, 106–22. Harrisburg, PA: Trinity Press International, 1997.
Said, Edward. *Culture and Imperialism*. New York: Vintage Books, 1993.
Testament of Solomon. In *The Old Testament Pseudepigrapha*. vol. 1. Edited by James H. Charlesworth, 960–87. Translated by D. C. Duling. Garden City, NY: Doubleday and Company, 1983.
Theissen, Gerd. *The Miracle Stories of the Early Christian Tradition*. Edited by John Riches. Translated by Francis McDonagh. London: T & T Clark, 1983.
Toussaint-Samat, Maguelonne. *A History of Food*. Hoboken, NJ: John Wiley & Sons, 2009.
Waetjen, Herman C. *A Reordering of Power: A Socio-Political Reading of Mark's Gospel*. Eugene, OR: Wipf & Stock, 1989.
Watts, Rikki E. *Isaiah's New Exodus in Mark*. Grand Rapids, MI: Baker Academic, 1997.
Williamson, Lamar, Jr. *Mark*. Interpretation. Louisville, KY: Westminster/John Knox Press, 2009.
Witherington, Ben. *The Gospel of Mark: A Socio-Rhetorical Commentary*. Grand Rapids, MI: Eerdmans, 2001.
Yarbro Collins, Adela. *Mark*. Hermeneia. Minneapolis, MN: Fortress, 2007.

Chapter Twelve

The End of the Road

Jesus, Donkeys, and Galilean Subsistence Farmers

Matthew Valdez with Kendra Haloviak Valentine

Too often our interpretations of Jesus revealed in the four gospels relegate his ministry to the private sphere. We seem to be limited by the narrow horizon of privatized American capitalism that dictates and defines social relations as the nuclear family, private devotional religion, and the constant acquisition of private property. The great myth of our time is reading this privatized society onto a time and place far removed from our current social relations, which renders the actual situation of first-century Palestine unrecognizable.[1] Even worse, our misreading of their social relations leads us to draw conclusions about Jesus's activity in the gospels in ways that promote and support our destructive way of life, retroactively naturalizing it. To put it simply, we misread the gospels when we claim Jesus was on the side of the ruling class or that his ministry somehow aligns or supports capitalism and "free markets." A different reading of Jesus is necessary if this common reading is to be properly subverted, a reading that more closely resembles the actual social relations of first-century Palestine. As Fernando Belo has shown, this reading calls for a new perspective.[2] Instead of reading from the angle of the ruling class, which narrows the horizon of social reality since it relegates the rest of society to a subordinate and subservient role, we must read from the viewpoint of the majority of any society, that of the working class.[3] Looking outward from this standpoint gives us a broader and more complete picture of the social reality assumed in the gospels. This allows us to concretize the liberating social practice of Jesus that certainly contains challenging modern-day implications.

This study aims to combine narrative and social-scientific criticism with ecotheology in viewing the world of Mark's gospel and, more specifically,

Jesus's entry into Jerusalem (Mark 11:1–11). I will attempt to show that in a decisive way, Jesus, along with his group of peasant farmers and day laborers, moves southward to challenge the corrupted temple institution that impoverishes and dehumanizes them. I will describe the setting of Jerusalem and the temple system's symbolic order while explaining its oppressive effects upon those following Jesus from Galilee. I will then describe the emancipatory "way of Jesus" and his action against the temple system's oppression by using symbols of the agrarian peasant class and by differentiating Jesus's politics from that of the popular Davidic kingship. The last section will include some modern day connections. Ultimately, I intend to make the case that Jesus took sides with the peasant farmers to fight systems of oppression toward the complete liberation of the land, the human and even the nonhuman life that rely on the land for survival.

The narrative critical method analyzes texts as story. Narratives usually include a narrator that guides the reader or hearer through the plot and provides us with a consistent point of view. Throughout the plot, characters and themes are developed. The narrator explains particular settings, conjuring up cultural meanings for the audience, staging the action between characters and their scenes, and disclosing character attributes.[4] As David Rhoads, Joanna Dewey, and Donald Michie indicate, when the narrative critical method is used to analyze Mark's gospel, we can encounter a rich story full of suspense, atmosphere, and drama.[5] This gospel engages the reader with its own "story world."[6] Like novels, films, and episodic shows on television or Netflix, the author of Mark seeks to draw his audience into a place that is foreign yet familiar. It is foreign in the sense that the story world is not an exact replication of the world it portrays. This means that the author of Mark is less concerned with historical accuracy and instead prioritizes rhetoric that radically transforms the way the audience views their real world. However, Mark's story world is still a familiar one for its original audience. Its setting is first-century Palestine; it deals with existing socioeconomic-religious systems; and it portrays momentous events that occurred in history.[7]

The fact that Mark's story world is similar to the actual lived-in world and experiences of its original audience shows why a social-scientific approach is vital for the twenty-first-century reader. Mark's story world and the real world it comments on are both vastly different from our world. Therefore, if we are to glean from Mark its intended meaning, however partial, we must make attempts to understand the world in which Mark comments. The social-scientific method seeks to understand biblical texts in terms of their social-historical location. Our modern lives exist in an interconnected web of particular symbols and signs that provide meaning and ultimately give our society form. This process is studied today by social scientists, but in practice these symbols are interpreted reflexively. For example, if I'm on the highway, and I drive past a brand new 2016 Chevrolet Corvette Stingray, I interpret the car as a symbol of wealth. The driver of this car must have enough disposable income to afford a $55,000 vehicle. However, when I read Mark 11 with Jesus riding on a donkey into Jerusalem, I feel less clear as to what this means. Mark, in writing to his first-century audience, makes no attempt to explain his world of symbols. The text assumes that we understand its "social system" as well as its economic and religious culture.[8] If we cannot understand the world that Mark is commenting on, we will miss critical points about the gospel.[9] Jesus will simply be a healer of sick people, an exorcist of demons, or some weird guy who rode a donkey into some random city. Even worse, if we are unable or unwilling to learn about the social systems at play in Mark, we may misunderstand the gospel. Divorced from its social-historical location, the weight of Mark's highly intentional narrative is lost.

Mark's gospel was most likely written either during or shortly after the Roman-Judean war in 66–70 CE.[10] The consensus among New Testament scholars is that the composer of Mark was writing to a group of people who had been rebuffed or mistreated for Jesus's name by both Roman and Judean authorities.[11] While this chapter does not seek to cover the history of the Judean revolt against the Roman occupiers, this struggle was certainly in the air during Mark's composition.

THE CENTER: JERUSALEM, THE SYMBOLIC ORDER, AND SYSTEMATIC OPPRESSION

As Jesus arrives at the outskirts of Jerusalem (11:1–11), it is important to highlight the setting of this passage that is introduced in 11:1a, "When they were approaching Jerusalem. . . ." While not yet in the city itself, the narrator, as has often been the case in this gospel, sets the stage for the episode by giving the reader or hearer a sense of place in citing a concrete geographical location.[12] Here we find Jesus with his followers approaching Jerusalem. As was already revealed to the reader in 10:32, those following Jesus on the road to Jerusalem were both "amazed" and "afraid." In order to understand the amazement and fear of the crowd following Jesus, we have to unpack the symbol of Jerusalem. What was this city to these particular people following Jesus? Why go there now? In a sense, Jerusalem, and more specifically the temple, was the center of the cosmos, "a flat earth with heavens extending from the earth up to where God dwells."[13] When traveling to Jerusalem, regardless of approach—north to south or east to west—the traveler always goes up (10:32–33) and so ascends to Jerusalem. In this way, the cosmos stretches horizontally from the temple toward the four corners of a flat world and vertically with Sheol below and the multi-tiered heavens above.

Jerusalem and its temple represent the center of the cosmos, so it is only fitting that the symbolic order that regulated life and the ruling class that enforced it resided here. By symbolic order, I mean the thing that "regulates relations"[14] between people. For Jews, this thing that regulated all relationships between each other and Yahweh was the Torah, or Law. Adherence to the Law meant purity and freedom/offerings with its opposite possibilities: pollution and debt. Pollution has to do with what is pure and impure, clean and unclean. One aspect of pollution has to do with compatibility, or what can be combined with what: "You shall not sow your vineyard with a second kind of seed, or the whole yield will have to be forfeited, both the crop that you have sown and the yield of the vineyard itself. You shall not plow with an ox and a donkey yoked together. You shall not wear clothes made of wool and linen woven together" (Deut. 22:9–11).[15] According to Fernando Belo, "wheat and vine, ox and donkey, wool and linen are *incompatible* pairs."[16] Once combined, these things are considered impure or "out of place,"[17] "a confused hybrid."[18] As well, the blind, lame, deformed, those with crushed testicles and missing limbs are impure in the sense that they lack proper form. Contact with the dead, semen, menstrual blood, and urine also brings impurity.[19] Since pollution and purity have to do with relations to each other and to things, there was always the possibility of "contagion,"[20] meaning an out-of-place or impure person or object coming into contact with someone or something else and so spreading the impurity.

The temple stands as the center of purity and is the heart of the Law and so the symbolic order that all were required to observe. Those seeking to become pure, which meant improving their public reputation and social status, performed redemptive rituals and sacrifices here.[21] As a center of purity, the temple and its rituals had to be attended by pure persons. The priestly class (Levites) was considered most pure. Through the symbolic order of the Law, Jerusalem, and its temple stand as the center of cosmos, purity, and even economics.[22]

Debt, which is the second facet of the Law, required Jews to bring their sacrifices and tithes to the temple. Of course, the priests were the ones who benefitted from this most of all. During the time of Moses, a redistributive economy was established so that not only the farmers but also the nonproducers, trades people, or handicraft workers, "generally weaving women and artisans," could eat.[23] However, by the first century, things had drastically changed since the days of Moses, and many of the priests now owned their own land and grew their own crops.[24] The tithe of crops received from the peasant farmers was no longer necessary for the survival of the nonproducing priests in the temple.

AMONG THE PERIPHERY: GALILEAN SUBSISTENCE FARMERS

Jesus is not alone in his approach toward the center of the cosmos. "The crowd," a character in itself, is following Jesus here. By this time Jesus's movement has grown large. As Rhoads, Dewey, and Michie suggest, the size of the crowd is revealed by the different locations where the people meet with Jesus.[25] At the start of Jesus's ministry of healing and exorcising unclean spirits to the north in Galilee the people gather together in houses (1:29). Then, whole cities of people gather at the door of the house where Jesus is (2:2). This forces Jesus to move his ministry to a shore by the sea (4:1). Here, he has to teach from a boat in the water to avoid being crushed; finally, he moves to the even more open area of the desert, where he feeds the people (6:32).[26] The crowd that follows Jesus is not some arbitrary group of curious onlookers. In Mark's story world, the crowd represents the social outcasts.[27] These are the symbolic order's delinquents: the impure, the impoverished, and the periphery. The peasant farmers and day laborers of Galilee lived in constant threat of contagion. Contact with dead animals, dead people from widespread starvation, feces, urine, and blood were commonplace among the peasantry. These people were systematically impure also because they lacked the economic means to go through the appropriate purity rituals.[28]

Peasant families had to accomplish three things in order to live. (1) "Above all they had to grow enough food to feed themselves and their animals, and to have seed for the following year's crop."[29] (2) They also had "a need for a surplus because of the demands of the reciprocity and redistributive systems."[30] The reciprocity system required surplus to provide for neighbors in need and to contribute to local festivals,[31] but these agrarian peasant farmers produced the minimum needed to get by. In an industrial agricultural economy—like the one we have today—surplus is produced for the purpose of profit and to satisfy the unending hunger of the "overloaded bodies" of the United States.[32] We live in a culture that accumulates excess goods and generates massive amounts of waste that we do not know what to do with.[33] However, any excess generated by first-century subsistence farmers was stored for emergencies and hard times, not profit. Surplus was considered insurance against "bad harvest, drought, burned crops, animal disease, or any other untoward but all too common event that threatened survival."[34] It is the surplus produce needed for the redistributive system that saw wealth moving in the wrong direction and perpetuated the never-ending cycle of poverty for the peasant farmer.[35] (3) A Galilean farmer had to pay a land tax to the king or to a Roman landowner,[36] and, as mentioned before, the farmers also had to provide tithe in the form of crops to the priests in the temple. The tithing structure, according to rabbinic tradition, required one-tenth of the crop yield for priests and for one-tenth of what was left over for the Levite temple workers who assisted the priests.[37] The tithe system corresponded to the symbolic order of debt that was established to feed nonproducers, or those who did not work the land.

The way of life for day laborers and tenant farmers was defined by a sense of alienation from culture and the daily wage.[38] The subsistence farmer's way of life was communal in that kinship groups lived and worked the land together to survive with the gifts of the land being allocated to those who needed it. But the day laborers' way of life was landless, as they worked in the fields of the ruling class or on construction projects.[39] This labor on land that was not their own pulled them away from the kinship groups (presumably disrupting family ties) and further distanced them from the means of production.[40] The agrarian way of life and the economy of subsistence that allowed for survival in the past, as Wendell Berry writes of the present, "feels threatened and sickened when it hears people and creatures and places spoken of as labor, management, capital and raw material."[41] Whether it is the ruling class of first-century Palestine or of twenty-first-century America, people, creatures, and land are subjugated under these terms. The destruction of the kinship group and alienation from the land for the day laborer spelled disaster for future generations of farmers, for the "knowledge and know-how of good caretaking" is always handed down to children.[42] We can imagine the children of the landless day laborers knowing nothing of subsistence farming and feeling a perpetual alienation from the way of life that allowed for the survival of so many past generations. They were born as slaves to the destructive redistributive system that saw their crops appropriated.

These land estates were granted to priests and other bureaucrats by Jewish rulers and colonial Roman authorities for the sole purpose of producing goods that benefited those in the ruling class to the detriment of society as a whole.[43] With farmable land being a limited resource, the rise of estates meant forcing the subsistence farmer either to continue to work the land as a tenant farmer paying taxes to the landowner and having no control over distribution of crops or to work as a day laborer on another estate. The Galilean peasants' agrarian way of life (along with family ties) was now eroding and being replaced by an economy that benefited the ruling class, which at almost every point in history only represents one to two percent of the total population.[44] The delicate balance between starvation and surplus for subsistence farmers was tilted toward starvation with surplus crops being appropriated by the temple tithe and the landowners' tax. Here, the land, the people, and animals that work it were exploited as a means toward the ultimate end—profit.

The attractiveness of the Human One (Son of Man) who "declares all foods clean" (7:19), touches the dead (5:41), restores the impure (1:41), and provides unlimited bread and fish (8:8) cannot be overstated. This crowd that was made pure, complete, and included by Jesus is approaching head-on the very institution that impoverishes them. The Human One, who has constantly challenged the symbolic order of purity and debt on the periphery in rural Galilee, is approaching the center of the cosmos, which for Jesus is now the center of injustice. The setting conjures both dread and excitement for the reader or hearer. For we already know from his three pronouncements (8:31, 9:31, 10:33) earlier in Mark's narrative that Jesus walks the way or road (Greek, *hodos*) of death on a cross. Yet, there is also excitement. What will Jesus do to confront these systems of oppression? Well, ride on a donkey, of course.

> When they were approaching Jerusalem, at Bethphage and Bethany, near the Mount of Olives, he sent two of his disciples and said to them, "Go into the village ahead of you, and immediately as you enter it, you will find tied there a colt that has never been ridden; untie it and bring it. If anyone says to you, 'Why are you doing this?' just say this, 'The Lord needs it and will send it back here immediately.'" They went away and found a colt tied near a door, outside in the street. As they were untying it, some of the bystanders said to them, "What are you doing, untying the colt?" They told them what Jesus had said; and they allowed them to take it. Then they brought the colt to Jesus and threw their cloaks on it; and he sat on it. Many people spread their cloaks on the road, and others spread leafy branches that they had cut in the fields. Then those who went ahead and those who followed were shouting, "Hosanna! Blessed is the one who comes in the name of the Lord! Blessed is the coming kingdom of our ancestor David! Hosanna in the highest heaven!" Then he entered Jerusalem and went into the temple; and when he had looked around at everything, as it was already late, he went out to Bethany with the twelve.
> —Mark 11:1–11[45]

CONFRONTING THE CENTER: JESUS ON A DONKEY

The author uses familiar military themes juxtaposed by symbols of the agrarian peasant class to portray Jesus's entry into Jerusalem. Jesus is portrayed as being intentional about the way in which he will enter the Holy City. He commissions his disciples to "procure"[46] a donkey (Greek, *polos*[47]) from the village ahead of them in the same way that a military commander acquires his resources for the upcoming battle. Jesus even instructs his disciples to exercise his authority as "Lord" (Greek, *kurios*) if they meet any resistance. The donkey is an interesting choice in that kings who rode into the city that they conquered typically rode the strongest horse or drove a war chariot, which represented his own as well as his horse's prowess in battle.[48] However, Jesus requires a donkey that "has never been ridden" (11:2) and that "has as yet not been trained to carry a rider," as Fernando Belo writes.[49] Donkeys were the common beasts of burden for transporting commodities and human riders.[50] Here, the donkey would have been the pack animal that transported tithe crops from Galilee southward to the temple storehouses in Jerusalem. Instead of carrying the tithe that served as a death sentence for the Galilean peasant farmer, the donkey now carries the Human One who is working toward its liberation. The donkey will no longer be relegated to a system that deems it the pack animal for the oppressive redistributive economy.

While riding on an untrained donkey toward Jerusalem was certainly choreographed by Jesus, the acts of spreading cloaks and leafy branches on the animal and the road seem to be spontaneous acts on the part of the people following. These acts of the people are better understood as Mark's intentional use of agrarian symbols rather than as Jesus's character imposing action. Cloaks and leafy branches from the fields are associated with the poor. Beggars "spread out their cloaks to receive alms,"[51] and peasant farmers would have the proper tools to cut the leafy branches from the fields to place on the ground. These reedlike branches stand in as weapons of the rural poor, now laid down at Jesus's feet. Entering into the temple upon his arrival (11:11), Jesus finishes his staged procession by participating in reconnaissance—military theme again—for the following day's assault against the symbolic order and the authorities that uphold it (11:15–17). In the end, these symbols of the peasant class subvert the common image of a warrior king and instead resemble the imagery of the peasant king who rides into Jerusalem on a donkey and commands "peace to the nations."[52]

The people scream, "Hosanna!" or, literally, "Save us!" "Blessed is the one who comes in the name of the Lord! Blessed is the coming kingdom of our ancestor David! Hosanna in the highest heaven!" (11:9–10).[53] It is here that the crowd misunderstands Jesus's politics in the same way that his disciples have misunderstood him all along the way to Jerusalem.[54] The people's cries are nationalistic in nature because they desire salvation from the Roman occupiers and the reinstatement of the Davidic dynasty. This sentiment among the people here is not much different from a familiar campaign slogan, "Make America great again!" It is as if the crowd is saying, "Save us from the Romans so that Israel can be great again!" The people are still caught up playing the game of thrones, which Jesus explicitly opposes earlier in the story.[55]

THE END OF THE ROAD

In Mark's story, 11:8 stands as the end of "the way" motif (or end of the road) that begins in 8:27, when Peter identifies Jesus as the Messiah. "The way" (Greek, *hodos*[56]) to Jerusalem (8:27–11:8) is one setting "where Jesus instructs his disciples on the expectations and the cost of following."[57] *Hodos* can be translated as "journey," "road," or "way." As Rhoads, Dewey, and Michie suggest, "the way of God" symbolizes the way Jesus's disciples ought to follow along. It is the way of self-denial and the taking up of one's cross (8:34). Those who seek to save their life will lose it, and those who lose their life for the good news will save it (8:35–36). Those who want to be first must be the least and a servant to all (9:35). The kingdom can only be received as children, who represent the lowest in the social order (10:15). To the rich, "the way" requires that they become poor and follow Jesus along the road toward the cross (10:21). It is in 10:41–45, after James and John request to sit at his left and right hand in glory, that Jesus explicitly condemns Roman rule and opposes his messiahship as Davidic:

> So Jesus called them and said to them, "You know that among the Gentiles those whom they recognize as their rulers lord it over them, and their great ones are tyrants over them. But it is not so among you; but whoever wishes to become great among you must be your servant, and whoever wishes to be first among you must be slave of all. For the Son of Man came not to be served but to serve, and to give his life a ransom for many."[58]

It is important to note here that in most cases Mark uses the designator "Son of Man" to describe Jesus instead of "messiah."[59] The full weight of this designation is felt here in Jesus's opposition to the title of "anointed one" in the Davidic sense, which would surely "lord it over them." Instead, Jesus identifies himself as the Human One, who has come to serve humanity and to die for them. Rhoads, Dewey, and Michie see verbs, such as "sent," "goes ahead," and "follow after," in Mark as "the pattern of life that is 'the way of God'. . . . Jesus was sent by God, proclaimed, was handed over, and was put to death."[60]

When we reach the end of "the way" motif in 11:8, the crowd meets Jesus with misunderstanding, revealed in their naming him the messiah who would return Jerusalem to its seat of power by reinstating the Davidic dynasty (11:9–10).[61] However, it is in examining the nature of this particular misunderstanding that we are led to define Jesus's practical social strategy: real solidarity with the poor and socially outcast means becoming poor with them, meeting them in their social location and together fighting systems of oppression, not toward becoming rich and powerful but toward their liberation to live full, complete lives. This is "the way of Jesus." As I have previously shown, the corrupted temple system with its symbolic order of the Law regarding pollution and debt was systematically dehumanizing and impoverishing the masses. Jesus's ministry liberates the people by declaring the polluted pure, completing the incomplete, and feeding the masses. Along with the liberated crowd, his ministry takes a turn southward to challenge the institutions of oppression on their own turf even unto his death.

THE WAY OF JESUS CONTINUES

Jesus's concrete social strategy outlined in "the way" stands in direct opposition to today's bourgeoise Christianity.[62] Like the ruling class of Jesus's time, we, too, give "lip service to eschatological eulogies"[63] of liberation while we secretly hope that Roman rule and its economic benefits last forever. Is this not the case with our acknowledgement that poverty in the United States is a problem that we should remedy even while we also say that raising the minimum wage, raising taxes on the rich, creating new systems of free healthcare, and providing free education are "un-American," "communist," and impossible? Meanwhile, we reap economic benefits from a capitalist system that values the rich and continually dehumanizes the poor. In the same way, do not our police shootings of black people and our systematic incarceration through the war on drugs[64] resemble the temple system's mass social exclusion and dehumanization of the impure Galilean peasantry? Former convicts and parolees are often treated no better. As Michelle Alexander notes, "[o]nce you're labeled a felon, the old forms of discrimination—employment discrimination, housing discrimination, denial of the right to vote, denial of educational opportunity, denial of food stamps and other public benefits, and exclusion from jury service—are suddenly legal."[65]

Mark's story makes explicit Jesus's commitment toward the liberation of the poor and their agrarian way of life yet is silent about what this liberation means for animals in general, specifically for the donkey, which most likely resumed its role as the beast of burden, a silent slave whose rights are never codified and whose body remains distantly other.[66] In Mark's depiction of Jesus's entrance, the donkey remains relegated to a symbol of the oppressed peasant class and is not depicted as oppressed in its own being. If the donkey receives any liberation from the intentional action of Jesus, it is merely a symbolic liberation. It is here that moving beyond the scope of Mark's story becomes necessary if we are serious about animals, their rights, and the nature of our relationship toward them. In light of the continual mass killing of animals in slaughterhouses,[67] the liberation of the oppressed humans that Jesus fights and dies for needs to be extended toward the oppressed animal today. The animal cannot simply be the metaphor or symbol of human oppression: it is, instead, the very subject of oppression itself.[68] The oppression of animals today comes from our systematic commodification of animals, revealing that they have no other value than how they are used by humans.[69] The availability and consumption of meat was infrequent throughout the history of ancient Israel,[70] but the Galilean farmers obviously utilized animals for many things, such as plowing and hauling, and so their relationship with animals was vital for survival. Today, we have perverted this sacred relationship with animals through our commodification of them in concentrated animal feeding operations (CAFOs) and the slaughterhouse. Animals are no longer required for life itself to go on, yet we continue to breed and slaughter them at a feverish pace. Millions of hogs are slaughtered each year in the United States with most living in CAFOs and never experiencing the basic benefits of animal life like "soil or sunshine."[71] Ellen Davis describes the conditions for these animals: "covered with sores . . . legs planted in urine and excrement."[72] Hogs are "stunned, slashed, hoisted, and scalded at the rate of 2,000 per hour."[73] The first-century Galilean subsistence farmer's relationship with animals marked survival and life. Today, our relationship with animals marks widespread death and disease.[74]

It is clear in Mark's story and in Jesus's choreographed procession into Jerusalem that Jesus is on the side of the oppressed. He has met the poor in their social location, becoming poor and liberating them from dehumanizing and oppressive powers into full humanity by making them pure, complete, and in proper form. We know Jesus's way is that of servanthood and the cross. We know that Jesus follows through in his way and is executed on a cross. However, his foreshadowing of his death three times also anticipates his resurrection.[75] The young man in the empty tomb informs the women that "he is raised; he is not here . . . he is going ahead of you to Galilee" (16:6–7). "The way" has not ended after all but begins anew in Galilee, where Mark's story began. Once again we find Jesus, not among the rich or in centers of power but along the periphery, among the poor, the animals, and the land, and we are called to go out and meet him there.

NOTES

1. See Fernando Belo, *A Materialist Reading of the Gospel of Mark* (Maryknoll, NY: Orbis Books, 1981) and Ched Myers, *Binding the Strong Man: A Political Reading of Mark's Story of Jesus* (Maryknoll, NY: Orbis Books, 1988).
2. Belo, Introduction to *A Materialist Reading of the Gospel of Mark*, 1–6.
3. Georg Lukács, *History and Class Consciousness: Studies in Marxist Dialectics* (Cambridge, MA: MIT Press, 1971), 19–20. Or in Marxist terms, the *proletariat*. See also Belo's second chapter, "Palestine in the First Century A.D.," in *A Materialist Reading of the Gospel of Mark*, 60–86.
4. David Rhoads, Joanna Dewey, and Donald Michie, *Mark as Story: An Introduction to the Narrative of a Gospel*, 3rd ed. (Minneapolis, MN: Fortress Press, 2012), 63.
5. Rhoads, Dewey, and Michie, *Mark as Story*, 2–5.
6. Rhoads, Dewey, and Michie, *Mark as Story*, 4.
7. Such as the Roman occupation of Palestine.
8. Bruce J. Malina and Richard L. Rohrbaugh, *Social-Science Commentary on the Synoptic Gospels*, 2nd ed. (Minneapolis, MN: Fortress Press, 2003), 9–10.
9. Malina and Rohrbaugh, *Social-Science Commentary on the Synoptic Gospels*, 10.
10. Rhoads, Dewey, and Michie, *Mark as Story*, 2
11. Rhoads, Dewey, and Michie, *Mark as Story*, 2.
12. To list a few, see Mark 1:16; 1:29; 2:1; 2:13; 3:1; 3:7; 3:13; 4:1; and 5:1.
13. Rhoads, Dewey, and Michie, *Mark as Story*, 64.
14. Fernando Belo, *A Materialist Reading of the Gospel of Mark*, 37.
15. New Revised Standard Version.
16. Belo, *A Materialist Reading of the Gospel of Mark*, 38.

17. Malina and Rohrbaugh, *Social-Science Commentary*, 395–96.
18. On the other hand, certain things can be combined with others only if they are different. This is why incest and same-sex relations are considered impure. Here, sameness is out of place. See Belo, *A Materialist Reading of the Gospel of Mark*, 38.
19. Ched Myers cites m. Kelim (1:3) in *Binding the Strong Man: A Political Reading of Mark's Story of Jesus* (Maryknoll, NY: Orbis Books, 1988), 75.
20. Belo, *A Materialist Reading of the Gospel of Mark*, 38.
21. Myers, *Binding the Strong Man*, 74.
22. Rhoads, Dewey, and Michie, *Mark as Story*, 64.
23. Thomas F. Carney, *The Shape of the Past: Models and Antiquity* (Lawrence, KS: Coronado Press, 1975), 173, quoted in Myers, *Binding the Strong Man*, 48.
24. Myers, *Binding the Strong Man*, 77.
25. Rhoads, Dewey, and Michie, *Mark as Story*, 67.
26. Ibid., 134–35.
27. Jesus's ministry in Galilee places him inevitably among the peasant class (tenant farmers, day laborers and otherwise social outcasts) who, because of the transition from subsistence farming toward a redistributive economy that displaced farmers and eroded the kinship group, it is safe to assume, were attracted to the Son of Man who makes them pure, feeds them, and raises the dead.
28. Myers, *Binding the Strong Man*, 75–76.
29. Myers, *Binding the Strong Man*, 51.
30. Myers, *Binding the Strong Man*, 51.
31. Carney, *The Shape of the Past*, 198, quoted in Myers, *Binding the Strong Man*, 51.
32. Ellen F. Davis, *Scripture, Culture, and Agriculture: An Agrarian Reading of the Bible* (Cambridge: Cambridge University Press, 2009), 77. Davis cites obesity as "the single greatest threat to health in the United States and a rising threat in Britain" and correlated with these countries' surpluses of food.
33. Davis, *Scripture, Culture, and Agriculture*, 76.
34. Boer, *The Sacred Economy of Ancient Israel*, 66–67.
35. Myers, *Binding the Strong Man*, 77.
36. Myers, *Binding the Strong Man*, 52.
37. Myers, *Binding the Strong Man*, 52. See also Malina and Rohrbaugh, *Social Science Commentary*, 420.
38. Myers, *Binding the Strong Man*, 51.
39. Richard A. Horsley, "Ancient Jewish Banditry and the Revolt against Rome, A.D. 66–70," *Catholic Biblical Quarterly* 43 (1981): 416ff, quoted in Myers, *Binding the Strong Man*, 51. I follow Boer's definition of "class" as determined "by access to and control over the means of production, as well as location in the division of labor" (122).
40. See Roland Boer, *The Sacred Economy of Ancient Israel*, 115–21, for the relationship between the estate owner and the laborer.
41. Wendell Berry, *The Art of the Commonplace: The Agrarian Essays of Wendell Berry*, ed. Norman Wirzba (Berkeley, CA: Counterpoint, 2002), 239.
42. Berry, *The Art of the Commonplace*, 240.
43. Myers, *Binding the Strong Man*, 52. Myers highlights Galilee as the "breadbasket" of the region and as an ideal location for the ruling class to appropriate goods for municipal areas (*Binding the Strong Man*, 53).
44. Boer, *The Sacred Economy of Ancient Israel*, 123.
45. *The New Oxford Annotated Bible: New Revised Stand Version* (New York: Oxford University Press, 2010).
46. Myers, *The Sacred Economy of Ancient Israel*, 295.
47. Literally means any young animal. Jesus's entry on the young animal seems to allude to the prophecy in Zechariah 9:9, which describes a peasant king riding on a "donkey" into Jerusalem. In order to maintain thematic consistency, I translate *polos* as "donkey."
48. Belo, *A Materialist Reading of the Gospel of Mark*, 178.
49. Belo, *A Materialist Reading of the Gospel of Mark*, 178.

50. For commodity transport, see Gen. 42:26–27; 44:3, 13; Exod. 23:5; Josh. 9:4; 2 Sam. 16:1–2; Judg. 19:10. For human transport, see Exod. 4:20; Josh. 15:18; Judg. 5:10; 2 Kgs. 4:22, 24; 2 Sam. 17:23.

51. Myers, *Binding the Strong Man*, 282. Immediately before Jesus's entry into the city, Bartimaeus is the first to throw his cloak on the ground and follow Jesus along the way (10:50–52).

52. See Zechariah 9:9–10.

53. New Revised Standard Version.

54. See Mark 8:31; 9:31–32; and 10:33–34.

55. See Mark 10:42–45.

56. Used eight times: 8:27; 9:33; 9:34; 10:17; 10:32; 10:46; 10:52; and 11:8.

57. Rhoads, Dewey, Michie, *Mark as Story*, 68.

58. New Revised Standard Version.

59. Rhoads, Dewey, Michie, *Mark as Story*, 104–5. See also Malina and Rohrbaugh, *Social Science Commentary*, 409.

60. Rhoads, Dewey, Michie, *Mark as Story*, 72.

61. See Rhoads, Dewey, and Michie, *Mark as Story*, 135.

62. See Belo's introduction to *A Materialist Reading of the Gospel of Mark*, 1–6.

63. Myers, *Binding the Strong Man*, 82.

64. Michelle Alexander, *The New Jim Crow: Mass Incarceration in the Age of Colorblindness* (New York: The New Press, 2012), 6.

65. Alexander, *The New Jim Crow*, 2.

66. J. M. Coetzee, *The Lives of Animals* (Princeton, NJ: Princeton University Press, 1999), 35. Through the fictional character of Elizabeth Costello, Coetzee asserts that the capacity of human reason is not sufficient for a response to the suffering of animals; rather, it is sympathy and the ability to imagine oneself as another that is necessary (34–35). See Allison Carruth, "Compassion, Commodification, and *The Lives of Animals*: J. M. Coetzee's Recent Fiction," in *Postcolonial Ecologies: Literatures of the Environment*, ed. Elizabeth DeLoughrey and George B. Handley (New York: Oxford University Press, 2011), 208. If anything, it is our confidence in higher reason and its misinterpreted absence among animals that has relegated them as completely other, justifying our mass killing in slaughterhouses.

67. United States Department of Agriculture & National Agricultural Statistics Service, "Livestock Slaughter," accessed May 19, 2016, http://usda.mannlib.cornell.edu/usda/current/LiveSlau/LiveSlau-05-19-2016.pdf. 2.41 million cows and 9.37 million pigs killed from April 2015–2016. I could not find the number of poultry killed since the USDA measures poultry slaughtered in weight instead of individual birds.

68. See Carruth, "Compassion, Commodification, and *The Lives of Animals*," 208, for a discussion of how Coetzee's fictional character Costello turns an object and its metaphor around.

69. Carruth, "Compassion, Commodification, and *The Lives of Animals*," 204.

70. Davis, *Scripture, Culture, and Agriculture*, 97.

71. Davis, *Scripture, Culture, and Agriculture*, 98.

72. Davis, *Scripture, Culture, and Agriculture*, 98.

73. Davis, *Scripture, Culture, and Agriculture*, 98.

74. Davis mentions "mad cow disease" emerging out of the social conditions of animals living in CAFOs (*Scripture, Culture, and Agriculture*, 98).

75. See Mark 8:31; 9:31–32; and 10:33–34.

REFERENCES

Alexander, Michelle. *The New Jim Crow: Mass Incarceration in the Age of Colorblindness.* New York: The New Press, 2012.

Belo, Fernando. *A Materialist Reading of the Gospel of Mark.* Maryknoll, NY: Orbis Books, 1981.

Belo, Fernando. *Introduction to a Materialist Reading of the Gospel of Mark*. Maryknoll, NY: Orbis Books, 1981.

Berry, Wendell. *The Art of the Commonplace: The Agrarian Essays of Wendell Berry*. Edited by Norman Wirzba. Berkeley, CA: Counterpoint, 2002.

Boer, Roland. *The Sacred Economy of Ancient Israel*. Louisville, KY: Westminster/John Knox Press, 2015.

Carney, Thomas F. *The Shape of the Past: Models and Antiquity*. Lawrence, KS: Coronado Press, 1975: 173, 198. Quoted in Ched Myers, *Binding the Strong Man: A Political Reading of Mark's Story of Jesus*. 1988. Reprint. Maryknoll, NY: Orbis Books, 2008, 48, 51. Page references are to the 2008 edition.

Carruth, Allison. "Compassion, Commodification, and *The Lives of Animals*: J. M. Coetzee's Recent Fiction." In *Postcolonial Ecologies: Literatures of the Environment*. Edited by Elizabeth DeLoughrey and George B. Handley, 200–213. New York: Oxford University Press, 2011.

Coetzee, J. M. *The Lives of Animals*. Princeton, NJ: Princeton University Press, 1999.

Davis, Ellen F. *Scripture, Culture, and Agriculture: An Agrarian Reading of the Bible*. Cambridge: Cambridge University Press, 2009.

Horsley, Richard A. "Ancient Jewish Banditry and the Revolt against Rome, A.D. 66–70." *Catholic Biblical Quarterly* 43 (1981): 416ff. Quoted in Ched Myers, *Binding the Strong Man: A Political Reading of Mark's Story of Jesus*. Maryknoll, NY: Orbis Books, 1988, 51.

Lukács, Georg. *History and Class Consciousness: Studies in Marxist Dialectics*. Cambridge, MA: MIT Press, 1971.

Malina, Bruce J. and Richard L. Rohrbaugh. *Social-Science Commentary on the Synoptic Gospels*. 2nd ed. Minneapolis, MN: Fortress Press, 2003.

Myers, Ched. *Binding the Strong Man: A Political Reading of Mark's Story of Jesus*, Maryknoll, NY: Orbis Books, 1988.

Rhoads, David, Joanna Dewey, and Donald Michie. *Mark as Story: An Introduction to the Narrative of a Gospel*. 3rd ed. Minneapolis, MN: Fortress Press, 2012.

United States Department of Agriculture and National Agricultural Statistics Service. "Livestock Slaughter." Accessed May 19, 2016. http://usda.mannlib.cornell.edu/usda/current/LiveSlau/LiveSlau-05–19–2016.pdf.

Index

abuse, 28
accountability to God for evil toward nonhumans and the earth, 5
acid rain, 67
activists, 114
Adam, 87, 90
aesthetics, 53, 58n23, 134
Agape, 35–36, 37
agency, 28, 85
agents, 28, 103
"Agnus Dei", 133
agrarian : peasant life, 222; symbols, 224; way of life, 222
agroecology, 174n23
alienation from land, 222
allegorical, 132, 133
altruism, 92
ammunition selection, 123
amphibians, 72
ancient social order, 202
angels, 132
anglers, 125
animal(s): advocacy, 33; in captivity, 73; companion, 9, 32; cruelty towards, ix; emotions in, 27; farm, 9, 221; game, 118; husbandry, 26, 202, 203; inclusion of in moral regard, 31; as individuals, 63, 73; inherent value of, 26, 29, 31, 36; liberation, 25, 37, 68–69, 226; rescue, 14; rights, 8, 25, 26, 27, 29, 30; sacrifice, 6; scientific use of, 25, 29; societies, 15n1; theology, 5, 7, 18n53; unethical use of, 26; welfare, 13, 26, 28, 31, 40n50, 63, 64, 67, 71, 72; wild, 72, 135, 138
Animal Cruelty Act, 2
animal rights manifesto, 2
ant, 51, 53
Antarctica, 73
anthrax, 126n17
Anthropocene, 81–82, 85, 88, 92, 98
anthropocentrism, 33, 55, 63, 191
anthropogenic, 63, 64, 68, 75. *See also* climate change
anthropological, 25, 26, 31, 180, 202
anthropomorphic, 133, 134, 156, 165
anti-imperial, 199, 206, 207, 209n5
anti-vivisection, 2. *See also* vivisection
Appalachia, 11, 101–114
apocalyptic, 146. *See also* eschatological
Aquinas, Thomas, 26, 35, 36, 38n3, 38n25
Arctic, 72
arid, 203
aristocratic, 203
Aristotle, 9, 19n62, 51, 51–52, 52, 57
ark : of the covenant, 86; Noah's, 65
art, 86
Asian dog-meat trade, 2
assisted reproduction, 63
Augustine, ix

Bartholomew, Patriarch, 183, 184

Bauckham, Richard, 6
beast(s), ix, 1, 137
beast-like, 202
beef, 93
Belo, Fernando, 217, 223
Benedict XVI, 188, 190
Bentham, Jeremy, 27
Bernstein, Ellen, 6
Berry, Thomas, 179, 183
Berry, Wendell, 8, 11, 55, 101, 109, 111, 114, 168, 222
Bethany, 223
The Bible and Ecology, 6. *See also* Bauckham, Richard
biocentric, 49
bio char, 94
biodiversity, loss of, 5, 10, 15, 63, 73, 185
biological, 33; agent, 47; processes, 119
biomimicry, 171
biopsy, 63, 73
biosphere, 63, 82
biotic community, 68–69
bird, ix
birth control, 124, 126n16
bishops, 102, 148; Canadian, 183
Black Beauty, 1, 15n1, 15n3
Boer, Roland, 200, 203
bourgeoise, 226
breeding cycles: disruption of, 63
breeding sites, 74
brothers, 54. *See also* fraternity
buck, 117
Buddhism, 108
butcher, 112

CAFO's, 13, 226
Callicott, J. Baird, 68, 69
canine, 85. *See also* dogs
"Canticle of Brother Sun" ("Canticle of the Creatures"), 54, 192
canticles, 131
capitalism, 217, 226
capital punishment, 43
carbon emissions. *See* CO_2
care ethics, 9
carol, 134
carrier pigeon, 125
Carroll, Lewis, 2. *See also* Animal Cruelty Act

categorical imperative, 8, 83. *See also* Kant, Immanuel
caterpillars, 53
cattle, 71, 203
Cecil the Lion, 14
celebration, 148, 152, 156
CFL's, 68
chains, 201, 202, 212n37. *See also* shackles
chants, 131
character, 44, 45, 50, 56
charity, 35, 40n43
chemical killing, 47
chimpanzee, 33
China, 2
choir, 134
chora, 202
Christological, 31, 32, 37; hymn, 90
Chrysostom, John, 54
chytridiomycosis, 74, 78n55
The City of God, ix
civil rights movement, 26
clams, 44
clean, 202; animals, 65, 66. *See also* purity
clergy, 145, 146
climate, 65; change, 10, 73, 75, 185
climate science, 65
Clough, David, 7, 11, 20n86, 118, 118–119, 120, 122
CO_2, 64, 67, 68, 69, 82, 92, 166, 170
coal, 67; mining, 101
Cobb, Jr., John B., 5
Coetzee, J. M., 229n66
coinhere, 89
collaring, 73. *See also* radio-tagging
colonialism, 82
colt, 223. *See also* donkey
Columbia spotted frog, 74
commodification of animals, 226
communion, 88
communist, 226
community,: of compassion, 5, 179
compassion, ix, x, 4, 7, 34, 102, 108–109, 110, 165, 186, 213n60
conception rate, 71. *See also* frog reproduction
conservation, 69, 76n14, 118, 124
consumerism, 12, 145, 156, 188
consumption, 123

"contact zone", 67
contagion, 219, 221
conversion, 183, 186
coral reefs, 141
I Corinthians 13, 35
corporate worship, 131
covenant, 154
cow(s), 93
creation, 81, 86; account, 65; community of, 164; short-term interpretation of, 65; temple, 87
creation care, 5, 11, 12
creativity, 87. *See also* Holy Spirit
CreatureKind, 13
cricket, 45, 51
crop(s), 182, 219, 220, 221, 222, 223; surplus, 203, 221, 222
cruciform, 92
crush fetishism, 47
cultivated, 200, 202
cultural revolution, 190

Darwin, 90
data-logging devices, 63. *See also* tracking devices
David, 223, 224
Davidic kingship, 217, 224, 225
Davis, Ellen, 4, 6, 226
day laborers, 217, 221, 222, 228n27
day lighting, 170
Deane-Drummond, Celia, 7, 10
debt, 219, 220, 221
Decapolis, 201, 202, 203, 205, 210n10
deforestation, 124
De Grazia, David, 26–28, 29–30, 33, 39n30
dehumanizing, 217, 225, 226
dehydration, 63
deliverance : from demonic possession, 199, 207, 208
demon(s), 199, 206–208, 218
demonic colonial forces, 201, 207; *see also* unclean spirits
Department of Agriculture, 122
deontology, 8, 18n55, 31. *See also* duties; Kant, Immanuel
Descartes, Rene, 53
desert, 221
desertification, 192

destruction, 65, 67, 200, 208, 209, 213n60; environmental, 181
destructive way of life, 217
devotional, 131
dikaiosune, 36, 57. *See also* justice
disciples, 121, 224, 225
disciplined, 109
discrimination, 226
disease: animal, 63, 221
displacement : animals, 63; human, 200
divine image. *See* imago dei
DNA, 90, 191
doe, 117
dog(s), 2, 44. *See also* canine
dog-meat market. *See* Asian dog-meat market
domestic animals, 203
domesticated, 63, 67, 69, 69–71, 77n39
domination, 212n52
dominion, 132, 187, 191
Dominion, 3. *See also* Scully, Matthew
donkey, 218, 219, 221, 223, 226, 228n27
Douglas, Mary, 12, 200, 202, 210n15
doxological, 87, 148
drones, 47
drought, 4, 221
drugs, 226
ducks, 123
duties, 26, 28, 29, 48, 49. *See also* Kant, Immanuel; deontology

earth care, 5
eauton ekonôsen, 90
ecological education, 189
economy: allocation, 203, 211n22; extraction, 203, 209; industrial, 218, 221; local, 209; redistributive, 221, 223; subsistence, 203, 222
ecosystems, 63, 68, 182
elephants, 2, 3, 4
elk, 166
emancipatory, 217. *See also* liberation; "Way of Jesus"
emergence theory, 81, 84, 92
emissions, 69. *See also* CO_2
empathy, 53, 105, 166
endangered species, 69
endocrine disruption, 69
Enlightenment, 26, 52, 108, 135

enslavement, 82. *See also* slavery
Episcopal Church, 147, 157n5
epistemology, 81, 84
"equal consideration sense", 27, 30–33. *See also* De Grazia, David
equality, 30
equivalent, 53, 57
Erlich, Paul and Anne, 53
Esau, 66
eschatological, 65, 151, 226
eschaton, 90, 120, 121
ethnic, 200
ethnographer, 102
ethology, 31
Eucharist, 122
eudaimonia, 55
evangelical, 64, 65
evangelization, 131, 154
evolutionary theory, 33, 65, 84, 118–120
ex nihilio, 94
exorcism, 200, 218, 221
experiential subjects, 28. *See also* moral considerability
exploitation, 65, 101, 113, 121–122, 125, 182, 222
extensionist ethics, 29, 30, 31, 33
extinction, 63

factory farm animals, 4, 5, 13. *See also* CAFO's
faith communities, 65
the Fall, 66, 82
fallow, 63
famine, 82, 83
farmers, 200, 203, 204, 209; agrarian peasant, 217, 221, 224; Galilean subsistence, 221–223, 226, 228n27; peasant, 217, 220; tenant, 222
farms, 118; factory, 9; fur, 9
fauna, 93
fellowship, 145, 147, 148, 149, 150
felon, 226
fertilizer, 82
festivals, 221
fiddle, 112
fields, 200, 202
fish, 82, 113, 121, 138
fishing, 118
fitness, 63

flesh, 32, 122, 164
flora, 93
fodder, 204
folklore, 111
footprint, 188
forest(s), 140, 171, 184, 203
forgiveness, 121, 185
fortifications, 205
fossil fuel, 93, 170
"The Four Seasons", 142n11. *See also* Vivaldi, Antonio
The Foxfire Books, 11, 111–113
Francis of Assisi, 5, 54, 179, 183, 184, 185, 187, 191, 192. *See also* "Canticle of Brother Sun"
Francis, Pope, 12, 81, 83
Franciscan, ix, x
fraternity, 192
freedom, 15, 180
free markets, 217. *See also* capitalism
Frey, R. G., 27–28
friendship love, 40n41
frogs, 72, 73–74; reproduction of, 73

Gadara, 205, 210n10
Galilee, 217, 221, 227, 228n27; Sea of, 202
garbage, 182
garden, 152
Garden of Eden, 6, 88, 172
Gatta, John, 148
Genesis, 64, 65, 87, 88, 93
Genesis 1, 90, 136, 137
genetics, 33
genocide, 82
Gentiles, 200, 202, 202–203, 208, 225
geoenergy, 92
geological, 81
Gerasa, 205, 210n10
Gerasenes, 201, 202, 203–204, 208, 210n10
GHG's, 72
globalization, 82
global warming, 10, 63, 185. *See also* climate change; temperature increases
gluttony, 93
gnat, 44
goats, 203
godhead, 85, 90, 92. *See also* Trinity
Golden Rule, 48, 49

goods, 204
grace, 154–155
grasshoppers, 46
greed, 167
Greek, 90, 202, 206, 207
green buildings, 170
green design, 170
"green teams", 145, 156
greenhouse gas, 64, 75, 82
groaning of creation, 4, 66, 168, 172. *See also* Romans 8

habitation, 81
habitats, 63, 68, 118, 205–208, 209
harvest, 221
harzardous, 202, 203, 209
healing, 221; spiritual, 206
healthcare, 226
heat stress, 63, 71
heaven, 132, 161
Hellenistic, 202
herd, 201, 203, 204, 206
hermeneutic, 81, 199
hierarchy, 84, 123
high-density housing, 92
hodos, 224
hogs, 102, 112, 226
homoousial, 87
honesty, 56
hormonal treatment, 71
horses, 69
Hosanna, 223, 224
hostility, 207
humanities, 25
human rights, 29, 31. *See also* civil rights
humble, 90
humiliation, 90
humility, 4, 15, 52, 121
hunt: inability of polar bears to, 73, 78n43
hunting, 3, 4, 11, 69, 72, 117–125; community, 118, 125; season, 118; trophy, 123
hybrid, 219
hydraulic fracturing, 101
hymnals, 131
hymnody, 11

Idaho Great Basin, 74
idolatry, 87
idols, 81
imago dei, 31, 92, 180
imperialism: Roman, 200, 206, 207, 208, 209
incarnation, 36, 92, 119, 123, 125, 146, 164
indigenous : knowledge, 73; people, 182, 208
industrialization, 124
Industrial Revolution, 82
insect(s), 10, 43–57
integral ecology, 189
interests, 27, 28, 31, 33
intervention, 73, 74; of God, 164
intuitions, 49, 50, 56
invasive species, 63
invertebrates, 44, 75
Isaiah 65:25, 77n29
Israel, 224
ivory import/export, 2, 4

Jerusalem, 217, 219, 220, 223, 227
Jesus, 164, 199–208, 221; as human, 90; mission of, 201; as model for creation care, 10; in solidarity with the poor, 225
Jesus's ministry, 217, 221
Jesus's parables, 66, 67
Jewish, 86, 199, 202, 203, 208, 210n13, 210n16
the Jewish war, 203
Jews, 202, 212n50
Job, 87
John of Damascus, 86
John, Pope, 181, 186
John Paul II, Pope, 183, 186
Jordan River, 202, 205
Josephus, 205
joy, 137
Judaism, 14, 200
Judeo-Christian, 5, 64, 65–67, 186, 187
"The Judgment of the Nations", 54
justice, 10, 26, 55, 57, 86, 189, 191, 192; as virtue, 36; making, 35, 36, 37; social, 145, 180

Kabbalah, 89
Kant, Immanuel, 8, 26, 31, 83
Kantian ethics, 14, 56. *See also* deontology
Kauffman, Stuart, 84

kenotic, 10, 35, 81, 83, 90–92
kill, ix
Kingdom of God, 120
kinship, 37, 148, 191, 199, 222, 228n27
kittens, 51
Küng, Hans, 81, 83, 94

labor, 203
Laissez-Faire Intuition (LFI), 67
lamb, 133
"Lamb of God", 133
land: arable, 203, 222; tax, 221
land-clearing, 82
The Land Ethic, 101; *see also* Leopold, Aldo
landfills, 171
Latin, 137, 206
the Law, 219, 220, 225
Legion, 12, 199–209
Leopold, Aldo, 55, 68, 69, 101
Leviathan, 89
Levite, 220
Levitical law, 63, 66
liberation, 154, 208, 217, 223, 225, 226
Linzey, Andrew, 16n8, 18n49, 25, 31, 32, 39n29
Lion of Judah, 133
livestock, 122
Lockwood, Jeffrey A., 10
Lyme Disease, 126n17

MacIntyre, Aladair, 34, 39n37
madness, 207, 210n15
male chick maceration, 3, 16n17
mammals, 31, 32, 85, 182; marsupials, 85; placental, 85
marginal cases, 29, 30, 33, 34, 43
marine fish capture, 82
Masai, 93
mascot, pigs as, 206
materialism, 132. *See also consumerism*
Matthew 10:29, 7, 57
McKibben, William, 68
Medieval, 12
megafaunal, 82
menuha, 88
mercy, 4, 52, 53, 55, 138
messiah(ship), 224, 225
metaphysical, 90

Midgley, Mary, 29, 30
migration, 73; patterns, 125
military : command, 206; forces, 200. *See also* Roman army
milk, 203, 204
mining industry, 101
misanthropic, 55
mission of church, 146
missionaries, 131
misuse of animals, ix, 1, 26. *See also* use of animals
Moltmann, Jürgen, 5, 10, 89
monastic spirituality, 161
monks, 46
monitoring wild animals, 73. *See also* collaring; radio-tagging; tracking devices
moon, 135
moonshine, 102, 111, 112, 113
moral : community, 26, 29, 30; consideration, 27, 28, 29, 30, 35; cultivation, 113; patients, 28, 29. *See also* Regan, Tom; regard, 4; sphere, 29, 33; standing, 53; status, 26
morally considerable, 49, 53
Mormon ecology, 13
Moses, 66, 220
Most High God, 201, 206
moths, 46
mountain-top removal, 101, 112, 167; *see also* Appalachia
Murdoch, Iris, 8, 11, 109–111

narrative critical method, 218
narrative symbols, 13
natural gas, 101
natural rights, 49
neighbor, 35
neoplatonism, 83
the Netherlands, 3
neuroscience, 92
New Age Movement, 65
new creation, 164
new earth, 132, 141
new heavens, 141
New Testament, 66, 88, 219. *See also* Jesus's parables
Niebuhr, H. Richard, 11, 102, 105–110, 115n7

Nimrod, 66
nitrogen, 82
Noah, ix, 63, 65, 66
Noddings, Nel, 9
nomadic pastoralists, 204
nourishment, 204
nuach, 87
nutrients, 84
nuts, 204

ocean acidification, 4, 64, 82, 94n1
oil, 72, 172
Old Testament, 63, 66, 86, 152
omnivorous, 125
ontology, 81, 84, 85, 181
oppression, 207, 217, 225; colonial, 200, 201. *See also* Roman rule
ownership, 26
ox, 219

pain. *See* suffering
Palestine, 217, 218, 222
Palmer, Clare, 67. *See also* Laissez-Faire Intuition (LFI)
panentheism, 81, 90
pantheism, 65
parables, 66. *See also* Jesus's parables
parasites, 63, 71
Parliament, 2
Passover lamb, 121, 122
Pastoral, 6, 142n11
pathogens, 43, 71
Paul, 4, 35, 86, 90, 132
peace, 83, 182
peasant king, 224
peasantry, 221
Pentecost, 164
perichoresis, 10, 86
perinatal survival, 71
pest(s), 93; control, 44
Pharaoh, 206
photovotalic cells, 170
phronēsis, 9, 55
pickling, 113
pig(s), 4, 12, 112, 199–209
pig owners, 208
pilgrimage, 132
Planetary boundaries, 81, 82, 94n1. *See also* Anthropocene

plastic, 189
Platonic, 36, 109
plow, 111
poaching, 2
poisonous : insects, 47; substances, 184
polar bears, 72–73, 75
political, 31
pollutant, 64, 72
polluted stream, 167
pollution, 200, 219, 225
polos, 223, 228n47
population(s), 82, 124; declines, 73
pork, 204, 206
possession, 206, 207, 212n50
postcolonial, 12, 199, 200, 201, 207, 208, 209
post-Enlightenment, 52. *See also* Enlightenment
poultry, 122, 229n67
precipitation, 64
predation, 49, 84; human, 121
predator-prey relationships, 11, 29, 69, 72, 117, 120–121
prenatal care, 71
preservation, 118
prey, 63, 72, 118. *See also* predator-prey relationships
priest(s), 164, 203, 220, 221, 222
Prince of Peace, 120
private sphere, 217
prophets, 67; of Baal, 94, 97n84
protest, 207, 208
Protestant, 131
Psalm(s), 6, 17n39, 131; 104, 85, 87, 89
Psalm of Ascents, 88
public domain, 30
purity, 200, 203, 210n13, 219, 220, 222
Purity and Danger, 202. *See also* Douglas, Mary
purpose of God's creation, 4, 7, 107, 113, 119, 156

quality of life virtue, 27, 28. *See also* Frey, R. G.

rabbinic tradition, 221
radio-tagging, 73
rain, 139
rainfall, 74, 203; patterns, 64

rainforests, 141
ransom, 225
reciprocity, 32, 34, 36, 89, 221
recitations, 131
reconnaissance, 224
reconciliation of all things, 118, 119, 149, 154, 157, 165
recreation, 123
redeemed living, 118, 120
redemption, 84, 148; for animals, 118–120; narrative, 118–121
redistributive, 221
reforestation, 94
refugees, 74
Regan, Tom, 25, 28–31
rehabilitation, 67, 73
relocation, 63, 73, 74
remediation, 69, 74
renewable energy, 93
reparative action, x, 10
repertoires, 131
reproduction control. *See* birth control
resistance, 207–208, 208
restored, 208. *See also* deliverance
resurrection, 121, 164, 227
retrain, 133
Revelation, 67, 86, 120, 132
"reverence for life", 7, 18n50, 49, 51, 53
the righteous, 54
righteousness of God, 36
rights language, 26–33, 41
rituals, 220
river bank, 204
robin, 45
Rolston II, Holmes, 92
Roman : army, 200, 205, 206, 207, 212n48; authority, 222; colonizers, 206, 207; land owners, 221; occupiers. *See* Roman land owners
Roman Empire, 205
Roman-Judean war, 219
Romans 8, 5, 66, 156
Rome, 205, 206, 207, 208
ruling class, 222
ruminants, 203

Sabbath, 66
Sabbatical year, 6, 63
sacrament, 133, 145, 151

The Sacred Economy of Ancient Israel, 203
sacrifice, 121, 134, 135, 147, 165
sacrifices, 92, 220
saints, 67
salvation, 145, 146, 149, 150, 152. *See also* redemption
sanitation, 92
Schweitzer, Albert, 7, 49
sea level changes, 64
sea lions, 72
seals, 72
Second Vatican Council, 180, 185
seed, 219
self-emptying, 84
selfishness, 92
self-sacrificing behavior of women, 40n39
sentience, 3, 4, 27, 29, 30, 49, 53, 102, 105, 108
sentient, 68, 69
servant(hood), 224, 225
seventh-day Sabbath, 13, 88
Sewell, Anna, 1–2. *See also Black Beauty*
shabbat, 10
shackles, 201, 202. *See also* chains
shalom, 164, 165, 169
Shema, 86
sheep, 138, 203, 204
shepherds, 5
shooting, 3, 44
Sierra Club, 148
Singer, Peter, x, 6, 7, 8, 17n24, 18n51, 27–28, 34, 38n5
Sittler, Joseph, 149, 152
slaughter, ix, 2, 200, 207
slaughterhouse, 3, 226
slave(s), 90, 222, 225, 226
slavery, 154, 180; spiritual, 200
social conscience, 1, 3
social-scientific critical perspective, 12, 218
Socrates, 52
SOI Foundation, 3
soil, 141
solar, 93, 161; *see also* sun
solidarity, 118, 180, 181, 185, 187
Solomon, 88, 135
"Song of Moses", 212n46
sophia, 9, 19n70
soteriology, 87

sparrows, 57. *See also* Matthew 10:29
speciation, 39n31
speciesism, 27, 28, 33. *See also* Singer, Peter
spider, 51
squirrel, 45
stars, 135, 136, 155
starvation, 63, 222; of polar bears, 73
stewardship, 65, 66, 141, 148, 149, 153, 191
stratosphere, 92
subdue, 136, 137. *See also* Genesis; Genesis 1
"subjects of a life", 29, 31. *See also* Regan, Tom
subjugation, 137
suffering, 102; of animals, 27, 34, 63, 69, 72, 73, 75, 85, 119, 125, 229n66; of humans, 139, 140, 155; of insects, 43, 46, 47, 50, 52, 53; of God, 81, 90, 92
sulfur, 92
sun, 139. *See also* solar
supplementation of vitamins for animals, 71
surface tension, 82
sustainability, 199, 208
swine. *See* pigs
symbolic order, 217, 219, 222, 225, 226
systematic theology, 119

Tabernacle, 88
technai, 111, 114
technocratic culture, 188, 190
teleological, 85
temperance, 51
temperature increases, 64, 71, 72. *See also* climate change; global warming
tempests, 137
temple, 13, 85, 87, 224; system, 217; workers, 221
Ten Commandments, 35
terrestrial biosphere degradation, 82
terrorism, 43
testimony, 207
theocentric, 106
theodicy, 90
theos-rights, 31. *See also* Linzey, Andrew
tithe(s), 220, 221, 222

tombs, 201, 202, 207–208, 209, 210n12, 210n13
top-soil erosion, 5. *See also* soil
Torah, 219. *See also* the Law
tormented, 206
tormenters, 207
tracking devices, 63
transcendent, 109
transfiguration, 148, 164
transformation, 36, 120, 148, 163, 179, 192
trapping, 122
Trinitarian, 10, 119, 180
Trinity, 81, 90, 149; economic, 86
Triumphal entry, 217, 223
tropical climes, 71
tubers, 204
Turere, Richard, 82

unclean : animals, 65, 66, 199, 210n13. *See also* pigs; land, 200, 208; spirits, 199, 200, 202, 212n54
unforested, 203
United Egg Producers, 3
urban contexts, 190
U.S. Fish and Wildlife Service, 15
utilitarianism, 8, 28, 29, 31, 35, 45–48, 49, 50, 55, 56, 57, 63, 69, 81, 169

vaccines, 14
veganism, 119
vegetarianism, 93, 121, 122
vertebrates, 75
Vespasian, 205
victims, 206
village(s), 200, 202, 203, 204, 205, 210n10, 219
vineyard, 219
violence, 93, 200, 206, 207, 209, 213n59; human-to-human, 15, 25, 26
virtues, 8, 25, 28, 29, 139, 165–169; cardinal, 50; classical, 34; theological, 35, 50
Vivaldi, Antonio, 142n11
the vulnerable, 30, 34, 35, 37, 191, 201

war, 83
warrior king, 224
wasp, 51, 53
waste, 167, 168, 171, 173n16, 182

water shortage, 203
water stress, 74
Watts, Isaac, 136
"Way of Jesus", 217; motif, 224, 225, 227
weapon(s), 123, 224; nuclear, 82
web of life, 102
Webb, Stephen, 32
Webster, John, 86
Weil, Simone, 124
Weinberg, Stephen, 84
Western : culture, 180; thought, 26, 33, 45; tradition, 50
wetlands, 141, 185
White House, 2
White Jr., Lynn, 5, 6
white-tailed deer, 124

Whitman, Walt, 53
Wigginton, Eliot, 111
Wilberforce, William, 16n4
wild animals. *See* animals, wild
wilderness,: conservation, 101
wild justice, 31, 35
wildlife, 72; preservation, 125; rescue, 67
wind, 93
wisdom, 9, 37, 165, 172, 187
wonder, 52
wool, 204, 219
working class, 217
worms, 44, 53

zoos, 73, 75

About the Contributors

Melissa Brotton is associate professor of English literature at La Sierra University, California. She teaches courses in nineteenth-century British literature with special attention to Elizabeth Barrett Browning and Robert Browning. She has edited and contributed to a collection of essays, *Ecotheology in the Humanities: An Interdisciplinary Approach to Understanding the Divine and Nature* (Lanham, MD: Lexington Books, 2016). She is a contributing editor to *The Works of Elizabeth Barrett Browning*, edited by Sandra M. Donaldson, et al. (2010). Her PhD is in English literature from the University of North Dakota, Grand Forks.

Jerry Cappel is an ordained Episcopal priest currently serving as the environmental network coordinator for Province IV of The Episcopal Church in Tennessee. Jerry's professional interests are in adult education, ecology, and faith. Jerry serves as president of Kentucky Interfaith Power and Light and is a fellow with the Center for Religion and the Environment (Sewanee, The University of the South) and GreenFaith. He has worked as an author and editor of youth and adult education materials for Smyth & Helwys Publishing in Macon, Georgia, and as a learning consultant for Humana, Inc. in Louisville, Kentucky. He is a graduate of Harding Graduate School of Religion (MDiv) in Memphis, Tennessee, and Southern Baptist Theological Seminary in Louisville, Kentucky (PhD).

David Clough is professor of theological ethics at the University of Chester, Cheshire, UK, and the president of the Society for the Study of Christian Ethics. He has previously written on the ethics of Karl Barth in *Ethics in Crisis: Interpreting Barth's Ethics* (2007), and the ethics of war in *Faith and Force: A Christian Debate about War*, with Brian Stiltner (2009). His current research concerns the place of nonhuman animals in Christian doctrine and ethics, focused on a two-volume monograph, *On Animals*. Volume I, *Systematic Theology* was published by T & T Clark/Bloomsbury in 2012, and Volume II, *Theological Ethics,* is in progress. He has also coedited with Celia Deane-Drummond two related books: *Creaturely Theology: On God, Humans, and Other Animals* (2009) and *Animals as Religious Subjects: Transdisciplinary Perspectives* (2013).

Celia Deane-Drummond is full professor in theology at the University of Notre Dame, Indiana. Her research interests are in the engagement of theology and natural science, including, specifically, ecology, evolution, animal behavior, and anthropology. She has published widely, including more than thirty papers in internationally recognized scientific journals and more than twenty books, either edited or as sole author. She is joint editor of a new journal launched in 2014 with Mohr Siebeck (Germany) titled *Philosophy, Theology and the Sciences*. Her most recent books include *Wonder and Wisdom: Conversations in Science, Spirituality and Theology* (2006); *Genetics and Christian Ethics* (2006); *Future Perfect*, ed. with Peter Scott (2006, 2n ed. 2010), *Eco-Theology* (2008), *Christ and Evolution* (2009), *Creaturely Theology,* ed. with David Clough (2009) *Religion and Ecology in the Public Sphere*, ed. with Heinrich Bedford-Strohm (2011), *Animals as Religious Subjects*, ed. with Rebecca Artinian Kaiser and David Clough (2013), *The Wisdom of the Liminal: Human Nature, Evolution and Other Animals* (2014); *ReImaging the Divine Image: Humans and Other Animals* (2014).

Robert (Robin) Gottfried, professor of economics, emeritus, serves as the executive director of the Center for Religion and Environment at Sewanee, The University of the South, Tennessee. Long known for his passion for environmental economics and sustainable development, he has conducted research on land use change and forest policy as well as the economic impacts of development and other economic activity in the United States, Costa Rica, and elsewhere. Gottfried helped spearhead the creation of Sewanee's environmental studies program and served as its first chair. He also teaches occasionally in the school of theology. He is the author of *Economics, Ecology and the Roots of Western Faith: Perspectives from the Garden* as well as articles addressing the interface of social science, ecotheology and spirituality. Gottfried is a facilitator for the "Opening the Book of Nature" program and a speaker on theoecology and sustainable development. Robin received his PhD from the University of North Carolina, Chapel Hill.

Kendra Haloviak Valentine is associate professor in the Department of Biblical Studies in the H. M. S. Richards Divinity School at La Sierra University, California. She has served as a pastor in Ohio, Michigan, and Maryland, and has taught at Adventist colleges and universities in the United States and Australia. She completed her doctoral studies at the Graduate Theological Union at Berkeley with a dissertation on the hymns of the book of Revelation. She has authored numerous articles in her field, including "The Book of Revelation" in *The Dictionary of Scripture and Ethics* (2011). Recent publications include *Worlds at War, Nations in Song: Dialogic Imagination and Moral Vision in the Hymns of the book of Revelation.* (2015), and *Signs to Life: Reading and Responding to John's Gospel* (2013).

Perry Hodgkins Jones was the first student to graduate with an MA in religion and the environment from the University of the South's School of Theology in Sewanee, Tennessee. Her thesis applies an environmental lens to twentieth-century Christian spiritual writings and seeks spiritual direction for the environmental movement within the Church. She graduated from Wellesley College in 2011 with a BA in international relations: political science. Perry currently lives in Macon, Georgia, with her husband, where she continues to write and explore the practical implications of ecotheology.

David Kendall is assistant professor of music at La Sierra University, California. His interests in music history include the Spanish colonial world, particularly the Philippines. He has performed documentary research in the Philippines and Mexico and has presented his findings at local, national, and international conferences. Additionally, David is interested in organology (the study of musical instruments), with a particular focus on brass instruments in the nineteenth century and how they influenced the Bach and Handel revivals late in that century. He directs a Civil War–era brass ensemble, playing on period instruments as well as modern reproductions. This ensemble has been featured in sound tracks and on the screen for films and television. David received his PhD in historical musicology from the University of California, Riverside.

Jeffrey A. Lockwood is currently director of the MFA program in creative writing at the University of Wyoming. He earned a PhD in entomology from Louisiana State University. He worked for fifteen years as an insect ecologist at the University of Wyoming, publishing more than one hundred scientific papers and pioneering a method of integrated pest management (IPM) for rangeland grasshoppers. In 2003, he metamorphosed into a professor of natural sciences and humanities in the philosophy department and the creative writing program, where he teaches environmental ethics, philosophy of ecology, and nature/environmental writing. He has published three collections of environmental/spiritual essays through Skinner House. His other books include: *Locust: The Devastating Rise and Mysterious Disappearance of the Insect that Shaped the American Frontier* (2004), *Six-Legged Soldiers: Us-*

ing Insects as Weapons of War (2008), *Philosophical Foundations for the Practices of Ecology* (2010), and *The Infested Mind: Why Humans Fear, Loathe and Love Insects* (2013). His work has been honored with a Pushcart Prize, the John Burroughs award, and inclusion in the *Best American Science and Nature Writing*.

Bryan Ness is currently professor of biology at Pacific Union College, California, where he teaches a portion of the freshman majors' biology sequence (Mendelian genetics, evolution, biodiversity, and ecology) and upper division courses in genetics and biotechnology. He also teaches a major's writing course called Introduction to Research Methods. His research interests range from molecular plant taxonomy and biotechnology to environmental science and evolutionary biology. He was editor of *Magill's Encyclopedia of Science: Plant Life* (2003) and the Second Edition of the *Encyclopedia of Genetics* (2004). Bryan received his PhD in Botany from Washington State University.

Mick Pope is a meteorologist and faculty member of the Bureau of Meteorology Training Centre, Melbourne, Australia. He is coordinator of Ethos Environment, the environmental working group of Ethos: EA Centre for Christianity and Society. Mick was the invited speaker for the 2013 Tinsley Institute annual lecture and presented "Preaching to the Birds: The Mission of the Church to the Creation," also published in *Speaking of Mission: Volume 2*. Mick recently published a book with Claire Dawson, *A Climate of Hope: Church and Mission in a Warming World* with UNOH Publishing. He has two published papers in ecotheology in *The Australian Journal of Mission Studies* (2012) and in *Anglican EcoCare Journal of EcoTheology* (2014). Mick received his PhD in meteorology from Monash University in Melbourne, Australia.

Andrew R. H. Thompson is postdoctoral fellow in environmental ethics at the University of the South, Sewanee, and assistant director of the Center for Religion and Environment at Sewanee in Tennessee. His book, *Sacred Mountains: A Christian Ethical Approach to Mountaintop Removal* was published in 2015. Andrew earned his doctorate in religious studies at Yale University.

Matthew Valdez is currently enrolled in the master of theological studies program in the H. M. S. Richards Divinity School at La Sierra University, California. His focus is on studying the gospel of Mark through the work of narrative and Marxist biblical scholars. In 2016, he presented a paper on a narrative, sociological reading of Christ's triumphal entry at Inclinations, a graduate and undergraduate humanities conference held annually at La Sierra

University. Matthew plans to pursue an advanced degree in biblical studies once he completes his current program.

Cristina Vanin is associate professor of theology, associate dean, and director of the master of Catholic thought theology program at St. Jerome's University in Waterloo, Ontario, Canada. Her research focuses on examining the role that theology can have in helping us respond adequately to the ecological crisis. Recent publications include: "The Significance of Lonergan's Method for Ecological Conversion," in *Lonergan's Anthropology Revisited: The Next Fifty Years of Vatican II*, edited by Gerard Whelan, S.J. (2015) and "Understanding the Universe as Sacred: The Challenge for Contemporary Christianity," in *The Intellectual Journey of Thomas Berry: Imagining the Earth Community*, edited by Heather Eaton (Lanham, MD: Lexington Books, 2014). Cristina received her BA from St. Jerome's University, her MDiv from the University of St. Michael's College, Toronto, and her PhD in theology from Boston College.